Child care experts, educators, and working parents all agree—
***The Working Mother's Guide to Life* is a must-have reference!**

"A working mother can thrive only if her children are thriving. Linda Mason's compassion for both mothers and young children is the very heart of this practical, uplifting guide for everyday life."
—Dr. T. Berry Brazelton, child development author and pediatrician

"It's exciting to see such a comprehensive approach to the myriad of issues and opportunities for working mothers today; as a working mother myself, I can relate to many of the challenges presented here and found the advice quite practical and useful."
—Joy Bunson, senior vice president, JP Morgan Chase

"I wish I had read Linda Mason's fine and useful book when I was rearing my children. I'm glad they will have this practical parenting guide as they assume and share work and family responsibilities. I applaud her for trying to help other working parents ensure supportive work and home environments and safe, affordable care as they raise their families."
—Marian Wright Edelman, president, Children's Defense Fund

"Linda Mason has taken on the challenging task of really listening to employed mothers' questions and then culling through this research and drawing on the best of mother wisdom to answer them. A wonderful map to anything and everything you want to know."
—Ellen Galinksy, author of *Ask the Children,*
and president, Families and Work Institute

"Working mothers, run—don't walk—to get Linda Mason's powerhouse book. It provides poignant, honest responses to all the questions we dared to ask and hoped someone would answer . . . (but never did!). Based on first-hand research with working mothers and filtered through Mason's clear and experienced lens, the book is delightful and demanding. It allows us to confront our deepest selves and lets us know that and how working motherhood can be done well and rewardingly. At once, this is a terrific, timely read and a durable reference for contemporary women."
—Sharon Lynn Kagan, Ed.D., professor of early childhood
and family policy, Teachers College, Columbia University

"Challenging and reassuring, inspirational and practical, *The Working Mother's Guide to Life* is a valuable and wise book. Speaking with an authority and humility born of experience, Linda Mason blends her extraordinary insights with the compelling stories of mothers from all walks of life—teachers, doctors, businesswomen, factory workers, choreographers, and writers—creating a beautiful tapestry of diverse voices. All of us who are working mothers live with a chronic sense of guilt, ambivalence, and everyday weariness. Linda Mason's sage counsel will not make those feelings disappear, but her book assuages our worst fears, offers us new perspectives, terrific ideas, and pragmatic solutions to daily dilemmas. And, perhaps most important, Mason helps us celebrate those rare and wonderful moments when we are able to balance our deep dual commitments—to love and work—with alacrity and grace."

—Sara Lawrence-Lightfoot, professor of education, Harvard University

"It's important to me to do a great job as a mother and as a professional. Linda Mason's powerful and comprehensive book covers every aspect of working motherhood, and she helps us all to see that it's possible to succeed and find satisfaction in both worlds. This should be required reading for any woman—or man—starting a family while maintaining a career."

—Indra Nooyi, president and chief financial officer, PepsiCo, Inc.

"As a child developmentalist and advocate, I found myself thinking from the first few pages of the vast numbers of children who would love (and benefit from) finding this book for their parents. First, kids are keenly aware of and worried about the stresses their moms and dads are feeling these days about balancing family and work. Second, they would want their dads to read it when mom was finished. And so would I; fathers are welcomed and their needs addressed in every chapter. Compassionate, smart and practical, Linda Mason replaces working parent guilt and doubt with encouragement and solutions. You, and your kids, will feel better for reading it."

—Kyle D. Pruett, M.D., clinical professor of child psychiatry, Yale School of Medicine, and author of *Fatherneed: Why Father Care Is as Essential as Mother Care for Your Child*

The WORKING MOTHER'S GUIDE to LIFE

STRATEGIES, SECRETS, AND SOLUTIONS

Linda Mason

 THREE RIVERS PRESS • NEW YORK

Published by Three Rivers Press, New York, New York.

Member of the Crown Publishing Group, a division of Random House, Inc.

www.randomhouse.com

THREE RIVERS PRESS and the Tugboat design are registered trademarks of Random House, Inc.

Printed in the United States of America

Design by Robert Bull Design

Grateful acknowledgment is made to the following for permission to reprint previously published material.

Catalyst, Inc.: Statistics from the booklet "Two Careers, One Marriage—Making It Work in the Marketplace." Reprinted by permission of Catalyst, Inc.

Dutton Children's Books: Excerpt from the poem "Halfway Down" from *When We Were Very Young* by A. A. Milne, illustrations by E. H. Shepard. Copyright © 1924 by E. P. Dutton, renewed 1952 by A. A. Milne. All rights reserved. Reprinted by permission of Dutton Children's Books, an imprint of Penguin Putnam Books for Young Readers, a division of Penguin Putnam Inc.

MCS Music America Inc.: Excerpt from the song lyric "One Glass of Water" by Si Kahn. Reprinted by permission of MCS Music America Inc.

Library of Congress Cataloging-in-Publication Data

Mason, Linda, 1954–
    The working mother's guide to life / Linda Mason.
    1. Working mothers—Life skills guides. 2. Work and family. I. Title.
    HQ759.48 .M346 2002
    646.7'0085'2—dc21   2002006447

ISBN 0-609-80735-8

10 9 8 7 6 5 4 3 2 1

First Edition

To Farrell, Lucas, and Gracie

and, of course,

to Roger

Acknowledgments

I would like to extend my deepest gratitude to all the mothers interviewed for this book. Your honesty and openness made this project come alive, and I have attempted to capture your insight, strength, and love for your families in these pages. It is your voices and wisdom that I hope will now guide so many of us in our family lives.

I want to thank my large extended family at Bright Horizons. I love you all, and my life has grown immeasurably by working side by side with you on behalf of young children and families. Your passion for and devotion to young children have made this world a better place. Roger and I learned to become parents by watching our skilled and caring teachers. You have made a lifelong impact on our children and family. Thank you.

Thanks also to the many, many directors, teachers, regional managers, trainers, members of our education department, and all the other educators in Bright Horizons who have enthusiastically traveled the journey of this book with me. Many of your suggestions and strategies are tucked into this book. I loved all our lively exchanges over the past few years on this project. I want to especially thank Susan Brenner, Linda Whitehead, Jim Greenman, and Dana Friedman for reading the entire manuscript and offering your wise and experienced counsel. I also want to thank Debbie Cohen, Eileen Smith, Katherine Palmer, and Jean Ann Schulte, who read and commented on specific chapters. Angela Lyons, Doris Fantasia, Arlene

Ruisi, and Nancy Lague were all wonderful assistants at various stages of the process. I want to thank my board of directors and advisory board, who enthusiastically embraced this project and have encouraged me along the way. In particular, thank you, Sara Lawrence Lightfoot. I feel blessed to have you as a friend and mentor.

Rachel Rock and Allison Daskal Hausman were my two intelligent, perceptive researchers. I appreciate your help with the interviews, and I loved all our initial discussions when I was just forming my ideas for the book. I want to thank several individuals who graciously offered or agreed to read parts or all of the manuscript: Alice Honig, Lisa Groos, Mary Lou Mason, Sam Mason, Hilary Pennington, Molly Aalyson, and Anne Holton. Also thanks to Stacey Gibson, Candi Lange, Joy Bunson, and Phyllis Stewart Pires for your thoughtful input. Jessica Fein and Ilene Hoffer have been, and continue to be, two incredible resources for this book. Their creative ideas and talents are inspiring. I want to thank those who spent hours transcribing the interviews for me: Doris Fantasia, Carol McClusky, Jennifer McClusky, Kathy Patenaude, and particularly Angela Lyons, who spent hours and hours faithfully listening and typing—all while laughing and crying along with my mothers.

What would I do without my soul sisters: Jane Levitt, Mary Brown, Karen Harris, Molly Aalyson, Sally McAlpin, Jody Judge, Hilary Pennington, Cindy Link, Barb Caddell, Ingrid Markman, and Lisa Groos. And, of course, my adored real sister: Lisa Pullman. We are each other's sustenance, support, and source of laughter and tears. I value so much the community we have created for ourselves and our families. Our friendships have helped so much throughout the process of writing this book, and even more important, in life. Thanks to Marlene O'Halloran, who has been like a cherished and beloved aunt to our family over the years.

It's been fun to go through the book-writing process with my two good friends and fellow writers, Scott Brown and Jim Levitt. Our mutual encouragement and sharing of stories have made the endeavor more interesting and fun. I also want to thank Mark Albion for his advice, friendship, and candor along the way.

To my mother and father, Mary Lou and Sam Mason, who are the absolute best parents anyone could ever dream of. I hope Roger

and I can be for our children what you have been to me and my siblings, Sam, David, John, and Lisa. I know that our notions of good
parenting have been inspired and modeled by you and Roger's parents, Roger and Carolyn Brown.

Thanks to Jim Levine, my agent extraordinaire. You have been
my partner, friend, advisor, and supporter throughout this project.
Thanks for being there for me in many different ways. Becky Cabaza,
my editor at Crown Publishing—how did I get so lucky? You have been
tirelessly supportive, encouraging, and optimistic. Your skills as an
editor never cease to amaze me. And, of course, I appreciate that you
went ahead and had a baby in the midst of this process so we could
witness, firsthand, the ways this book could be helpful!

Farrell, Lucas, and Gracie—you're my inspiration for this book!
I have loved all your ideas and suggestions and all your curiosity
about book writing. And, most of all, I just love you more than words
can describe. And, finally, to Roger—I am so blessed to have such an
amazingly wonderful life partner. You have brought such happiness,
passion, and meaning to my life. You have been there every step of
the way in this book process—and in our journey through life.

Contents

The WORKING MOTHER'S GUIDE to LIFE

Introduction

As I carry my sleeping six-month-old daughter, Farrell, into the child care center, I can't take my eyes off her tranquil, sweet face. She is so trusting and comfortable in the world. I sit down in the center on the couch with Farrell asleep on my lap. It's still very early. The center is quiet, and I can have a moment of peace. My mind drifts off to our board of director's meeting that will be starting in an hour. I have all the financial reports stuffed in my briefcase beside me; I rehearse in my mind yet again the explanations for our shortfall against budget. I'm anxious about what lies ahead in our meetings today. Farrell murmurs and then nestles in closer to my body. I lift her up to feel her breath on my face. I nuzzle and smell her baby skin. As her tiny hand wraps tighter around my finger, my eyes start to well up with tears. Am I doing the right thing? Should I be staying home with Farrell, or should I be working? Certainly today, as I anticipate a tough few hours with our investors, all I want to do is cuddle up with Farrell on my bed and make her smile and laugh.

My husband, Roger, and I are working hard to get our fledgling company off the ground. Everything is still so unsure. Every month is a constant struggle as we try to build our organization and convince clients, investors, and employees to join with us. The work is intense and stressful; it's unclear whether our company will survive. But regularly throughout the day, my mind brings up the sweet image of Farrell's fuzzy little head, her rosebud mouth, and her toothless drooling smile. A baby sock I found in my suit coat pocket remains there as a tactile connection to my baby.

Dozens of times each day, I question my choices as a new working mother. Is there any way I can cut back at work? Can I do some of the work out of my house? How much does my company need me? How much does Farrell need me? The most sobering question is whether I am doing right by my child. As we set up the philosophy and design of the child care centers our company develops, I read everything I can on the effects of child care on children. I know that excellent child care can be wonderful for a child. But will it be right for ours? Is it excellent enough? Are we women all just kidding ourselves—after decades of fighting for the right to have a career, are we now just rationalizing that it's okay to be a working mother?

I find myself obsessing about time, always counting hours. How many hours is Farrell in someone else's care? How many hours is she with us? How many of those hours is she awake or asleep? Roger and I are constantly reconfiguring our schedules to stagger our day and maximize the time Farrell can be with one of us. Though the mission of our company is to provide high quality child care at the workplace, and though I've interviewed every teacher in the child care center at our office where Farrell is enrolled, I am still constantly wracked with guilt and questions. I am never sure that we're doing the right thing. This is such a different model than what I grew up with, and there is no "proof" that it's the right one. If I'm wrong, by the time I find out, it will be too late.

How can I be a devoted, effective mother and do my job? This is the question I am trying to answer with my book. As I have faced different crises and challenges in my personal, family, and work lives over the years, I find myself regularly and emotionally questioning my decisions and path. If I had not continued with paid outside work, would my life have been smooth and easier? Are there strategies that can effectively guide us through the large and small challenges of a working mother's life? To find these answers, I have turned to other mothers. In this book, we will enter into the lives of many mothers who have discovered how to create thriving family and work lives. We will learn about their secrets and strategies and techniques. They will share with us their steps to create lives that work for them and their families. I started this book to answer some questions for myself, and in the process I entered a sisterhood of working mothers who are all seeking these answers.

Over the past fourteen years, I have had three children, three miscarriages, and a four-month pregnancy bed rest, all while we were trying to launch and grow our child care organization, Bright Horizons. Through the book, I will share my own journey and struggles into working motherhood as I offer you the perspectives and strategies of other working mothers I interviewed from a broad range of backgrounds who have been able to make it work.

For years I have lived in a world of working mothers. Our company, Bright Horizons, serves tens of thousands of working mothers and their children every day through our network of child care centers. We also employ thousands of working mothers. Daily, I witness many good examples of mothers who are working in responsible positions and who are also effective, engaged, devoted parents.

In my research, I attempted to find and interview the true experts—those women who are doing an excellent job of mothering while working. Most profiles you encounter of successful working mothers portray those who have succeeded at work. It is harder to tell if they are succeeding at home. Our work at Bright Horizons puts us in the privileged position of intimately knowing the parents and children in our care. We interact with parents, in their parenting role, every day over a period of years. We see the good examples and the not so good. More important, we also know the children well and see how they develop and grow as children of working parents. This book is based on what is going on with expert practitioners—the moms who have figured out how to make it work in many large and small ways.

To find these excellent examples, I turned to the parenting specialists and child development professionals within Bright Horizons. I selected a handful of experienced, mature educators who have worked for years in early childhood education and whose judgment I value. I then asked them to select a few mothers who, in their view, are excellent, engaged, devoted mothers and whose children are thriving. It is this group of mothers I have interviewed, each person individually over a number of hours. I came away from the interviews deeply impressed with their mothering skills. I came away impressed with their ability to create lives where they and their families can grow in healthy ways. Their lives are not perfect; some of the mothers I interviewed were navigating their way through crises, disappointments, and setbacks. And, in fact, it is especially through their challenges that many gained strength and insight, much of which I hope to share in this book.

I use the term "working mother" broadly in this book, since many "stay-at-home" mothers do substantial volunteer work outside the home in addition to their significant work at home. I have therefore included mothers who hold volunteer positions in the community (that consume twenty or more hours a week) and who, in my opinion, are also doing an excellent job of mothering and working.

In interviewing, my two researchers and I covered a broad range of subjects with seventy mothers, then held shorter interviews covering more targeted subjects with another thirty-five mothers. The mothers we spoke to relied on a variety of child care options, as you'll see. I have also incorporated mothers' views as expressed in a parent survey of twelve thousand working parents conducted by Bright Horizons in the spring of 2001.

Among the excellent mothers we interviewed were a construction manager, a nurse's assistant, a choreographer, a president of a large public company, an architect, a factory assembly-line worker on the night shift, a graphics designer, a student in occupational therapy, an author, an entrepreneur who runs her own trucking company, a secretary, a management consultant, an operations manager, a benefits clerk, a software engineer, a senior research scientist, an administrative assistant, an elementary school classroom volunteer, a medical school admissions officer, a bookkeeper, a senior partner in a law firm, a teacher, an office administrator, a saleswoman, a banking executive, a truck receiver, a venture capitalist, a pastor, an ophthalmologist, a lab technician, an auditor, a machine assembler who bolts twelve hundred parts a shift, a managing director of a global health care business, a college trustee, a volunteer elementary school PTA president, and many others—all of them working mothers.

My group of mothers:

Description of Mothers		Range of Employment	
Single mothers	22%	Volunteer	4%
Ethnic minorities	25%	Freelance/self-employed	8%
Mothers who had a child as a teenager	6%	Shift workers	10%
Mothers who had a child after age forty	12%	Entrepreneurs	5%
Mothers handling crises	19%	Students	3%
Mothers with fertility issues	12%	Small organization	18%
Adoptive mothers	9%	Medium organization	28%
Lesbian mothers	3%	Large organization	21%
Mothers with children who have special needs	16%		

Range of Income Levels		Employment Status	
Low	13%	Full-time	71%
Lower/middle	25%	Part-time	25%
Middle/professional	53%	Volunteer	4%
Upper middle	9%		

I did not interview working fathers, though I believe their role is critical to both the child's development and the mother's sense of well-being and partnership. And you will see that throughout the book, I frequently discuss the role and responsibility of the father. However, as a woman, I felt drawn to the experience of other women moving into motherhood while working. I decided to keep the book focused on the mother's experience and have recommended books throughout that address working fathers.

I spent much of my early adult life working and living over-seas. Now, as a mother, I am struck by how differently our culture approaches working motherhood than many other cultures abroad. In talking to many different mothers across the United States, my eyes were also opened to just how differently mothers approach working motherhood throughout our own culture. There is certainly no one common approach to doing it well. In Part I, I discuss different styles and approaches to working motherhood. You'll probably recognize yourself in one of these categories.

In Part II, I identify and explore in depth each of the "Three Pillars of Successful Working Motherhood": a partner-in-parenting, a supportive employer, and excellent child care. The pillars are the key supports that make it easier for you to get everything else done, and I'll show you ways to put them into place.

In the chapter on partner-in-parenting I discuss how partners—whether a spouse, close family member, or friend—can help the entire family dynamic. I describe the three types of marriages that working mothers tend to have; the important role of the father; and how single mothers find partners-in-parenting. In the chapter on the supportive employer, I discuss a family-friendly work environment and how it can help you as a parent. I give you information to help make your current work environment more family-friendly and show you how to negotiate for flexible work options. The chapter on excellent child care presents the four child care options—child care centers, family child care homes, nannies, and care by relatives—and how to find high quality care in each option. Since early education and care is the world I'm immersed in every day, I will share with you my "insiders' tips" on what is most important to look for in each option.

Part III, "Making It Work for You," is the last and longest section. This is where I offer practical advice and tips to help you deal with aspects of your life as a working mother: I'll show you how to manage your pregnancy and maternity leave, and how to handle the practical and emotional dimensions of your return to work. I'll help you figure out an approach to balancing work and family that takes advantage of your personal style. I'll help you create healthy and happy family morning and evening routines—the two family times that wrap around your workday. I'll point out how other working mothers create a strong family culture, and how you can, too. I'll show you how to manage the common pressure points of a working mother's life. Last but not least, I'll show how you, like other successful working mothers, can build a community of support to envelop and nourish you through the vicissitudes of your life.

I hope that with this book, I can help expand your range of choices in how you live your daily life as a working mother. I hope to be able to give you some tools to help you and your family to thrive. As I spent more and more time talking to working mothers, I felt a powerful sense of kinship with them. We shared the same language of concern, of desires, of aspirations for our families. Although working mothers are diverse, we all share the same powerful goal—to do the right thing for our children and families. You and I *can* work and be devoted, effective mothers. Our children can thrive while we work. We can learn from one another's tried-and-true strategies to find our own chosen path. We may have different approaches to combining working and mothering—but with thoughtfulness and conviction, our families can thrive and so can we.

PART I

You're on Your Way

ONE

"Go Pick Up a Hoe"
Different Approaches
to Working Motherhood

Petronila, my friend in rural western Kenya, sits in the shade under a small tree in a congested and lively marketplace in a small hillside village. It is hot and dry. Petronila's hardened, dusty feet are set off by the brilliant patterns and colors of her long skirt wrap and head scarf. Her round face is deep brown; she has a wide, bright smile. She readily breaks out into laughter, particularly with Westerners, who she feels often have odd ideas and notions.

Petronila and her husband, Moses, have eight children. They live in a small three-room cinder-block bungalow without plumbing or running water. Petronila squats to cook over a wood fire outside the back door. They have several chickens running in the back of the house, two goats, and a large, well-tended vegetable garden.

Petronila spends several mornings each week in the village marketplace selling her vegetables and crafts spread out on a blanket. She uses the money earned to buy needed items for the family and herself. She and the other women merchants are friends or acquaintances. She has known most of them since childhood. They have an easy banter. She and the woman next to her, Esther, like to tease and laugh. This morning they are laughing about their husbands' eating habits. They mimic their husbands, bent over their bowls of *ugali*, chewing and talking simultaneously.

As the women sell, barter, and examine one another's wares, children are seen everywhere. Petronila frequently nurses her youngest child, Litonde, who is two. Her four-year-old leans against her side. Her five-year-old is chasing his friend behind the market. Her children frequently run off, often with Litonde bouncing on a sibling's hip, to play with other children in the marketplace, all of whom they seem to know very well.

As I watch Petronila and her small village community, I marvel at how naturally blended their work and family life are. In fact, there is no sense of *work life* and *family life*. It is just *life*. Somehow, Petronila is raising eight children while engaging in the productive life of the community. It is natural and expected. There is no guilt. It seems uncanny to me.

Throughout all the hardship that rural Kenyans suffer, their communal structure gives them a great deal of support. There is comfort in the society of women and children. It is a hardworking culture that emphasizes responsibility and contribution to the family and community. All members of the village, male and female, young and old, are expected to contribute what they can through their labor.

I spent much of my twenties and early thirties traveling, living, and working in small rural villages in Africa and Southeast Asia. During these years, I became very interested in the life and customs of the women, particularly mothers. I was an active participant in their daily lives. I spent mornings with my Thai women friends in the village marketplace while they bartered, bought, and sold. I walked with them to a little pond where we squatted and fished, holding large "umbrella" leaves over our heads to shield us from the sun; I sat in the shade under their hut on stilts while they chopped, pounded, and prepared food for their extended family. I spent long afternoons in Sudanese family compounds while the women tended their vegetable gardens, wove baskets, fed and cared for their children, scrubbed clothes, and meticulously applied henna designs to one another's hands and feet.

Although the cultures vary, there is a strong common thread in the life of many third-world village women. Women play an integral part in many economies. They produce goods to sell in the local market. Many marketplace vendors are women. Families often live together in compounds of extended families where women work together to grow and prepare food, care for the children, produce textiles and crafts, and perform myriad other family-sustaining duties.

Throughout most of the developing world, there is no concept of a "working mother." Every mother works. In fact, it would be quite unacceptable for a mother not to be a productive part of community life. Children and women spend much of their day in close proximity. Babies stay with their mothers throughout the day. Family life and work life are blended in a very natural way. Children are cared for by a community of aunts, neighbors, older siblings, and their parents. They grow up observing and participating in the adult world.

Although our society thinks of the stay-at-home mother and breadwinning father as the norm, it certainly is not. In fact, it is a recent phenomenon of the last few generations. In the United States, child rearing has changed dramatically from one generation to the next. What had remained constant throughout history until recent times are variations of the model described above, one that was based on a productive extended family unit where work and family functions were integrated on farms and in small towns. In the industrial and postindustrial eras, men left the home and family farm to go off to factories and offices in the cities. Domestic life and work life became highly differentiated.

It would be wrong to idealize the developing-world model. Much of what I witnessed was constant struggle, deprivation, and severely limited options for everyone, particularly women. But is it possible for parents to combine working and parenting in a healthier balance? Could there possibly be a more integrated model as technology transforms the work world and people develop more flexibility in their place and mode of work?

As I spent much of my twenties living and working in the developing world, this view of an integrated work and family life became an important backdrop for me in my thirties when my husband, Roger, and I decided to have children, and we embarked on our own journey of combining work and family.

As I talked to Petronila about all these concepts, she laughed. It was just like a Westerner to waste time thinking and worrying about such issues. Petronila knows no other model. She told me, "You young American people think and question too much. Go pick up a hoe, girl, and get to work. That will help you with your questions." Petronila thinks that all our choices have just confused us. But then again, she doesn't have the luxury of choice.

I have picked up the hoe, and so have millions of my sisters in the United States, but it's a vastly different world than Petronila's. We have both the benefit and the complications of greater choices and control over our decisions. Women can decide whether or not to have children. We can have them and work outside the home or stay home. We can have children early or late in our careers. How women make these choices deeply affects the outcome.

Unlike many young women, I never visualized myself as a mother while growing up. I had a strong adventure-seeking streak, and spent my early adult years moving around a lot—living for periods of time in Europe, Africa, Asia, and different cities in the U.S. Roger and I worked together both on the Cambodian border and in the Sudan, where we ran refugee relief operations for people fleeing war and famine. With this work we lived in primitive, and at times harsh, conditions. Although we worked with families and children, I did not yet have any desire to have my own.

We finally returned to the States in our early thirties, wanting to take a break from this intense refugee work. Most of our overseas programs had been with young children, since they are the most affected by war and famine. Once back in the States, we decided to create an organization of our own, one that would focus on young children and have a societal impact. We started Bright Horizons, a network of child care centers, when I was thirty-two.

The start-up years were exciting, difficult, stressful, a real roller-coaster ride. It certainly wasn't the easiest time to have a child. But after a couple of years, Roger and I started to really want a baby. We were now well into our thirties, bathed in the world of babies and young children and early childhood education. We spent our days thinking about the quality, educational philosophy, and design of our child care centers. We were hiring teachers who emanated a passion for babies and children. We, ourselves, began to want a baby, and began thinking and talking about babies constantly. We knew that it was crazy to develop a company at the same time that we were start-ing a family. But what was the alternative? We just plunged in and somehow had the faith that we would figure it out. We didn't create a grand plan; we just took the leap.

I later learned through interviewing many mothers for this

book that this approach is not typical. I had assumed that most working mothers think and act like I do. I couldn't have been more wrong. There is no one common approach to working motherhood; there is no one "right" way to be a devoted, effective mother. Wonderful mothers are mothering in different ways, reflecting their personalities, orientation to the world and life, and cultural and religious backgrounds. I found this liberating, since I never seemed to mother just the way my best friends were.

One of the first differences I noted was in *style of mothering*. I found that, in general, the working mothers I interviewed reflected one of four different styles: the Strategic Planner, the Camp Counselor, the Earth Mother, and the Passionate Spirit. As I describe each type, see if you can find yourself. Many moms fit squarely in one category; other mothers use a blend of styles depending on the situation or phase of family life. By understanding that there are many ways to be a good working mother, you may feel freer to find your own personal path.

THE STRATEGIC PLANNER

The Strategic Planner lives her life very intentionally. Things don't simply happen to her; she crafts her life. This planning starts early, long before she has her first child. The Strategic Planner wants to make sure that she is settled in the right job and home before she has

THE STRATEGIC PLANNER'S FAMILY PLANNING

- Finishes her education or times the pregnancy to fit within the academic schedule
- Settles into the home where she and her partner want to have their baby; thinks about location in terms of proximity to work or a desired neighborhood
- Scrutinizes her job to make sure it will accommodate and support having a baby; and if it doesn't, she makes a change; makes sure she is valued and secure in her position before having the baby
- Achieves some degree of financial stability

a baby. If she has a partner, they take time to think about the right timing for their family and how to organize their life around working and parenting.

Rebecca,* who works in the community affairs department of a hospital, and her husband, Carl, are very thoughtful about each step in their life together. They met in their early twenties, and they wanted to have plenty of time together before having children:

We purposely waited five years after getting married before having a baby. We knew that life would be different with kids. We did a lot of traveling. We wanted Carl to finish his education and training. And I wanted to be more settled in terms of being in a work environment that could support me as a working mother. These were all conscious decisions.

Some moms have had their strategic plan worked out since childhood. Shalisha, born of a Jamaican mother and a Russian father, and now working as an author and product manager, spent her first four years living with a foster mother who was caring for ten children. Shalisha then moved in with a Jamaican aunt who had six other children, and at age nine, she went to live with her mother, who was working two jobs to support her two children. Shalisha grew up witnessing this incredible struggle and became determined to create a plan ahead of time that would work for her:

I always had the plan. Back in the seventh grade, I would have told you I was going to get married at thirty and have my first child at thirty-five. And that's exactly what I did. I wanted to make sure I had finished all my education, that I was comfortable financially, and that I had done the things I really wanted to do. I tell a lot of my friends that you just need to make sure you've got all of your ducks in a row.

---

*I have changed the names of all the mothers I have interviewed (as well as other family members). Mothers were incredibly open and honest about the joys and struggles in their lives, and I would like to repay this honesty with privacy.

Some moms, such as this one, work out their family planning in such detail that they know exactly what day they want to conceive:

I was in my first year of graduate school. My husband was actually still living overseas. I figured out the exact days to conceive so that I could work a summer internship and then have my baby. He flew in for four days and did his duty. I had it planned to get ten weeks of internship in, have the baby, and have six weeks before going back to school. I finished my internship and had the baby the following Friday. I thought that was how the world works.

For the Strategic Planner, a key part of being ready to have a family is being in a job that will support her as a mother. Originally, Rebecca had been working in a fast-paced and intense management consulting job. The hours were long, and she traveled each week. She loved the work, but she knew it wouldn't be the right environment for having children. Rebecca researched other work options carefully. She wanted to find a new job in which she wouldn't have to travel, and an environment where she would feel supported as a working mother. She found a "family-friendly" job in a large hospital. Rebecca worked hard for two years to establish herself in this job.

Once she got pregnant, she started to think that her supervisor might not be very supportive, so she arranged a transfer before she had her baby:

My current boss had a very traditional life at home with two young children and a stay-at-home wife. He couldn't quite comprehend how you work and manage a family. But I adored this other manager. He was at a later stage in his life, and he had two grown daughters who were balancing work and family. He really understood the struggle. So I engineered a switch to this other manager before I had my child. And he was great! He was the most supportive boss.

It is certainly not common or even possible for an employee to choose her own supervisor, but you can think about your current position. You may have more choices than you think you do. I cover this more fully in chapter 3.

Many Strategic Planners develop goals for their parenting and new life as a family. Colleen, a financial planner, wrote up her own list of parenting goals while she was still pregnant:

1. *My husband, Jack, and I should try to go out on a date once a month.*

2. *Never complain that you don't have enough time. It's your life, so if you're really having that much trouble, you have to change it.*

3. *Give my full attention to whatever I am doing with my child. There are times when I have read* Cat in the Hat *from beginning to end and realized that I hadn't even been paying attention. I'm thinking about what I have to do, making some list in my head.*

4. *Have "hanging around" time. Don't be so scheduled. Maybe I'm living in a fantasy world, but I'm hoping that our child is just going to be able to go to a friend's house and ring the doorbell and say, "Can someone come out and play?"*

5. *Do lots of fun outdoorsy stuff with our child. I need to do it, too, not just my husband. I don't want to be home cooking while they're out fishing or something.*

REGARDLESS OF YOUR MOTHERING STYLE, IT CAN BE HELPFUL TO CREATE INITIAL PARENTING GOALS:

- *What approach to baby care feels best to you?* Constant holding and feeding on demand or getting your baby on a schedule as quickly as possible; taking the baby everywhere with you; or acclimating your baby to sleeping in her crib in a quiet environment?

- *What kind of atmosphere at home do you want to establish?* Quiet and pulled in to the nuclear family; open to extended family and friends who hold and interact with the baby; music, liveliness; serenity, quiet?

- *What kinds of activities with the baby are important to you?* Outdoor activities—lots of walks with the baby in a stroller or Snugli; stimulating activities at home; quiet nurturance; just hanging out?

- *What would you like your social life to look like?* Continue as before with little change, with or without the baby; pull back on social life to cocoon as a family?
- *How would you want your married life with baby to evolve?* Maintain regular alone time with your partner; include your baby in nearly everything?
- *What adult activities are important for you to maintain?* What should you give up?
- *What values do you want to stress in your new family?* Religion and spirituality; fun and humor; service to others; organization and discipline; togetherness; independence; sports; learning; being laid-back or active?

When the family planning doesn't work out exactly as hoped, it can be disappointing for any mother, but particularly for the Strategic Planner, who puts great importance on following a careful plan. When Susana, a business manager in a high-tech firm, and her husband, Antonio, had a baby, they decided to relocate to their hometown for more family support. She was the primary breadwinner of the family at that point and had interviewed with several potential employers:

> *I had a great offer letter in hand, and I was in the midst of negotiating the package when I found out that I was pregnant again. We were specifically not trying to get pregnant. In fact, I had had fertility issues! We were flabbergasted. We were trying to make this huge decision with a new job. We were relocating; our baby, Andres, was just five months old; and we were still adjusting to being new parents. We really didn't want this to happen. When I got pregnant with Andres, we were so ecstatic. When I got pregnant this second time, I just sat down on the floor and cried. "This is not the plan! This is not the plan!"*

But, good Strategic Planner that she is, Susana eventually adjusted to her present reality, threw out the old plan, and created a new plan. Strategic Planner moms are not necessarily rigid; they just feel more comfortable with an operating plan, even if that means rethinking midstream.

Once the Strategic Planner has her children, she uses her organizational skills to run a smooth-functioning household. She thoughtfully crafts the influences her children are exposed to, whether it is type of friends, family experiences such as sports or cultural activities, or spiritual pursuits. Patricia, an architect, is very intentional about her family life:

> You have to decide and plan all the things that you are doing when you have children. You have to say to yourself, I want my children to have this kind of experience, and then that experience will influence your child. If you want to make it work, with some will and planning you can.

Strategic Planners are often fairly neat and well organized. They have found that daily routines—whether they're for getting the family out the door in the morning or for household chores—can make family life flow more smoothly. Wendy is an operations analyst in a large company and the mother of two young children:

> Having a routine really reduces our stress. Our mornings go smoothly. We have everything pretty much laid out. At night I pack a big bag and make sure we have everything our kids need for child care and what I need for work, so in the morning everything is ready to go. As long as we follow the order, everything works.
>
> As far as household chores, I try to break down tasks and have routines. Monday is laundry night—just like in the old nursery rhyme. I even have a routine and schedule for dinners. Every Monday we have pasta, every Tuesday we have chicken, and so on. I pick out the recipes and just write them on a calendar. The preplanning works out well.

The Strategic Planner uses her skills both at work and at home. Her natural focus on results helps her in the workplace, and she knows how to get a job done. She continually reevaluates her job situation to see if it works for her. Leah had a job she loved in a small international development agency that was known for its supportive work environment. However, after a few years, a new CEO came in and changed the culture. Leah also started working for a supervisor who was unsupportive of her challenges as a working mother. What was once a good work situation was no longer. Through careful planning, Leah left that organization and set up business on her own as an independent consultant working out of her house. She now sets her own hours and combines work and family in whatever way she chooses on a daily basis:

For me, what was successful was creating my own track and my own route. That I've been able to make it work is a function of my own deliberate action to make it work for me.

We can all learn from the Strategic Planner's ability to thoughtfully chart a personal and family plan, to set goals and to operate by them. We can benefit from her ability to take control of the direction of her life and get things done well. The risk for the Strategic Planner, however, is that life doesn't always conform to planning. Conceiving children and then raising them does not always turn out exactly as you want. The Strategic Planner is used to successfully mastering her situation. It is sometimes harder to let go. Sometimes she would like to just "hang out" without an agenda or a to-do list.

THE STRATEGIC PLANNER

- Has strong planning and organization skills
- Develops a long-term vision of how she wants her work and family life to develop
- Is very intentional about crafting her and her family's daily life
- Is determined and careful about the boundaries between work and family
- Is well organized about household chores, meals, family schedules, etc.; sees the value of routine

VULNERABILITIES

- Can be inflexible or unnerved by the unforeseen or uncontrollable
- May lose the beauty of the moment by planning for the next step

THE CAMP COUNSELOR

For the Camp Counselor mom, attitude is everything. Her strong, confident demeanor and enthusiasm for what she is doing carry everyone along. Action is key; she doesn't stop to ponder for long. Her positive outlook on life helps her push through disappointments and setbacks. In fact, problems have no chance of sticking long to this positive, can-do woman. One Camp Counselor, Erin, a banking executive, describes her approach this way:

> I have such a rich life. Some people could look at my life and say, "It's so busy," but I look at it and say, "It's so full!" I've made sure that I'm in a good place. I have enough of a risk-taking mentality that if it doesn't work, then I change it, and I feel I have a right to do that.

While the Strategic Planner spends time articulating a vision for family and creating an overall family plan, the Camp Counselor is comfortable just taking the plunge. Like a sky diver, she jumps and has confidence that it will all work out. She has no detailed plans, because either she has an aversion to that kind of planning or she doesn't realize that more planning might be useful. When asked if she had a vision for mothering, family, and work prior to having children, Helen, who works part-time in a small employee placement firm, responded:

> I knew it would be fun to have kids. So we said okay, and immediately I got pregnant. It was almost better that it happened so fast. It didn't give us a lot of time to think about it. We were just kind of thrown into it, like it's happening. Our vision is to keep rolling and enjoy life.

The Camp Counselor's confidence, energy, and sense of conviction about what she does help her in many work situations. Announcing a pregnancy at work is often a situation fraught with anxiety, but not for the typical Camp Counselor mom. Carrie found out she was pregnant when she was in the early stage of her medical residency. This is a stage of medical training when doctors-in-training are intensely focused on working long hours in positions that are highly competitive. Carrie didn't spend a great deal of time pondering how she would break this potentially difficult news; she simply confidently plunged into the situation:

> *I was so happy that I was pregnant that I marched into my program director's office and just said, "I'm pregnant. I'm having a baby!" It was sort of a horrible thing to do to your training. I suppose I should have been incredibly nervous breaking the news, but I wasn't. They would either have to deal with it gracefully, or deal with it rudely, but either way I didn't really worry.*

The Camp Counselor mom often brings her gusto and energy with her to work. Just as she throws herself into activity at home, she throws herself into productivity at work. As Helen puts it: "I don't want to be halfway with work or with children or with my husband or with anything at all in life. I like to throw myself fully into each part of my life."

Camp Counselors are not afraid to face their situations and quickly make a change if necessary. Erin returned from maternity leave with her second baby to a new supervisor in the financial institution where she worked. She knew on the first day back that this relationship wasn't going to work when her new supervisor said, "Oh, you're back?"

> *I couldn't believe that is how he welcomed me back. In my mind, I wanted all sorts of drum rolls: "She's back!" It was not a great situation, and after just a few weeks, I knew I had to leave. Of course, this was insane when you think about it. I had two babies, and I'm now starting a job search. But if I'm going to work, I want to feel good about it, so I knew I had to change.*

The Camp Counselor's home life reflects an orientation toward fun and activity. Anna, an athletic mother of four who works in a medical school admissions office, loves outdoor adventures and indoor games that family and friends can all get involved with. Her husband, Jerry, has the same approach. Their home is always a focal point of activity:

> *There always seems to be a fun project going on, whether we're flooding the yard to make an ice-skating rink or building a tree fort. I don't think we've really developed a philosophy about that; it's just what we enjoy. We want to be involved with our children's lives because it's fun.*

Some parents like a calm, settled family evening after a day at work, school, and child care. The Camp Counselor's evenings are often full of activity. It's a chance to turn off work and have some fun. Adah, a sales and client relationship manager and a mother of two young children, sees her house largely as a springboard for activity:

> *Usually we'll come home, settle in for a half hour, and then go walk in the park, go bike riding, or go swimming. We definitely do some activity most nights. We also eat out a lot. I do not like to cook. I do not like to waste my time in the kitchen.*
>
> *We're constantly on the go during the weekends. My mother will call at nine A.M. on Saturday and leave a message saying, "Where are you? You're already out of the house at this hour? It's okay to be home sometimes, you know." But that's our style—to be active.*

Soon after Yvette, a student, and her husband had their second child, their marriage started to deteriorate and her husband left. Yvette was now a single mother of two small boys. After the difficult breakup, Yvette had some severe health problems and spent time on welfare. Like most of us, she has had some struggles in her life, but like many Camp Counselor moms, she is very good on the rebound. She pulled herself up, completed her college education, and became determined to apply to law school. She knew it was a long, hard road, but Yvette had unflagging energy and a resolute can-do attitude about her life:

*When it becomes very tough trying to do my schoolwork and
take care of my children all on my own, I'll say to myself,
"Yvette, what's your option? Flunk out of school? No. Be a
bad mother? No. If there are no other options, then just do it."
It's all about determination and spirit. I can make it happen.*

Amanda, a treasurer for a small investment management firm
and the mother of a two-year-old daughter, sums up well how many
Camp Counselors view working and mothering:

*I don't feel at wit's end too much. I don't let things affect me
too much. I know I'm a good mom. I know I'm doing a good
job, and don't tell me otherwise. And if you do, that's your
opinion. I just let things roll off my back, and I stay confident.*

We can all learn from the Camp Counselor's positive attitude. It
takes a lot to get her down. She pushes through difficulties and challenges with gusto and strength. She makes things happen. Her enthusiasm and positive attitude make her fun to be around. But sometimes
her preference for action and taking charge can run up against the will

THE CAMP COUNSELOR

- Is strong-willed, confident, and upbeat
- Is oriented toward action, not long reflection or planning
- Embodies a determined, can-do attitude; knows she can make things fall into place; doesn't spend time worrying how things will turn out
- Carries an enthusiasm for the journey
- Sees her home as a springboard for activity, with fun projects and activities often going on
- Doesn't agonize about changes; just goes ahead and makes them without looking back

VULNERABILITIES

- May not be tuned in to subtle cues or needs of others
- Allows little time for reflection or introspection

and needs of her babies or young children. The Camp Counselor's vulnerability is that she sometimes may not realize that others may want to go in a different direction than she does.

THE EARTH MOTHER

The Earth Mother has a calm, accepting approach to life. She doesn't worry about or try to change things that are out of her control. She takes life as it comes, enjoys what is good about it, and lets the rest go. Jaclyn, a budget clerk and the mother of four children, three of whom are adopted, aptly describes how an Earth Mother approaches her life:

> *Just take one day at a time and go through it and enjoy it. If you think too far ahead of yourself, it just gets all out of whack. If you let it, things will just work out. It all falls into place.*

The Earth Mother embodies a natural, instinctual approach to motherhood. She always knew she would be a mother. She made her early decisions based on that awareness. She doesn't spend much time pondering, worrying, or planning and feels that having children is a natural, normal, and expected part of life.

Alena, who works in an audit department, grew up in a large, extended Armenian-American family where family was central to her life. She was surrounded by children and mothers and always knew that she would be a mother, and a good one:

> *My husband and I didn't feel we needed to have our careers first and have every "i" dotted and every "t" crossed. I knew mothering would be an easy thing for me, that it would be a natural thing, that I would love my child to pieces the moment she was born.*

The Earth Mother handles her pregnancy calmly and naturally. She doesn't ignore it, but she also doesn't obsess about it. She has an intuitive sense of what needs to be done, does it, and then relaxes.

She has a quiet confidence in herself as a mother. Chavonne, a safety associate in a biotech firm, is a mother who serenely adjusted to pregnancy and motherhood as a single mom:

> *I was very confident. I used to talk to my baby, Gabriel, a lot when I was pregnant with him. I was really very calm. I had no worries. I had family support and I had friends' support.*

The Earth Mother is able to take many of life's disappointments in stride. She accepts the direction her life has taken and embraces what has been given her. Jaclyn and her husband, Clement, had one daughter, Desiree. After giving birth to Desiree, they found out they couldn't have any more children. Jaclyn accepted that, and they raised Desiree as an only child. When Desiree was a teenager, she volunteered with her mother in a homeless shelter. Jacyln accepted what came her way:

> *One day the shelter social worker called me and said, "We have a baby here, and no one's here to take her home." Her mother had been a substance abuser; the baby was on a heart monitor. I went in to the shelter. I sat down in the rocking chair, and the social worker handed me the newborn, Jamila, to hold. It was like she was giving me this baby. I just looked at the child and I knew. "Okay, I'm taking her home with me, we've got to take care of her."*
>
> *The same thing happened with Amina two years later. I went to the shelter and I saw her. The shelter worker said she needed a loving home. I knew I could provide that for her.*
>
> *I hadn't planned on adopting any more, but Amina's biological mother had another baby and just abandoned him at the hospital. The social workers knew I had his sister and called me to see if I could take Ezekial. I'm thinking that this is crazy, I can't take care of another baby. But I did. It's what life has handed to me.*

The Earth Mother tends to have an easier time with her newborn baby than many other mothers. She enters into a rhythm with her newborn and is tuned in to his or her subtle cues and needs. Like Janet, below, she doesn't try to *accomplish* a lot with her maternity leave but sees this as a wonderful time to bond with her baby and just *be* with him:

> *I got into a rhythm with my baby son, and I wasn't too tired. I slept when he slept and just took it easy with him. It was fine and a nice time off. It didn't feel too overwhelming. I think I learned to let go of things, just to let them happen.*

The Earth Mother often has a very child-centered home. It is comfortable and well used, not designed to be admired or fussed over. She does not try to create action-packed evenings after work and school or busy weekends. She doesn't necessarily plan and organize experiences every day. She simply enjoys her children and allows them natural, unstructured playtime. As Theresa, a teacher and administrator, says:

> *I'd say our home is more of a family place—we just spend time with the children. I don't like to be running around every day doing everything. I just like to take them outside and let them play and be in a happy place.*

The Earth Mother also has a relaxed approach to household chores. Although she may like a comfortable, clean house, she doesn't become preoccupied by cleanliness or organization. Her priorities are spending time with her children. Silvia, a real estate project manager and mother of a four-year-old boy, would let things go from time to time:

> *We don't have an impeccable house, and I can tell you I am not bothered by it. I do not want a child who feels that we never pay attention to him because we are all stressed out trying to clean and keep a neat house. We live simply, too. My husband and I bought a small house knowing we were both going to work. We were not going to take care of an enormous house or enormous yard.*

By not focusing too much on plans, to-do lists, or crafting life experiences, the Earth Mother is able to enjoy life as it happens.

Jaclyn accepts life's difficulties and challenges and doesn't let them stress her:

> *Don't take life too seriously. Always have a hug and kiss and smile for your children. When you or your children have a bad day, just come home, lie down on the floor or on the sofa with each other, and hug and show one another a lot of love. Watch a movie, talk, or just joke around and laugh. This can heal the soul.*

The Earth Mother's approach carries over into her work life. Some mothers feel very anxious when home and family issues intrude into their work day. The Earth Mother can take things in stride. Once Shoshanna, a computer programmer in a technology company, came back to work after her maternity leave, she wanted to pump breast milk throughout the day. Shoshanna didn't have a private office, but that didn't faze her:

> *I was very casual about the whole thing and just pumped in my cubicle. Some people feel it's a big deal and make all sorts of special private arrangements. I felt that was unnecessary. Feeding your child is a natural part of life.*

No matter what the internal work environment is, the Earth Mother is often able to let stress slip off her. She goes at her own pace and is able to keep her equanimity. Although Chavonne works in a very fast-paced, intense work environment, she carries her tranquil manner into work:

> *Work is my relaxation. I don't let my job become stressful. It is high-volume but not high-stress. Some people are workaholics in my department; I refuse to be like that. My days are manageable. If it's a nice day, I'll go for a walk during lunch.*

Myrna works on an assembly line in a factory where the pressure is always on. But she enjoys the change of pace at work, where she can actually have a little solitude:

I look at work as my own time. A lot of people, they run back and forth all day long. They're talking all the time. I don't do that. This is my quiet time.

We can all learn from the Earth Mother's ability to take things in stride, to keep life in perspective, and to avoid getting stressed easily. We can learn from her ability to be tuned in to her children's needs and rhythms; and she has confidence in her ability to do a good job as a mother. The Earth Mother's vulnerability is that she is sometimes passive in the face of challenges and accepts difficulties rather than trying to change the situation. At times, she avoids complex or thorny emotions and situations as she accepts what life hands her.

THE EARTH MOTHER

- Has a calm, natural attitude toward life
- Sees family life as easy and natural; takes difficulties in stride, enjoys easy time with her children.
- Does not try to jam-pack too many activities into a day but "goes with the flow"
- Is drawn to a child-centered family life; doesn't try to carefully craft childhood experiences but responds naturally to life as it happens
- Focuses her time at home with her family and is not too focused on high standards of organization and cleanliness

VULNERABILITIES

- Can subvert her life to the needs of others
- May have limited expectations for her children and herself

THE PASSIONATE SPIRIT

Whereas the Earth Mother is calm and serene, the Passionate Spirit mom lives in her emotions. She vividly feels the highs and lows of life; she embodies an artistic temperament. The Passionate Spirit's love for her children, friends, extended family, and even coworkers creates an environment that is rich and warm, where all in her care thrive. She does not rely on planning skills and is often not very organized. Emotions and relationships are everything. She frequently stops to "smell the roses."

The Passionate Spirit mother believes in the mystery and beauty of life. She understands that having a child is not entirely a rational decision or a step that can necessarily be fully planned, organized, and implemented. She embraces the miracle of creation and is transformed by the experience.

A deep emotion or deeply moving experience may launch the beginning of family life for some Passionate Spirit mothers. Rather than just accepting what life has given her, she allows her passions to set her path. Catherine, a woman who started and built her own trucking company, has always been motivated by her passions. She worked hard, had an active social life, and assumed that someday she would get married and have children. Although her life didn't work out that way, her passion launched her in a direction that she deeply embraced:

> *I was in a long-term relationship, and I was about thirty-seven when it ended. As the years went on, I had this terrible sadness that I might not have a child, and I had always envisioned myself as a mother. I knew my biological clock was ticking. At forty I was still not in another relationship. I had always had a deep yearning for a child. I never questioned it—someday I would be a mother.*
>
> *One night I couldn't sleep. I turned on the TV, and there was a documentary called* The Dying Rooms, *about Chinese orphanages. Sometimes you see something that is really poignant and it affects you deeply. It changes your life. I then gave up all ideas of getting married and pregnant, and thought, "I am going to China to adopt one of these children."*

Catherine's depth of emotion for what she saw the Chinese babies enduring created a deep desire and conviction to adopt one. She went through many struggles to adopt her baby, but her passionate commitment could not be broken.

The transition to motherhood can often be a transforming and even overwhelming experience for the Passionate Spirit. She lives in her emotions, which can sometimes overpower her, as Chloe, who works as an education consultant, attests:

Part of me was reveling in what a miracle this baby was, and then another part of me was absolutely panicked and overwhelmed. I didn't know that you just love your baby so much. The love was just overwhelming and just so scary.

The Passionate Spirit's vision of family embodies relationships and the spirit of the child. Home is the fertile bed where the emotional connection is made. Things might not get done and schedules may get off track, but that is because the Passionate Spirit mother will stop and focus on her child, her friend, her spouse, and let everything else go. Chloe believes that the human connection is the most important thing:

For me, it's not about tricks or strategies or keeping a neat house; it's about a relationship. Since my kids were babies, it's been a relationship; I've been deeply guided by that.

Dionna, a factory worker and a Passionate Spirit mom, finds that she focuses most on her child's spirit and soul:

I have to remember that my daughter is only mine for a short time. I want to help her be the person that she is intended to be, and to stir up those gifts and not to hinder the growth of her spirit. I want to make sure I'm nurturing her soul.

The Passionate Spirit's children thrive in this cocoon of her passion for them. They know that she will always relish a special moment with them or will come back for that extra hug and kiss. Small and large moments are appreciated and savored in family life, even if that means the dinner dishes don't get done until morning.

The Passionate Spirit's home is often inviting and warm. I met several whose homes felt comfortably chaotic. As I sat in the home of Josie, an artist and a wonderful Passionate Spirit, we suddenly heard a crash. A shelf loaded with piles of laundry had crashed to the floor.

So the laundry may not get done on time, but you can always have a warm conversation or a much-needed hug. Household chores, systems, goals, and plans can be a distraction to her.

The Passionate Spirit mom will often carry that spirit to work with her. She takes time for people there, and her relationships are central. Francesca quit her job as a construction manager when she had her first baby, and set up her own small construction management firm in her home so that she could control her hours. She has become very personally involved with her few employees. She helps them in their personal lives and, in turn, feels comfortable involving them in her family's life. Although Francesca wanted her own company in order to control her hours, she becomes so engaged in a work project, a client issue, or an employee's personal life, that she invariably works long into the night after she puts her children to bed. Her life is rich and full and somewhat unbounded.

Dionna carries her passionate spirit into the workplace on the factory assembly line:

> *We are with our coworkers more than we are with our family. We are each other's family, so it's very important, very vital, that we treat one another with love and respect. Two older ladies on my line, "Auntie" Gina and "Auntie" Lillian, they're always laughing at me because I will often say, "Everybody, stop, stop, stop. Can't you feel the love that's in here?" and they say, "There she goes again!" But everyone loves the atmosphere in our shop. People see the love and the involvement and they say, "Well, hey, I want to participate in that."*

The Passionate Spirit mom will often throw herself into a work project with the kind of zeal that dominates her life. Chloe's three-year-old daughter adored animals and wildlife. When Chloe couldn't find quality children's videos on wildlife, she threw herself into a new project:

> *I just thought, "Well, why hasn't anyone produced a great wildlife video for kids?" So then I became obsessed with the concept of what a video could be, and I thought, "I can do*

that!" I felt I just had to do this, and if I fail, well, I've tried to pursue a wonderful dream. I worked really hard. I did a lot of work in the middle of the night when the girls were sleeping. I lost a lot of sleep, but that was okay, I was inspired.

We can all learn from the Passionate Spirit's healthy approach to embracing and accepting the depth of her feelings and focusing on the people around her. She understands that motherhood is a deeply emotional and life-changing experience. Her ability to relish the emotional connection allows all in her care to thrive. The Passionate Spirit's vulnerability is that her life can feel unbounded. She sometimes misses schedules or deadlines. Her powerful emotions can sometimes become a quagmire for her.

THE PASSIONATE SPIRIT

- Embraces a passion for life and experiences
- Immerses herself in the emotional connection with those close to her
- Realizes the beauty, mystery, and importance of each life
- Wears her emotions on her sleeve; feels the highs and lows of life intensely
- Sees her family life as revolving around relationships, conversations, physical affection
- Lives in the moment; does not focus a great deal of attention on planning and organization

VULNERABILITIES

- Life can sometimes feel unbounded or out of control
- Powerful emotions can overwhelm her and make it difficult to move on

---

FINDING YOUR PATH

A mother's style of parenting reflects her personality and worldview. The beauty of her mothering emerges when she realizes the great strengths of her style and draws on them for the benefit of her children and family—and ultimately for herself. No one mothering style is better than another. I saw with the working mothers I interviewed that you can thrive in many different ways. Don't pressure yourself to conform to a style that is not really you.

I realized, through this process, that I started in parenting twelve years ago as largely a Camp Counselor and Passionate Spirit mom, and I had no carefully specified plan for work or family. In fact, I embarked on several paths that made no sense for work/family sanity. In retrospect, I don't know what possessed me to want a child so much when we were in the midst of our start-up of Bright Horizons, at a time when every day was action-packed, full of intense highs and lows, and everything was still so unsure. But we welcomed Farrell with enthusiasm and passion, and we reoriented our lives for her. Then, two and a half years later, we were struggling through the most difficult time in our company's history. Our new concept of worksite child care was still unproven, and in a recession, we couldn't convince employers to sign on. Month to month it was unclear whether our company would survive. Amid all this uncertainty, we joyfully plunged into having our second child. After a miscarriage and a difficult pregnancy, Lucas was born. Perhaps due to his miraculous arrival against this backdrop, I felt stronger, more resolute, and more joyful myself. In reaction to all the stress and potential distractions of our work, my priority of children and family above all else now suddenly became clear and simple.

With a healthy girl and boy and major work challenges on our plate, we should have stopped there. But I knew that Gracie's spirit was yearning to be born and felt that she had spoken to me in my dreams. After two more miscarriages and a four-month pregnancy bed rest due to complications, Gracie arrived triumphantly in this world. Even with three young children, my deep interest in third-world cultures and issues had not been dampened. Throughout these early child-rearing years, my mother, who also shares this interest, and I have taken my young children off on many adventures to Africa, Southeast Asia, and Central America. Although my path has not always been practical or rational, I have now started to understand that is who I am.

Through all my interviews with other mothers, I came to realize that I could have benefited from more strategic planning, particularly early on. When pregnant with Farrell, I never thought ahead to register her for child care at our center, although I knew it was full. When she was born and I finally did, the waiting list was six months long, and they could take her only a few mornings a week. I didn't feel that we could jump ahead of all the people on the waiting list, so Roger and I began to work shifts to cover the time we didn't have child care. And here it was, our own center—I should have known better. We also made the poor decision to move to a new house in a new town just months after Farrell was born. We took on greater expenses just when our company was most unsure and were now in a community where we knew no one.

Over time, I have managed to adopt some strategic planning in a few areas—and that has helped immeasurably! I often wish that I could have a more "go with the flow" attitude, and be more laid back like our Earth Mothers, but I somehow doubt that it will ever happen.

You may recognize yourself principally in one of the four categories described in this chapter, or you may find that you vary your style depending on the situation, time of day, or phase of family life. Throughout the book, I will point out how different mothering styles can help in certain situations. Embrace the strengths of your style and feel free to borrow from the other styles depending on the circumstance. Perhaps we can learn from one another to incorporate a broader range of skills in our parenting and liberate ourselves from thinking that there is just one right way to mother. The goal is not to have it all perfectly figured out, but to enjoy the journey along the way. As Denise, a mother of two young children, said:

> *I think I am a really good mom, but definitely not perfect. In fact, I do not aspire to be a perfect mom. That sets up too much pressure. I want my children to understand that I'm human—that I enjoy them and love them without having everything all figured out.*

Being a good mother does not depend on being a Strategic Planner or an Earth Mother. It does not depend on whether you work or stay home. It does not depend on how big your house is, whether it is neat and well organized, whether you have a nice yard. Married, single, young, old, gay, straight are not the critical variables. It's less important to look at how all your neighbors and friends are living their lives than to look inside and understand how you want to live yours.

You can lead a quiet life that is pulled in close around your nuclear family and your job. Or you may build a big community and immerse yourself in neighborhood, church, synagogue, mosque, work community, or extended family. You may want a challenging career, or you may prefer a job that is satisfying but not too demanding. You can lead a blended life where work and family are closely enmeshed, or you can keep the two worlds healthy but separate.

A major message of this book is to take the effort to try to find *your* path—the path that makes you feel fulfilled and comfortable as a working mother. If you are thriving, feeling good about yourself and your choices, then it is more likely that your children will thrive. As one mother, Paige, said:

> *I believe that being a good mom means being happy at the end of the day. That happiness ultimately translates into your kids, and maybe your partner, being happy at the end of the day. It's curious to see, but if I'm happy, everyone tends to be happy.*

Having a child brings great joy and mystery, and also an enormous number of activities, chores, and sometimes complicated logistics. Your daily life will need to change, both to accommodate the large number of new tasks associated with being a parent and also to allow time with your child. You will be a much better parent and a much better worker if you've been thoughtful about your choices—for both work and family. And know that these choices may change over time.

PART II

The Three Pillars of Successful Working Motherhood

I started my conversations with mothers looking just at what the working mother could do, but I discovered that many flourish not only due to their efforts, but also due to what *others* are doing with and for them. Many working mothers rely on outside support. Although their support structure is varied, mothers continually focused on the same three major sources of strength, what I call the *Three Pillars of Successful Working Motherhood:*

1. A partner-in-parenting
2. A supportive employer
3. Excellent child care

Although our media and public debate often focus on the working mother as an entity unto herself, she actually exists within a constellation of influences that helps or hinders her ability to mother effectively while working. It is not the mother's abilities alone that allow her and her family to thrive.

When things go wrong in families, too often we, as a society, point a finger at the working mother. If only she didn't work, or didn't work such long hours; if only she weren't so stressed. She is the one who needs to accommodate and change, society says. It's as if media and society believe that a child has only one influence in his or her life—the mother. And it's as if there is only one characteristic of motherhood that is important—her constant presence. Mothering *is* a critical skill that will have a powerful effect on a child's development. Yes, a mother is vitally important. But *how* she mothers is the important factor—and how the father parents is an important factor, too. Much of the public debate about working motherhood ignores the role that other elements play in a family life. They carry a great influence and also a great responsibility for the well-being of our children and families.

PILLAR ONE: A PARTNER-IN-PARENTING

Parenting can be confusing, exhausting, joyful, life-changing, or overwhelming. Doing it all alone can be very difficult. Having a partner-in-parenting (whether a spouse, a family member, or a friend) to share the joys and daily responsibilities can help make your parenting journey easier and more meaningful.

If there are two parents present in a child's life, the child can benefit from both parents' devotion and involvement. While a mother's contributions are essential, the father's role should not be ignored. He, too, is responsible for the well-being and care of his child, and deserves more recognition for his involvement.

The father of your child can be a partner-in-parenting even if you are no longer together. He can still maintain a primary caregiving role in his child's life. Or this partner may not be your child's father, but may be someone else who is close to you and your children. Your partner-in-parenting may be a close friend, your life partner, your child's stepfather, or perhaps your own mother, father, sister, or brother. It helps to share the joys and burdens of a household and family with someone else who is close to your children.

PILLAR TWO: A SUPPORTIVE EMPLOYER

Most of us spend many hours of our day in a workplace. The culture and values of this workplace play a strong role in our family's healthy functioning. An unhealthy, unsupportive work environment is just as toxic for our family life as living in a home with asbestos and lead paint. Environment counts—physical and psychological. To be healthy, well-functioning employees *and* healthy, well-functioning parents, we need work environments that support us as whole people.

A supportive organization and supervisor can help you to succeed both as a worker and as a parent by offering you support, flexibility, and respect. More and more organizations are starting to understand that a supportive work environment helps to create and keep good employees. If you know you have the support to be a responsible, engaged parent at home, it helps you to be a responsible, engaged worker as well.

PILLAR THREE: EXCELLENT CHILD CARE

An excellent child care provider can make a big difference in your children's development, security, and happiness. She or he can also become essential to you in your journey through working parenthood.

You'll have greater peace of mind being away from your children during the day if you know that they are well cared for while you work. The first years of life are vital to your children's development. A skilled and committed caregiver can help foster your children's sense of security and love and desire to learn. Excellent child care can also help give your children the foundation of skills necessary for later school success.

Also, an experienced caregiver can offer you invaluable parenting advice and support as you adjust to your new role. Your caregiver can become another devoted adult who loves your children and provides a stable, constant presence in their and your lives.

Without confidence in her children's care, no mother can thrive at work. Conversely, if her children are thriving, a mother is better able to both work and parent more effectively.

You can certainly be a good mother without these three pillars. But when you do have them, they can make your various roles easier and more enjoyable. If things are not working in your life, don't look only to yourself for blame and guilt. Look to see if one of the three pillars is missing. If we can understand the importance of these pillars, we can work to ensure we have them in our lives. In this section I will discuss in greater depth each of these pillars of successful working motherhood, and I will show you some paths for finding them for yourself.

TWO

A Partner-in-Parenting

*When I think about being a good working mother, it helps to
have my husband, Andrew, right there with me. When you
work, part of the mothering thing that you worry about is
whether your child has enough of that "mother love." But
when I see Andrew, who is so in touch with our kids and who
does so much at home, it takes a lot of the burden off me.*

—Carrie

Whether you are married, have a life partner, or are single, sharing the joys and responsibilities of caring for your child can
make your parenting more enjoyable and less overwhelming. It can
also make a difference in your ability to effectively combine working
and parenting. The thrill of your child's first step, the charm of your
three-year-old's imagination, the philosophical musings of your
seven-year-old—all this joy, wonder, and mystery are wonderful to
share. It is just as helpful to share the challenging moments of your
child's sick days while you're working, discipline issues, and the complicated logistics of school, child care, lessons, and activities. This is
not to say that you can't do it on your own, because you can. But your
life as a working parent can be eased if another devoted caregiver
shares this job with you.

    If you are married, your partner-in-parenting is most likely
your spouse. For some married mothers, their partner-in-parenting is
instead another close family member or friend. Most single mothers I
interviewed also have partners-in-parenting. This partner is some-

times the child's father, who shares custody of the child and is actively engaged as a primary caregiver. In other instances, this partner-in-parenting is a member of the mother's family—sister, brother, parent—or a close friend or two. In addition to a partner-in-parenting, many mothers, married or single, have other sources of support—child care providers, neighbors, religious institutions. I discuss these communities of support in chapter 14.

In this chapter I will talk first about the spouse as a partner-in-parenting. I will describe the three most common types of marriage for working couples—what I call the Equal Partnership marriage, the Manager/Doer marriage, and the Traditional marriage. Mothers and other experts will explain why the father also matters so much in a child's life. Other working mothers will tell you how they found partners-in-parenting when the father was not available. With this chapter I hope to show you the value of partnership and help you think about what kind of partnership you would most like to seek.

THE SECRET TO MAKING IT WORK: A GREAT PARTNER

Mothers told me time and time again how indispensable their partner's support was to their ability to function at work and at home effectively. I heard stories about the father's responsiveness to a crying baby, his ease in changing diapers and bathing a newborn, his adeptness at handling the busy morning routine, his commitment to the nightly bedtime rituals. Many dads are the ones who cook dinner every night, or clean up the kitchen after the mother cooks. I began to see that the reason many working mothers feel they are thriving is due to this support. One mother, Sondra, is a machine assembler on a factory line. Both she and her husband, Cody, who also works on an assembly line, often have to work a fifty- to fifty-five-hour week due to mandated overtime. They have a four-year-old son, Bryant. Listen to what Sondra has to say about the value of a supportive partner:

I always thought that this life as working parents would be stressful and really hard, but it's just not as hard as I thought it would be. I think it's because my husband does so much. It just amazes me. What's the secret to making it all work? A great husband.

But a number of people can potentially fill this partner-in-parenting role, and every mother varies in how much of a partnership she wants. Let's look at the various models, starting with the different marriage models.

MARRIAGE MODELS

When working couples organize themselves for new parenthood, husband and wife evolve into new roles to reflect the new responsibilities. Some couples discuss and define the obligations and consciously organize their respective tasks. But many couples move into new roles without consciously designing them or even sometimes realizing the evolution. Many of the married mothers I interviewed have husbands who are partners with them in parenting, an essential support that allows the mothers to feel good about working and parenting. Far fewer mothers have husbands who are also partners in the domestic chores around the house. I have included both aspects of domestic roles, in addition to the wage-earning role, below.

Generally, mothers described to me a marriage that fell into one of three marriage models:

- *Equal Partnership marriage:* Husband and wife consider themselves a balanced team. They share the domestic responsibilities for both parenting and household chores and also share the "breadwinning" responsibilities.

- *Manager/Doer marriage:* One spouse, usually the wife, organizes and plans the domestic life and care of the children. The other spouse, usually the husband, is an engaged participant. Often in this model, the husband is a partner in the parenting responsibilities but not in the domestic chores. Primary wage-earning responsibility varies widely in this model.

- *Traditional marriage:* The wife takes full responsibility for domestic life and does most of the tasks—in both parenting and household chores. Although the husband may be a loving father and husband, he does little of the domestic work. He is often, but not always, the primary wage earner.

My group of mothers had these types of marriages:

Equal Partnership: 36%
Manager/Doer: 50%
Traditional: 14%

MAKING CONSCIOUS CHOICES IN MARRIAGE

I was initially surprised to see how many of the mothers I interviewed are in Equal Partnership and Manager/Doer marriages—marriages where they have a partner-in-parenting—and how few of the mothers are in Traditional marriages. I doubt if these percentages are reflective of working couples in general. However, let's remember that the mothers I interviewed were chosen because they seem to be effective, thriving working mothers: Perhaps having a partner-in-parenting is a major reason.

As you read through the marriage models, think about what model feels right for you. Read this chapter together with your partner. Any one of these three models is fine, *if you and your partner are both happy with it*. Although many couples "just fall into" certain models, you and your partner can make deliberate choices in your marriage. Just as there has been enormous flux in work roles over the last few decades, there has also been change in roles at home. If you and your partner both have some choice and control in how to define your roles at work and home, you will more likely embrace them.

Working parents have three areas of family responsibility:

	Parenting	Housework and Home Management	Wage earning
Equal Partnership	Mother and father share	Mother and father share	Mother and father share
Manager/Doer	Mother and father share	Mother takes the lead; father participates	Varies widely
Traditional	Mother takes the lead; father usually participates	Mother	Father usually takes the lead; mother participates

Equal Partnership

An Equal Partnership marriage is one where there is generally a balanced split of responsibilities for child care, maintaining the home, and earning money. Many couples in this category have consciously chosen and worked at this path. Since cultural expectation calls for a more traditional gender split in roles—father as primary breadwinner and mother as primary caregiver—these couples explicitly decided on a path that worked better for them. Monique, a financial manager, describes how and why she and her husband, Patrick, also a financial manager, developed the roles in their Equal Partnership marriage:

> *Since I grew up in a single-parent environment, my mom taught me how to jack up a car and change a tire, and my brother can iron and cook better than I can. So the idea of gender-specific roles never even entered into my head. Our son cooks with Dad and does laundry with Mom.*

Either before they had their first child or shortly thereafter, many Equal Partnership couples sat down and talked about how they want to live their family and work lives, and how they want to design their roles. They valued the sense of teamwork they had created before children and want to continue along this path. Sarah, an academic administrator, and her husband, John, an architect, chose to share the home roles:

> *What John and I think is most important is acting as a team and making all our decisions as a team. We share the responsibility at home. We share a vision for our family and what we want for our children. We've made decisions together about our careers. And we've created a home together that we both maintain. We've purposely moved away from traditional roles to create a balanced, shared life.*

Some of the couples in this category do most of the domestic chores interchangeably. Others split the chores, with each spouse taking responsibility for certain tasks. Silvia, a real estate project manager, describes how she and her husband, Justin, an attorney, approach their home life:

> *We don't need to discuss that this or that thing needs to get done. We both pitch in to take care of things. If I have a really stressful week at work, Justin can sense it and he will take over more of the housework and spend more time with our son. And I'll do the same if he is having a hard week at work.*

Equal Partnership couples demonstrate a wide variety of ways to organize their family and work lives. They follow no standard model. Since, in many ways, they are departing from the traditional, they have charted their own course in ways that are unique to them. Some of the ways they have organized their lives include:

- Husband and wife continue in the same full-time jobs they had before children. Through great planning and determination, and often by limiting their outside commitments, they create a balanced and shared approach to domestic roles and responsibilities.
- Mother and father stagger their full-time daily work schedules so that one parent is present for the morning routine and one parent is there for the late afternoon or evening routine. They all gather together at the same point later in the evening.

- Each parent chooses a new job in a "family-friendly" company where family issues are supported. They often take advantage of available flexible work options.

- Both mother and father telecommute (work from home) a day or two each week.

- The mother and father "sequence" their careers. The mother stays home for several years during childbearing and babyhood. She then goes back to work, and the father stays home for several years.

- The couple chooses to have just one child, and therefore feel they are better able to be fully responsible and engaged both at home and at work.

- Both parents choose less ambitious career tracks, possibly at lower pay, in order to be more available at home.

Not only do father and mother share the domestic responsibilities in an Equal Partnership marriage, they also share the wage-earning responsibilities. Again, there is no one set model. In some cases, the father brings in more income; in other cases, the mother earns more; and some earn roughly equivalent incomes. But they both share in the financial planning and responsibility.

I was struck by how many mothers in this category talked about how happy they are in their domestic arrangements. They have some control over their lives. They and their partners decide together what would work best for them. Patricia, an architect, describes her husband, Ralph, an entrepreneur, and marriage this way:

I have an incredibly sensitive and supportive husband. He gives the time that is needed. He doesn't say, "Oh, I can't do this. I can't do that." We do look at our marriage and our parenting as a partnership. We pick up each other's slack. It makes our marriage feel—well, magical.

Characteristics of an Equal Partnership marriage:

■ Wife and husband share the domestic responsibilities: both care for the children and household chores.

- Wife and husband also share household management responsibilities: being aware of what needs to be done at home, prioritizing tasks, and scheduling the tasks.

- Both parents share wage-earning responsibility; they may not have equal salaries, but they share the financial concern and planning.

- If one partner goes away for several days, the other partner can run the home successfully with no extended "to-do" lists or other direction and guidance.

Manager/Doer

In most Manager/Doer marriages, the mother is the household manager and takes the lead at home, and the father is an active participant. The father is often very engaged with the children and, in many cases, is a primary caregiver along with the mother.

I saw a great deal of diversity of reactions and work/family arrangements in this category. Many of the mothers in this category feel very happy and fulfilled. They take great pride in being able to both work and be devoted mothers. Many of the Manager/Doer mothers greatly appreciate that their partners share with them in parenting, and accept that their spouses participate less with the household chores. Chloe, an education consultant, knows that she could not do so well at work and at home without the support and involvement of her husband:

I am really appreciative of all that my husband does. I think that we are really very comfortable in each of the roles we are taking. I do a lot more of the housework. I also do more of the traditionally female jobs—you know, I'm the fixer-upper of the house, and he kills the bugs and changes the lightbulbs. So we're pretty traditional in household chores, but I think that in the ways of the really important things, like deciding what we want for our children, we're not.

Many of the Manager/Doer mothers feel that they and their spouses operate as a strong team. They both work (most full-time), and they are both devoted to their children. They are partners in the parenting of their children.

In most Manager/Doer marriages, both parents do household chores and tasks, but as I mentioned above, the mother is the household manager. As one mother put it, "I set the agenda; he comes to the meeting." The mother is typically the one who devotes the substantial time and mental energy to planning, organizing, scheduling, and delegating. She takes the lead on many of the household chores, then assigns the tasks. Although some mothers feel fine with this arrangement, many resent carrying the larger burden of domestic work while also working outside the home. Janet, who works in human resources for a hospital, sees it this way:

> *I have really turned into the taskmaster at home. I am the one who sees that the carpet needs vacuuming, or that laundry needs to be done. My husband doesn't pick up on that. I could give him a list of ten things and he will do them all, but he will not take the initiative to do it. That bothers me. It is not romantic or sexy to be the one saying, "Can you clean up the kitchen or vacuum the rug?" It gets to the point where I feel like I am everybody's mother.*

The chores for which the father has primary responsibility often carry great discretion about when and how they are done—yardwork, home equipment purchases, furniture and toy assembling, car repair and servicing, household repairs. They often are not daily tasks and can be done on his own schedule, whenever he chooses. The chores that the mother has primary responsibility for are frequently daily tasks that can't be put off—cooking meals, doing laundry, sweeping and mopping floors, picking up the house.

Several mothers who hold more demanding jobs than their partners still carry the household-manager role at home. The following mother holds a senior corporate position and travels a great deal, and her husband works flexible hours in an office near home:

> *I do a lot of the daily stuff around the house, even though he's there much more than I am. I am the spark for how the house*

is managed. I wish that both of us were equally responsible for everything at home. That responsibility for me is the impetus for a negotiation, how to delegate it, how it's going to happen. It's just something that I do on a pretty conscious level. You know, thinking about what has to be done, organizing it—all that just occupies a big part of my mind each day. Any way you cut it, that's gonna be, yeah, me.

Characteristics of a Manager/Doer marriage:

- Both spouses play an active role in the parenting of the children; they make decisions together about the children.
- The mother usually keeps track of family life: daily activities, scheduling doctor and dentist appointments, children's functions, etc.—in short, she is the master planner and organizer around the home.
- The mother usually notices when chores need to be done around the house, then asks her spouse to help out with certain tasks.
- The mother is the one who gets called at work when their child is sick and is usually the one who stays home when a repairman needs to show up.
- Wage-earning responsibility varies widely in these couples.

Traditional

In a Traditional marriage for a working couple, the mother has responsibility for the home and children in addition to working, and the father usually, but not always, has the primary wage-earning role. In this category, the mother not only manages the household but does all or nearly all of the domestic tasks for both children and home.

Some of the couples in this category explicitly *chose* to live in a more traditional marriage. In these cases, the mother had long looked forward to devoting the bulk of her energies to children and home, and the father feels most comfortable in the primary bread-winning role. Often the father is devoted and loving, but neither one expects him to do much of the domestic work. In some cases, the mother does not seek rapid career advancement or additional work responsibilities. She works either because she enjoys doing so or out of financial necessity. Alena, who works full-time in an auditing department, would prefer to stay home with her children, but due to financial necessity, she has to work. She wants to have primary responsibility for her children and home:

> It has always been very painful for me to be working, but it's just a necessity right now. I like being home caring for the children and the home. It's an innate desire. Most of the time these responsibilities fall on me because I want them to.

Although some couples have chosen this path and are happy, many more of the mothers I interviewed have just fallen into these roles, and they express acute frustration. The telling element is choice. For many mothers it is not by choice that they shoulder the domestic load; it is by default. The father expects the mother to take responsibility for children and home. Cynthia, a corporate executive, describes her relationship with her husband, another senior professional:

> My husband really leaves it all to me. I can be very angry about his level of responsiveness, why he does so little. The biggest wish I have for my husband is for him to give more. If you are going to be married, have a family, and both work, you have to be a team. It has to be a partnership. My husband is just not tuned in.

Several of the mothers in the Traditional category talked about resenting doing all the "second shift" of work at home after putting in a full day at work. Many feel exhausted, stressed, and resentful. Joyce, a mother of two, puts it this way:

> When I got pregnant, I knew that my husband's job was pretty demanding. He said that I could work or not work, but I would need to handle the house and kids. I do feel that our relationship changed after we had kids. We really went into these gender-traditional roles. I resent it. Why do I have to do everything when I also work? Why is it just assumed that the

mother does it all? It was a huge problem when I worked full-time, but now I've cut back to part-time and am just resigned to it.

The father's and mother's paths have dramatically diverged; as she does more and more of the domestic work, he spends more and more time at his job. Many ultimately find themselves living very different lives. In some of the marriages, the mother has accepted the situation and focuses on creating a wonderful home where her children can thrive. But I found more deeply frustrated mothers in this category than in the other two. There may not be as much resentment in marriages where the wife is not employed outside the home. A Traditional marriage in which a mother also has a paid outside job puts a great many additional burdens on her shoulders that are not shared by her spouse.

Characteristics of a Traditional marriage:

- The mother is responsible for the bulk of the domestic duties—both child care and household chores.
- The mother plays the primary emotional and logistical planning role at home, not only thinking about what needs to be done at home but doing it, too.
- The father carries the primary responsibility for the economic security of the family.
- The father's career takes precedence over the mother's job or career.

DECIDE WHAT WORKS BEST FOR YOU BOTH

In each of the three marriage models, the mothers who felt happiest (and there were happy mothers in each category) were those who sat down with their husbands or partners and together decided on their roles.

There are two parts of work at home—parenting work and housework. One of the challenges with deciding domestic roles is that it is a lot easier to have enthusiastic participation with the parenting work. Many fathers seek to play an active role in their children's lives, and are actively engaged in the nightly routine of baths, stories, and bedtime. But it is a lot harder to enthusiastically jump in and mop the kitchen floor, clean the bathroom, and fold laundry after a long day at work. Deciding what works best for the household should also include a discussion of housework. (I cover household chores more fully in chapter 11.) It is easy to "get stuck" in certain roles. In the sections below, I discuss common patterns in working-couple marriages.

As you think about your respective roles, you and your partner can discuss the following questions:

WORKLIFE

- How important to each of you is your career and job? How ambitious are you? How much do you want/need to devote to work?
- What are the financial commitments in your family? How can your combined incomes cover those financial needs?
- How comfortable does each of you feel with primary wage-earning responsibility?
- Does either of you want to cut back at work to spend more time at home?
  - If so, how should your lifestyle change to accommodate a reduced income?

CHILDREN

- How much time do you feel comfortable placing your children in nonparental care?
- What importance do you place on each parent playing a primary role in your child's life?
- How many children do you want to have and feel you can care for?

MAINTAINING THE HOME (see chapter 11)

- How can the household chores get done so neither spouse feels they're unfair?
  - Are there chores you each prefer?
  - Can some chores become less important or can standards decline?
  - Can some chores be outsourced?

BEWARE OF DRIFTING INSTEAD OF DECIDING

Many couples move into more traditional views of their roles by cultural expectation, rather than by choice; and therefore many mothers end up feeling frustrated by the ultimate arrangement. Sue, a software engineer, described to me how she and her husband, Dan, a budget analyst, fell into a path that they did not consciously design. Ultimately they both felt frustrated and dissatisfied. Sue and Dan met in their twenties and spent several years together before having children. During their childless years as a couple, they were very much a team. They shared many interests and activities together. They loved to camp and hike and participated in these activities with friends. They both did the minimal housework and were often fairly lax about it. They have similar educational backgrounds. They each were pursuing a career.

Then they had their first child, Jillian. Without consciously understanding it or discussing it, they each started to assume more traditional roles. Even though they both worked full-time, Sue took on more and more of the domestic duties—both in taking care of their baby and managing things around the house. It just seemed that she noticed when things had to be done, and more often than not, she did them. Dan loved coming home from work and playing with the baby, but he didn't notice when diapers were low or when the next pediatrician's appointment needed to be scheduled. If Sue asked him to do something around the house, however, he usually did it.

With the arrival of Jillian, Dan felt greater responsibility as the provider. He started to spend longer hours at work. He moved ahead in his career, and when he got his next promotion, he no longer felt he could take days off when Jillian was sick. During Jillian's first year in child care, Sue was frequently called out of work to pick up Jillian when she had a fever or cold. With Dan spending longer hours at work and feeling greater work stress, Sue took on more and more of the household chores and errands. When Sue's supervisor offered her a position that would carry greater pay and also greater responsibilities, she turned it down, feeling that it would add too much stress to their lives.

Dan often got home from work just in time to tuck in Jillian. He felt bad when Jillian wanted only Sue to put her to bed, or when

Jillian wanted only Sue to comfort her as she cried. He felt he really missed something when his daughter took her first steps and three days passed before he was able to see it.

Although they had not planned it, Dan is now in the primary wage-earning role, and Sue is in the primary domestic role. Dan feels removed from the emotional center of the family and left out of his baby's daily milestones. He feels bad that he does not have the easy intimacy he sees between Sue and Jillian. Sue resents doing most of the housework and being the one who is always interrupted at work for home issues. She dislikes carrying the bulk of the domestic responsibilities while trying to also have a career. Because of this, she feels that she has fallen back in her career while Dan is moving ahead:

> *Although I love Dan and I love being a mom, I can't help but resent the situation we're in. I don't feel as much a partner as I used to, because now my main job is home and family, and his main job is to make the money.*

BEWARE OF ACCEPTING INSTEAD OF CHOOSING

Many mothers who did not choose the primary domestic role live with it, justifying that their husbands are doing a lot more than many others they know.

> *The relationship works. If I specifically ask him to do something, he will do it. My husband comes from a very traditional family where his every need was catered to. I am very appreciative that he grocery-shops and does the cooking. That is really great.*

This mother looks at the glass as half full, rather than half empty, even though she works longer hours than her husband and has less job flexibility.

Other mothers find that it is easier to do the work themselves:

> *As far as the cleaning or the grocery shopping, it would be great if my husband said he'll go do that. But I know it's more*

*hassle to ask him to do it, or want him to do it, when I know
he would be absolutely miserable doing it. It's just not
worth it.*

Myrna and Eugene are both assembly-line workers who earn
the same wage and work about the same hours. Myrna, however,
shoulders nearly all of the housework. She accepts it because she
feels Eugene is such a good husband in other ways:

*It really doesn't bother me, because I guess I'm kind of old-
fashioned. He's always so good to me. He's always concerned
about my health; and financially, I couldn't ask for anything
better. He'll drop the check on the table every week, he doesn't
care. Anything for me, anything for the kids. We enjoy each
other's company. We rarely argue. I'll come home after my
shift at two A.M., and we'll sit in bed and talk.*

Are you accepting the domestic responsibilities because:

- He's better around the house than most dads and you're
grateful for that?
- You just want to keep the peace and know he'll never change,
so why start a war?
- He supports you in other ways—love, friendship, psychological
and financial support—and this is more important to you?
- He's a good dad, your children love him, and that's more
important to you than getting him to share the housework?
- You believe there really should be a gender split in roles, and
you feel more comfortable in traditional male and female
roles at home?

If you're comfortable with the arrangement, that's great. If not,
go back to the questions on page 55 of this chapter as a point of
departure for a conversation with your partner.

Many of these issues are deep-seated and can impact marriage
dynamics broadly. There isn't usually a quick fix. If you are unhappy

with the domestic dynamics in your marriage, it will require a sincere commitment on the part of both spouses to grapple with these issues. Resolving deep unhappiness and frustration in marriage roles may require professional help. However, many times it is more a matter of raising awareness, and following some of the guides in this chapter and in chapter 11, which deals with household tasks, will help each spouse to understand the other's perspective. The important point is to be sensitive and respectful of each spouse's situation and find solutions that both of you can embrace.

BEWARE OF GATEKEEPING

It is interesting to see that many moms serve as "gatekeepers" in the family dynamic. Even though they may complain about having to do most of the work, and want their husbands to do more, some may really want the control and ultimate authority over what happens with the children and home. Perhaps they don't want their husbands to be equal partners. Particularly if you are a Strategic Planner or a Camp Counselor mom, you should watch out for this. You may be used to taking charge and making decisions; maybe you don't want to share this with your spouse. Lena, an entrepreneur and mother of three children, guards all the decision making at home:

> It was really my decision which child care center we would enroll our children in, but I had my husband go to the last few. It got him involved a little bit, as if he were part of the decision. My husband feels that I pretend that I don't have a husband. But I always have all the responsibility—I take them to school, to the doctors' appointments. I am always carrying them around with me. So why shouldn't I have the last word?

Jessica is a senior executive. She is the primary breadwinner of the family. She works long hours on top of a fifty-minute commute. Even though her husband works shorter hours at an office close to home, she still carries the household manager and primary caregiving role. She will drive back home in the middle of the day to take her children to their pediatrician appointments, even though her husband is nearby. She is stretched by her more than full schedule, but she won't give up that role:

> *The children cry if I'm not the one to put them to bed, if I'm not the one doing story time. But I created that. I want to be the primary person for them. I think I've overcompensated for working. I definitely have more on my plate, and I let my husband know that sometimes. But I don't see how I would let any of it go, either.*

Roger and I have moved between the Equal Partnership and Manager/Doer marriage models at different points in our marriage. In the early childbearing years, I took on the household management role. I would have liked to spend less time on it, but I also found it difficult to give up control over the home and children decisions. Without consciously realizing it, I was often a gatekeeper; I really wanted to decide how things would get done.

Then when I was pregnant with our third child, Gracie, I developed some complications and was confined to strict bed rest for the last four months of the pregnancy. I was suddenly removed from the daily operation and logistics of our family. In the early days of the bed rest, it was difficult for me to give up control of the details of our family life. I would lie upstairs confined to bed and fret about whether Roger was doing things "right." I would yell instructions downstairs, but after a while it seemed like no one heard me. Undaunted, I picked up the phone by the side of the bed and called downstairs to the kitchen on our second line to see if Roger had packed the kids' lunches and bundled them up in hats and mittens before going off to school. Oh, and another thing, had he brushed Farrell's hair, and I don't think Lucas should wear his Batman costume to preschool a fourth day in a row. After a couple of days of the kitchen phone ringing off the hook, Roger tactfully explained that he would let me know right away if either of the children got frostbite or were sent home because of undesirable attire. And until that point, maybe I should sit back and relax, since that was the point of the bed rest.

Roger developed his own approach to children's fashion and

daily activities, and they developed their own routines and habits. Roger developed his own style of cleaning up. In fact, he experimented each evening to see how dirty the dishes could be when he put them in the dishwasher and still come out clean. Roger quickly assumed complete management of the household. Although friends who trooped up into my bedroom to visit would report to me that the house certainly looked "different" now, I became blissfully unaware of the myriad small changes in our family's daily life.

Our children thrived through this period and enjoyed the activities their dad engaged them in. Roger, though harried by the never-ending domestic duties while trying to get his work done, also clearly thrived in his deepening relationship with the children. Roger and I had to come to understand that my way of doing things wasn't necessarily the only way, just my way. If I wanted him to shoulder more of the household responsibility, I also had to relinquish control of determining exactly how things would be done.

Are you a gatekeeper?

- Do you feel that your way is truly the right way to do things?
- Do you feel that your partner should conform to your standards?
- Do you feel uncomfortable when your partner does things very differently?
- Do you feel uncomfortable if your children go to their father to be soothed instead of you?
- Do you really want to be the one to make the decisions about child care, children's clothes and activities, etc.?

THE WORK/FAMILY TRAP

Arlie Hochschild, a sociologist from the University of California at Berkeley, wrote a best-selling book entitled *The Second Shift*. In it she chronicled how most working mothers return home after a day's work and then start their "second shift" of domestic work. Hochschild wrote about the added number of hours per week that a mother works, compared to the father, by doing and planning the household and parenting work.

But both mothers and fathers can feel caught in a work/family trap. Let's look first at the mother. When she takes the bulk of the responsibility for domestic life, she often is more distracted and interrupted at work with family issues; and she pulls back somewhat at work in order to get the housework done. In fact, on average, full-time working mothers work six hours less per week than full-time working fathers.[1] Much of this extra time is spent on household chores. Mothers may have trouble achieving parity with men at work in the face of these two disadvantages. If working dads can invest six hours more per week on their careers, without interruption for home issues, they may be better equipped to get ahead.

I think about this second-shift issue a great deal at Bright Horizons. Ninety-five percent of our employees are women. If the majority of our employees assume the second shift at home, that puts an added strain on them that a largely male organization does not have. They are being distracted and interrupted at work when their husbands are not. Is this affecting the productivity in our organization in a way that a largely male organization does not feel? I have often been tempted to give all our employees a copy of Hochschild's book. I distinctly remember one of our former salespeople, a recent graduate of Harvard Business School, saying she had to leave work early every night because her husband expected a cooked dinner when he arrived home. Why was her husband not leaving work early to cook dinner for her? Again, if it was something they both wanted, then it was a wonderful thing to do. But if he expected a cooked meal every night and she just complied, then frustration is the likely outcome.

But dads in our culture can get caught in a work/family trap as well. What happens to the working father in this scenario? After the birth of their child, the father feels greater responsibility to provide for the family. After all, the father's traditional role has been to provide economic security for his family. So he devotes more time and energy to work, and begins to work longer hours. He is then less available for domestic duties and feels less motivation to take responsibility for them, since his wife is the capable manager at home. As his career moves forward faster, his work demands become more important and take precedence over his wife's work demands. He then becomes less central to family life, does not participate fully as a decision maker regarding the children and home, and is marginalized there. Children adjust and accommodate to his absence. Both he and his family suffer from his less than full engagement in the family.

Surveys have shown repeatedly that many men yearn for a fuller, more involved life with their families. They want to play a central role in their children's lives.[2] For example, a national survey conducted in 2000 by the Radcliffe Public Policy Center and Harris Interactive found that 82 percent of the men surveyed at all income levels stated that it was "very important" to them to have "a work schedule which allows me to spend time with my family." In fact, it was the most crucial job characteristic listed for both men and women.

At the same time, women want equal challenge and meaning at work. This same survey found that 74 percent of the women surveyed said that it was "very important" to find work that "challenges me to use my skills and abilities," compared to a similar 76 percent of the men. Men's and women's views are converging, particularly when looking at surveys of couples in their twenties and thirties. Both want to be devoted parents *and* contribute to the broader work world in a meaningful way. And children should have two parents who are fully engaged at home and fulfilled and actualized as people.

As a culture, we know well about women's quest for equality and equal opportunity at work. However, we do not recognize men's quest for fuller involvement with their families. In the last twenty-five years, with the rise of the women's movement, men's and fathers' roles started to dramatically change as well. This change has included much more involvement in parenting and child rearing on the part of the father, yielding benefits for the entire family.

THE IMPORTANCE OF THE FATHER IN THE CHILD'S DEVELOPMENT

While a father's active involvement at home greatly facilitates his wife's ability to do a good job at work and at home, perhaps an even more compelling argument to dads is that it will have a significant impact on how their children develop. Regardless of whatever marriage model you are in, if your husband or partner can see the important benefits to his children of his active engagement, he may want to play a greater role at home.

It has been only in recent decades that child-development experts have started to understand the role of the father in child development. Before the 1970s, researchers assumed that the father played a limited role in child rearing. They studied almost exclusively the many ways mothers shape and influence the child. Starting in the 1970s, fathers became much more involved in intimate family life and the daily nurture and education of children.[3] As studies began to address the impact of this involvement, the results have been no less than astounding. Children raised with involved fathers have shown distinct benefits in terms of greater cognitive development and academic success, higher self-confidence and self-esteem, and a better ability to handle risk and challenge.[4] By learning to relate intimately with the father as well as the mother, a child can develop more confidence in his ability to forge close relationships with different kinds of people. A child benefits from a dad's different set of skills, his different set of expectations for his child, and from the intimate presence of another adult who unconditionally loves him.

Fathers can bring their own set of skills to nurturing and caring for a child. Many fathers approach child care, even infant care, in a much more physical and playful manner, whereas mothers may emphasize a softer, nurturing approach. Neither is the one right technique; both offer vital developmental resources for a baby. Myrna, a mother of two girls, sums up her and her husband's roles this way:

> *The girls love Eugene to death, that's for sure, and he's more of the play person. They know that's where they get that from. And with me, I'm more of the hugs. They want a hug, they want a kiss, they want love, they can come and get that from me all day long. When they want to play and wrestle, they go to him.*

Recently, I was on an airplane seated next to a man in his midthirties. As we got to talking, I learned that he was an investment banker who worked in an intense, fast-paced business environment and was married with two young children. He was clean-cut, dressed in a conservative business suit, and very focused on the financial statements in front of him. Once I asked him about his children, however, he wouldn't stop talking. He put aside his computer and calculator and switched rapidly from intense business mode to parent mode. He talked about what a wonderful, loving mother his wife was. I asked him what he did when he got home at night. He described how his six-month-old daughter was trying so hard to crawl. He loved to get down on the floor behind his baby and "head-butt" her bottom as she struggled to crawl. His baby would squeal with laughter and inch ahead, then he would head-butt her again to keep her going. Both Dad and baby loved this game. His wife watched this activity, not quite sure of its value. As I sat and listened to this man, I marveled that this was a conversation I never would have expected to have a few years ago.

Much of the research on the impact of the parents' involvement focuses on the father's more active, physical, challenging approach and the mother's nurturing, intuitive, emotive approach. However, in talking to a range of working mothers, I saw a wide diversity of styles that did not necessarily fall along gender lines. Mary loves to organize neighborhood touch football games; Max loves to cook and paint; Lisa loves to wrestle with her three little boys; Paul loves to garden; Karen loves to go on adventure treks and ride horses bareback. Myrna, quoted above, talks about her husband's deep sense of nurturing—a more classically "female" approach:

> *Eugene seems to know our littlest, Bethany, better than I do. They're really connected. Eugene will walk into the house and say, "Where's Bethany, is she okay?" Often it turns out she's running a slight fever or her stomach is bothering her, and I'll not have noticed. He just seems to know what is going on with that little girl.*

Much of what a child gains from having both an engaged mother and father is a wider range of approaches that serves to expand her repertoire of experiences and capabilities—the "dual parent" advantage, as referred to by psychologists. Just by dint of being two individuals who see and experience life through different eyes and have distinct skills and values to relay to the child, the mother and father together can foster a fuller development. If one parent loves to read to the child, and the other parent loves to do physical activity together, the child develops in both arenas.

This diversity of styles and skills can happen with any set of partners-in-parenting: a mother and grandparent, a mother and her sister or brother, two same-sex parents, etc. The father can and should play this role even if the parents are separated. Dionna and her husband, Robert, separated shortly after their daughter, Jamilla, was born. Even though Dionna has primary custody, she has worked very hard to keep Robert actively involved:

> There are things that he can teach that I can't. Now that we're split up, people say to me, "Well, you're her mother and her father now," and I say, "No, I'm not her mother and her dad. I'm her mother." I don't see through the eyes of a man. We each bring different things.

BOOKS ON THE IMPACT OF FATHERING ON CHILD DEVELOPMENT:

- *Fatherhood*, Ross D. Parke
- *Fatherneed: Why Father Care Is as Essential as Mother Care for Your Child*, Kyle D. Pruett, M.D.
- *The Role of the Father in Child Development*, edited by Michael E. Lamb

USEFUL WEBSITES:

- www.fathersforum.com
- www.fathersworld.com
- www.fatherhood.org

Yes, Dads Are Just as Good as Moms at Taking Care of the Kids

Our culture often makes the assumption that mothers are more innately skilled at baby and child care than fathers. But many women today arrive at motherhood with very little or no experience with babies. They are just as mystified and perplexed as their husbands by their newborn baby. Researchers find that fathers who care for their newborns are as responsive to the baby's cues as the mother and as adept in infant care. Michael Lamb, one of the nation's foremost researchers on the impact of fathering on child development, says, "We do know . . . that both mothers and fathers are capable of behaving sensitively and responsively in interaction with their infants. With the exception of lactation, there is no evidence that women are biologically predisposed to be better parents than men are. Social conventions, not biological imperatives, underlie the traditional division of parental responsibilities."[5]

It's a great benefit for a child not to rely on one parent alone to fulfill all his needs. In fact, the mother as the sole provider of care, comfort, and nurture can lead to insecurity when the mother is absent. Sondra and her husband, Cody, chose to work opposite shifts in a factory for a few years so that one parent could always be with their child, Bryant. Because of this work arrangement, they are each intimately involved in Bryant's life and are each primary caregivers. Sondra describes this benefit:

What I feel really good about is my son got to bond with both of us. Bryant isn't just attached to one of us. If he gets hurt, he might cry, "I want my daddy," or he might cry, "I want my mommy." I feel that he got a good start in life with that.

Cody recently got laid off from the factory. When I asked Sondra if he was upset or depressed by this event, she replied, "Oh no, he's happy to have this extra time with Bryant. They do all kinds of things together. He knows that he'll go back to work and he won't have this time again."

Encouraging your partner to be actively engaged:

- Your partner can be encouraged from the outset to care actively for the baby. Research shows that fathers are just as adept as mothers in newborn care. You can both learn together.

- Your partner should be allowed and encouraged to care for the baby and children in his style, not yours. He will become increasingly comfortable if it is his approach.

- This divergence in approach is a benefit for the baby or child: His or her adaptability and repertoire of competencies will expand with this diversity of mother and father approach.

- The father's comfort level will increase, along with the benefit to the child, if he has stretches of time where he interacts with his child alone.

- You will be less apt to serve as the gatekeeper, and your partner will be less reticent, if you both understand the clear developmental benefits to your child of two engaged parents.

FINDING OTHER NONSPOUSE PARTNERS-IN-PARENTING

For some married mothers, their partner-in-parenting is not their spouse but a close family member or friend. It can also be a child's nanny or other close caregiver—I discuss this more fully in chapters 4 (Excellent Child Care) and 13 (Ongoing Involvement in Child Care and Elementary School). Most of the single mothers I interviewed also have a partner-in-parenting. A single mother's partner-in-parenting is often the child's father—although they may live apart—a close family member, or a close friend or two.

A partner-in-parenting can give you needed support, both emotionally and logistically, even if this person does not live with you. It is someone who can give you a break when you are exhausted or at your wit's end. This partner-in-parenting gives your child another person to go to for comfort and fun. Let me share with you some of these partners-in-parenting.

The Child's Father, Even When Divorced or Separated

Even if your child's father does not live with you, it may be possible to keep him engaged in your child's life. I found many instances where the mother and father have developed ways to work productively as a team for the well-being of their child. The mother still has a partner in the major decisions in the child's life, as well as with many of the daily logistics.

Joan, a corporate vice president, felt controlled and unsupported by her husband, Gary, while they were married. Gary never spent much time with their son, Simon. After their marriage broke up, and Joan and Simon lived apart from him, Gary woke up to the fact that he might lose a relationship with his son. He started to work hard at being a good father. Ironically, he became a much greater support for Simon, and ultimately for Joan, after they were divorced. Now Gary shares custody, never misses soccer games or school events, and attends every single parent/teacher conference:

> *Gary was a lousy husband, but he's a great ex-husband. We have excellent, much better, communication now than when we were married. The day he moved out and I knew the marriage was over, we both decided we are going to be the best coparents we can be. And the whole focus has been on Simon's well-being. What we care about is that this child knows he has two comfortable homes with two people who love him more than anything. We get along well because we both love Simon so much.*

Joan also has a partner-in-parenting in her mother. Joan's mom stays with her on the two nights during the week when Joan has to start work early, and stays with Simon whenever his mom has to travel for business. Simon's grandmother is a very important part of his life.

Chavonne, a safety associate for a biotech company, had two children with Abram. Although Abram has never lived with Chavonne, he has joint custody and is deeply involved in the children's daily lives:

> *Our kids really love their daddy. Abram has always been involved in their lives, and he loves his kids. He picks our son up every day after school, and they spend every afternoon together until I come home from work. Abram goes to school activities and field trips.*

A Family Member

Many single mothers talk about the valued assistance of a family member—a parent, a sister, a brother. Both Tina, an operations manager, and her brother, Joe, were divorced and raising their children on their own. Joe moved in with Tina, and for years they supported each other:

> My brother and his kids lived with me for a long time, and he was great. If I had to go on a business trip, he said to do it, that he would be there with the kids. So we had this big house together with all these kids. We took vacations together. We helped each other a lot. The house worked so well. I'd cook, and he'd sit and read to the kids. We did a lot of sharing.

Alissa's partner-in-parenting is her father. Alissa, who is receiving state assistance for child care until her income moves above the low-income threshold, moved in with her parents after she had her second child. Her father, who is retired, is there every day as her partner-in-parenting:

> It's wonderful. You can see how this relationship makes my dad and my kids so happy. My dad always gets up in the morning as soon as he hears we're up. The kids adore him. My two-year-old daughter is completely in love with my dad. She calls him "Bumpy," and she'll always say, "Where's my Bumpy?" if he's not right there when we come in the kitchen. It's hard to be a single working mom, and his support helps us all so much. My dad is big on the cooking thing, and he will make dinner for us at night. When we get home in the afternoon after work and child care, he'll cut up fruits and vegetables for the kids and serve them glasses of Ovaltine. He has a little "happy hour" for us.

Dionna, a factory worker, has a daughter, Jamilla, who is now four years old. In addition to her ex-husband, her mother has become an important partner-in-parenting:

After my husband and I split up, I made the phone call and asked my mother to come live with us. She was living alone, and now so was I. We've been living together ever since. It's an awesome thing. She works the day shift, and I work the evening shift. When she gets off work, she often picks Jamilla up from child care.

Dionna and her mother share a life together, and Jamilla gets the benefit of two devoted caregivers in her home.

A Close Friend

Joyce, a married mother whose husband works long hours and is not available much at home, has two partners-in-parenting in her best friends from childhood:

I've known Stephanie and Lisa since I was a little girl. We all had children at the same time. We talk or see each other every single day. I don't know what I would do without them. I can talk to them about things I wouldn't tell anyone else. They understand. If I have to work late, I can drop the kids off with either of them. They'll give them dinner; give them baths. They support me in a way no one else does. Whatever it is, we're there for each other.

Olive, an educator, and her husband, Les, have always had a close friend or relative sharing their home. For eleven years, their friend Frances and her son lived with them. Frances was a partner-in-parenting:

We were all very committed to each other. It really felt like there were three parents and three children. If one of our children would act out, Frances would discipline them. Likewise, we would love and care for her son. We played parental roles with each other's children. I had to go out of town for two summers for graduate school and work, and Les and Frances just took care of the kids.

Can you find a partner-in-parenting?

- Someone who loves your child and with whom your child likes to spend time
- Someone who is close by and available to pick up your child from child care or school if necessary and can keep your child if you have to work late or travel, etc.
- Someone you feel comfortable turning to when you're at wit's end
- Someone with whom you can share your child's milestones and successes
- Someone you can confide in about challenges with your child's behavior and child rearing

The partner-in-parenting role can be filled by any of a number of people who are important in your and your child's life. The number of partners—one, two, or three—is not as important as their devotion and availability. Your partner-in-parenting can be a regular daily presence in your life, or someone you can turn to easily in a happy or challenging moment—to share the highs and lows of parenting. Of course, many mothers do a good job on their own. But if you can share both the benefits and burdens, your parenting job can seem easier and more enjoyable.

THREE

A Supportive Employer

*I am so grateful that I am working where I am. My boss is
so supportive. It's an environment where people focus on
the work you do, and that's it. That helps me so much as
a working mother. No one is ever watching what time I
come and go. My boss knows that I will get the job done
and do it well.*

—Susana, manager in a high-tech firm

A supportive employer is the second pillar of successful working motherhood. A supportive employer creates a "family-friendly" work environment—one where your supervisor understands that you have a life and responsibilities outside the job, and creates an environment that supports success in both work and family.

A supportive employer does not penalize you or your opportunities for advancement due to the fact that you are a mother. A supportive employer allows you to craft your work schedule to focus at work and get your work done well *and* be available for important family issues and events. A supportive employer understands that if you are supported and respected at work, you will work harder and smarter in return. Most of all, a supportive employer helps you feel successful as a mom.

In this chapter, I will define a family-friendly work environment and how it can be helpful to you. I will give you tips on how to negotiate flexible work options with your current employer. If you are looking for a new job, I will show you how to find a family-friendly workplace. And finally, I will offer tools to help convince your supervisor that family-friendly is the way to go.

SUCCESSFUL WORKING MOTHERS WORK FOR SUPPORTIVE EMPLOYERS

When I started to interview "successful" working mothers, I fully expected to hear stories about how they manage to sneak out of work, cover up their absences, and try to fool their supervisors and coworkers into thinking they are working longer hours than they actually are. I thought mothers would tell me how they hide the fact that they have children at home.

But I was wrong. Mothers didn't tell me these stories. The mothers I interviewed work in diverse environments—large and small organizations; for-profit, nonprofit, and government agencies; small entrepreneurial ventures; large conglomerates; factories. But what these work environments have in common is that for the most part, they are supportive, respectful environments where family issues are understood and supported. The mothers I interviewed do not have to sneak out of work to deal with child care issues. They have support as working mothers, whether it is through flexible work schedules, parent support groups at work, or on-site child care. Their value as employees is joined with a recognition that they are also parents. In fact, an astonishing 70 percent of the successful mothers I interviewed describe their workplace as a family-friendly environment.

Listening to my group of mothers, you would think that we now live in a world of supportive, family-friendly workplaces. Although tremendous progress has been made in the past twenty years, we are still far from that reality. But most women I interviewed feel successful as working mothers in part because they work for employers who support them as parents. Many mothers spoke passionately about this. Patricia, an architect, started her career in a small office:

> *My husband and I had very understanding bosses. We were in situations where we knew we would be supported in our parenting roles. I can't say enough how this whole aspect of*

life makes it easy or hard in terms of having children and working—having the freedom to take the time off if you need to, or having a boss that understands. If I needed to leave to take care of a sick child, I knew I wouldn't be penalized.

ARE YOU IN A FAMILY-FRIENDLY WORK ENVIRONMENT?

Does your work environment support you as a working parent? Let's talk about what a family-friendly workplace looks like, and then about how to get the support you need. A family-friendly environment essentially has three characteristics:[1]

1. Policies, programs, and services that support working parents
2. A track record that shows employees at various levels actually use these programs without being penalized
3. A supportive, respectful supervisor to whom you report

Policies, Programs, and Services That Support Working Parents

The following list is a range of family-friendly programs used by organizations. You can check your employee manual to see which of these programs your organization provides. Also check the website of your organization, consult with your supervisor, or talk to your human resources officer if there is one.

FLEXIBLE WORK OPTIONS

- Flextime: flexibility in when you start and end your day
- Varied schedules: alternative hours/days
- Part-time: less than full-time; hours can vary widely
- Job share: two people sharing one full-time position
- Compressed work weeks: working forty hours a week in four days or less; typically used for hourly, not salaried, workers
- Telecommuting: based in an office but can work at home part of the time
- Remote work: work from home

TIME-OFF POLICIES

- Family leave for the birth or adoption of a child or for elder care, both paid and unpaid, may have a phase-back to work after family leave
- Personal days, paid and unpaid
- Paid sick days for care of children/elders

DEPENDENT CARE SUPPORT

- Dependent Care Assistance Program: pretax deduction of child care/ elder care tuition and expenses
- Resource and referral program for child care, elder care, and adoption assistance
- On-site child care; child care subsidies or tuition assistance
- Support for community child care centers; efforts to accredit centers, enhance quality, extend hours
- Breast-feeding room
- Emergency backup child care, summer camp, and vacation child care
- Sick child support
- Access to family child care homes, before- and after-school care
- Adoption reimbursement or subsidy
- College scholarships or loans

COUNSELING AND TRAINING

- Prenatal and postnatal education
- Parenting education
- New-parent support groups
- Work/life balance seminars and training
- Work/life training for supervisors
- Employee Assistance Program (EAP)
- Employee opinion surveys

HEALTH AND FITNESS

- Health coverage that may include:
  - Prenatal and postnatal care
  - Psychological counseling
- Fitness or exercise facility and/or subsidies
- Health and wellness seminars

Very few organizations offer all of the above. Given your family situation and the nature of your job, think about which of the above policies, programs, and services are most valuable to you. Although some of the programs are costly and only rarely offered, others are inexpensive. In general, a supportive work culture, a respectful management, and flexibility do not require outlays of money yet are highly valued.

A Successful Track Record

Some organizations track usage of their family-friendly programs, particularly flexible work options. Most organizations, however, do not. Whether or not employees are penalized for choosing programs such as flextime, part-time work, or other flexible work options is usually "known" throughout the work culture.

Look around you to see if people in various levels of the organization and in various departments use these programs and services. Talk to your coworkers; talk to human resources about the use of flexible work options. Through conversations and observation, you'll get a sense if these programs are offered just on paper; you'll find out if few people use them, and whether those who do seem to be penalized in their advancement or recognition at work. Also, are there senior-level people who have young children or are in dual-career situations? If everyone who succeeds has no children or stay-at-home spouses, beware.

Look at the track record of people who have used family-friendly programs and services:

- Are they in respected positions and valued for the work they do?
- Are they in a variety of areas within the organization or with one specific supervisor?
- Do they have the option to progress within the organization if they want to?
- Are supervisors trained in managing employees with flexible work options?
- Is the use of family-friendly programs part of the culture or isolated exceptions?

A Supportive, Respectful Supervisor

This is the most crucial characteristic of a family-friendly work environment.[2] Regardless of your organization's stated policies, how your supervisor treats you will most determine whether you feel you are supported as a working parent. Your supervisor will be either a roadblock or a facilitator. In fact, work/life experts now understand that supervisor training in managing family-friendly practices helps employees to use them effectively. And supervisors are able to be consistently supportive of work/life issues only if their senior management is also committed. Otherwise the support will be undermined over time.

A supportive supervisor:

- Is clear with you about what constitutes successful performance, especially what results you need to deliver
- Is realistic about work expectations
- Provides opportunity for advancement
- Allows autonomy in working on tasks
- Respects that you have a life outside of work
- Is understanding when you have a family need; supports a solution that will work for both you and the organization
- Informs you of available family-friendly programs and assistance within the organization

YOU KNOW YOU ARE IN THE RIGHT PLACE WHEN . . .

Whether you have a supportive supervisor will become vividly apparent when you announce that you are expecting a baby, whether you are pregnant or adopting. Sarah, an academic administrator, was nervous about her supervisor's reaction. She was pleasantly surprised once she shared the news:

When I told the chair of my department that I was pregnant, having only worked for him for four months, he got up from the table, walked around, and gave me a big hug, and I burst into tears. He was an unusual boss. Most men would not be thrilled that their newly hired employee was taking a maternity leave. He set the tone for the entire department.

Adah, who works in sales, was interviewing for a job while she was already pregnant, though not yet showing. She didn't want to tell her future supervisor that she was pregnant because she worried that she wouldn't get the job. Once she landed the job, she then anxiously told him:

Without hesitation, the gentleman did not even miss a beat and said, "Absolutely, that does not make a difference." It was a very nice learning experience for me. It was also a nice way to change my cynicism of organizations.

This was a good omen for both these mothers that they might have wonderfully supportive supervisors. And indeed, both women had a positive experience at their jobs.

YOU KNOW YOU ARE IN THE WRONG PLACE WHEN . . .

Other mothers are not quite so lucky. Unfortunately, many work environments are still very old-fashioned in their views of pregnancy and working mothers. One mother talked about being treated as if she had a problematic disability when she was pregnant. Another talked about no longer being viewed as a serious professional when she started to look pregnant.

Isabelle worked in human resources at a large company while she was pregnant. She carefully prepared the department and company for her absence during her family leave. She clearly communicated her schedule and the plan for how her work would get done. It was a work environment where she felt there was often insensitivity to the individual. As she headed off into labor for her first child, she felt the brunt of that insensitivity:

> *I knew I had a problem at that company when I got a call from a senior manager when I was actually at home in my early stage of labor. I was having contractions, and he's calling me and telling me that he suddenly decided after all this time that he wants to fire his secretary and needs my help. And I said, "You know, I was there for six months, you watched my stomach get bigger and bigger. You knew this was something we would have to work on. Why did you suddenly wait until now? I'm sorry, I can't help you. I'm going into labor. I'm actually having contractions as we speak." I knew then that things had gone too far.*

Some mothers feel blatant discrimination once they become pregnant. Hong, a software engineer for a small high-tech company, explained to me that after she announced she was pregnant, her work situation changed dramatically:

> *Once I told them I was pregnant, they put me on hold. I was assigned to a kind of side-way project, not the mainstream project that I had been on. They thought maybe my energy level would not be as it used to be. They put me on a slower track.*

Hong works in an all-male environment where none of the men have responsibility for child care. Although her work ability hadn't changed with pregnancy, they assumed that she no longer was on an equal level with the men, and they downgraded her assignments. Hong had no other support in her department, so she accepted their assumptions. However, she is an ambitious woman and frequently mentioned the fact that she had been put on a slower track.

It would be understandable for Hong's supervisors to move her off a fast-track project that could be negatively impacted when she left to have her baby. It is not unrealistic to move off time-sensitive projects as you prepare to go on family leave. But in Hong's case, her supervisor kept her on a slower, less important track even after she returned to work.

Hong explained to me that her company expects workers to regularly put in a minimum of fifty hours per week. Her supervisor carefully watches hours in the office. Once Hong came back to work, she continued to work fifty hours a week but shifted to an earlier schedule—eight A.M. to six P.M.—to accommodate the child care center's hours. The other workers in her department arrived between nine-thirty and ten A.M. They were all still working when she left at six P.M. It seemed like she was leaving work early when everyone else was staying on:

> *It affected my career advancement. Even though I worked the same number of hours, they thought I was leaving work early every day. When it came to my promotion, I didn't get it. When I asked my boss why, he said that he wished I would put in more hours. My boss doesn't have children. The group leader's wife doesn't work. They come to work late, and they leave late. That is hard for me.*

It is interesting that Hong's supervisor didn't talk about her results or performance on the job. He talked about visible (to him) hours. Hong had wanted to continue breast-feeding once she came back to work; however, her first week back, her supervisor assigned her to a week's training program out of town. She had to leave right away. She felt the obstacles were too great, and she gave up breast-feeding.

Surrounded by the skeptical and unsupportive attitudes of her supervisor and coworkers, Hong will never be allowed to get ahead. Hong is an ambitious woman, but she is in a situation where her contributions, and even her abilities, are minimized because she is now a mother. Her self-esteem has eroded enough that she has come to accept their placement of working mothers on a slower track with lower pay.

If you find yourself in this kind of environment, the best thing to do is face the issue honestly with your supervisor. If you believe your performance has not changed, show your manager measurable results. If you feel that his or her views will not change, start looking for another job before your self-confidence suffers and the stress gets too high. Some mothers I spoke to are in personal situations where they feel they cannot change an unhappy job right now, whether due to serious financial stress, a crisis at home, or the like. It is still helpful for you to understand your options; you may be in a position to change sometime in the future.

IF YOU FEEL YOU ARE BEING JUDGED UNFAIRLY AS A WORKING MOTHER:

- Together with your supervisor, clearly delineate expected results and deadlines. Understand what results would mean success in your supervisor's eyes. Agree on realistic expectations.
- Set up a future meeting to review with your supervisor whether you are meeting performance expectations.
- If you continue to believe that you are being judged unfairly, talk frankly with your supervisor about how you feel you are being treated. Focus on the facts; use specific examples. Use a constructive, not confrontational, tone.
- If the situation still does not change, talk to your organization's human resources officer, if there is one. He or she can be a coach and ally as you try to constructively work through these issues.
- You may want to start looking for another job, either with a different supervisor at your organization or with another organization.

HAS MOTHERHOOD SLOWED DOWN YOUR CAREER?

Examine how motherhood has affected your career where you're working. Many mothers purposefully slow down their career pace once they have children. They may want to reduce their stress or hours. But many other mothers may feel even more ambition once they have children. Every mother is unique. How you feel about your workplace will depend a great deal on whether you have the freedom to make that choice yourself once you have children. We asked this question to twelve thousand working parents across the country on a Bright Horizons annual survey in the spring of 2001. Mothers answered the question in one of three ways:

1. No, being a mother has not slowed my career.
2. Yes, by choice. I wanted to slow down after I had children.
3. Yes, unfortunately, my career has been negatively impacted and not through my own choice.

No

Forty-three percent of the mothers surveyed said no, having children did not slow down their careers. Many of these mothers have the three pillars of support that allow them and their children to thrive: They work in supportive work environments; they have engaged partners or other personal support; and they are confident of the high quality care their children are getting. Says Natalie, a human resources professional:

> *I focused more on my career after my second child was born. I moved to an exciting company that had progressive employee practices. I was then really able to bring everything together— my career took off, I was where I wanted to be in terms of a socially responsible company, and I felt great about the care my children were getting.*

For some mothers, having children has not only *not* held them back, but they now have higher aspirations at work. Dionna, a factory worker, states:

> *Once I had Jamilla, I became a lot more serious about my work. My job now has become more important to me. I need my job, and I need to do well at my job. I have become more ambitious. I feel like I was too limited before. I want to be more knowledgeable and more skilled. It's a way to be a better provider for my daughter. I want to feel like I'm a role model for her by always growing and developing.*

Some mothers have shifted professional direction, discovering paths that have brought them new, and possibly greater, meaning. Chloe, who pursued a graduate degree in education, has three young children. After watching her children develop a passion for animals and wildlife, Chloe decided to create her own children's wildlife video. She plunged into a creative video venture, raised money, and filmed an award-winning wildlife video that she showed at a number of film festivals. It was a fabulous and totally unplanned shift in her career:

> *Actually, when I think about my career, that whole experience was the most rewarding work I have ever done. It was so creative, and the whole process was so exciting. It was great. But I never would have thought that I would produce a film.*

Becoming a mother opened new professional vistas and interests that Chloe did not have before. She threw herself into this work more intensely than she ever had in the past.

Yes, by Choice

A similar number (44 percent) of mothers surveyed by Bright Horizons said that their careers slowed down after having children because they wanted them to. They purposely pulled back on their ambitions in order to focus more of their time and energies on family:

> *Well, to some degree, yes, motherhood has delightfully held me back at work. I definitely slowed down. I'm sure I would be here working significantly more hours if it weren't for my kids—so thank you, Molly and Brett! It really does keep my life in check and gives me a mental balance.*
> —Helen, consultant in employee placement firm

> *When you're younger, you think you can just go out there and conquer the world. I question now whether or not I want to make the commitment to get far ahead. I enjoy work, and it's very stimulating and very gratifying, and I'm glad I can work, but I've gotten over the point where my job is my self-worth.*

So, have my priorities changed? I would say yes. Would they have changed regardless of having my daughter? Maybe, I don't know, but for sure they have changed now.

—Shalisha, product manager

Many mothers look at their lives in phases. Parents often cut back during different stages of family life to be able to devote more time to their children during critical periods. Some scale back during childbearing and early childhood years. When their children are in elementary or middle school, they gear back up again. Or some cut back during adolescent and teenage years. Chloe's mother taught her a very important lesson:

One thing I learned from my mom is that a career is really long. My mom graduated from law school at age thirty-eight. She's now sixty-one and at the peak of her career. She now has a really exciting job. Her career really happened from age forty on. I have a lot of ambition, and I see her and I think—I have twenty years, I really have time. I can look at life as a series of phases.

Yes, Unfortunately

Thirteen percent of the mothers surveyed said that their careers were unfairly held back due to children and that their employers were not supportive of them as working mothers. Colleen, a financial planner with one young child, felt that the firm she had worked at for years no longer supported her once she had a baby:

I stayed in the same job after I had my baby, but I changed the way I did things. I continued to do a great job, but I set limits and just was not available to work the sixty hours a week that I used to. I became more focused and efficient, but I started to feel like I was being judged on hours of "face time," not work produced. When I would leave the office, people would say, "Oh, you're going now?" Just the way they said it, I knew they were judging me.

Now I feel like my career path is stalled because I'm not here the hours I used to be. I think it's not fair, since I still produce the same quality work, and it's still a professional job. I want to be rewarded on output, not hours. I handle more clients now than I used to, even though I'm working less time. But I'm operating here under the old model, of watching hours. It's really hard to break that model.

Colleen realized that she would never get ahead in that firm. She eventually left to set up her own financial-planning business with a partner, where she now has control of her schedule.

Think about your own personal situation and whether you are in the right work environment that supports your choices on work and family. Understanding how much time and energy you want to devote to a career will help you identify the kind of position you would like to be in. Once a woman has children, her work objectives often become more tightly focused. Now that you have children, do you want to:

- Continue on your same career track?
- Get more ambitious and achievement-oriented?
- Slow down during the early childhood years and then rev up later? Or work hard now and slow down during the adolescent and teenage years?
- Indefinitely turn down your career aspirations a notch so that you can focus primarily on family?

Any one of these models is fine. Don't let society, Grandma, Dr. Laura, or your next-door neighbor tell you what to do. Make your plan and know that any decision you make now does not have to be forever. You can view your life and career in phases and revisit your decisions later. Try to understand your goals now. That will make a difference in what kind of career path you follow and what kind of hours you want to work. If you have a partner or spouse, discuss with him his goals for work and parenting. He may also want to see his work and family life in phases. Together you can plan how to focus on work and children.

HAS BEING A MOTHER SLOWED DOWN *YOUR* CAREER?

- No. *That's great.*
- Yes, by choice. *That's great, too.* You may:
  - Have changed life priorities
  - See life in phases
- Yes, unfortunately. *Then you'd better go back and check the Three Pillars:*
  - Do you have enough support at home? Is your spouse or partner engaged enough in child care and household chores? Or do you have other partners-in-parenting who could be more engaged?
  - Do you have peace of mind with your child care choice? Should you make a change in your child care support? (See chapter 4.)
  - Do you work in a family-friendly work environment? Is your supervisor supportive of your family role?

Let's focus on this third factor in this chapter, a supportive workplace.

IT'S IMPORTANT TO KNOW: WHY DO *YOU* WORK?

Most mothers work because their families need the income—it's a necessity. However, mothers also work because it provides a source of personal development, self-esteem, and gratification. Women, like men, gain a great deal from working—personally, professionally, and economically. In a recent large survey of salaried workers conducted by Catalyst, an organization that researches women's issues, 67 percent of women responded that they would work in some capacity even if money were not a consideration. This is only slightly less than the 69 percent of men who said they would continue to work even if they did not have to.[3] The 2001 Bright Horizons survey found similar results. Seventy-two percent of the mothers and 74 percent of the fathers surveyed said they would work even if money were not a factor.

What are your reasons for working? Let me take you through some of the benefits of working that mothers talk about, which might help to clarify what is most important to you. As stated above, first and foremost are the *financial benefits* of working. Evelyn, a research scientist, remembered when her father deserted her family when she and her brother were young. Their mother made very little money, and Evelyn grew up in poverty. Evelyn's childhood experience was deeply influential:

> *I am not going to be in that situation—not ever. I've got to be financially independent, period, regardless of marriage or not. When we had our first baby, I remembered what happened to my mother when my father walked out—all that dependence, the troubles, the lack of money. I made sure it was going to be different for me.*

For Sarah, an administrator in an academic department, working not only gives her financial security, it seems a *natural part of a mother's identity.* The women in her family have always worked:

> *That's the model both my husband and I grew up with. I had never even thought about staying at home full-time. It's just part of who I am. I couldn't be financially dependent on someone else.*

Sondra, who works on an assembly line in a factory, finds that her work gives her a great *sense of pride:*

> *I enjoy working. It's very rewarding to think I'm doing a job that a man does. It's very fulfilling that way. I feel like I am growing.*

Leah, an independent research consultant and a creator of children's curricula, enjoys the *intellectual stimulation* of her work and *the chance to be on her own:*

> *It is important to me to have that adult breathing space. I like the intellectual challenge. I like the balance. I can see that my days with my children are much better when I have my days at work. I feel more energy and enthusiasm. It makes me a better parent.*

Elizabeth, an attorney, feels it is important to be *a contributing member of the community*:

> *I always want to work. I think work is about being integrated within a larger society. You are really part of your community, a productive part of your community. I think working gives you a chance to test yourself and see what's possible in the world and what's not.*

Claire, who works as an active volunteer in her children's school and a local environmental organization, believes that her work *establishes important values for her children*:

> *My children are very proud of what I do; they are very aware of my volunteering work. I think it is very important that they see me involved, beyond my parenting role, in education and the environment. I want them to know how important it is to give back to society and to the community.*

Myrna, a factory worker in an automotive plant, values her work for the *independence* it gives her and the *respect it creates in her relationship with her husband*, Eugene:

> *My father instilled in me when I was little that you should never need to be taken care of—that it's important to be financially independent. I just need to know that I will always be all right on my own. Eugene respects the fact that I earn a good wage. In fact, I think that was one of the things that attracted him to me in the first place—the fact that I was independent and I wasn't just looking for someone to leech on to. I knew what I wanted to do.*

Chloe, an education consultant, sees herself as being a *role model* for her children:

> *I want my children to see me as a person who has other interests. I have three daughters, and I want them to see their*

future as full lives, that they should develop their talents and use them productively in the world. It is so important to me that I am a working person.

Denise, a staff member in human resources at a public agency, values *the friendships* she gets at work. This gives her a separate and enjoyable role outside of the family:

I am not kidding myself. I work mainly because I like to. It gives me interaction with a lot of people. When I am home, I can really focus on the kids because I get my social interactions at work. I think it is important to have an identity separate from the kids.

What do *you* value about working?

- Financial security and providing for your family
- Higher standard of living for your family
- Development of your skills and abilities
- Intellectual challenge
- Contribution to community and society
- More balanced relationship with spouse or partner
- Self-exploration
- Role model for children
- Friendships

NEGOTIATING FLEXIBLE WORK OPTIONS

You may have decided that you would prefer to work part-time or choose another flexible arrangement for a defined period of time or indefinitely.[4] You are now ready to ask. Many mothers find that negotiating is easier once they are firmly established within their organization and their work is respected and valued. It is also easier to negotiate if your workplace already has a track record of flexibility so that you do not have to be the trail blazer. As listed earlier, the typical flexible work options are the following:

- Flextime: flexibility in when you start and end your workday
- Varied schedules: alternative hours/days
- Part-time work: less than full-time; hours vary widely
- Job share: one position shared by two people
- Compressed work week: work forty hours a week in four days or less; offered typically to hourly, not salaried, workers
- Telecommute: office-based but work from home or another location on an occasional basis
- Remote work: work from home or another location

First think about whether your job would accommodate a flexible work option. If it requires your physical presence, or if its content requires specific hours, a flexible work option may not work for you. A teacher in a classroom or a surgeon in an operating room may have less flexibility than those in other positions. Always start with the question: Can I do my work just as well or better if I work different hours or in a different place?

If you are considering remote work or telecommuting, think hard about whether working at home would work for you. Do you get easily distracted? Can you work independently? And very importantly: Working at home is not a substitute for child care. It is unrealistic to expect that you can work while caring for a baby or young child. You, your child, and your supervisor will just end up getting frustrated. So you'll need to line up child care while working at home.

Think about your work style and how you can be most effective. Some people like early mornings better, or would rather get into the "flow" during a couple of long days and then have more rest time. Some like to work at home once in a while to have "thinking time" or uninterrupted work time.

If your workplace offers flexible work options, you should not have to present your personal reasons for wanting to take advantage of them. Make the distinction in your mind that you are not asking for a favor to help you as a mother; you are asking for a different way to get your job done as well or better. When preparing for your request, look at your work situation from your employer's point of view. Show your supervisor how this arrangement will help you perform and meet customer or coworker needs better; or, at the very least, how it won't hurt your performance. You want to make this a situation that will work for both you and your organization. If it does not ultimately meet both of your needs, it will not work out for the long term.

Once you start in your new work arrangement, document your results. If it means you won't be as physically visible in the workplace, make sure that your performance and results clearly are. This is important for two reasons: Your visible successful performance will help ensure that you can continue using your flexible work option. Second, your success will make it easier for others to use flexible work options. It validates to your employer that flexibility makes good business sense. But also understand that if you do cut back significantly to part-time work, you you shouldn't expect to progress as fast as full-time workers.

Set up a review date with your supervisor after a few months. Discuss whether the arrangement is meeting the organization's needs; also consider if it is meeting your personal family needs. Often a flexible work option will need to be adjusted as time goes on. Neither workplace nor family needs are static. For flexibility at the workplace to succeed, it needs to work both ways. Be willing to be flexible if something urgent comes up at work, or if the work situation changes and your supervisor needs you to alter your arrangement—just as you would expect your workplace to adapt if something crucial came up at home.

NEGOTIATING A FLEXIBLE WORK ARRANGEMENT:

- Investigate your organization's track record with flexible work arrangements. Try to understand where it has worked well and what options the organization commonly supports. Talk to your human resources officer or the appropriate manager about how to proceed.
- Talk to coworkers who have successfully negotiated similar arrangements. Ask their advice.

- Prepare your case well. Look at the situation through the eyes of your supervisor. With your plan, show how you will get your work done as well or better. Prepare answers to all possible concerns.
- Write up a thorough proposal that covers:
  - How you will get your work done—outline specific areas of responsibility
  - Expected results—defined and measurable
  - Suggested schedule
  - How your supervisor and colleagues can get in touch with you when you are not in the office
  - Compensation and benefits
  - How you will handle sudden, unexpected work needs and regular peak periods; be clear about where you can be flexible
  - Your participation in department (or other) meetings and training; any changes in interactions with your coworkers and customers
- Be clear that if the arrangement does not work for the company or for you that you both will revisit the situation.
- Set up a three-month review period. Establish in advance with your supervisor what desired results would mean success. This review period will give both sides a chance to see if it can work and to make necessary adjustments.
- Outline any advantages to your organization: saved costs, increased productivity, increased coverage in the department (through longer days with compressed work weeks or flextime), and so on.

Wendy had worked as an operations analyst for a large consulting firm for several years. When she became pregnant with her first child, she wanted to work part-time. She did her homework thoroughly and then presented her supervisor with a carefully worked-out plan:

> *I felt like I was perfectly positioned to ask to work part-time because I had been with the firm for over five years and had performed well. When I wrote my proposal, I said that in the spirit of making our company the greatest place to do great work, allowing flexibility would embody that spirit. I wrote a two-page memo proposing an arrangement, saying I would like to take sixteen weeks off for maternity leave, and I would*

like to come back part-time, and this is what I feel my contribution can be. I was very specific. I really didn't get any resistance.

Wendy took the initiative to propose what would work for her and looked at her proposal through her employer's eyes to craft an arrangement that would work well for them. She was clear about her expected contribution and performance.

Isabelle and Claudia both worked in human resources, and they each had two small children. They decided to look for a new job together. They wanted to share one position in a job share arrangement, with each working three days a week and one day of overlap. They worked hard for weeks preparing their case before they tried to market their proposal; as Isabelle explains:

I would go over to Claudia's house with my kids, and she'd have her two babies. We'd have these four little kids, and we'd have papers taped to the wall trying to write out how we would do it. We said if we're going to do this, we've got to have this airtight case that we can sell. So we really went through scenario after scenario—how would we hand off work to each other during the week, how would we handle sick time, how would we handle urgent, time-sensitive projects, etc. We sat down and hammered through exactly how we would envision it working, down to file systems, phone, e-mail. We wrote it all up, and we still refer to these guidelines.

The two created a "terms and conditions" job share document that covered all the various elements of their work agreement and work relationship, including how they would handle conflict if they disagreed on a work-related issue. Their thoroughness paid off. They landed an excellent job share position. They have now job shared successfully for six years.

The following are websites useful in crafting a proposal for a flexible work arrangement. They offer excellent on-line books that guide you, step by step.

USEFUL WEBSITES:

- www.workoptions.com: offers the book *Flex Success: A Proposal Blue-print and Planning Guide for Getting a Family-Friendly Work Schedule,* by Pat Katepoo
- www.jobsandmoms.com. offers the book *Flex Jobs: The Smart Mom's Guide to Finding and Creating a Great Flexible Job,* by Nancy Collamer

LOOKING FOR A NEW JOB IN A FAMILY-FRIENDLY WORKPLACE

How do you go about finding a family-friendly organization? Fortunately, some of the homework is now being done for you. Every October, *Working Mother* magazine publishes the highly touted "100 Best Companies for Working Mothers," and every January, *Fortune* magazine publishes the "100 Best Companies to Work for in America." Both issues are terrific resources for identifying good companies and understanding what to look for.

USEFUL WEBSITES:

- www.workingmother.com
- www.fortune.com/lists/best companies
- www.flexibleresources.com
- www.womans-work.com
- www.jobsharing.com

In addition, many regional business magazines and newspapers publish lists of local and regional family-friendly employers, corporate and nonprofit. This may be a way to find smaller or local organizations. Consult with your local Chamber of Commerce, which may be able to steer you in the right direction. Network; talk to friends and acquaintances who might also be resources.

If lists of local family-friendly employers do not exist, you can do your own research on a prospective employer. Before going in for an interview, call the human resource office for available materials on the company; these may give you a feeling for the culture and values. Check out their website. Ask the human resources officer about family-friendly programs and services. Make sure that any organization you interview with has the programs that are most important to you.

Although it is harder to investigate whether family-friendly programs are indeed utilized—and to determine that the culture is supportive and respectful—there are ways to do so. Now that "family-friendly" is becoming "trendy," you must investigate whether the organization's commitment is more than skin-deep. You can learn a great deal through two additional steps: 1) your interview with your prospective supervisor, and 2) walking the halls and reading the bulletin boards.

You Can "Interview" Your Supervisor, Too

When you're going to a job interview, you should be interviewing the boss as much as the boss is interviewing you. Ask about their philosophies about flexibility and your work. I will never, ever work for somebody who watches my time versus my work. And there's a way to tactfully interview for that without asking questions that would make you appear not dedicated or committed.

—Stacy

I was surprised and pleased by the number of mothers who talked about how forthright they were in their job interviews. Many were determined to learn as much as they could about the culture of the organization and the supervisor's views of working mothers. They asked specific questions about flexible work options, systems of reward and recognition, and how many women were in positions of senior management. As more and more prospective employees ask these kinds of questions, employers will realize that a family-friendly culture is key to recruiting the people they want.

Just asking these questions can sometimes signal to an employer that you are confident of your worth. I remember when Roger and I first started Bright Horizons and were working out of our small house in Cambridge, Massachusetts. We were recruiting a center director for our first child care center and looking to hire the very best. I interviewed candidate after candidate in our living room. One candidate, Eileen Smith, asked me several questions about employment policies—a Dependent Care Assistance Plan, flextime, a 401(k) plan. Roger and I had just returned from working in the Sudan for a few years, and I had no idea what Eileen was talking about; we had none of these programs. But she impressed me—in being informed enough to know what programs were important to her, and in being confident enough to ask for them. She got the job, and we implemented all those programs and many more. Fourteen years later, Eileen is still with us. Employers want to hire the best, and if the best require family-friendly programs, employers will implement them.

Even if you don't feel comfortable being so direct, there is still a great deal you can determine during your interview about both the organization's culture and the supervisor's approach to working-parent issues. The following is a list of what to look for in your interview. Of course, for small organizations or for some positions, some of these issues are irrelevant. Adjust the list accordingly.

DURING YOUR INTERVIEW WITH THE SUPERVISOR:

- Draw her into a conversation about the people in the department. You can get a good sense of the makeup of the team she has hired: men, women, minorities, young, old, parents, single. Watch for the way she talks about them to get a sense of the work culture, sense of teamwork, her level of respect and support.
- Ask about typical work schedules in the department and about regularly scheduled department meetings. See if the supervisor schedules his meetings early in the morning or late in the afternoon. Get a sense if he regularly schedules work on the weekends.
- Ask if it's possible to see an employee evaluation form (it may be proprietary). Ask how often the supervisor evaluates her subordinates. Ask her what she looks for in employees, what is most important to her. How do people advance in the department?
- Ask about work travel. How often is it expected? Is it typically sched-

uled in advance, or are there quick-notice trips? Do they use phone or teleconferencing in place of some trips?

- Ask whether there is training in skill development. How often is it provided?
- Does the organization have regular employee opinion surveys? Ask about the survey and results. Ask about turnover rates—how quickly people leave the organization.
- Ask for a copy of an organization newsletter, if there is one: It can tell you a lot about the organization culture and what is valued.

One mother, Sarah, saw a photograph of the supervisor's large family as she walked into his office for her first interview. He was a man in his early sixties with a nonwage-earning wife at home. It was unclear to Sarah whether he was progressive or old-fashioned in his views of working mothers. It was important to her to find out:

I saw a picture on his desk of five children. That gave me a chance to ask him what it's like to raise such a large family. He promptly launched into this wonderful description of his family. It was clear he was an incredibly devoted and involved father. I had wanted to see what kind of a dad he was, so that was great.

Walk the Halls

Ask for a tour of the workplace. Make sure you get to places where people would commonly congregate: the kitchen, the mailroom, the cafeteria. There is much you can glean if you are observant.

DURING YOUR TOUR:

- Keep tuned in to the atmosphere. Is there a feeling of congeniality in the workplace? Do people seem to like one another? Are people hidden behind closed doors, or are there natural places of interaction? Does the atmosphere feel calm, chaotic, tense, friendly?
- Take your time as you walk around and meet your future colleagues. You can get a feel for the team composition: men, women, old, young, parent. If appropriate, engage them in conversations about their work

and their outside lives. Look to see if they have family photos displayed—you can see if there are other parents of young children.

- Go into the kitchen and cafeteria, if there is one. Are people sitting alone or in groups? Do they seem to be enjoying one another?
- Glance at the bulletin boards. Look for notices of parent or other support groups; for company sporting events, sports leagues, or other company events. Are families invited?
- Do you see information on wellness and fitness programs?
- Do you see indications of employees' outside lives? Are they celebrated?
- Do a website tour. Many organizational values—and a mission statement—may be reflected on the website.
- Check the parking lot in the early morning or evening and even on the weekend. You can get a sense of work routines by how many cars you see during off hours.

OTHER IMPORTANT JOB CONSIDERATIONS

What Kind of Job Suits You Best as a Working Mother?

As you think about your job, either current or prospective, consider the characteristics that can impact your ability to comfortably work and parent. One of your decisions is whether to be an "individual contributor" where you can work independently, or to work in a team or management position where you may be responsible for other people.

Some mothers prefer to be individual contributors, with their own projects or assignments. You may not want other people depending too much on you on a day-to-day basis. One mother, Rebecca, felt that such a position would give her more flexibility at work:

> I was very conscious of wanting to find a job where I could have kids. I thought about the type of role I should be in. I thought that if I am managing other people, it would be very hard to take time off or to work four days a week. I would always be ultimately accountable. That would make it hard to

*leave work for a family issue. If I worked more independently,
I thought I would have more flexibility.*

However, some mothers purposely choose a position in which they can manage and interact with other people. Often parents find that skills they have developed at home help them to better manage and interact with people at work. They gain energy and inspiration from working directly with other people, in the same way they enjoy nurturing and encouraging their own children. Susana manages a large department in a high-tech firm:

*My work is very people-intensive, and I really enjoy
managing, seeing people accomplish things and moving their
careers. I mentor and coach people. That really drives and
inspires me. And I think I am really good at what I do.*

Find a Place Where Your Skills Can Be Appreciated

Some mothers look for a job niche where their particular skills are needed and appreciated. Sarah, a business manager who had always worked in very stressful, fast-paced management positions, decided when she had children that she wanted a different kind of job environment. She interviewed for a position as an academic administrator in the medical research department of a university. She brought her business and management skills to a department that had very little of that expertise:

*I have found a wonderful job for my skills and desired
lifestyle. The medical researchers in this department know
nothing about management or administration or money. My
skills complement theirs, and I bring something valuable that
they do not have. They greatly appreciate the contributions I
make, so I feel fulfilled professionally.*

Carla, who graduated from a top law school, decided to work as a legal-aid attorney in a small office in a small city:

I deliberately chose to be a bigger fish in a smaller pond for much of my working career—working where some thought I was overqualified. I was such a valued employee in those environments that I could write my own ticket. I still had lots of great professional opportunities.

In fact, Carla became so esteemed in her work that she ultimately became a judge. She crafted her own path where she was valued and could more confidently ask, and get, the work arrangements that suited her goals as a working mother.

Small or Large Organization?

Large or small—you can't be sure which is better. It depends on the unique work environment of the individual organization. In general, large organizations provide more work/life benefits, resources, and services.[5] They can offer a more stable environment than small organizations and are not so dependent on one individual. Sarah appreciated the size and stability of the university where she found her job:

This university has been around for years and years. There's never any question that the organization will rise or fall on my efforts. I wanted a job in a major, stable environment.

It is more likely that a large company or organization will have flexible work options in an established program. However, studies show that employees in small organizations rate their work environments as more supportive and flexible. But the environment is usually dependent on management attitudes and specific supervisors rather than fully developed policies or programs.

Some mothers find that the informality of a small organization works to their benefit. Since there is often no established track record of family-friendly programs, the employee can sometimes chart her own course. Joanne works for a small hospitality consulting firm. She had worked there several years before she got pregnant. She had developed strong friendships with her supervisor and coworkers in her small office. They liked and respected her. Since there was no established policy, she thought about what she wanted and had the confidence to ask for it:

> *There was no road map. I basically just suggested to them that I would work four days a week and would like to get paid four-fifths my normal salary. If I worked that fifth day, we would figure it out, and I could be paid on a monthly basis for those extra hours. They would let me do as much as I wanted, so it was up to me to decide. It's definitely a very supportive environment.*

But sometimes informality can mean that there are fewer boundaries in the work environment and it is harder to leave—physically and psychologically. There is no one right answer for a small or large organization. A supportive work culture is organization-specific.

BE AN INTERNAL CHAMPION!

Convincing Your Employer to Offer Family-Friendly Programs

Most organizations evolve into more family-friendly workplaces because their employees want them to, ask them to, and present good reasons why it makes business sense. In fact, it's often due to one or several employees' initiatives that an organization creates such programs.

There has been a movement among employers over the last two decades toward understanding and creating family-friendly work environments. A new field of research and study, the work/life field, has been created to understand how a supportive work environment impacts employees' attitudes, company performance, and an individual's ability to perform at work and to parent at home. The work/life field has also studied the developmental outcomes of children of parents who work in supportive environments compared to parents who don't.

The research is clear. Creating a supportive work environment helps to make organizations stronger; creates more committed, effective employees; and helps an employee to be a more engaged parent, which leads to better developmental outcomes for children—what experts call the "virtuous circle."[6]

But many employers are still unaware of the benefits to an organization of a family-friendly culture. Many are afraid that employees will take advantage of flexibility to the detriment of the organization. And many are just entrenched in old work habits. There are several common objections that managers have to creating family-friendly programs. I have listed them and elaborated on your possible answers:

> *Objection:* **Most mothers stay home; let's just ignore the issue of working mothers. It's a passing phenomenon.**
> *Answer:* **Working mothers are now the norm.**

Whatever your supervisor's view of working mothers, the fact is that today most mothers work outside the home, and each year the percentage of working mothers grows. Working motherhood has now become the norm. Let me cite a few recent statistics:

- Seventy-seven percent of all mothers with school-age children are now working.[7]

- Even mothers of very young children are in the paid workforce. Sixty-three percent of mothers with children under the age of six are working.[8] Fifty-nine percent of women who had a baby within the last year are working.[9]

- Women who have achieved higher levels of education are more apt to work. Although 59 percent of mothers with babies under the age of one work, 68 percent of mothers who have achieved a college degree or above work, compared to 38 percent of women who have not achieved a high school degree.[10] This indicates that women are making the choice to work.

- Both spouses work in 51 percent of married couples with children—the traditional two-parent family model.[10]

- Twenty-three percent of all employees are single parents.[11]

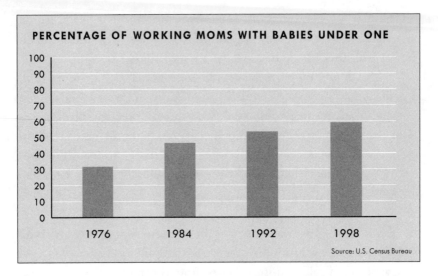

Our workplaces are now populated with working parents. Our workplace environments can no longer expect men to work long hours while their wives take care of the children at home. The wives are in the workplace, and the men are carrying their responsibility as involved parents and need to be present for their children as well. In addition, many mothers and fathers are single parents.

Half the workplace is now women.[12] Among the half that is men, an increasing percentage wants and is demanding family-friendly programs. There are more of you who want supportive workplaces than you think; as a group, you may be more influential than you realize.

> *Objection:* Family-friendly policies and programs are only for mothers who are not ambitious. I don't really need to offer them; my most valued employees are ready to "give all" to their work.
>
> *Answer:* High-performing employees value family-friendly programs and want access to them. In fact, a supportive, family-friendly environment creates and attracts more valued employees.

Traditionally, family-friendly policies were designed to help working mothers take care of their children. Organizations assumed that the primary users of these programs would be mothers who were not as ambitious or as committed to their work as other employees. Thus developed the notion of the "mommy track."

As I discussed earlier, there are indeed many mothers who choose to shift to a slower track or who do not seek rapid career advancement, especially when their children are young. But there are also many working mothers who are very ambitious—just as there are many working fathers who are very ambitious. Working mothers do not all fit into one mold. Choosing a family-friendly program does not necessarily reflect curtailed ambition or less commitment to work. *In fact, researchers are finding that the greatest users of family-friendly programs are their highest performers—both men and women.* High-performing employees seek out family-friendly programs at higher rates than other employees, and they are more apt to seek employment in only those organizations that have supportive workplace practices.[13]

In fact, implementing supportive workplace practices creates a workforce that is loyal to the company, more motivated to do a good job, and more apt to go the extra mile for the company.[14] In a business era where employees routinely jump from job to job, employers find that putting supportive practices in place enables them to keep

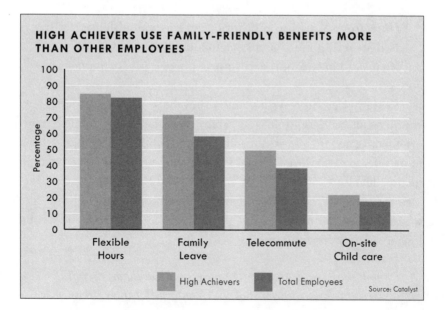

HIGH ACHIEVERS USE FAMILY-FRIENDLY BENEFITS MORE THAN OTHER EMPLOYEES

Percentage

Flexible Hours | Family Leave | Telecommute | On-site Child care

High Achievers | Total Employees

Source: Catalyst

their highest performers, who are not only loyal but know the business well and keep building organization-specific expertise. The result is a more effective workforce that takes pride in the organization and takes initiative to make it more successful.

FAMILY-FRIENDLY PROGRAMS CREATE MORE MOTIVATED, PRODUCTIVE EMPLOYEES:

- Dupont found that employees who use their family-friendly programs were 45 percent more likely to go the extra mile to ensure Dupont's success than other employees.
- Fleet Financial Group found that managers who used flexible work arrangements generated $16 million more in revenue per manager per year than their full-time colleagues.
- The National Study of the Changing Workforce found that workers who use flexible work options stay more committed to the organization and show more initiative on the job than other workers.
- JPMorgan Chase discovered that employees who had control over their time at work demonstrated 10 to 13 percent higher satisfaction levels than other employees.

Source: Families and Work Institute; Work Options, Inc., JPMorgan Chase[14]

> *Objection:* **Working mothers aren't as valuable; parenting is distracting and harms performance at work.**
> *Answer:* **Parenthood can improve work performance.**

Many parents say that once they have children, their focus sharpens at work and in life. Many become more achievement-oriented, strategic, and serious about their work, which makes for a more effective employee. I heard about this increased drive from all income levels.

Yvette was on welfare at home with two young children. She was unhappy and unproductive. Now that she had children, she no longer wanted this kind of life:

I knew that I had dreams. If I didn't pursue them, I would never show my children that they could fulfill their dreams,

because I had never gone after mine. That wasn't the life I
wanted for them. Everything was based on my children.
I decided to go back to school and get a good job for that
reason.

Yvette pulled her life together, went back to school, got her degree, and got off welfare. She is a motivated worker, and she makes sure that she will succeed. At work, she is now extremely focused:

I have become so efficient and effective. I don't have time for
all the pettiness and backstabbing at work. I won't waste my
time with it. My priorities are more clear.

Selena is the managing director of a successful and highly visible venture capital company that targets its investments for minority-owned businesses, and she is the mother of two young children. She feels that she is a more productive professional now that she is a parent:

Becoming a mother has made me more effective in the
workplace. I have more maturity and better perspective. I
have a better sense of what is important. I'm really focused on
conducting efficient, strategic meetings. I don't want to waste
my time, and I don't want to waste other people's time. I don't
do a lot of extra schmoozing around the watercooler. Why
would I sit around and talk to a coworker for a half hour
when that means then I'll have to stay at work a half hour
later at night?

Selena attributes her parenting experience to making her a much better professional. Good parenting skills are, in fact, directly relevant to good management skills. This is a view that is now being understood and promoted by some of our nation's leading business thinkers. Peter Senge, professor at MIT's Sloan School of Management and author of the bestselling business book *The Fifth Discipline: The Art and Practice of the Learning Organization,* is one of the nation's most respected thinkers on effective organizations. He says,

"The values and habits learned by practicing the disciplines of a learning organization serve to nurture the family as well as the business. It's a virtuous circle: not only is being a good parent a training ground for being a learningful manager, but being a learningful manager is also good preparation for parenting." He goes on to quote one of his corporate executives: "The more I understand the real skills of leadership in an . . . organization, the more I become convinced that these are the skills of effective parenting. Leading in a learning organization involves supporting people in clarifying and pursuing their own visions, helping people discover underlying causes of problems, and empowering them to make choices. What could be a better description of effective parenting?"[15]

In the Bright Horizons spring 2001 survey, *78 percent of the mothers and 73 percent of the fathers stated that their parenting skills have helped them do a better job at work.*

> **Objection: Aren't there plenty of people out there looking for jobs who don't care about a family-friendly culture? Can't I just hire them?**
>
> *Answer:* **The new job hunt: Employees—men and women—only want family-friendly workplaces.**

Women and men are putting family-friendly programs and supportive culture right at the top of their job criteria. Attitudes have changed dramatically. People no longer think of choosing either a career or a family. They want both, and they want to do well at both. A study done by the Radcliffe Public Policy Center in 2000 found that 80 percent of U.S. workers, male and female, at all income levels, report that one of their top job priorities is to have a work schedule that allows them to spend meaningful time with their families.[16] Young people are emphatically making that statement. A study conducted by PricewaterhouseCoopers found that nearly 60 percent of current business school students, both men and women, state that that their top career goal is to "attain a balance between personal life and career." This job goal is rated above compensation.[17] Savvy employers understand this and are crafting internal practices that will allow employees to achieve this balance.

In our 2001 Bright Horizons survey, 74 percent of the mothers and 65 percent of the fathers said that *finding a family-friendly work environment definitely factored into their decision to either take a new job or stay with their existing job*—powerful information for employers to understand. If organizations want to attract and keep good workers, they must offer a supportive work environment.

Organizations are starting to realize that these programs are important not only to mothers but to *all* valued employees—male, female, married, single, highly ambitious and not.[18] They're a competitive and business necessity. As one mother, Wendy, said:

> *At my company, flexible work options are not really viewed as an employee perk just for mothers. They are viewed as meeting a business need. We have to accommodate people with flexible schedules. Our managers talk a lot about how much it costs to lose good people. It's come a long way here. Alternative work schedules are now really accepted. Even the men make use of these programs. They take paternity leaves. Some guys now work at home.*

Objection: **But what about my business? I can't afford family-friendly programs and still be competitive in the marketplace.**

Answer: **Family-friendly companies are stronger, more competitive companies.**

As the interest in family-friendly practices has grown, so has research and media interest. Major business publications have studied, surveyed, and identified the leading organizations in America in regard to supportive workplace practices. Companies are very eager to be chosen for the "Best Place to Work" lists offered each year by *Fortune* magazine and *Working Mother* magazine. It is a highly sought-after honor.

Researchers have found that organizations on these lists, all having supportive workplace practices, achieve better financial results than their competitors. And as we have discussed earlier, the most valued aspects of a work environment—a supportive work culture and respectful supervisors—cost nothing. As the following chart shows, these organizations significantly outperform the marketplace.

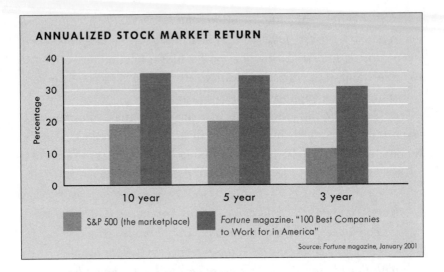

ANNUALIZED STOCK MARKET RETURN

S&P 500 (the marketplace)

Fortune magazine: "100 Best Companies to Work for in America"

Source: Fortune magazine, January 2001

Researchers have found that companies on these lists demonstrate superior results across a variety of performance indicators. They show higher productivity, increased ability to recruit and retain high-performing employees, and better earnings. In short, they are more effective organizations.[19]

Objection: **Will a family-friendly work environment really make a difference to children and families? To society?**

Answer: **Family-friendly organizations help employees feel better about themselves and their lives; they help employees to be better parents.**

Not only do family-friendly organizations create and attract motivated workers, good ones help employees feel better about themselves and about their lives in general.[20] When an employee feels supported and valued at work, she brings that sense of well-being into other aspects of her life. Her sense of competence at work spills over into her family. As Peter Senge says, "There is a natural connection between a person's work life and all other aspects of life. We live only one life."[21]

People who work for organizations that value them for their contributions and support them in being engaged parents develop a sense of gratification and accomplishment. Employees feel that they are developing as full, integrated human beings. They feel good about making contributions to the larger world. Susana, who works in a supportive work culture, says: "I have a great sense of accomplishment at work as well as at home. I think I am contributing to something greater than myself. That gives me a great sense of fulfillment."

Children are the indirect beneficiaries of good workplace practices.[22] Studies have shown that if a mother feels fulfilled and her self-esteem is high at work, she will show more sensitivity in her interactions at home and will become more involved in her child's daily life, school, and homework.[23] Typically, if a mother works outside the home, the father will be more actively engaged with his child's daily care than a father whose wife stays at home. As discussed in the previous chapter, children benefit greatly from the involvement of their father as well as their mother.

Developmental psychologists have found that girls in particular profit from the positive example of their mothers contributing and thriving in the external world. In fact, many mothers talked to me about the emphasis they place on being a role model for their children, both sons and daughters, by doing a good job at work. As Sarah states:

> I like to work, and I feel that it is important to work. Because I am the mother of boys, I've always felt that I have the responsibility to show these young boys what a strong, independent woman does.

Maria grew up in an inner-city housing project, dropped out of high school, had two children with an abusive boyfriend, and went on welfare. As her children grew, she became determined to turn her life around for their sake. She did not want them to make the mistakes she did, and knew how vital it was to set a good example, especially for her now adolescent daughter. Maria left her boyfriend, got a job, and after years of hard work and several promotions, she is now the office manager for a small nonprofit organization. She loves her work and is deeply engaged as a mother:

> I want to grow as high as I can. It feels like such an honor. I know it's good for my daughter, too. I see her talking to her friends, and she is so proud. She says, "Look how far my

mama is going." She is proud. She pushes me all the time, and then she pushes herself to achieve, too.

So there are many reasons a supportive work environment would be helpful to you. You can actively work to help your managers see why it makes sense for both the organization and the employees. Or you can focus on your own job situation and work with your direct supervisor to achieve the support and flexibility you need. And if you are looking for a new job, you can look for those work environments that you feel will support you in doing well both at work and at home.

FOUR

Excellent Child Care

*I don't think I could possibly go to work every day if I didn't
know that my children were in excellent care. There would
absolutely be no way. I know that my kids are thriving and
growing with the great care they are getting—and then I can
devote myself to doing a great job at work. It's essential to
making this whole working-mother thing work.*

                                                              —Cynthia

Excellent child care is the third pillar of successful working motherhood. If you know that your children are thriving, you will have
greater peace of mind while you work. I heard this from almost every
mother I spoke to. An excellent caregiver can be a great help to you
as well as your children. An experienced caregiver can help you
through challenging and confusing moments of parenthood and can
be a valued source of parenting advice. Excellent child care can also
be a beneficial element in your child's development and can augment
your child's foundations for later school success. Finding the right
kind of care for your child and your family's needs, and finding high
quality care, are the focus of this chapter.

There are several options to choose from in child care: child
care centers, family child care homes (where a caregiver takes care of
several children in her home), nannies, and care by a relative. No one
option is always right. I will go through the advantages and drawbacks
of each option to help you decide which one would work for your
child and your family. I will give you some of my "insiders' tips" on
what to look for in quality. I will also discuss how to find good after-
school child care for your elementary school children.

USING COMMON SENSE ABOUT CHILD CARE

Shortly after my husband and I enrolled our first child, Farrell, in child care, a research study announced that infants who are in child care for more than twenty hours a week risked becoming "insecurely attached." The concern was that the strength of the baby's bond with her* mother would weaken if she had other caregivers during the day. I remember driving along on the way to child care, with Farrell in the back in her baby seat, when I first heard about this study on the radio. When I got to the center, I just sat in the car in the parking lot, with Farrell asleep in her seat, as I thought about whether we were doing the right thing.

It was all so confusing. I knew that the caregivers in Farrell's infant room were warm, compassionate women trained in early childhood development and had years of experience caring for babies. To me, it seemed clear that they were experts in the nurturance of my baby, and Farrell was thriving. But this was also an "expert" who had conducted this research study and frowned on infant care. Was he right? Was I deluding myself?

That morning, as I made my tentative way into the infant room with Farrell, I cautiously and skeptically watched all the interactions. Was Farrell showing traits of being insecurely attached? What was her bond like with her caregivers? What was her bond like with me? All of a sudden I wanted Farrell to cry vigorously when I handed her to her caregiver, in order to prove that she was securely attached to me. But I also felt reassured that she had such a warm bond with her caregiver. It was clear that Farrell loved being with her, too.

As the years have gone on, and we have had two more children who also traveled through child care, I have seen a variety of studies for or against child care. Every couple of years, some new issue hits the headlines, and working parents are launched on another round of intense guilt and anxiety. After we have worried about whether our children will be insecurely attached, we then worry about whether our children will get into good colleges if they can't say their ABC's and

---

* To keep gender pronouns from getting confusing throughout this book, I have alternated the use of "he" or "she" chapter by chapter when referring to children.

have all their preacademic skills in place by the time they are four and a half. We worry that they will be sunk for life if their brains have not been optimally "wired" by high-caliber learning experiences and language by the time they are three.

When my colleagues and I get frantic calls from parents, media, and clients after the latest research comes out for or against child care, I always feel it is important to stop and look at the broader picture. There are some things we know and some things we don't know about what is good for children. We know that a child's development is impacted by a complex set of family and environmental factors—no one factor should be taken in isolation. This includes child care. The strength of our family system and our ability to sensitively parent are the most critical factors by far. We know that high quality child care has many positive developmental benefits, and that poor quality child care hampers development.

We don't know how long a child can be left in nonparental care each day and still reach optimal development. We can believe that twelve hours of child care a day is too much. But what about ten hours, eight hours, four hours? What is too much, and how do we know? And what about if the parents are gone twelve hours a day, but most of that time the child is with an adored grandma, in addition to three hours a day in a terrific preschool? Then is twelve hours of nonparental care okay? How many hours can we work and still feel confident that our children are thriving?

Parents seek concrete answers to these questions. We all wish that things were black and white and that there would be a clearly stated recipe for success in child rearing and child care. We look for things that are easy to calculate—such as numbers of hours in child care and age of entry—to see if we should feel guilty or proud. I have to admit that I had another quick, intense anxiety attack when a recent study suggested that children who are in center-based care for more than thirty hours a week may show more mildly aggressive behaviors as preschoolers than those who are home exclusively with their mothers. I immediately starting counting hours and wondered if time in the car commuting to child care counted as time with parents. What about time at home when I am on the computer finishing up e-mail? Where should I put those hours?

I wanted to know if that study showed increased aggression or increased assertiveness—a very big difference. For my four-year-old daughter, Gracie, who is now in child care, aggression seems bad, but assertiveness seems good. And if the study showed minor differences in "aggression" between children in exclusive maternal care and children in child care, should I really be worrying at all? What about the major developmental benefits that this same study showed that they are getting from child care? Are the benefits big enough to negate the minor risks?

Parents can go round and round, driving themselves crazy looking for the one right answer. One thing that I have learned over my years following the research and writing on early childhood development is that the "experts" don't agree! Experts cannot agree on what constitutes good mothering, and they certainly cannot agree on what set of elements will lead to optimal child development. And definitely don't look back over time. Every generation has its own set of experts. The current generation of experts typically disagrees with the prior generation's experts. Your mother may disagree with how you are doing things, but very likely, her mother criticized her methods.

Perhaps it would be better to step back and look at our own individual children and our own families and use some common sense. We know when our children and family are thriving. We know if we are devoted, sensitive, responsive, and happy parents.

We also know if we have made time for our children, if we have reorganized our lives to make room for them, their needs, and their development. I do think this question of hours in nonparental care is important. I don't know if ten hours or eight hours or even six hours a day is the cutoff point for too much child care, but I do believe that having a child means making accommodations in your life. It's too much for employers to expect employees to consistently work long hours each day. Children are resilient and will do fine if parents have occasional intense spurts at work, but parents and children will miss a great deal if that is consistently the schedule. Somehow we as families and a society must ensure that children and parents—both parents—are able to spend meaningful time together. To do this, employers and spouses must understand the importance of engaged parenting for children and therefore for society.

As we embark on our discussion of what would work best for your child and family, let me summarize for you a few general points about child development and child care around which all experts seem to agree:

• The first few years of life are critical in a child's development. It is during these first years that important brain development occurs that launches a child on her cognitive, social, and emotional path in life. It is vital that your child receives excellent care—from you and others—during these early years before school.

• Your child's development is impacted by a complex set of factors. No one factor alone can determine how well she develops. These factors include parenting skills and sensitivity, family environment and stability, and quality of child care. Family factors are the most meaningful determinants of child development—regardless of whether both parents work or not.

• Children in high quality child care during the preschool years show developmental benefits, particularly in language, premath, and social skills. By contrast, the development of children in poor quality care is at risk.

• The child care system in the United States is highly diverse, with an extremely broad range of quality within each option: child care centers, family child care homes, nannies, and care by relatives. If high quality care is chosen, no one option shows distinct advantages. The right choice depends on your family and work situation and the nature of your child.

• In all child care categories, responsive, sensitive caregiving, and the caregivers' training and education, are the significant elements to seek.

THE IMPORTANCE OF EARLY BRAIN DEVELOPMENT

We are just now starting to understand the importance of a child's early experiences for brain development.[1] Up until recent years, the only way scientists could study the brain was through animal studies or human autopsies. With the advent of new technologies, scientists can now study how living human brains operate. Through noninvasive technologies, such as the PET (positive emission tomography) scan, ultrasound, MRI (magnetic resonance imaging), and the EEG (electroencephalogram), scientists can watch active brain processes as a baby or young child interacts with her environment.

By measuring brain activity when a baby or young child has a loving interaction with a caregiver, experiences fear or high stress, or actively engages in a learning activity, scientists can begin to understand just how the brain functions and develops while experiencing these activities. One of the most astounding discoveries is how incredibly active and malleable the brains of babies and young children are. The staggering activity of the brain during the first years of life far outpaces brain activity at all other phases of life. While in the past it was believed that brain development depended largely on the genes you were born with, now it is understood that it is not only your genes but also, very importantly, your early experiences that determine how your brain develops.

A baby is born with billions of neurons, or brain cells, in a highly unfinished state. In the first days, months, and years of life, neurons develop connections, or synapses, with other neurons to form complex pathways of connections throughout the brain—its "wiring." This wiring takes place through a baby's and child's experiences. Her active interaction with her caregivers and environment determines the specific pathways of connections. In the first years, the child's brain has a tremendous proliferation of synapses, or connections—far more than the brain will ever need or use. As certain synapses are used over and over again through repetition of certain activities and emotions, they become reinforced, and a permanent pathway is created. If synapses are not actively used, over time they are eliminated.

Therefore, the activities the baby and young child engages in, and the emotions and stimulation she receives over and over again in the first years of life, create the blueprint or architecture of the brain. This "wiring," or network of neural connections, sets a child on her initial path in life. The major developmental task during these early years is to establish healthy pathways for learning and relating to others through active interaction with close caregivers, other children, and the environment.

For a baby and young child, warm, nurturing, responsive relationships with parents and close caregivers are critical for healthy development. The foundation of these nurturing relationships serves a protective biological function that helps a young child meet the challenges and stresses of development. Your baby and young child will thrive with lots of holding, cuddling, and loving talk. For healthy growth, a young child needs these relationships, as well as a variety of opportunities to explore and discover her environment. She needs stimulating activities, and she needs to be bathed in language.

A young child's fabric of relationships is the most consequential part of her development. A young child can benefit from a variety of close, dependable relationships that offer her security, love, and stimulation. She develops her budding skills best through play and interaction. In fact, play is the work of childhood.

It is through play that a child starts to develop concrete skills that she will need for school and life. When she is building a castle with blocks, she is really learning spatial relationships, the rudiments of physics and math. When she does a cooking project, she is learning chemistry and math, measurement, and the fine motor skills of stirring and cutting. When she plays make-believe with a friend or sibling, she is developing imagination, language skills, and an ability to cooperate and share: She is learning negotiation skills. When she plants a garden with a parent or caregiver, she learns planning skills, learns about cause-and-effect, nurtures new growth, and learns to understand changes over time. Reading a book with a caregiver teaches the importance of language and builds an understanding of logical flow and sequence of events. Reading also expands her vocabulary, enhances reasoning skills, and develops patience and focus.

Fostering this development does not require expensive learning toys or intense stimulation. It requires exposing your child to a variety of everyday experiences and allowing her to stretch her skills and process their meaning in an environment of love and security. It means having a caregiver who is tuned in to the interests and developing skills of your child and who can show patience and nurturance of her budding abilities. It means having a caregiver who can help your child learn to do things herself and who can help her channel frustrations when mastering something that requires repeated trial and error—a caregiver who will say, "I know you're disappointed that your castle fell down. And you worked so hard at it. Do you think if we used a different-size block on the bottom that it might stay up this time? What size do you think will work? Let's go give it a try." A child thrives with a caregiver who takes seriously her play endeavors and stimulates her interest in and dedication to them.

A good caregiver models effective behavior and shows children positive ways to relate to others. Discipline becomes a constructive technique rather than merely punishment. In fact, the root word of "discipline" is "disciple"—one who is taught. When a sensitive caregiver sees one child hit another and then grab a toy, rather than banishing the transgressor to a time-out, the caregiver will bring the first child over to the one she has hurt to demonstrate how her actions made the other child cry. The caregiver can say, "Ellie, do you see how Sam is crying? And he was playing with that toy that I see you want so much. Is there a way that you can each play with the toy? What are some good ideas?" Invariably, the children will forge their own solutions—taking turns or playing together. The caregiver has found an opportunity to teach and guide behavior. The children feel proud for having figured out their own solution. With a talented caregiver, discipline becomes teaching.

Parents are often surprised to learn that babies need active interaction as well. When you hold your baby, you can look her in the eyes and tell her all that you are doing and thinking: "You are the sweetest little baby. Do you know that when you smile at me like that, my heart just melts?" She will then start cooing or "talking" back to you. This little interchange helps her to start understanding language and connection. You'll find that she gets animated when you interact with her. She then works hard to connect back, making sounds, smiling, waving her arms and legs, reaching out.

The more a baby or young child is talked to directly, the greater her vocabulary and language skills will be as she grows. Reading to a child, talking to her, and listening to her all encourage development of language, reading, and writing. These activities can also foster close, loving interactions—so essential to her development. If you can take your young child onto your lap and cuddle her and show her how happy you are to read together, she will learn to love reading, too.

Although a baby or young child does not need numerous special toys for a healthy development, her early environment *is* important. Development can happen at home with a devoted parent, grandparent, or nanny, or outside the home in a quality child care setting. In fact, if a young child has multiple devoted and dependable caregivers—mother, father, grandmother, child care provider—she will grow up feeling that the world is populated by loving, responsive adults who are devoted to her care and nurturance.

QUALITY CHILD CARE IS IMPORTANT

I can see the difference my kids' child care has made in their lives. They are curious and vibrant thinkers. They are really social, really nice. They get along well with kids and know how to share and cooperate. They can express themselves. It's exciting to see.

—Patricia

The key is quality care. A 1995 landmark study conducted by four universities across the country looked at a range of child care in the United States and the impact on child development. The study repeatedly stressed the importance of quality care: "The results indicated that children in better quality child care displayed more advanced language and pre-math skills, had more positive views of their child care situation and themselves, had better relationships with their teachers, and had more advanced social skills. . . . All of these are primary areas of development for preschool age children, and furthermore, are considered important to children's ability to be ready to learn and to succeed in school."[2]

What is quality child care? In later sections of this chapter, I will outline what to look for in each child care option. But there are some general characteristics that you will want your child to receive regardless of which option you choose:

- *A caring, responsive caregiver attitude.* The caregiver should be warm, nurturing, and deeply engaged with your child. It must be clear that your caregiver loves being with children in general, and with your child in particular. The caregiver should hold and cuddle your child frequently.

• *A caregiver's knowledge of child development.* A caregiver must understand that babies and young children go through different phases of growth and development and, therefore, the interactions and environment they provide must evolve as well.

• *Sensitivity to individual development.* Every child develops at a different pace, with her own interests and preferences. A caregiver should be responsive to the individual needs and preferences of *your* child.

• *Positive, constructive behavior management.* Children should be guided to learn positive behaviors. They should be helped to learn from their mistakes and redirected to acceptable behavior. Clear and consistent limits should direct children on what path to take. Discipline should teach children rather than humiliate them.

• *Importance of language.* A caregiver should actively encourage language and conversation. A caregiver should listen to children, encourage them to express themselves verbally, value and respect what children say, and explain clearly the reasons for things. A caregiver should understand the importance of books and reading, even in infancy.

• *A learning environment.* As children grow, they should have varied toys, materials, games, art, and puzzles that stimulate their interest and development. These materials should evolve in complexity as the child grows so she can test and stretch evolving skills. Children should be allowed some choices in their activities so they learn to think on their own. Activities should be varied: individual and with friends, quiet and active play, building, make-believe, music, art.

• *A safe and clean environment.* There should be good hygiene and hand-washing procedures, and a space free of hazards. Toys, equipment, and furniture should be in good repair. You should see sound nutritional practices.

• *Support for engaged parents*. Child care providers should see themselves as partners in caring for the child. Parents should be encouraged to be involved in the daily program and decisions.

WHAT ARE MY CHILD CARE OPTIONS?

If you are a working mother, you generally have four options for child care: a child care center, a family child care home, a nanny, or a relative. These options have evolved significantly over the past two decades as working mothers have become the norm. Relatives and child care centers are the most common forms of child care. The use

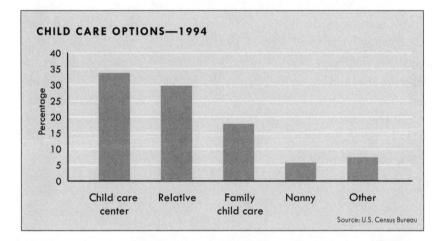

CHILD CARE OPTIONS—1994

Source: U.S. Census Bureau

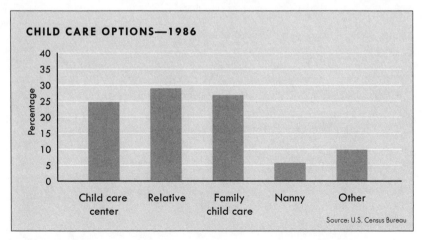

CHILD CARE OPTIONS—1986

Source: U.S. Census Bureau

of child care centers has grown over the last decade, and the use of family child care homes has dropped. The use of relatives and nannies has stayed about the same.

We have no comprehensive child care system in the United States. Child care regulations, standards, and licensing requirements vary, often dramatically, from state to state. In the United States, we have some of the very best child care that exists in the world, along with some of the worst. There are three important points to remember in your search for quality care: 1) Child care is highly diverse in our country; 2) much of the child care you will see will be poor to mediocre; 3) you *can* find high quality care if you know what you are looking for and what your child needs.

Although much of our nation's child care is, at best, mediocre, this is starting to change. Society is coming to understand the importance of early care, and a great deal of media attention has focused on this issue in recent years. Parents are becoming more knowledgeable and are demanding better standards; new public funding sources are opening up; and more and more employers are subsidizing child care of all types for their employees. There is wonderful child care available in all the option categories, and armed with the right information, you can find it.

USEFUL BOOKS:

- *Child Care That Works*, by Eva and Mon Cochran

Useful brochures by the National Association for the Education of Young Children (NAEYC):

- *What Are the Benefits of High Quality Early Childhood Programs?*
- *Choosing a Good Early Childhood Program*
- *Finding the Best Care for Your Infant or Toddler*
- *A Caring Place for Your Infant*
- *A Caring Place for Your Toddler*
- *A Good Preschool for Your Child*

To get a copy of these brochures, contact NAEYC at 1–800–424–2460 or www.naeyc.org.

Because every family has different needs and each child is unique, there is no one right option in choosing child care. In the next section, I will go over the benefits and drawbacks of each option and why parents make particular choices. I will also outline how to go about finding and evaluating the care, and I'll offer you some guidelines for finding high quality care.

Once you have settled on a child care solution, you'll want to forge a positive ongoing relationship with your caregiver. For tips on engaging with your child's teachers, family child care provider, or nanny, see chapter 13.

CHILD CARE CENTERS

I love the balance of learning activities and creativity and a certain level of professionalism, the cleanliness. I like the fact that the space was designed for children. It is a place of learning, fun, and love.

—Leah

Child care centers are the most common form of child care and are growing in demand. They can be fairly small, with just fifteen or twenty children of preschool age, or large centers with several hundred children ranging from infant to kindergarten age. Children are normally grouped by age: infants, toddlers (one- to two-year-olds), preschoolers (three- to five-year-olds) and kindergartners (five- and six-year-olds). Child care centers are licensed and regulated by state child care agencies that usually cover space requirements, materials and toys, ratios of children to caregivers, group sizes, and experience and training of the caregivers.

Benefits of Quality Child Care Centers

The teachers are trained and educated in child development. My kids learn how to cooperate and get along. And I can't believe the projects they do. I remember when my baby first started there. The teachers literally covered the infant floor

with paper and let the babies finger-paint all over it. They
were all so excited. There were little thumbprints, handprints,
and footprints all over the paper. And I'm thinking, This
would not be happening in my living room—with me or a
nanny.

—Helen

A quality child care center is designed as a learning environment with a developed curriculum. Quality centers are staffed by teachers who are educated and trained in early childhood development and education. The curriculum is designed to foster development—social, emotional, physical, and cognitive. A variety of age-appropriate materials, games, and equipment is provided. Teachers often receive ongoing training in early childhood education and are supported in their professional development. In excellent child care centers, children enjoy a foundation of learning that can serve as the basis for school success.

Vivian, an information technology specialist and the mother of twins, chose to put her babies in a child care center, in addition to her mother helping out, because she liked that the teachers were trained professionals and that her babies would receive important developmental benefits:

I knew that the center would give them developmental and
educational care. I know that they are going to do so much
more at the center than I would even dream of at home. It's
all new to me, but this is their job. The teachers have been
trained; I don't even have a manual. I am working on gut
instinct. And I am so protective, I am afraid to let them do
things and try things. I know the teachers will be protective,
but they will challenge my babies more than I would. They
will give them the toys and room and stimulation to do what
they can.

Child care centers are social environments where children learn from a young age to share, cooperate, negotiate with, and play with children their own age. These social skills encourage language development and help them ease into later school settings.

Taking care of babies and young children all day long is a hard job. It can have its frustrating and exhausting moments for even the most talented caregiver. In a good child care facility, the work environment is set up to support teachers in doing a good job. Teachers usually work in teams. One adult is not typically alone with the children all day long. Teachers take breaks and help one another out. Center directors supervise the care and pitch in when needed. One mother, Joanne, felt this was important:

> *I liked the idea of group care, because teachers who are in group care get lunch breaks, they come and they go, they can separate themselves from it. And if there's a problem, someone's going to be watching them.*

Care is always available, even when your child's primary caregiver is sick or on vacation. Child care centers are almost always open during standard work hours. If one teacher is sick, another will cover. This can help meet working parents' needs for reliability and constancy.

One variation on centers is employer-supported child care: centers sponsored by an employer that are located at or near the worksite. Employer-supported child care centers offer parents the convenience of having their young children nearby. The mother can continue to nurse after she goes back to work, and parents can join their child for lunch during the day and visit whenever they choose.

Child care centers have space designed expressly for children, with age-appropriate furniture and equipment, as well as safe environments with close attention paid to hazardous materials and safety precautions. Importantly, centers are licensed and accredited by external authorities.

A child care center can become a major source of friendship and support for parents and children. New parents often feel isolated. In good centers, there is a strong sense of community; both children and parents experience a sense of belonging and mutual support. For many families, the child care center becomes their "neighborhood"— a community where many devoted adults care for and look out for the children and one another.

Finally, the center director and teachers can be reliable sources of parenting information. They are trained professionals and can offer parents crucial support and knowledge. Many centers also offer resource libraries and workshops on a variety of parenting issues.

Drawbacks of Child Care Centers

If you work long hours, travel a great deal, or work nontraditional hours, the set opening and closing times of a center may not work for you. If you are arriving home late from a business trip or meeting, you won't be able to keep your child in the center later.

In order to make the right child care choice, you must understand the nature and personality of your child. Some children do better with one-on-one care and a very quiet environment and would not thrive in a group care situation. You may prefer to have your child in the quieter home environment.

Child care classrooms that do not have adequately trained or experienced teachers can become too noisy. If the numbers of children per adult or group sizes become too large, it can be difficult for teachers to have meaningful interaction with each child during the day. Long hours in a chaotic setting can exhaust or overwhelm a young child. The key, as with each child care option, is in the training and experience of the providers.

Some children or parents are slow to start in the morning. Many working parents feel rushed to meet an early work schedule. Many parents find it too stressful to get themselves and their child ready and out the door to drive to child care—perhaps over long distances and in sometimes inclement weather—do the drop-off routine, then get to work. It can become an exhausting and stressful routine in the morning and evening.

Parents find it harder to forge a close, continuing relationship with the teachers in some child care centers. Teachers typically work eight-hour days, and centers are usually open ten hours a day. You may see one teacher when you arrive and another teacher when you pick up. Unless communication is clearly established, it can be difficult to get in-depth information about your child's entire day. Some centers have high faculty turnover, with teachers always coming and

going. One mother who had her children enrolled in a center ultimately decided to seek a nanny instead:

With two working parents, my children had very long days. I
felt that they would be better at home and involved in local
play groups for shorter periods of time. Also, due to a
troubling staffing issue at the center, my children often had
substitutes and new caregivers. Consistency wasn't there, and
the care was not up to my expectations.

If your child is sick, she will not be able to go to the child care
center, and you will have to make other arrangements. The first year
that a child is in regular contact with other children, she will likely
become sick a number of times. You will have to set up some form of
back-up care—although this will happen when your child starts any
regular contact with groups of children, whether it's play groups,
group child care, or elementary school.

I never chose a child care center, because if I kept getting
called at the office to go pick up a sick child, that would just
be the end of my career. I don't have the kind of support at
work for that. And it is also just so hard to get my children out
of the house, especially during those first years.

                                             —Elizabeth

Child care centers are licensed and regulated and have established systems of operations. Regulations may leave less room for
individual family requests (for example, placement of a child in a certain classroom or administering medications). More informal child
care may allow greater flexibility in the program and policies.

And finally, as with all child care options, turnover of teachers
can be high. Teachers will remain longer if salary and benefits are
higher and the environment is rewarding.

BENEFITS OF QUALITY CHILD CARE CENTERS

- They are learning environments with a developed curriculum fostering cognitive, language, and preacademic skills.
- Teachers are trained and educated in early childhood education.
- The space is expressly designed for children with age-appropriate toys and materials. Safety precautions are in place.
- Teachers are supervised and work in teams. They can take breaks and get backup help when needed. If a teacher is sick or on vacation, care is consistently available.
- Children are in a social environment and are taught important social skills of sharing, cooperation, empathy.
- The center can provide a community for children and parents.
- The director and teachers can be an important source of parenting information and expertise.
- Centers are licensed and regulated. There is an external validation of quality.

DRAWBACKS OF CHILD CARE CENTERS

- Set hours provide less flexibility for parents.
- Less one-on-one care for children than nanny care or care by a relative.
- Long hours can be tiring for children.
- You'll need to get children up and out of the house in the morning, which may mean more rushed morning and evening routines.
- The first year that children are exposed to other children, they will likely get sick a number of times.
- As with all child care options, there can be high turnover of teachers.
- Many centers are expensive and may have long waiting lists.

How to Find Quality Child Care Centers

There are several ways to start your search, and I would recommend following a number of paths to make sure that you find a center that works for you. First of all, you will want to look only at high quality child care centers. In many instances, the quality centers are those that have some form of external subsidy in addition to tuition. The extra subsidy allows the center to achieve higher levels of quality. These types of centers could be publicly funded, located within universities and colleges, employer-supported, or with an established fund-raising arm.

Although you may start your search with subsidized centers, many nonsubsidized centers have achieved high quality, and you'll want to look at these as well. An important source of information is the National Association for the Education of Young Children. Centers can choose to undergo a rigorous evaluation of quality programming by NAEYC in order to become accredited; only 7 percent of all centers nationwide have achieved accreditation. You will certainly want to investigate any accredited centers located near you. NAEYC's website has a full listing of accredited centers.

Check your Yellow Pages to see if you have a local child care resource and referral agency. They will have a full list of all area licensed child care centers. States vary widely in their licensing standards, and some have different levels of licensing for different levels of quality. Your resource and referral agency can help you understand the levels of licensing in your state. Also ask them for their list of NAEYC-accredited centers. Put those on the top of your list to visit. If you cannot find a local resource and referral agency, Child Care Aware can direct you to the nearest one.

TO FIND LISTS OF ACCREDITED CHILD CARE CENTERS:

- Your local child care resource and referral agency
- Child Care Aware: 800–424–2246 or www.childcareaware.org
- NAEYC: 800–424–2460 or www.naeyc.org
- Also ask trusted friends and colleagues for their recommendations on child care.
- Check with the human resources office within your company to see if they support or recommend any area child care centers.

Now that you have a list of centers, take some time to visit and observe the programs. Never enroll your child in a program without having observed it yourself. Start early—preferably six months before you will need it. The best centers tend to be more fully enrolled and may have a waiting list, particularly for infants and toddlers. Call the directors of centers you want to visit and set up appointments. You can go with your spouse or partner or divide up the centers and then compare notes. Tell the director that you would like to visit the classrooms, particularly the one where your child would be enrolled. Give yourself plenty of time so that you can actually watch the activity for a while. Go to a couple of centers so that you can start comparing. Once you have narrowed your selection to one or two centers, return for a second visit and spend time both with the director and in the classroom again.

Insiders' Tips

In addition to my own views, I asked the center directors, regional managers, and education and training coordinators at Bright Horizons to tell me how they evaluate the quality of a center and its programs. In what kind of center would these educators want to enroll their *own* baby or young child? Below I share some of these views in addition to NAEYC and other expert guidelines.

The Owner

In many cases, the owner of the center is different from the director who operates it. The owner may be an organization that operates multiple centers, or an individual who operates one or several centers. Find out the owner's objectives and philosophy of child care. The owner or organization will often have a website that you can check. Most likely they can provide written materials about the center and its educational philosophy. You want to look for signs that the owner is motivated by a vision of quality child care. If the center is privately owned, you can also ask to meet with the owner. Investigate:

- The number of past licensing violations, if any, with the local child care licensing agency.
- How long has the owner been in business? What is the owner's background? Has there been stability in ownership?
- Does it appear that the organization has good systems for recruiting teachers and a director?
- Is there a system of teacher training and curriculum development? Are the teachers and director monitored, evaluated, and given opportunities for development?

- Is there a statement of educational philosophy? Is it one that you believe in and can support?

The Center Director

The center director is the key to a high quality center. A good director will know how to hire excellent teachers; how to motivate, guide, and evaluate them; how to keep center morale and creativity high; and how to engage parents and create a community.

- What do you think of the director? What is her or his background, experience, and training? How long has the director been there?
- Where is the director's office located? Does the director have easy access to the classrooms? Easy viewing of the front door?
- Is the director available at either morning drop-off or end-of-day pickup to greet and talk to parents?
- What is the relationship between the director and teachers— do they seem to have a positive, confident rapport? Does there appear to be mutual respect? Does the director seem to be a good manager?
- Does the director have good relationships with parents? Does she or he seem to know them and the children well?

Teachers

Your child's primary caregiver, as well as all the teachers in your child's classroom, will be important people to your child and you. As your child moves up in age, she will be changing classrooms or groups and will be with other teachers as well. Those relationships will have a major impact on your child. You will want to feel very good about the teachers who will be caring for your child.

- What are the backgrounds, experience, and training of the teachers? Many centers post short bios of all faculty outside the classrooms. Go read them all.
- What is the teacher turnover at the center? Ask every teacher you meet, "How long have you been here?" If everyone answers less than six months, that's a warning sign.

- Is there ongoing and periodic faculty training? What happens when a teacher is sick? Is there a ready list of substitutes?

- Do the teachers seem to like working together? In a good child care center, teachers work in teams—different from the K–12 model. Is there a feeling of camaraderie? Do they plan the program and activities together? Teacher/teacher relationships are important as well.

- Quality centers have a more intensive teacher-to-child ratio and smaller group sizes. This allows more one-on-one interaction and a calmer environment. NAEYC recommends, as a minimum, the following teacher-to-child ratios by age group:
  - One teacher for every 3 to 4 infants
  - One teacher for every 4 to 5 younger toddlers (12 to 24 months)
  - One teacher for every 6 older toddlers (2 to 3 years)
  - One teacher for every 9 to 10 preschoolers (3 to 5 years)

Classroom and Center Atmosphere

- Is there a sense of interesting, involved activity? The classroom should be neither too noisy nor too quiet. Are the teachers down on the children's level, engaged with them and facilitating activities? Do teachers seem to love what they're doing and love the children? Do you see smiling faces and happy, compassionate voices?

- The teachers should be talking primarily with the children and not with one another. Are the teachers spread throughout the room with small groups of children? Are children listened to and encouraged to express themselves? Is there an atmosphere of respect? Are the teachers warm and affectionate? Are they responsive to the children?

- Are children redirected from undesirable behavior and shown positive ways to handle issues and problems? Do teachers help children to understand their behavior and why they should and shouldn't do certain things?

- Do teachers find plenty of opportunity for warm one-on-one interaction—reading a book to a child on her lap, a warm hug and conversation, comforting a child? Do teachers use routine caregiving (such as diapering and feeding) as moments of one-on-one interaction for talk, nurturance, and affection?

• Is children's artwork displayed throughout the room? Are there pictures and artwork at child height?

• Is the classroom well organized and a pleasant, clean environment? Children learn respect for things if teachers model that for them. Are there clearly delineated learning centers throughout all the classrooms?

• Is there an outdoor play area that is easily accessible and well maintained? Are there climbing structures? Do children go outside regularly every day?

• Watch the drop-off times in the morning. Are the teachers and children happy to see each other? Does there seem to be a real bond? Are the classrooms set up and activities set out to interest the children?

Classroom Program

FOR INFANTS

• The most important factor for infants is one-on-one care and interaction—lots of holding, rocking, singing, and loving. Do the teachers talk to the babies?

• Babies should be held when fed. Babies should sleep and be fed on an individual basis, rather than being kept to a rigid schedule.

• Babies should be free to explore their environment. They learn through active exploration with their mouth, hands, and other senses. They shouldn't be restricted in chairs, swings, or bouncy seats for lengthy periods of time. Are there safe, clean, and interesting places for the babies to crawl? Is there a variety of textures and materials to experience? Are there toys within easy reach? Can teachers see babies at all times?

• Are babies responded to quickly when they cry? Is the classroom atmosphere settled, calm, and happy? Expect to see some crying, even in high quality settings, but watch carefully how caregivers respond—do they pick up the babies and comfort them? Do they talk in a loving and soothing voice?

• Is the room clean, the toys and floor washed? Are hand-washing procedures scrupulously followed?

• Do the teachers welcome and encourage parents to visit and moms to nurse—at any time of the day?

• Are babies taken outside every day?

FOR TODDLERS

• Toddlers are much more mobile. Their attention span is short; they are just beginning to talk. They cannot sit still for long and must be able to actively experience their environment, with plenty of opportunity for motor and sensory exploration.

• Is there a variety of choices for the toddler around the classroom? Is the room set up so that children play and participate successfully in small groups? Is there a minimum of large-group time?

• Do the teachers encourage the toddlers to use words to express themselves rather than grabbing or hitting? Do they model resolving issues with respect and understanding?

• Is the child free to move around the classroom environment with a minimum of restrictions? Is there flexibility in the schedule to meet the needs and moods of the children? Do teachers read to the children frequently and allow them to look at books?

• Are mealtimes a time for social interaction, conversation, and the beginning of some self-help skills (e.g., pouring from a small pitcher with a lid)?

• Do the toddlers have time each day to play outside?

FOR PRESCHOOLERS

• The preschool environment should be rich in activity and curriculum. Activities should take place in small groups. The classroom should be set up in learning centers such as dramatic play, art, music, reading, writing, puzzles and other manipulative toys, blocks, snack table, water table, science and nature area. Children should have a great deal of choice in their activities, as well as time to complete projects. Teachers can help facilitate and extend the play.

• There should be a planned structure for the preschool day, with learning activities and goals. Look to see if the daily or weekly lesson plans are posted. Ask the teachers how the curriculum is developed. A quality child care center usually has skilled teachers who create their own daily curriculum rather than using a packaged one.

• Preschoolers should be encouraged in social play—sharing, cooperating, planning together, sharing dramatic play.

• The classroom should be a very print- and language-rich environment: lots of books with a comfortable place to sit, frequent reading by teachers, books on tape, labeled shelves, lots of conversation.

• Mealtime is an important time for conversation. Children and teachers should be grouped together at tables for social interactions. Self-help skills should be encouraged, such as pouring, serving, and cleaning up.

• The classroom should be inviting and delightful for children. The toys and materials should evolve over time.

• Do the preschoolers have time to play outside each day?

Parent Involvement and Communication

• Are parents welcome at any time? Are they made to feel comfortable and part of the center? Is the director available to greet the parents?

• Are there bulletin boards with information for parents? Is there a resource library for parents? Is there a parent newsletter or committee?

• Is there verbal and/or written communication for the parents about the child's day? Are there regular parent/teacher conferences where the child's development is discussed? Are lesson plans posted?

• Is there a sense of community in the center? Do families know one another? Are there center family events? Go to the center at

pickup time and watch the mood and interactions. Do families socialize and seem to enjoy one another and the center?

FAMILY CHILD CARE HOMES

*I went through the list of licensed family child care providers,
and Mrs. Johnson was the first person I called. She told
me to come over whenever I wanted. I dropped in on her
unannounced, and what a wonderful sight. Her home was
clean, the kids were happy. She was feeding them this
wonderful home-cooked meal of green beans, pork chops,
and homemade applesauce. She has been so outstanding;
I am always well pleased and comfortable.*

—Myrna

A family child care provider is a caregiver who takes care of several
children in her home. A mother who wants to stay home with her
baby or small child may decide to take in a few other children for
extra income. Once her own children have gone off to elementary
school, she might decide to continue caring for other children. Sometimes women who love caring for children start a family child care
home once their own children are grown. Family child care is still a
fairly informal system. Although there are state regulations and
licensing, most family child care is not licensed.

Benefits of Family Child Care

*I wanted my son to be in an environment that was as close to
the home that I would provide for him if I had the ability to
stay home.*

—Stacy

A major benefit of family child care is that your child will be in a
home environment. She will be part of a small group of children in
an intimate, familylike situation and can participate in a daily family
life with its familiar rhythms and routines. An attractive benefit for

many parents is that if you have more than one child, they can be together during the day. The provider can understand both children separately and as siblings. Children are usually with children of various ages—approximating the familylike setting and dynamics.

Good family child care homes can be wonderful learning environments. Many providers are professionals who set up daily activities that foster development in a warm home setting. Much of the learning revolves around family and home projects: cooking, gardening, participation in simple building projects, etc. Children can play, learn, and make friends in a relaxed, intimate environment.

If a provider cares for just a few children, she may have more opportunity for one-on-one care. Your child can experience other children and learn social skills in a small setting. Parents and the care provider can develop a close personal bond that feels more like family or a close friend. A great deal of information is often shared about the child between the provider and the parents.

Many parents like the fact that the family child care home is in their neighborhood or community. Their children can be involved in community events, go to the local pool or library, and perhaps get to know some children with whom they will go on to elementary school. These relationships can ease their later entry into school.

Another benefit for parents is the flexibility in hours. Particularly if you work nontraditional hours, family child care may be more convenient for you than a child care center. Providers are often willing to take your child during off hours—early morning or evening. Some providers will even keep children overnight. Myrna, whose hours at the factory changed frequently, especially liked this aspect of family child care:

Mrs. Johnson took Valerie whenever I needed her to. There were some weeks when she would even have to keep Valerie overnight. She just loved babies. She kept a crib in her bedroom. She was definitely like a grandmother for us. It was beautiful.

One very talented and experienced family child care provider, Joy, described how she views her relationships with her families:

*We are really part of one another's family. I have a lot of
flexibility to support families when they experience a crisis.
The kids are excited to stay late at Joy's, even if it's because
Dad's car broke down or Grandma is sick.*

And finally, family child care is typically the least expensive of
the nonrelative forms of child care. Due to the informality of the
setup—usually a neighbor or friend who will take in your child plus a
few others—the provider will typically charge less.

Drawbacks of Family Child Care

Major challenges of family child care are the potentially difficult
working conditions the providers operate under and the stress that
puts on them. Many providers work long hours at low pay with no
benefits. They are typically isolated and unsupported, working alone
with several children all day. Most do not have a way to take a break
during the day or get some help if two or three children are needy at
the same time. Joanne is one working mother who felt uncomfortable
with this option:

*I didn't like family child care because I felt that people who
were taking care of kids in their homes never got a break from
what they were doing. What do they do when they're about to
lose it? I didn't want to worry about my child in that kind of
situation.*

The demands on the provider can be particularly difficult if she
takes care of several children, including infants. Many caregivers take
care of up to seven children. Without help, this can put a tremendous
strain on the provider and can amount to insufficient attention for
each child. That is why so many family child care providers resort to
TV and videos for the children during the day.

Most family child care providers are not trained in early childhood education, and because of the need to be constantly present, it
is difficult to pursue ongoing education and training—a significant
indicator of quality.

BENEFITS OF QUALITY FAMILY CHILD CARE

- Home environment; intimate, familylike feel
- Smaller group setting for young children
- Siblings can remain together
- If there are just a few children, there may be more opportunity for one-on-one care; continuous, caring relationship between the provider and child can take place over several years
- Close personal bond between provider and parents
- Greater communication about the child between the provider and the parents
- Can provide a community and neighborhood connection; children can make friends that they will maintain in school
- Flexible hours. Can better serve nontraditional work hours and sudden needs for more care
- Low cost

DRAWBACKS OF FAMILY CHILD CARE

- Difficult working conditions for the provider: often long hours at low pay with no benefits
- Provider is isolated and unsupported
- Lack of supervision of the provider
- Typically not trained in early childhood education; few opportunities to pursue ongoing training
- High turnover
- Closed if provider is sick or on vacation
- No control over what other people may be present in the house and in contact with your child

If the provider is sick, on vacation, or has a family emergency, parents may be left without care. Because of the difficult working conditions, there is high turnover of family child care providers, often with little or no notice.

Another crucial drawback is the lack of supervision of the family care provider. Typically, one woman is alone with a group of children all day, with no monitoring of care. Unless she is part of a network of family child care providers, there is no external evaluation of quality. This made Denise uncomfortable:

I didn't want to leave an infant who couldn't speak to me about what happened with any one individual. I wanted a child care situation where there could be some checks and balances—where people are watching what is going on.

Finally, one of the biggest disadvantages for some parents is the lack of control and knowledge of what goes on in another person's house. Parents cannot control other adults, teenagers, and older children who come in and out of the house. You don't want other adults whom you have not met and approved in contact with your young children.

How to Find Quality Family Child Care Providers

Most parents find family child care providers through word of mouth. They may have a trusted friend or neighbor who takes in a few children. Most providers do not advertise, so the best way is to talk to all your friends and acquaintances whose judgment you respect.

Go to your local child care resource and referral agency. They will have listings of licensed family child care providers. Although the vast majority are not licensed and regulated, research shows that the better ones typically are. It is best to start with that route. There is also a budding accreditation program within the family child care sector. The National Association for Family Child Care (NAFCC) has an accreditation process and list of accredited programs. Contact them to find local accredited programs.

TO FIND LISTS OF ACCREDITED FAMILY CHILD CARE HOMES:

- Your local child care resource and referral agency
- National Association for Family Child Care: 800–359–3817 or www.nafcc.org

---

It can be difficult to obtain an external validation of quality. Studies have shown that the majority of family child care is inadequate or merely custodial care, so you will have to work hard to make sure you find a good one.[3] There are excellent family child care homes available, so when you find one, it will be well worth the effort.

In general, family child care homes that are part of a network of providers deliver higher quality,[4] so investigate through your resource and referral agency whether there is a network in your community. If they are part of a network, they are better able to get backup and support, may have evaluation visits, and can participate in ongoing education and training programs. Some networks offer provider access to health insurance and curriculum resources.

Insiders' Tips

Start with the list of quality child care characteristics that I listed early in the chapter. These are also critical in family child care. To summarize:

- A caring, responsive caregiver attitude
- Knowledge of child development
- Sensitivity to individual development
- Positive, constructive behavior management
- Emphasis on language
- A varied and stimulating plan of activities
- A clean, comfortable space free of hazards
- Environment where parent participation is welcomed

You will learn a lot if you visit the home at different times during the day. You can even ask to help out for a day or two to really get a sense of the daily routine and atmosphere. Trust your instincts. How does this home feel to you? Would you be excited to have your baby or young child there?

The provider should have no more than three or four babies and toddlers in her care. Although many states allow six or seven children per adult, that is only reasonable if they are all preschool age. The following is a list of what else you should look for:

The Family Child Care Provider

- Why does she do this work? Her commitment will be greater if she sees this as a profession and a career rather than simply picking up some cash. How long has she done this work? Does she have any education and training in early childhood education? Obtain *and check* several references from current and past parents.

• Does she pursue any ongoing training programs? Is she part of a provider network? What does this network offer her?

• Watch how she interacts with the children—with respect, attention, responsiveness, and interest? Is she loving and nurturing? Do you hear a great deal of language from both the children and the provider?

• Does she read to the children often?

• How does she handle the needs of different-age children? For example, preschoolers need to work with small "manipulatives"—LEGOS, puzzles, scissors, pens, etc., but infants need to be kept away from these items for their own safety.

• Watch how she handles difficult behaviors. Does she redirect and explain rather than punish and humiliate?

• What happens when she gets sick, goes on vacation, or has a family emergency? Does she have any backup or access to help during the day? If so, who is this person and can you meet her? What is her background?

• Does she have first aid and CPR training? Has she ever had an emergency with a child in her care? How was it handled? Has she received training in risk and safety management?

Atmosphere

• You can tell a lot by staying for a while and observing. Do the children seem happy and engaged? Is there laughter and fun? Are the children settled and comfortable?

• Are there children with challenging behaviors who would make it difficult to add one more child—yours?

• How many children are currently in her care? What is the maximum number of children she plans to care for and at what ages? If the provider you are considering is currently caring for two children under three years of age and you want a very small group, you should know whether she plans to enroll more, including older preschoolers.

• Does she have a style and philosophy of caregiving that is in line with yours? Explicitly go over discipline approaches.

Daily Structure

• Does she plan activities for the children every day? What are these activities? What kind of learning activities take place? There are many natural learning opportunities in the home: gardening, cooking, even some laundry and chores. The preschoolers can start learning about family responsibility in an appropriate way.

• Does she vary the activities throughout the week? Is there a structure or schedule during the day? Do the children have opportunities to engage in art and music, books, dramatic play, games and puzzles? Do they have social time and time to be quiet by themselves?

• Do the children go outside every day?

• Do the children watch TV or videos? If so, how frequently and what do they watch? TV should be allowed only infrequently, if at all.

• Will children go outside the home property? On neighborhood walks? In cars? Are there car seats? Seat belts?

Home Environment

• Check childproofing, placement of hazardous materials, safety precautions, gates on stairs, smoke detectors, fire extinguishers, covered electrical sockets, etc.

• Is it a warm, inviting environment?

• Look carefully at the toys, games, equipment, art supplies, dress-up, etc. Are they organized and accessible? Are they well maintained? Are there enough for the number and ages of the children enrolled?

• Does she have a large supply of books readily available?

• Is there an enclosed outdoor play area with maintained play equipment?

- What does she feed the children for lunch? For snacks?

- Are there animals in the house? Any smokers in the house?

- What other adults or older children are regularly present in the home? Can you meet them?

Parent Relationships

- Observe at the family child care home during drop-off in the morning and, even more important, during pickup at the end of the day. Do the parents and provider have a strong relationship? Watch how she communicates about the day. Does she share developmental information? Is she constructive in her feedback?

- Do you feel that you can be partners with this provider in the care of your child?

- Is there a regular time set up to discuss your child's developmental progress?

- Explicitly discuss mutual expectations, policies, hours, payment, holiday and vacation schedule, sick-child policy, etc. Treat this as a professional relationship, with clear communication on both sides. Perhaps the two of you can develop a contract where these policies are laid out explicitly. Many bad feelings are avoided if you are each clear up front.

NANNIES

I was so conscious of how important the early years are and hoping to find someone who is bright and energetic to focus all her energies on our baby. Someone who could help make our lives easier, so that when we were home, we could focus on our baby.

—Rebecca

A nanny is someone who is hired to care for your child, usually in your home, although it may be in the nanny's home. A nanny is different from a family child care provider in that the nanny cares only for your children. The nanny may live with you or arrive every morning to care for your child. The nanny is hired to be your employee and is paid on an hourly basis or at a set weekly salary.

Parents use a variety of nanny solutions. Many hire professional nannies who are trained in early childhood development and nanny skills. These nannies, who are fairly expensive, are highly skilled and usually very reliable. They may have a degree in early childhood education from a college or university or accreditation from a nanny school.

Many parents use an au pair, a young person (between eighteen and twenty-five) from abroad who comes to the U.S. on a one-year cultural exchange program. The au pair lives with an American family and takes care of their children in exchange for room and board and a modest fee. The au pair agency stipulates the permissible number of hours and responsibilities the au pair can work. Au pair programs are administered through various agencies regulated by the U.S. Information Agency.

Other parents hire women or men who are not necessarily educated or trained in early childhood development but have experience caring for children and love doing this kind of work. These people come from a wide variety of backgrounds, countries of origin, and age. Pay varies widely.

Benefits of Nanny Care

We thought someone coming to the house would be the best thing for Aaron. It most simulated a stay-at-home mom. Aaron wouldn't have to share an adult's attention with anybody else in those very early months and years.

—Sarah

The biggest benefits of a nanny are that the child receives one-on-one care (or shares with a sibling or two) and stays in her home environment. There are some children who do not thrive in group care when very young, and benefit from more individual care. The baby can have a quieter, calmer day. The nanny can devote her or himself fully to the care of the child. The day can be organized around the baby's rhythms.

Your morning and evening routines can be less rushed and stressed with a nanny. If you have to rush out the door in the morning, your baby or child does not have to be disturbed. She can stay in her pajamas and have a more leisurely morning.

Another great convenience is the flexibility in the hours. If you have a job where you travel a great deal, work long hours, or have unexpected demands on your time, you can hire a nanny to accommodate these schedules. If your flight home is delayed or your car breaks down, you know that your child is already at home with her familiar nanny. That can reduce your stress level significantly.

You usually will not have to worry about the days your child is sick. If you have a job where you cannot easily take off for sick child care, a nanny will be there for you. You also may be able to postpone the frequent illnesses that come with a child's first exposure to many other children. Carrie, a physician, knew that it would be difficult to leave work if her child became ill:

I thought that child care centers and family child care homes would be a problem when my child is sick. The idea of having two conflicting responsibilities at once, both home and work, was overwhelming for me. I had to have someone else there. I also needed the flexibility for extra hours if I was on call.

Having a nanny gives you the greatest control over your child care situation. You have chosen this person, you set the hours and the policies, and you can come and go as you need and want. You can determine with whom your child can play during the day.

A nanny can help make life at home more manageable. You can arrange to have your baby or child fed dinner before you come home, so you aren't rushing around to feed a hungry child quickly. A nanny will often take care of some of the home functions that relate to your child: picking up toys, cleaning up after her, feeding and bathing her, and sometimes doing her laundry. This can free up more of your time to devote to your child when you come home from work.

Finally, an excellent nanny can become a treasured member of the family. An excellent nanny will be devoted to your children and will truly share in their care and development. She or he knows your children intimately and can share more information about your child's day and ongoing development. Many nannies become friends and important supports to the parents. The nanny becomes another devoted adult in your child's life.

From a nanny's perspective, this close personal relationship is one of the key benefits of the job. Listen to this nanny, Lynn:

> *The relationships I made with the family I worked for still exist today, some ten years after leaving that role. We became, and remain, close friends—the kind of friends you consider family. You build a deep relationship, being in a person's home every day. You experience their life firsthand as you become part of their total daily routine—being there for waking children, bathing and dressing, sidestepping parents as they prepare for their workday. As a nanny, I was also able to build strong relationships with the extended family. I became part of special celebrations and family events and got to know quite personally the aunts, uncles, cousins, grandparents, etc.*

Drawbacks of Nanny Care

A significant drawback of nanny care is the isolation for both the nanny and the child. Many mothers find it difficult to be home alone with their baby day in and day out. You can imagine how much more challenging it is for the nanny—who is not the child's parent and therefore may not have the depth of your unconditional love that carries you through the difficult and frustrating moments. If the nanny is from out of town or another country, that sense of isolation can be magnified tremendously. This is one major reason why turnover of nannies is so high. Sandra was a live-in nanny who loved working with the children but also felt lonely:

> *I did not like the solitude of working alone and did not have many chances to work with others. I was not aware of any*

professional organizations so did not have the opportunity to grow professionally. I felt very restricted by being available anytime. I also spent a lot of time alone when I went to my room at the end of the day.

Another drawback is that nannies work in an unsupervised environment. Many parents feel uncomfortable leaving a baby or small child in the care of someone for long hours where there is no direct knowledge of what is going on during that time. A baby or small child cannot communicate for herself. Without colleagues or a supervisor, a caregiver can find it difficult to continually generate the energy, initiative, and creativity to make the days interesting and developmental for your child. One mother, Paige, expresses a common concern:

I was very worried about bringing in a nanny with no other eyes around. I'm very trusting, so I worried that I would interview someone and think that they were great and later find out they weren't so great.

Although some nannies are professionally trained, many have had no formal experience in child development and child care. Whatever caregiver you choose should have a firm grounding in child development. She or he needs to understand how children grow and develop and be able to best nurture that development in your child. Some parents hire immigrants who have limited English-language skills. This can be a disadvantage unless the parents are explicitly trying to develop their child's foreign-language skills. A caregiver must be able to talk actively with children and foster language development in the first few years.

Since turnover is high, parents can be left high and dry if they suddenly lose their child's caregiver. You will also be left without care when your nanny calls in sick or goes on vacation.

Although many parents see the close personal relationships as an asset of nanny care, others feel that they end up filling a quasi-parent or counselor role to the nanny, particularly if the nanny is young or from out of town or another country. Some parents, like

BENEFITS OF NANNY CARE

- One-on-one care between caregiver and child in the child's familiar home environment
- No need to get your child up and out of the house in the morning, which can ease the morning and evening process
- Flexible hours: Your nanny can be there when you need her or him
- You don't have to worry about finding sick child care, which may lessen a child's early exposure to illnesses
- Offers greatest control over your child care situation, since you set the hours, policies, activities, friends, etc.
- Nanny may do housekeeping related to the children
- Siblings can remain together during the day
- Greatest amount of information communicated about your child
- Close, personal relationship—can feel like family

DRAWBACKS OF NANNY CARE

- Isolation and loneliness for nanny; no breaks or support during the day
- Lack of supervision and monitoring of care
- Typically little training in early childhood development
- Lack of care when nanny is sick, on vacation, or suddenly quits
- Loss of privacy for parents
- High turnover
- High cost

Adah, struggle with the loss of privacy in their home with a live-in nanny:

> *Having a live-in nanny turned out to be very difficult for us. We just didn't think about the fact that my husband and I really like to be together—alone. We didn't like having somebody in our house all the time. Then you get into trying to figure out how friendly and inclusive you should be. I like walking around naked. I couldn't do that anymore. She ended up leaving after about six months. Unfortunately, she decided one day that she was leaving the next day. That definitely put us into crisis mode.*

Some parents struggle with feelings of jealousy that the nanny is at their home with their child more hours during the day than they are. The child will often become attached to the nanny and at times prefers to be with her or him rather than the parent. Although the parents may want the nanny and child to have a good, close relationship, they can also have conflicting feelings. They don't want to feel displaced.

Although nanny salaries vary widely, a qualified, experienced nanny will be your most expensive child care option: $300 to $500 a week for full-time care. However, if you have more than one child, a nanny may be less expensive than a child care center or family child care home where you pay multiple tuitions.

Before Looking for a Nanny, First Define What You Want

It is important for you and your spouse or partner to sit down and think carefully about what you are looking for in a nanny. Think about your family style and atmosphere and what kind of person you would like to occupy this intimate role. Clearly discuss the personal characteristics that are most important to you. Do you feel it's essential to find someone of your faith or religion; someone who is vibrant and energetic or someone who is quiet and laid-back; someone who is artistic, creative, and spontaneous or someone who is efficient and organized? You should consider the mood and atmosphere you like established at home. Do you like a full and lively house with lots of activities and friends? Or do you like a home that is calm and settled? You should have someone who is the right match with your values and your goals for child rearing. Listen to a few very different sets of criteria used by parents:

I was looking for a woman who was nurturing. I am more practical, so I wanted someone who could be really sweet. I preferred that she speak Spanish, and I wanted someone who was a mother.

We wanted someone who could create a learning environment at home. We wanted someone bright who would talk to our child and who would have ideas about different activities to do—like go to museums, libraries, etc. We wanted someone who could follow our lead.

I wanted a gentle soul, someone who was content to just sit and hold and talk to my baby. I didn't need someone who could do tons of multitasking but just someone who would cuddle my baby and love him and walk him in a way that I would want to do myself.

We wanted a wonderful person who would bring their spirit and personality to the job, who needed as little direction from us as possible. We wanted someone who was interesting and interested, who would supplement our child's life—spunky, enthusiastic, adventurous.

In addition to personal characteristics, think through the responsibilities of the job. Will you require driving and carpooling, homework help, organizing and supervising play dates? Do you want to set the daily schedule yourself, or do you want someone who can plan the daily activities, outings, play dates?

How do you want the nanny to fit in to your family? Are you looking for someone who is part of the family, who eats meals with you, goes on vacations with you, and uses all the common areas of the house freely? Or, particularly with a live-in nanny, do you want to maintain as much family privacy as possible, with the nanny staying in her room or rooms in off hours? Are the nanny's friends welcome at the house? Overnight guests? What is your policy on significant others? Use of the car, television, and telephone during off-work hours? Does the nanny pay for long-distance phone calls or do you?

Do you require that the nanny have CPR and first aid training? This is important to know, since many nannies do not have this training, and you may need to provide it. How important are experience and education to you? How important are language skills to you?

Think through what you want for an approach to discipline. Be ready to describe a few potential scenarios of different child behaviors and how you would want those handled.

You should be very specific about what light housekeeping duties are expected. Typically, the nanny would be responsible only for those areas involving the children: keeping playroom and children's bedrooms picked up and beds made, preparing and clearing up children's meals, cleaning children's bathrooms after use. Sometimes the nanny will also do the children's laundry and shop for children's food. Nannies will vary widely in their willingness to assume some housekeeping responsibilities. Don't ask for or expect much housework if the nanny is also expected to do full-time child care. Remember that you are hiring a child care professional to care for your children.

It is helpful to define as much of the nanny situation as you can before you start looking. Much of this information will eventually go into the Caregiver Notebook (see page 164) that you will create once she or he starts.

Decide what is important to you:

- What personal characteristics are most important to you?

- What hours are required? How much flexibility? Any work on weekends or evenings?

- How do you want to see the day structured?

- Define the range of daily responsibilities.

- What role do you want to see the nanny play in the family?

- Clearly define your policies on use of the car, telephone, television, common areas, overnight guests, smoking, alcohol, etc. What is her driving record?

- How important are training and education to you? Language skills?

- Define your approach to discipline.

- Be clear if you expect the nanny to care for your sick child. Nannies will vary in their willingness to do so.

- Determine salary range, vacation and sick time, paid holidays. Will you provide medical insurance?

- Decide what you will do for child care when your nanny is sick or goes on vacation.

How to Find an Excellent Nanny

Parents follow several routes to finding a good nanny. Look in your Yellow Pages to see if there is a local nanny school where you can recruit. Also identify local colleges that have an early childhood education major; and contact their career-services office to place a job advertisement. These are both useful avenues to finding highly qualified, trained professionals.

Another avenue is through a nanny-placement agency, which usually charges an application and finder's fee. You can find lists of nanny-placement agencies in your Yellow Pages or in a local parent newspaper or magazine. Local child care resource and referral agencies may also have lists of approved agencies. There is considerable variation in agencies' standards. Look for ones that require or provide training in early childhood development and carefully screen candidates and do background checks. Ask about required experience.

Many parents find nannies through word of mouth. Ask trusted friends and colleagues who have children and may also know of candidates. One mother, Selena, sends out word to all her friends and colleagues when she is looking for a new nanny:

> I tell everybody I know that I am looking. I find that people who are especially good resources are those who are happy with their nanny. I then ask their nanny if they know of other great nannies. I have found that great nannies are responsible people and know other people like themselves. My best nanny came through that way.

Finally, parents can advertise. The best luck is often through local area newspapers rather than the larger regional newspapers; local papers also charge less for ads. Since you may get many calls from an advertisement, be as explicit as you can in your ad about what you are looking for. By listing requirements for the job, you will narrow the field of candidates to those who more closely meet your specifications. Read through the classified ads for nannies to get ideas for yours.

Elements of the advertisement can include:

- Brief description of family, ages of children
- Required schedule
- Live-in or live-out
- Education or training required; experience required
- Nonsmoking; driver's license required
- Fluent in English or other language if desired
- Length of time commitment needed (six months, one year, several years)
- Likes pets (if you have one)
- Telephone number to call

Thoroughly screen the candidates over the telephone; you will eliminate many right away. To determine whether a nanny candidate is right for you will require 1) an in-depth interview; 2) observation of the candidate with your children; and 3) thorough reference checks.

Candidate Interview

I asked the first nanny candidate, "Why are you interested in this job?" Her answer: "I need a green card." Bad answer. I asked the second nanny candidate, "Why are you interested in this job?" Her answer: "I love children." Much better answer.
                                                                    —Evelyn

The interviews are your opportunity to explore a nanny's motivation for wanting this job, background, relevant child care experience, and time commitment. Ask them why they have chosen to be a nanny and what it is about the job that appeals to them. Some people look for a nanny position because they have few other options. That is not the person you want to have caring for your child. Since most people care for children the way they were cared for, ask about their childhood and family model. You will want to explore how they would handle various daily situations, behavior issues, discipline, and emergencies. Ask them what age groups they have experience with and enjoy working with. If a candidate loves caring for preschoolers and is nervous around infants, and you just gave birth to infant triplets, that's a red flag.

The interview is important not only to inquire into the candidate's background and views but also to clearly outline the needs of the job and the full range of responsibilities. Be clear and realistic. The most common reason for a nanny relationship to not work out is a mismatch in expectations. This is the moment for both sides to share and get to know each other as much as possible. Beverly, a former professional nanny and now a mother who employs a nanny, has this to say:

> *It's important for the parent to be a good communicator about expectations. Talk about what your children are really like. Don't paint a rosy picture and then leave them alone with no advice when your child becomes a monster.*

Listen to and watch the candidate carefully during the interview. Trust your instincts. Would you feel comfortable with this person caring for your children? Is this someone you would enjoy in your home every day? Would you feel confident that this person could handle an emergency or difficult situation well? Does she or he seem to have good judgment and maturity? Are their values about family and children similar to yours? Listen to the answers and your intuition. Ellen, an experienced nanny, summed it up this way:

> *Similar to when you're looking for a roommate or life partner, you need to be able to live well together, and should agree on the little things as well as child care techniques. As a nanny, it is not desirable to have totally different values than the family you live with, since you are a reflection of their values to their children. For instance, my family did not believe in letting their children cry themselves to sleep, and it would have been*

improper for me to neglect their values and allow their children to cry themselves to sleep in my care. Communication and support between nanny and parents are key.

In the nanny interview:

- Explore the candidates' education and training, CPR, first aid. Ask about their childhood and what their family was like.

- Why have they chosen this profession? How long have they been doing it? How long will they continue? What is their time commitment?

- Explore thoroughly their past nanny experiences: the family situation, what worked and what didn't, why the job ended.

- Discuss their caregiving approach and philosophy. Describe hypothetical situations and ask how they would handle them. Discuss their approach to discipline.

- Thoroughly describe the job, the range of responsibilities, and the expectations.

- Describe your family and the ages, personalities, and interests of your children. Describe the family schedule.

- Listen to your intuition. Would you feel wonderful about this person caring for your children?

Observation with Your Children

If you are interviewing local candidates, invite your final candidate or two back to your home to spend some time with your children. Some caregivers who are good with children do not perform well in a formal interview situation; the opposite is true as well. Watch your potential nanny in action in a relaxed play situation with your children. Before the candidate comes, review the quality child care characteristics so that you will know what to look for (see pages 121–23). Perhaps you can all sit on the floor and start playing a game. When your children feel comfortable, you can excuse yourself and go about your business at home, quietly observing and listening to the interactions. A good nanny will look forward to that opportunity to interact with your children. Since this person will be with your children all day, the nanny will also want the opportunity to get to know them a little bit. As one nanny, Brandi, said:

My interview was an important part of the trust-building process. I was invited to a "tea party" with the whole family. I got a chance to interact with the children and answer the parents' questions in between cups of tea served by the three-year-old. It really got our relationship off on the right foot.

What you should look for in this initial get-together with your children is the nanny's attitude toward the children. Does she or he feel comfortable with children? Does the candidate know how to engage them in an activity, listen to them, and appreciate what they say? Does the candidate have a responsive, nurturing attitude? Don't expect your children to warm up to the candidate immediately during this get-together. Many children may be wary of a new person, no matter how friendly and engaging the situation. Again, listen to your intuition. Do you think this person will work out and be able to connect warmly with your children?

Reference Checks

Never hire a nanny without thoroughly checking references. You will be limited in what you will be able to learn through the interview and observation with the children. Augment these first two steps with in-depth conversations with prior employers and you will have a much fuller idea of the nanny's capabilities and potential for a match with your family. Through these reference checks, you will be trying to determine if your candidate has the following three essential elements:

1. Skilled understanding of child development
2. Good work skills and habits
3. Right match in personality and values

On your final candidates, check three to five references. Of course, it is most helpful if your candidate has prior nanny experience that you can confirm. Call the references and ask if they know anyone else who knows the candidate well and whose opinion would be relevant. It can be helpful to call people who aren't on the nanny's reference list, but check with the candidate first.

You will want to understand what the previous employer thought of the nanny's skills and capabilities. Thoroughly explore why the nanny left and if the family would enthusiastically hire the nanny again. Inquire about the strengths and weaknesses of the nanny and any areas where the family was disappointed or experienced conflicts. Give the former employer time to talk at length. If you sense any hesitation, probe the reason why. Ask if you can call back with any further questions. As in the candidate interview and observation, listen to subtle cues. How excited was this family to employ this candidate? Again, listen to your intuition, a lesson Selena shares:

> When I check references, I find that other moms are usually pretty candid. They may not say anything really bad, but if they don't give a glowing, really strong reference, that's a warning sign. I push pretty hard, and if it's just lukewarm, I don't go for it.
>
> Once we went against our intuition on a nanny. We hired her in the early summer. One morning at the end of the summer, she just never showed up. Can you believe it? She just never showed up, no telephone call or anything. We finally tracked her down. It turns out that she was a schoolteacher on vacation, and she had taken the job to make the extra money over the summer and never had any intention of staying. The one reference I checked had been her cousin. She just lied. And you know, I had an inkling that something was not quite right in the beginning. I really do believe in using your intuition as a kind of guide.

It's also a good idea to do a driver's-license check and a criminal-record check with the relevant state agency. If you are hiring a nanny through an agency, they will do those checks for you. Otherwise, do it yourself. Your local child care resource and referral agency will be able to point you to the right state agency.

Sample questions for the reference check:

- How long did the nanny work for you? What were the range of responsibilities and schedule? What was the split between child care and housekeeping responsibilities?

- Why did the nanny leave?

- How would you assess the nanny's skills in child care? Did the nanny have a good understanding of child development and a sensitivity to each of your children's needs and interests?

- Did your children like the nanny? How did they react to the nanny's departure?

- Was the nanny skilled in engaging the children in activities? Did the nanny plan interesting and varied days?

- Did the nanny develop opportunities for your children to play with other children and have social interactions? Did the nanny get the children outside to play regularly?

- Describe the nanny's work ethic. Was the nanny reliable and prompt? Did the nanny exhibit good judgment and maturity? Did the nanny ever have to handle an emergency? Was the nanny cheerful and emotionally stable? Did the nanny bring personal problems to the job?

- Was the nanny a good communicator? Did you feel that you got full information about the day and the child's development? Was the nanny honest and forthright?

- Describe your relationship with the nanny. Describe the nanny's personality and work style. How did the nanny fit into the family? Was the nanny able to follow your lead on child-rearing values and approach to discipline? Were there any problems with the nanny's personal habits?

- Summarize the nanny's strengths and weaknesses. Describe any conflicts or disappointments; anything you were uncomfortable with.

- Would you enthusiastically rehire this nanny? Why or why not?

- Is there anyone else you know who knows this person well whom I could call?

- Any final comments or observations?

Hiring the Nanny

Once you have completed the interview, observation, and reference checks and are enthusiastic about your candidate, you are ready to hire your nanny! Write up a clear job description, range of responsibilities, and schedule. Determine the pay, benefits, and time frame for performance review and salary adjustments. Be as explicit and detailed as possible about the terms and conditions of the job. This will avoid many problems down the line.

Sit down with your nanny and go over your write-up of terms and conditions. Put this document in the Caregiver Notebook (see page 164) that you have developed for the nanny, and keep a copy for yourself in your personal Nanny File. Although you may develop a close personal relationship, you are the employer, and you need to be very clear about the parameters of the job.

JOB TERMS AND CONDITIONS WILL INCLUDE:

- Salary and hours; expectations for evening, weekend, and vacation care; how to handle overtime hours
- Paid or unpaid vacation and sick time; paid holidays
- Any possible benefits, such as health coverage
- Annual salary and performance review
- Specific child care duties
- Specific household duties

Once you hire a nanny, you have become an employer. You will be responsible for payroll, income tax, and Social Security. You will need to provide the nanny with an annual W-2 form. There are a number of legal and tax requirements associated with employing a nanny; contact your local IRS office to get a list. You will need to have regular performance evaluations and make periodic salary adjustments. If you are serious about pursuing the nanny route, there are some excellent resources listed below that can thoroughly take you through each step of hiring and managing a nanny, and calculating and filing tax information, and serve as guides while you continue to employ a nanny in your home.

KEEP A CONFIDENTIAL NANNY FILE WITH ALL RELEVANT INFORMATION:

- Name, address, telephone number
- Social Security number
- Photograph
- Names, addresses, and telephone numbers of nearest family members
- Whom to contact in case of emergency with nanny
- Written references
- Driver's-license check
- Criminal-record check
- Health form with documentation of tuberculosis test (if desired)
- Job terms and conditions
- Your annual written evaluations

USEFUL WEBSITE OFFERING NANNY TAX FILING SERVICES:

- www.nannytax.com

BOOKS ON HIRING AND MANAGING NANNIES:

- *The Nanny Kit,* by Kimberly Porrazzo
- *Am I Hiring the Right Nanny?,* by Doris J. Pick and Michelle Hadley
- *The ABC's of Hiring a Nanny,* by Frances Anne Hernan

Develop Your Caregiver Notebook

Prior to your nanny's start date, develop your Caregiver Notebook. This will be a daily reference for your nanny and communication vehicle for you both. Keep the pages both in a binder and stored on computer disk, since you will frequently update things in the notebook. Separate the sections with tabs. Keep it in a central location so that mother, father, and nanny will remember to frequently refer to it. I have included the different elements for the notebook to guide your thinking. Choose the elements that relate to the age of your child and how your household is organized. Much of the Caregiver Notebook should also be compiled if you have a relative taking care of your child. This person will greatly appreciate having all the information in one central location. Remember, clear communication may prevent future issues.

ELEMENTS OF THE CAREGIVER NOTEBOOK

- *Developmental profile* of your child (see chapter 6)
- Statement of your *child-rearing philosophy*, including:
    - Your family's values; what's important to you for your child's infancy and early childhood
    - The way you want the caregiver to talk to your child, and your child to talk to the caregiver and others
    - Approach to discipline and manners
    - Ways to comfort and soothe your child
    - Desired social interaction among playmates and with adults
    - Desired atmosphere at home
- *Job terms and conditions* (see page 162)
- *Clear expectations* for the nanny regarding tardiness, backup when sick, communication, required notice at end of job
- *Medications* taken by your child
- General *daily schedule*, including suggested activities, outdoor time, meal and nap times, balance of physical outdoor play and walks with books and quiet games, arts and crafts, playmates
- *Rules and guidelines* for the nanny on the following:
    - Use of car, other passengers, car seats
    - Alcohol, smoking
    - Other adults around
    - Appropriate places to go with your child
    - Playmates—who and how much
    - Use of telephone
    - Use of television, for both nanny and child; which programs are allowed
    - Diet and nutrition/snacks
    - How much autonomy the nanny should have and what she will need permission for
    - Allowable expenditures
- *Housework responsibilities*, if any; should be minimal
- *Telephone numbers* (post another copy on the refrigerator):
    - Emergency: poison control, police, fire
    - Your work number, your spouse's number
    - Doctors, dentists
    - Key neighbors, friends, relatives
    - Playmates and parents
- Pocket for *local map* marked with key places

CARE BY RELATIVES

I love the fact that my twins are with their grandma every week. They see all sorts of other family, too—my brother, his little girls, my father, other relatives. I think it is important that they are part of my children's lives. I want my babies with family.

—Vivien

At one time, care by relatives was the most common form of child care. Even today many parents choose to have a relative—most commonly the grandmother, grandfather, sister, or aunt—take care of their child during the first year or two of life. Sometimes it is full-time care, but care by a relative can augment other child care options. Many arrangements are fairly informal, in which the relative is paid less than a parent would pay another child care provider or not paid at all.

Benefits of Care by a Relative

The biggest benefit of care by a relative is that you know and trust this person well. It feels like the closest thing to parental care. Many feel that this is particularly important during the first two years of life, when a baby cannot talk for herself and tell you about her day. Vivien loves the arrangement she has for her twins:

I feel very calm dropping my babies off at my mother's house. She knows their cries and routines. My mother adores my babies; she misses them when she's not with them. She gives them a million kisses a day. I don't worry about a thing.

A family member will more likely share your values, culture, language, and religion. You may also share a common approach to child rearing and discipline. Particularly if you are a first-time parent, watching your mother, father, aunt, or other relative care for your baby can be a great help in building your own parenting skills. You might feel more comfortable talking through various behavior issues and challenges with a close family member. Your relative may become a true partner-in-parenting.

A key indicator of quality child care is the strength of the attachment between caregiver and child. A family member can provide a child with devoted, warm care regardless of circumstances. This relationship will probably be a long-term, consistent one that will keep the child feeling secure in a stable, caring family environment. When Alena went back to work after the birth of her first child, her husband, father-in-law, and mother-in-law took care of the baby in their store for the first two years:

> *They were very excited about taking care of our daughter.*
> *That made it so much easier for me. When I look back and*
> *see the bond that our baby had formed with her grandparents,*
> *it is truly wonderful. The love and nurturing they were able*
> *to provide for her was wonderful. Nothing could have been*
> *better.*

In fact, caring for a baby will often bring the whole family together and strengthen the extended-family bonds. You as a parent can feel the support of this extended family, and your baby will thrive in an atmosphere of community and security. Often the motivation of the relative to care for your baby is for love of the child and to help the family rather than financial motivation. Giovanna was delighted to see how involved her family became:

> *I would drop our baby, Leonor, off at my parents' house, and*
> *my sister and brother were there, too. My father would come*
> *home from work early so that he could also be with Leonor.*
> *Everyone wanted to be with her. While my mother cooked*
> *dinner, my father and brother would play with the baby. They*
> *even changed diapers. So it was a wonderful thing for the*
> *whole family. Leonor had lots of family.*

For mothers who work odd-hour shifts, in the evenings, or on weekends, a family member is usually more willing to be flexible than other child care providers. It also reassures a child to spend your changing shifts and unusual hours with a close family member in a familiar family environment. This can greatly reduce the stress that shift workers, such as Giovanna, feel:

I would have to drop my baby at my mother's at four-thirty A.M. in order to make it to work for my shift. My mother was always ready. She would call me if she didn't hear from me by four A.M. I would arrive, and she would have coffee waiting and everything ready. What would I have done otherwise? She is quite a mother.

Many times a close family member is not the only child care option a parent will use. Sometimes parents will purposely choose to have both a relative and another provider care for their baby. Vivien found this offered some advantages and a certain security:

My babies are in a child care center two days a week and with my mother one day a week. I did that for a number of reasons. First of all, I love that they are with Grandma regularly every week. I wanted them with family. But I also wanted them in a child care center. I needed a guarantee. If my mother was sick or went on vacation, they could go to the center. The center offers stability and developmental care. I like both.

Silvia's little boy, Nate, is enrolled full-time in a child care center; but she loves to have the option of letting Nate go to Grandma's instead of the center:

I do feel guilty sometimes when I have had a week or two of long workdays and long days for Nate in the child care center. Those are the days I'll call my mom and say, "Nate wants a Grandma day," and she'll keep him for the day. It's nice to have that option.

Some parents find that if their child has a medical problem or special needs, a family member will be the best solution. A family member may offer patience and attention that would be difficult to find in another situation. However, if your child has special needs, be sure that she will receive comprehensive services and ongoing evaluation. Amanda was thrilled when her sister-in-law, Maggie, offered to take care of her baby, Julie, during the first year when Julie had severe eczema:

> It made a big difference leaving Julie with my sister-in-law. Julie would scratch until she bled, and Maggie was very familiar with her condition. She was so patient and comforting. It would be frustrating to other people who were not as accustomed or devoted to Julie. Family is a lot different. It was definitely a more comfortable feeling.

Some mothers talk about care by a relative being good not only for their child but for the family member, too. It can give a grandmother or grandfather a greater purpose and sense of meaning in their life.

And of course another benefit of care by a relative is that it is often much less expensive. The parent may pay the relative a nominal fee or provide food and equipment. It is estimated that at least one half of all child care arrangements with family members involve no money at all. Stacy did it this way:

> I had Jeffrey two and a half days a week with a family child care provider, Dana, and then two and a half days with my mother. I paid both of them. I paid Dana the regular child care tuition, and I paid my mother half that amount. She didn't really want to get paid much at all. So Dana got the big check, and my mother got half that.

Drawbacks of Care by a Relative

The biggest challenge with care by a relative is to create clear, open, and honest communication around potentially sensitive issues. Since by nature the relationship is more informal, parents and the family member might not sit down and discuss expectations, payment and hours, time frame, approach to discipline, etc. In fact, differences in child-rearing philosophies may be the biggest source of friction in this kind of arrangement. It may be hard to tell your mother that you want your baby's sleep schedule to be different, or that you want an alternate approach to toilet training or behavior management. Since it is a personal relationship, the family member can feel criticized, or you can feel resentful. Barbara's mother cared for her children after school, and she felt it was easiest on the relationship to skirt around touchy issues, even if she had to get a little creative:

> *My mother was very rule-conscious. One of the rules was that you could not eat before dinner—she saw that as an insult to the cook. This was always a big issue with the kids. I was so grateful to my mother for taking care of the kids that I really didn't want this to become a problem. So I would just buy the kids snacks and keep them up in their closets. "If you're hungry, go up to the closet and open a bag of chips and eat it. Let's not make a big deal of it with Grandma."*

Ongoing and open communication is key. Sometimes a family member will offer to help when a new baby is born; this offer then turns into a full-time expectation on the part of the parents. It can be exhausting for grandparents to care for a baby or toddler. They may have loved the idea of caring for their grandchild but underestimated how challenging caring for a young child can be. Subjects like this may be hard to bring up between family members.

Some mothers point out that the family member is not typically a child care professional; she or he may have limited training in early childhood education and care. Without that background, there may be less focus on providing a learning environment or developmental care for the child. The grandparent or relative may focus more on physical care and put less emphasis or energy into social or cognitive development. One mother had this concern:

> *My mother really wanted to take care of our baby full-time, but I thought it would be better if she were the backup to whatever primary situation I had. I didn't tell my mother this*

part of it, but I didn't want my child to just be fed and clothed.
I wanted him in a stimulating developmental environment,
something more than even I could provide.

Sometimes parents may start out using a family member for the first year or two. They may feel it's most important then to have the devoted one-on-one care and nurturance that a relative can provide. When the child turns two or so, they may want to then offer the child a more developmental environment with other children, as was Alena's case:

Family members took care of our baby at first. At about two
years, once my daughter was really all over the place and
very active, it started to seem like this situation was not
enough for her anymore. I struggled with the trade-off of the
nurturing, loving family versus needing her to be more

BENEFITS OF CARE BY A RELATIVE

- Someone you know and trust
- Closest to parental care
- Same language, culture, religion, values
- Long-term caring relationship; strong attachment
- Strengthens family bonds
- Flexibility in hours, shifts, sudden child care needs
- Easier when handling sick child care, special needs
- Relative can feel greater meaning and purpose in life
- Less expensive care

DRAWBACKS OF CARE BY A RELATIVE

- Potential differences in child-rearing philosophies
- Emphasis may be on physical care, and less on learning or social, cognitive, emotional development
- Can be exhausting for a grandparent not used to young children all day long
- Can be isolating for the relative and child
- Family roles may blur and can become stressful

stimulated. That was okay, because I was ready at that point. My daughter needed something more.

Family roles blur once a relative begins caring for a child on a regular basis. The relative is now an employee, with certain expectations. Some mothers, like Janet, below, do not like feeling dependent on a relative or comfortable with the changed family dynamics:

Both my mother and my mother-in-law offered to help with our baby. I thought it was not really fair for us to expect them to now take care of our baby. I am independent and wanted to take care of our situation ourselves. I didn't want to feel dependent on them.

REMAINING FLEXIBLE

Now that we have gone over the benefits and drawbacks of each child care option, what to look for in quality child care, and how to find it, you may feel a bit overwhelmed. Let's step back now a little bit and relax. No one approach will work out perfectly. You may have worked tirelessly on a list of what you would ideally want in child care only to discover you are just not able to find it. As Selena found, you may have to be more accommodating than you thought:

I remember that in midmaternity leave, I was really scrambling because all the nanny possibilities I had fell through. I was really set on having a live-in, but I was so stressed and just wanted someone who would be wonderful and warm and loving. The person I ultimately found was incredible but didn't want to live in. I went with that because she was just so great.

You may work hard at finding just the right child care for your child, and it may work beautifully for a while, then fall apart. People change, situations change, and your child care solution may not always work for you. Patricia had found a wonderful family child care provider for her first two children. By the time her third child came along, Patricia felt that the provider's standards had fallen dramatically:

> *She now had too many children, and she wasn't very organized. She was practically running a child care center, but she really wasn't capable. Early on, she had only two other children there. By the time our third child arrived, she had seven other children, and it was just a nightmare.*

Many parents find that their needs, and their children's, change over time, and their child care has to change as well. Some parents want their child at home during the first year, then later want to enroll their child in a child care center where they will get more socialization with other children and more learning opportunities. Erin put it this way:

> *When my baby was first born, what I really was looking for was a calm, nurturing woman. I was only looking at a one-year horizon. I knew he would change so much. I won't know what he will need in a year. I just took it one step at a time.*

The first decision may not last forever. You will regularly need to reevaluate your child care choice.

AFTER-SCHOOL PROGRAMS FOR ELEMENTARY SCHOOL CHILDREN

Although this chapter is primarily about child care options for children under elementary school age, you can use a similar approach when looking for and evaluating formal after-school child care programs for your elementary school child.

More and more school systems are creating after-school programs in the elementary schools. Many towns also have community after-school programs at Boys & Girls Clubs, community centers, at the Y, or in private programs. Although after-school programs have traditionally been fairly uninspired, there is more interest today in creating quality as more families need this care. Many of these programs are wonderful places of enrichment and friendship. The National School-Age Care Alliance (NSACA, at www.nsaca.org) has established national standards and developed a national accreditation program.

Before you check out your local after-school program, log on to NSACA's website and print out their "Standards at a Glance" to take with you. A good after-school program should allow the children a fair amount of choice and independence in their activities—but always under skilled, low-key supervision. Children should have time and a quiet place to do homework or talk quietly with friends. They should get daily play outside on a playground. There should be a range of activities to allow children to follow their own interests or learn new skills. The program can be fairly relaxed, since the children will just have completed a structured school day. Staff should work with the children to plan activities and encourage them to offer ideas.

What to look for in an after-school program:

- A schedule that allows for a fair amount of choice and independence by the children, but always under skilled supervision
- A chance for the children to play some role in planning the program and activities
- A quiet place to do homework and quietly talk with a friend
- Active, outdoor play period at a minimum of thirty minutes
- A range of activities where children can pursue their interests: art, dramatic play, reading, computers
- A healthy snack
- Ratio of one staff member for ten to fifteen children
- Maximum group size of thirty in each room

After-School Baby-sitter

It has been a challenge, because both my husband and I work far from where we live. So there was a really difficult period of time when it seemed I was always late for everything, always rushing through the commute to pick up the children from the after-school program before it closed. Then I hired a wonderful person. She picks up our children from school and schleps them to all their after-school activities. She gives them dinner at an hour that is a little more reasonable. Often she will give the children a shower or bath. When we arrive home, we can sit down with them and help them with their homework.

—Natalie

Some mothers express a preference for an after-school baby-sitter at home rather than a formal program. This offers the advantage of allowing your child some downtime at home after school. If your baby-sitter drives, your child can participate in after-school sports and activities as well. How do you find a person who is available for those afternoon hours? Natalie, the mom quoted above, works in human resources and used her professional skills to find a good person. We can learn a bit from her effective example:

We were pretty clear about what we were looking for. Since we both worked far from home, we wanted someone who was connected in the community, someone who has lived here for years, had family here, knew the area and people. We needed good local back-up. We said right in our advertisement that we wanted someone who would do light housekeeping before she picked up the kids and who had a car. We interviewed a lot of people and found this wonderful person who has now been with us for years.

Parents have followed several avenues to find good after-school baby-sitters. These include:

- Advertise in your local newspaper.

- Contact a local college, technical school, or community college. Many students are looking for part-time jobs. The after-school hours may work perfectly with an academic schedule. Post a job announcement in the career services office, student lounge, financial aid office, or on the jobs-listing page on the school website. Start with schools that have an early childhood education major.

- Some students or graduate students are interested in exchanging after-school help for a place to live for the school year. They also may be able to tutor your child if needed.

- Contact your local high school for responsible students looking for work. However, most high school students do not have a car, or you may not be comfortable with their driving skills. If a car is not necessary in your circumstance, this may be a very good avenue.

- Contact local nursery schools and post job announcements. Many nursery school teachers are interested in additional work.

- Also post an announcement in the area elementary schools. Teachers and teacher aides sometimes take on afternoon or evening part-time work.

- Post notices in local churches, synagogues, and community centers. "Empty nesters" may be interested in some part-time work.

- Ask all your neighbors and friends.

HANDLING THE HIGH COST OF CHILD CARE

With the nonfamily child care options discussed in this chapter, a highly skilled provider will be expensive. Quality child care in the United States is costly. In many industrialized Western nations, child care is a public service and is subsidized and provided by the government in a manner similar to public elementary schools. In the United States, the high cost of child care is supported by the parents through high tuitions, and also by the caregivers through low salaries and limited benefits. If care providers were paid comparably to public school teachers, the care would be unaffordable to most parents.

Until we find adequate subsidies for child care in the United States, our child care system will remain vulnerable and inadequate. Child care is a profession that has a deep and long-lasting impact on our children's lives. It should be a well-paid and highly respected profession. We are far from that reality in the United States today. Child care providers are among the poorest-paid workers in our country. That is a tragic reflection of our national priorities. What more important job is there than to care for and nurture a child during the critical first years of life? For the benefit of our children and society, we should all look for ways to increase the value and respect of the child care profession.

The lack of a national, publicly subsidized child care system means that our children suffer in mixed quality child care; parents pay extremely high fees; and providers are underpaid for their value. Fewer and fewer talented people will want to enter the profession unless salary and benefits improve significantly. Because pay is so low, turnover among providers of all types is very high. It will continue to be so until wages increase substantially. In order for that to happen, either parents will pay much higher fees or external subsidies must be found. All of us who use child care should understand this dynamic and lobby where we can for increased public or private support.

Parents use a variety of methods to help pay for child care. Some states, towns, and employers offer tuition assistance. In fact, more and more employers each year offer some financial assistance for a family child care provider or an on-site child care facility. Unless there is subsidized child care, your costs will take up a large portion of your income. But remember that an investment in these first years of life is probably the most important one you will make in your child's future. Excellent care in the first five years will make a significant difference in your child's lifelong success.

Child care is not a household expense where you want to find the best bargain. Generally speaking, the higher the cost, the higher the quality. Although you may want to haggle and pay the lowest price for a new car, you don't want to do the same with child care. This may be painful advice, since parents usually have children fairly early in their working lives, when their incomes are lower.

Here are some of the methods parents use to help pay for high quality child care:

• *State-, city-, or town-funded preschools.* Some states have passed universal preschool legislation for four-year-old care. As this legislation rolls out, more state-subsidized preschool spots will open up. Many cities, towns, and counties already provide public preschool programs in the schools.

• *University and college lab schools.* Many universities and colleges with majors in early childhood education have created "lab schools" on campus, where students and teachers work with and care for young children as part of their education. Some of these lab schools offer subsidized care.

• *Employer-sponsored child care.* The fastest growing area of subsidized child care is with employers. Many employers are finding that they cannot find and keep good employees because there is inadequate quality child care in the community. More and more employers are building new child care centers or subsidizing existing community child care for their employees.

• *Dependent Care Assistance Program (DCAP).* Many employers offer a DCAP benefit, which allows employees to pay for their child care with pretax dollars, offering significant savings for both employee and employer. Some employers also match these pretax contributions.

• *Child tax credit.* Individual taxpayers can claim a credit on their taxes for each child. This credit has recently been increased from $500 to $1,000 per child.

• *Dependent care tax credit.* For taxpayers who do not work for an employer with a DCAP benefit, there is a tax credit for some child and dependent care expenses.

• *State child care vouchers.* Many states provide subsidized child care vouchers for low-income parents. This voucher may help a parent who is earning very little, completing an education or job-training program, or on disability.

• *Head Start programs.* Low-income parents can also access publicly funded Head Start preschools, which exist in many communities across the country. Some programs have extended the care to the infant and toddler level.

• *Military child care.* The U.S. military provides a high quality, subsidized, fairly extensive system of child care at military bases, both domestic and abroad.

PART III

Making It Work for You: Tips and Strategies for Everyday Life

FIVE

Living Your Pregnancy and Maternity Leave

I loved being pregnant with my first child, Farrell. I relished watching my belly get bigger and bigger. I had a flourishing nesting instinct and spent lazy Saturday afternoons picking out things for the baby's room. I loved to go into the room at night to look at the tiny socks and T-shirts, washed and folded and ready for our newborn. Due to a pregnancy complication, I had to have an amniocentesis. I was in North Carolina on a business trip when I called the hospital in Boston to find out the results. My heart pounded when I heard the news that we had a healthy girl. In one powerful moment, I knew I was now a mother. I just sat still for about an hour, stroking my belly and my sweet baby girl, letting the realization soak in. I loved Farrell's every little movement and kick. I felt an incredible passion for her as she grew inside me. In fact, strangely, I felt no rush for her to be born. I loved the fact that I was nourishing her directly day by day.

I worked hard throughout the pregnancy, traveling until early into my eighth month. Our company was in its vulnerable, rickety, start-up phase. I was nervous about what would happen when I went on maternity leave. Although I looked forward to it, I didn't see how I could possibly leave work even for a day. I went into labor when Roger and I were out at a company dinner, celebrating the promotion of a new center director. Twelve hours later, I gave birth to Farrell. Roger and I had gone through many intense and transforming life experiences overseas, but none were as powerful as going through the labor and delivery together. I didn't want him away from me for a moment; we were both overwhelmed with emotion when Farrell was born.

I had read reams of parenting books while I was pregnant. I observed our experienced teachers in the infant rooms in our centers. Dr. T. Berry Brazelton was our pediatrician and friend. I was in the early childhood education field. I felt that things would be easy. I spent the few days in the hospital after Farrell was born in a fog of euphoria. Roger stayed in the hospital with me, and Farrell was with us the whole time. I loved nursing, and she had a great appetite. Friends and relatives came and went.

Roger, Farrell, and I were blissful in our new little family. I was mesmerized by the miracle of her arrival. I couldn't take my eyes off her. I loved to smell her newborn skin, I loved to feel her chest rise and fall with her breathing, to feel the life pulsating in her tiny body. I loved to nestle into the sheets with Farrell, her naked body against mine. She seemed so pure, so perfect. I wanted to offer up the world to her. All the stress and worries of our start-up company were now suddenly far away. I reveled in Farrell and the moment.

I was almost taken by surprise the morning of my checkout from the hospital. It took me ages to pack up my bag, Farrell's little things, and the array of products and supplies given to us by the hospital. The walk down to the car took forever. As we drove down Memorial Drive in Cambridge to our home, a route we had taken hundreds of times before, I was surprised at how normal the world seemed. People were going about their business, unruffled by the miracle of Farrell's birth. How could we have gone through such a momentous, life-changing experience without the world taking notice? I felt like an incredibly brave heroine, to have gone through such an excruciating labor for such a noble cause, yet here in front of me were all sorts of other mothers with their children. Were they heroines, too?

We walked in our front door. Everything was as we had left it, and I burst into tears. I had the powerful sense that we had gone through both the miraculous and the mundane. How could we step back into our prior life when we were so transformed by this experience of birth and becoming parents? Irrationally, I didn't want to believe it was also so common.

It was only ten in the morning, and I was already exhausted. What would we do for this whole day and for the duration of every other day in front of us? I was disoriented by the comfortable sight of our couch, our chairs, our things. In Africa and Asia, when we lived through adventures, risks, and seeming miracles, we were living in a foreign, exotic environment where it seemed more likely that transforming experiences could happen. Here, everything seemed too familiar.

I understood now why, in the Sudan—where I had just been living—mothers stayed in bed for forty days after childbirth and were cared for by others. The newborn was admired, adored, and blessed. The mother was nourished and honored for the experience she had gone through and the vital role she played in life. She was accompanied almost constantly by her relatives and neighbors, who formed a tight community around her, helped her, and celebrated the new life with her. In many cultures where I had lived and traveled, life paused for a while to absorb a birth. Why does our society push through this experience so quickly? Why do we try to be so independent and self-sufficient? I just wanted to lean on everyone around me. I wanted everyone to cherish and admire my baby.

The next many days were a roller coaster of emotions. My friends kept saying it was just the normal flood of hormones after childbirth. I knew better. It was really understanding the awesome nature of bringing a child into this world and becoming a parent—forever. I couldn't bear to be away from Farrell for even a moment. But I also felt that I was losing myself in her. I couldn't understand why things weren't working out perfectly. Why was she so fussy for hours on end? Why did she need to be awake all night? Why did we have to be so completely sleep-deprived? Perhaps, as Roger believed, it was to tear down our normal way of living our days; to rebuild according to Farrell's needs, not ours. We needed to reshape our lives into a new family. This tiny eight-pound baby was insisting on and achieving dramatic changes in our lives so that she would necessarily be central. I marveled at the power of this precious tiny being.

The maternity leave had looked to me like a wonderful time to indulge. I had all sorts of plans to take up painting, resume the piano, write, and read. But instead I just felt incredibly incompetent as, day after day, I barely got around to taking a shower until the day was almost over. How could it be so difficult for me to "master" this role when I had mastered countless other challenges in my life? I gradually learned that it was less about mastering and more about letting go. I had to follow Farrell's plan, not mine.

Work, which had seemed a few days ago so urgent, so compelling and all-absorbing, was winding its way to my back burner for a while. I thought our little company couldn't survive a day without me, but I found that I went days without thinking once about work—and steadfastly refused to think about it. And somehow the company seemed to be doing just fine without me. But that also bothered me—how could the company thrive when I wasn't there? Was work really not so compelling?

I was making my bumpy adjustment to motherhood and my maternity leave. Roger and I traversed the passage in our own way as we embraced the fact that Farrell was now the most important thing in our lives. In this chapter, I talk about this transition to motherhood and how mothers undergo it so differently. I talk about strategies you can use to live your pregnancy while working, and how to prepare to leave work for the period of your maternity leave. I share strategies to make the most of your maternity leave, and I talk about the role work plays during this time. My goal here is to help you understand how normal it is to have complex and difficult emotions during this time, and to help you accomplish the most essential goal of your maternity leave—that of embracing your role as a mother and getting to know and bond with your baby.

EXPECTING A BABY

If you are a working mother who has put off having children for years in order to devote yourself to work, this moment of finally realizing you are going to have a baby can seem especially fraught with all kinds of emotions. In fact, their intensity can start right when you do that drugstore pregnancy test, as they did for these two women:

I was scared when I saw the pink stripe on the pregnancy test, and I walked out and said, "Well, we did it." And my husband said, "We did?" He didn't even move off the couch; he sat there, stunned, for the longest time. Then we took a walk for an hour and just wandered around thinking about it, and I said, "Gosh, I think I had a glass of wine last week."

—Amanda

I was dying to find out if I was pregnant. I woke up at four A.M. because they say not to do the pregnancy test until morning. So I thought well, four in the morning is morning. I did the test, then I started jumping up and down on the bed, going, "Brian, Brian, we're pregnant!" I was just so ecstatic, just so overwhelmed that we had conceived, because I had this huge fear that we might not be able to. Now we were going to have a family!

—Erin

You know in that one instant that your life is going to change dramatically and forever. Catherine was in her office when she got the call from the adoption agency that a baby had been identified for her. She had waited years for this moment:

The woman at the agency told me my baby's name was Hisheng Sheng. I was overcome by emotion. I can get teary now, thinking about it. I immediately called my brother and asked him to go with me to the adoption agency, where they had a photo of her for me. I just ran out of work to get there. I found a roomful of people, and they were yelling out names and showing the photographs. I couldn't even look at it. I gave the photo to my brother. He said, "Catherine, she is beautiful. She is beautiful." I looked at the picture and felt overwhelmed. She is my baby.

For many mothers, like Myrna, priorities suddenly change, and they see their lives differently:

I knew that the baby was now my priority, and I wasn't. My work wasn't. I had a dog, and the dog wasn't. I suddenly thought, "I have to have more life insurance. We need to put locks on the basement windows, somebody might try to get out with the baby." I felt like a different person. It just softened my heart.

However, the waiting period, through either pregnancy or adoption proceedings, is not always positive. Some women, such as Elizabeth, don't like being pregnant at all:

Pregnancy was not a very happy time for me. Once the baby was born and I was sure there was nothing wrong with him, I was fine. But I was just so anxious through the whole pregnancy. And it was hard for me to talk about it. I was embarrassed to share it at work, and I didn't know if I was ready to be involved with children, which was ridiculous since I had been trying for years.

As much as some mothers don't enjoy pregnancy, others love it and continue to savor the experience every time they are pregnant. As Alena said, "I loved the way I felt. I was overjoyed from start to finish."

Carrie's husband, Andrew, was diagnosed with cancer just as they were deciding to conceive. Although the prognosis for his illness was positive, it looked unlikely that they would be able to have children. They were devastated. For years they had put off trying to have a child so that they could finish their education and training and become established in their work; they now regretted that decision. While they were mourning their situation, Carrie suddenly discovered that she was pregnant:

We were ecstatic. Andrew was going through radiation treatment, and he was throwing up all the time. But it was just unbelievable; we were walking on air. She was our miracle baby. I was never sick for one minute, so it was like Andrew had to have the morning sickness, but that was okay. It was a miracle, totally a miracle.

USEFUL BOOKS DURING PREGNANCY:

- *The Girlfriends' Guide to Pregnancy,* by Vicki Iovine
- *What to Expect When You're Expecting,* by Arlene Eisenberg, Sandee Hathaway, and Heidi Murkoff
- *On Becoming a Family,* by Dr. T. Berry Brazelton
- *The Expectant Father,* by Armin Brott

USEFUL WEBSITE:

- www.childbirth.org

USEFUL BOOKS ON ADOPTION:

- *Is Adoption For You?,* by Christine Adamec
- *Adoption Nation,* by Adam Pertman
- *The International Adoption Handbook,* by Myra Alperson

USEFUL WEBSITES:

- www.adoption.com
- www.adopting.org
- www.childofmydreams.com

WORKING WHILE WAITING

So now you're pregnant—but you're also still working. Many women feel anxious about announcing their pregnancy at work. You may be worried about how your supervisor and colleagues will react or how your role at work will now be viewed. Many women delay announcing their pregnancy until they absolutely have to—when they start to look pregnant rather than a little bit "chubby." Monique hid her pregnancy for several months:

> *My husband and I had code words that we would use when we called each other after the doctor's appointments. We made up euphemisms, because I worked in an open-space environment with people right across from me. So that was*

difficult. I was a nervous wreck when I got ready to announce my pregnancy. There had been only one other woman in a department of fifty who had gotten pregnant.

Mothers' tips for announcing the news at work:

- Wait until after the first trimester, or until you are "showing."
- Don't be ashamed to announce that you are pregnant, but also don't gloat about it. Just be confident and happy about the announcement and then move on.
- Be prepared for a range of reactions from supervisor and coworkers: happy for you, supportive, jealous, competitive, etc.

Before you announce your pregnancy or adoption proceedings, have a clear idea of your plan for work, since that is the first question your colleagues and supervisor will ask. Investigate the family leave policy of your organization so you will know how much time you can take off. Quietly research the available policies and benefits. Talk to your human resources officer and consult any benefits manual. Also talk to other mothers who have recently taken a maternity leave.

If your organization has more than fifty employees, it may be subject to the 1993 Family and Medical Leave Act (FMLA). If you have been working for this organization for at least twelve months and at least twenty-five hours a week, you will be entitled under this legislation to twelve weeks of family leave, and your position, or an equivalent one, will be safeguarded for you. Find out if you can negotiate for more leave or if that is the limit in your organization. Learn how much of the leave is paid or unpaid (most organizations do not provide paid leave). Find out if you can use accrued sick, vacation, and personal days to partially pay for the leave or to extend it. If you are covered by a short-term disability plan, you will most likely receive partial pay for six to eight weeks.

WHAT KIND OF FAMILY LEAVE CAN YOU TAKE?

- Does the federal Family and Medical Leave Act (FMLA) apply to your organization? To you?
    - Organization needs to have more than fifty employees in one location
    - You need to have worked there at least twelve months and more than twenty-five hours per week
    - For more information on the FMLA and how it pertains to your situation, consult the government website: www.grlaw.com/fmla.htm
- If your organization is not covered by the FMLA, what is the leave policy?
- Are you on a short-term disability plan that will partially cover your leave? What percentage of your salary is covered and for how many weeks? Is there a waiting period before you start receiving payments?
- Can you use accrued sick, vacation, and personal days either to extend your leave or increase the amount of paid time?
- Has there been a history of employees negotiating for more than the standard leave?
- Can you start your leave before you deliver?
- Is there a phase-back-to-work policy? A telecommuting policy?

Plan for Your Absence

You have the right to take a maternity leave, free from the pressures of work. But to do so, you need to plan with your supervisor and colleagues for your absence. Also, come up with a contingency plan in case you deliver early. Much of the stress that mothers feel is over leaving work undone at the office. Plan for such an eventuality.

Strategic Planners naturally know how to plan ahead for their maternity leave. The rest of us need to consciously learn to do so. Look ahead to when you expect to go out on leave. Will there be major projects on which you are expected to participate? Should you move off any fast-track project whose deadline is in the middle of your maternity leave? Work out a proposed plan for the date you will go on leave, how much time you will take, and how your job will be covered while you are on leave. You will determine much of this with your supervisor, but it will help to know what you want before you head into that discussion.

Also think about whether you want to change your job schedule or functions at work once you've had your baby and return to work. Does your employer offer flexible work options? If you want to propose one, use some of the guidelines and strategies presented in chapter 3 to help you plan and present your proposal. But keep your options open. As I discuss in the next chapter, some mothers do not know what they want to do regarding work until after they have their baby.

Pregnancy, adoption proceedings, and the birth of a baby are all fraught with uncertainty and emotion. It is hard to predict how you will react and how your views on working will change until you have your baby. This is just what worries many supervisors. Don't bring your uncertainty and emotional highs and lows in to work with you. Your supervisor and coworkers will be looking to you for a clear and solid plan, a professional attitude, and commitment. Do all your thinking, vacillating, worrying, and changing your mind at home with close friends and family, but *come to work with confidence and certainty*. Show your colleagues that you are committed to your work and the organization, that you take work priorities seriously, and that you are a reliable, steadfast worker they will want back on the workforce. So make your plan—and know that, if need be, it can always change later.

PLAN FOR YOUR ABSENCE AT WORK:

- Supervisor and coworkers will want to quickly know about your plans and how your absence will affect them. Think through these plans *before* you announce. Be clear and straightforward about:
  - Any anticipated changes in schedule or job functions while pregnant or adopting
  - Date you plan to go on leave
  - Length of family leave you would like to take
- Together with your supervisor, create a plan for how your work will be covered while you are gone:
  - Should someone fill your position in your absence?
  - Should your work be divided among colleagues? Make sure they are aware of it.
  - Can some work or projects be put off until your return?
- Write up any work procedures that your replacement will need.

- Who should coworkers go to for answers when you are not available? They will need someone else to turn to, or they will call you at home.
- Be clear about the areas where you want to be kept informed. Tell them how they should contact you: voice mail, e-mail, phone call, memo, etc. Be clear about the limits.
- Let them know if you don't want to be involved at all once home with your baby. Don't leave it unsaid. Understand that it is perfectly legitimate for you to have a complete break from work; don't feel guilty about it. Before you know it, you'll be back at work, and they will have forgotten about your absence.
- Make a contingency plan in case of premature delivery.
- Create a specific plan for your return—any changes in schedule or job function (these plans may change later).

Dealing with Reactions at Work

Some mothers feel that they are suddenly viewed differently once they announce they are pregnant. One day you are a worker valued for your skills and expertise, and the next day you may seem like a "pregnant belly":

When I started to show, I felt that people were making some assumptions about my life that they never had before. Would I come back to work? Would I lose my ambition? That didn't feel very comfortable. For the first time, my life outside of work was showing visibly.

—Erin

What I didn't like was that I was trying so hard to prove myself as a professional, confident woman doing my thing—and pregnancy is so public. So here I am trying to make it in a totally male environment, and the first thing colleagues see when I enter the room is this very pregnant belly. I just didn't want them to focus on that.

—Stacy

As I discuss in chapter 3, the kind of company you work for will impact how you are viewed once you announce that you are expecting. Mothers who work for family-friendly companies more often feel supported and valued. Their employers understand that major life events are part of every employee's life and should be met with sensitivity and support. Whether it is the arrival of a baby, the death of a close family member, a serious illness or disability, the active pursuit of an athletic or artistic achievement outside of work, or any other significant life events, a supportive workplace understands that these are aspects of life that cannot be completely ignored at work.

Although some mothers feel that their pregnancy can negatively impact them at work, other mothers, such as Sarah, feel it can bring them closer to coworkers:

> *I discovered when I was pregnant that men love to talk about their families, too, and somehow they feel they have a license to do that when they're talking to a pregnant woman. My pregnancy was an enormous icebreaker, and suddenly people at work talked to me about all sorts of things.*

Even if you try to proceed through your pregnancy as if nothing were different, it may just intrude at work in ways you wouldn't foresee. When I was eight months pregnant with Farrell, I was being interviewed on television about our work with young children. Suddenly, in the midst of the interview, I could feel my breasts start to leak milk—actually spout milk. I was totally shocked, especially since this was my first pregnancy and I was not prepared for such an event. What could I do? I was live and on-air. I wanted to look down to see what was happening, but I didn't dare. I picked up the folder of papers I had in front of me and held it to my chest as I continued the interview. The male interviewer looked at me strangely, but we both just went on. I'm sure he was very perplexed, because even after the interview, as I sat and met with him and the television crew, I continued to clutch the folder to my chest, trying to figure how I could bolt and get my coat on.

Maintain a Professional Attitude: Be Clear About What's Going On

You should not be made to feel embarrassed or self-conscious about being pregnant, but be sensitive in turn to how it impacts your work. For many women, becoming pregnant is an emotional roller coaster, and it can be difficult to keep those emotions from affecting your workday. You may have a hard time becoming pregnant, you may have to go through long months of fertility work, or you may have to undergo a long and sometimes arduous adoption process. You may feel sick and exhausted. You may also feel distracted by the arrival of your baby and impending life changes. As one mother said, "I have to say I spent a lot more time thinking about my family and what it would be like to have a baby than I did thinking about my job. I spent a lot of time daydreaming." Of course, no employer wants to hear this. If you count on coming back to work as a valued employee, don't undermine your performance when your supervisor and coworkers may be watching for just such a thing.

Some mothers advise confiding in a friend or two at work, but make sure you don't dwell on your pregnancy and all your bodily changes with those around you. Monique offers this advice:

> *Once you announce your pregnancy, be sure to be professional. Show your boss and colleagues that it is not going to hinder your performance, and whatever you do, don't run around the office complaining about how tired you are and how much morning sickness you have. If you've got it, deal with it.*

After all, no matter how supportive your supervisor is, he or she is ultimately concerned that you'll continue to focus on your job and do it well.

But sometimes it's unavoidable; you can't help but be distracted. At times during your pregnancy, you may feel too sick or tired to carry on exactly as you did before. If that is the case, you may have to make some accommodations. Elizabeth described how she went through extensive fertility work to become pregnant. Although she lived in one city, she traveled daily to another city for a round of fertility treatments:

> *It was terrible. I would get up at five A.M., travel a couple of hours to the clinic, travel back, and arrive in the office at ten A.M. I remember one of the managers saying to me when I arrived in the office midmorning, "Oh, you slept in!" I just burst into tears in front of him. I didn't tell him the reason. I hadn't told anyone what I was doing.*

If you have a circumstance with your pregnancy that is negatively affecting your work, don't try to hide it. It is better to clearly communicate with your supervisor and relevant coworkers that you need to make some changes with your schedule, explain why, then make the appropriate adjustments. "Covering up" usually doesn't work, and you risk losing everyone's confidence if you aren't clear and forthright.

Evelyn, a research scientist who had her first baby in her late thirties after years of professional work, had some serious pregnancy risks. Although she was distraught and distracted at work, she didn't let anyone know what was going on. Her work slipped. She later regretted that she didn't communicate with her department, and she felt that it took her years to recover professionally:

> *I always felt invincible at work, and when I got pregnant, I felt that nothing had changed. I can do this. And then I found out I had placenta previa, and then one of our baby's brain measurements was wrong. They were talking about whether or not she was going to have hydrocephalus. That changed everything. All of a sudden I didn't care what was going on at work. I became completely self-absorbed. My work started to slide like crazy. It was the worst performance of my career, in the most critical time at work. I wouldn't talk to anybody at work about my pregnancy because I still had this weird idea of invincibility—that nothing had changed.*
>
> *I made a lot of mistakes. I didn't count on the people at*

work like I should have. I should have walked in and said, "Look, this is what is going on in my life. I'm scared to death. I need help." They would have helped me. I paid for those mistakes for five years.

Her supervisor didn't know what was going on. All he knew was that Evelyn's work had deteriorated significantly for no apparent reason.

Since our workforces are now populated with women of child-bearing years, it has become more and more common for women to be pregnant or waiting for adoption while working. There are some important guidelines that can help you navigate this phase of waiting:

- This is your baby and your life—be confident and self-assured. You are about to have one of the most important experiences in your life; you can embrace it. Don't feel you need to hide your condition or apologize for it.

- But don't dwell on your condition at work. Maintain your professionalism and focus on your performance. No matter how supportive your supervisor and coworkers are, they still rely on you to get your job done well.

- If you can, seek support and community with one or two other pregnant or adopting parents. It's nice to be able to share this important experience with others.

- Remember that you may have coworkers who have been trying to have a baby and have not yet succeeded. Not everyone may want to talk about or celebrate what is happening to you.

- Be clear with your supervisor if your responsibilities or hours need to change due to pregnancy complications or a time-consuming adoption process. *Come with a plan for how your work will get done.* You and your supervisor must communicate regularly and openly about responsibilities, expectations, and output.

Investigate Child Care Now

This is the time to start investigating child care options. Don't wait until you have your baby. It's a gift to yourself and your child to be able to relax during your maternity leave and focus on him and your new life as a parent; you don't want to spend the bulk of your maternity leave searching for child care. Go back to chapter 4 and decide which option would work best for your family. Visit child care providers during your pregnancy or while waiting for adoption. Do as much of the footwork as you can before you have your baby, so you don't have that pressure when you are home with a newborn.

You will need particularly to search in advance if you want to find a child care center or family child care provider. Many of the high quality providers have long waiting lists—six months or more. If you wait until you have your baby before you select a provider, there may not be space available when you need it. You don't want to be in a position where you have to accept your second or third choice.

THE NESTING INSTINCT

Like many mothers, you may decide to move to a different apartment or house near the arrival of your first child. It may seem to you that your place is now too small or in a location that isn't ideal for young children. Some mothers talk about the "nesting instinct," when all of a sudden they start thinking about creating a wonderful new environment for their baby. *But do you know what? Don't move!*

It's exciting to think about creating a warm, welcoming environment for your newborn. But I was surprised to find that so many mothers add moving stress to their lives at a time when they could benefit from relaxing and getting themselves physically and psychologically prepared for their transition to parenthood. You can still fulfill your nesting instinct by creating a wonderful little spot for your baby in your existing home. After all, he won't take up much space.

Like many parents-to-be, Abigail and her husband, Bill, moved during her pregnancy, to a larger apartment in the same city. Their baby, Garrett, was born prematurely, and they were far from ready:

Garrett came six weeks early, while we were still painting our new apartment. His room was our paint room. It was horrible. We should not have moved then. I think it would have been important to have had plenty of adult time in the new place before we had Garrett. I was exhausted, and the place was in a mess when my water broke.

We were also new to our neighborhood. If I had known, I would have done it differently. If I had lived in the neighborhood a year ahead of time, I would have met other parents. You know, just to take a walk together. As it was, I felt very alone.

In order to buy or rent as big a place as they can, many couples end up moving farther from work and their existing community, which makes getting to and from work just that much harder. Community and family will become even more precious once you have children. This is the moment when you may want to stay close to them.

A network of support can be incredibly helpful while you are home with a newborn. You may want to get together with other mothers and their babies to go for a stroll. You may want to lean on your mother or sister or other close family and friends for help. If you stay within your existing community, you may be better able to seek support. That network is also important for the myriad needs you will have—most important, looking for child care. Many parents choose their child care based on trusted friends' and neighbors' recommendations. If you are fresh to a community, it may be harder to get those recommendations.

Selena and her husband, Peter, moved during her pregnancy with their first child, to a town that was far from where they had been living:

Don't move right before you have a baby. We did that, and it was a real challenge. We didn't know anyone, and I needed to network to find a great local baby-sitter. I now look back and regret how I spent my maternity leave, because I was in the middle of unpacking. I don't feel like I got to enjoy that special time. I think that there is this instinct that comes over

*you when you're pregnant and you think, "Oh, it's time to get
a bigger place." But it really doesn't make sense.*

Moving to a larger place usually means added financial burdens. As I discuss more fully in the next chapter, think about whether
you really want to lock yourself in to greater expenses right now. You
are just forming your family. Having a baby brings significant financial expenditures; why add a larger rent or mortgage burden at this
moment? Particularly since you don't know yet how you and your
partner will react to parenthood, you may want to have the financial
flexibility to cut back at work for a while.

A larger house or apartment also means a lot more cleaning,
just when household chores start to skyrocket with the baby. Also,
those extra rooms will just go empty. Crawling babies, toddlers, and
preschoolers will always be by your side, no matter how wonderful the
playroom is in the basement. Your world will be very small for a while,
and you and your spouse will be too tired to clean the house, so why
not stay small? Remember my friend Petronila in Kenya, who was
raising eight children happily in a three-room bungalow. That may
seem a bit too cramped to us, but we could all probably be happy with
less. As one mother, Janet, said after the birth of her first baby:

*We were living in just a small one-bedroom apartment when
we had our baby. It was a very nice one-bedroom apartment,
but we knew that we would need to find a bigger place at
some point. So we were thinking about that, but it was on the
back burner. We just left it there for a while.*

Okay, If You Are Going to Move, How Do You Look for a New Community?

You may decide to disregard this advice and go ahead and move anyway. Or you may be at a phase where your child is already a couple of
years old, you're out of the stressful early phase, and you're ready to
move. I don't want to leave you stranded, so let me share with you
some mothers' wisdom about choosing another location. There are
many models of looking for a neighborhood or community. Think
about what is most important to you as a working mother.

Close to Family

Many parents choose to find a place close to extended family. Having family nearby who can help when work and family conflicts arise can be very helpful. Many mothers lean on family for friendship, advice, and help when they encounter the expected periodic break-downs in child care. As Janet recounted:

We lived in a small apartment near my mother and mother-in-law. They could be there in a matter of minutes. The laundry was in the basement of the building; they would even come over to watch the baby while I did the laundry. If I had to do something for work, they could be there. It was wonderful to have them so close.

One mother left an abusive relationship and moved back to the neighborhood where she grew up and still had family:

My social worker advised me not to move back to where my family was. They were afraid that it was where my son's father would look for me first, the place where I grew up. But I told them that I would feel safe there because all my family is in this town, and that's where all the support is. I knew that my mother is a mile away and my sister is a mile in the other direction. As a single working mother, I knew I would need that support. It was a good move.

Close to Work

Other parents seek a place close to their place of work. Particularly if you and your partner both work in the same area, it can reduce your logistical challenges significantly. You can reduce your commute time, you may be able to eliminate the need for a car, and it makes life easier to have work, home, and child care all in close proximity.

Monique and her husband, Patrick, found an apartment that was just a couple blocks' walk to both their places of work and their son's child care:

That alleviated a tremendous amount of stress. It's reassuring knowing that we're a few blocks from our son, Tyler, and a few blocks from home. We've simplified logistics, and we're all home at a very reasonable time and have all evening to play with him. It makes no sense to be an hour away if someone gets sick.

Choosing Quality of Life

Some parents choose a community because they are seeking a certain quality of life, in an environment they value.

Colleen and her husband, Jack, love the ocean and the beach and decided to live in a beach community even though it meant a fifty-minute to sixty-minute commute to work each day:

It would be a lot easier for working if we moved closer to the city, but we would give up this kind of life. It's a whole different dynamic living here. Like this weekend, we went to the beach three times. We went for a walk, took the dog for a walk in the water. Our son, Alexander, ran around on the beach. We don't want to give that up. When I leave work and come home, I feel that I have really gotten away.

Patricia and her husband, Ralph, love the dynamism and culture of city living and chose to live in an urban environment:

We decided that the advantages of living in the city outweigh what we would gain from living in the suburbs or country. It was our choice. Every weekend we go to museums and children's bookstores. We go to musical and sports events. Our kids love doing this stuff. A city has wonderful advantages. They walk just twenty yards to their public school.

Natalie and her husband, Ron, placed more emphasis on finding a place with a strong sense of community, where people look out for one another and are friendly and helpful. They didn't want an anonymous urban environment or a spread-out rural environment:

Since I'm not at home during the day with other mothers and children, it was important to me to find a welcoming community with a small-town feel. We now have a lot of good friendships that we have developed over the years. Everybody gets together on the Common. We meet at the ice-cream store. We help each other out a lot. That's particularly valuable to me as a working mother. That's why I continue to do this long commute.

Seeking Important Values

Some parents want a living situation where they can live out their values. Some want to live in or close to their religious community. Others desire to live in ethnic communities where they can feel more connected. Olive and her husband, Les, looked to live with another family in a shared home. They felt that would bring a richness to their family life. Olive had spent time in Israel on a kibbutz, where adults and children live together communally. Shared living also supported a mortgage and helped with child care as they worked. Olive and Les bought their house jointly with Les's sister and brother-in-law:

We didn't think we had enough money to get into the housing market by ourselves. With the four of us together, we could. We first rented a house together and then saved up and bought it. We had grown up together at summer camp, so it didn't seem strange. We were all very close friends. It seemed like a positive thing to do.

For decades, Olive and Les have lived communally, first with Les's sister's family, then for years with a single woman and her son, and later with their grown daughter and her husband. Particularly when the children were young, the arrangement helped them a great deal. They were able to share the child care so that there was always a parent at home with the children. A strong sense of belonging, mutual responsibility, and love permeated the household. As Olive says:

When I was working, I knew my children were well cared for and loved. The adults also felt committed to each other. We helped each other through all of life's ups and downs.

Selecting the Right School

Some parents choose their home by first finding the school they desire for their children and then moving close by. They look for either academic excellence or a particular cultural environment in the school. One mother got the name of the PTA president in the community they were looking at and called her to get a sense of both the school and the parent community. She also wanted to know if there was a large working mother population; she knew that would be helpful for mutual support and acceptance. Look ahead to see if there is a quality after-school program for children of working parents. If the town is made up primarily of mothers who are home after school, there may be inadequate after-school care.

Sarah was particularly thorough about investigating a school and community before deciding to move. Her first step was to make an appointment with the principal of the nearby elementary school. She interviewed him to determine his academic priorities and his view of the parent community and children:

> *I also wanted to make sure I looked through the school. I wandered around the playground to get a sense of the atmosphere and interactions. I wanted to make sure that this was where we wanted to settle. It's like the book* Make Way for Ducklings—*I was looking to see if this was where we wanted to make our nest. I walked through the town, went to the town center. I talked to people on the street, talked to other people who knew the town. I got the real estate agent to give me all the comparative schooling information and test scores and all that stuff.*

Think about what's most important to you:

- To live close to extended family?
- To live close to work?
- To find a desired quality of life?
- To live in a community of similar values?
- To live close to a desired school?

YOUR MATERNITY LEAVE

Coming Home with Your Baby

You now have your baby. Many moms experience a jarring transition from the daily world of working and anticipating their newborn to actually coming home with one. As Sarah described:

We arrived home from the hospital. My husband, John, carried little Aaron's car seat into the apartment and put him on the living room floor, and Aaron started to scream. Of course he hadn't screamed while we were in the hospital, and John looked at me with this look of horror on his face: "Oh God, what do we do now?" I think the reality hit.

This can be a very emotional time; you may feel things you never have before. One mother, Pamela, described the experience of first picking up her adopted baby:

I came home on Friday afternoon after work, and my husband was there. He flung open the door. When I saw him, I thought, "What is wrong with him? I've never seen him look like this." He looked like he was crying, but he was smiling. He told me, "We have a baby girl!" He had just gotten the call. He told me that we were going to go tomorrow to get her, the next day, the very next day! We went at nine in the morning to the foster-care home. Our baby was crying and crying and crying— but the minute they put her in my arms, she stopped crying. It was very symbolic. I felt that we were destined for each other.

You are now home and ready to start your maternity leave. Your world now dramatically changes. Unlike in other times and cultures, many of us today grow up and begin our adult life far from the world of babies, immersed in our world of work. Suddenly being home on maternity leave with a newborn can feel overwhelming and disorienting. I heard many different reactions to bringing the baby home. Let me share a few very different stories, starting with Carol's:

I was so unprepared for what this little person was going to mean. Our baby, Michael, never slept. The first night we came home from the hospital, he slept forty-five minutes, and that was it. There were two or three nights of this, where I was getting very little sleep, and I hit the wall.

It seemed like Michael cried all day long. I was so tired and so overwhelmed; nothing was right. I was angry with everyone. I remember sitting in the bathtub one night and saying, "What have I done to my life? What have I done to my career? Why did I think this was a good idea? This is nothing like I thought it was going to be, and how am I going to do this?"

My whole life, I had had it together. Everything was in control; I was a successful professional. This threw me so much. I would sit in the rocking chair at night, just sobbing, while my husband and mother sat at my feet trying to console me. What I hated most about that time was that I didn't enjoy my baby at all, not one bit. He was just this little anxiety-provoking, scary thing.

Carol had a rough initial transition, but she eventually got through this challenging time; both her baby and she eventually settled into a comfortable rhythm. She went on to have a second baby two years later. Listen to another mother's story of new motherhood and her maternity leave. Tina had an entirely different experience:

It was probably the greatest feeling I had ever felt. I loved every minute of my maternity leave. I was really grateful that my daughter was healthy. I couldn't believe I had this beautiful baby. I was sitting there saying, "I can't believe that this little person is mine, and I have to take care of her." It was just the greatest joy to take care of her.

I really enjoyed my maternity leave. My baby and I bonded and became great friends, and I loved being with her, just hanging out with her. I discovered how to take care of her, which was my goal. The best thing I probably did was buy a rocking chair. We would sit in the rocking chair and spend long quiet times together.

Tina achieved happiness despite great odds. She had been confined to strict bed rest during the last trimester of her pregnancy. She and her husband had just moved to a new place far out from the city where she had lived for years and where she had a strong network of support. As African-Americans, they did not feel embraced by the largely white community. They were stretched financially, and her bed rest caused her to lose valuable months of income. Finally, her marriage had deteriorated significantly through the pregnancy, and she and her husband ultimately divorced. Yet despite all this, she felt transformed by the birth of her baby girl and relished her maternity leave. Nothing was going to stop her from feeling the deep bond with her baby.

It's difficult to avoid having a romantic notion of coming home with your baby. Particularly when you're at a point in your life when wanting a baby is all you think about, you imagine tender moments of love and bonding. Reality, of course, can be far more complex. The following mother, Catherine, took an honest look at how her hopes and expectations didn't line up with reality. Catherine, who had adopted a year-old baby girl from China, confronted a number of emotions and challenges that many mothers (who either give birth to or adopt a child) also face:

As soon as our group of adoptive parents arrived in China to get our babies, we found out that all the children were already at the hotel waiting for us. There, a woman brought out a screaming baby who had a terrible rash all over the bottom of her face. She was the only baby who cried, and she was my baby. It turned out that she had impetigo, conjunctivitis, and a terrible yeast infection. The poor thing was so miserable.

I put my arms out, and she kept screaming. I took her. My mother and I went to our room, and I rocked her back and forth for an hour, and she wouldn't stop. She just clutched on to me and tried to crawl up me like a monkey. She did that for the first three days straight. I think she was afraid. Really afraid.

I had this overwhelming feeling that this baby was now mine. I was entirely responsible for this helpless little creature. Going from imagining what it would be like to actually being there was very difficult. It was a struggle to come to terms with my feelings.

When we came home from China, it was wintertime—dark and bitterly cold. I was really isolated. The first week back was awful. It was just horrible. Then it settled into monotony. It was dreary outside and cold, and she was fussy. We played with the same five toys over and over, week after week. We did that throughout the whole maternity leave. It was tough.

Some Babies Are Just More Difficult Than Others

These women all became great mothers, but they had dramatically different experiences of new motherhood and maternity leave. A big factor in your experience of maternity is your newborn's disposition. Babies are very different; some are much more challenging than others. If you have a colicky, fussy newborn who will not sleep easily, it is much harder to feel blissful about your maternity leave. Although you can do many things to help make the leave easier, you cannot transform a colicky baby into a settled, quiet one. If your baby has health issues, your challenges may be greater.

In his classic baby book, *Infants and Mothers,* Dr. T. Berry Brazelton describes various temperaments of babies and gives wonderful advice on caring for them. Dr. Brazelton often talks about how difficult the first three months of a newborn's life can be, and it is in this period of time that you are home on maternity leave. By four

USEFUL BOOKS

- *Infants and Mothers,* by Dr. T. Berry Brazelton
- *Your Baby and Child,* by Penelope Leach
- *Oneness and Separateness,* by Louise Kaplan

USEFUL WEBSITES

- www.zerotothree.org
- www.parentstages.com

months a newborn usually settles in to a fairly predictable routine. He may still be waking in the night, but you can probably count on a predictable set of naps during the day. Also, babies typically become more responsive by four months. Seeing that wonderful toothless smile meant only for you, getting those loving wet kisses, or hearing him giggle when you play peekaboo or blow on his belly all go a long way toward compensating for those sleepless nights. Remember that the fussiness usually passes in a few months, even for the most colicky baby.

"I'm Totally Exhausted; This Is Overwhelming!"

Don't underestimate the impact of sleep deprivation. Lack of sleep and near-constant baby care may make the first weeks of your maternity leave strenuous. Make sure you have enough time at home to get through this period and see your baby settled. And even a normal delivery, free of complications, will leave the healthiest new mother tired and in some pain; labor and delivery are hard work! If you have had a difficult labor and delivery, or an episiotomy or caesarian section, your recovery will take much longer—sometimes a few months.

Pamela and Ned had gone through years of fertility work and then a long adoption process. When they finally received their baby, Hannah, their joy was beyond bounds. Although that happiness did not abate, the reality of a newborn quickly set in:

> We were so ecstatic to bring Hannah home. I was so happy and so excited most of the time during those first weeks of maternity leave, but it was also pretty hard and stressful. Hannah was very colicky; she would cry nonstop. She never seemed to sleep. I remember on our thirteenth day of having her, Ned came home, and I just blew up. I handed Hannah to him, and I got in the car and left. I thought, "Where can I go?" I thought I'd like to go to a bar, but it's so uncomfortable sitting in a bar, you know, as a woman, that I just couldn't do that, so I just drove around for a really, really long time, and I came back, and I was better then.

Pamela just needed to blow off some steam and get a quick break. The sleep deprivation is the element that takes the greatest toll on new parents. One mother, Monique, put it well:

The first week, I was in the hospital, and it was really exciting. I went home the second week, and I felt like it was a slumber party. You're up a few nights and thinking, "Oh, this is great, it's just like college." You're doing an all-nighter, isn't this fun. By week two to three you're thinking, "Oh, I'm kind of tired now." By week three to four, you're realizing why sleep deprivation is a form of torture according to the UN. It was so exhausting. I really lost all sense of time. You really migrate into this sort of twilight zone, wondering if you're ever going to get out again.

New moms sometimes experience a feeling of betrayal. It's almost as if there's some dark secret that all other moms know but them. Some, like Yvette, blame others for not getting them more prepared:

I was very angry at my aunt, my mother, and all the other women I knew, because nobody told me what it was really going to be like. I'd call and say I haven't slept in a month, and they'd say, "Yeah, I know." I was like, "What do you mean, 'Yeah, I know'? How come you didn't tell me this before?"

The best advice I heard from any of my mothers for this early newborn phase was: *"I guess it's like the weather—wait a day, just wait a day, because everything changes in a day."*

Babies change so rapidly in the early days and weeks, and mothers change as well. The difficult moments are short-lived. Most babies become settled by the twelve-week mark. Don't think that this stage is forever. Just focus on each day as it comes.

"I Feel Totally Unprepared; I Don't Know What To Do"

I had absolutely no experience with babies. I was sort of
afraid of them. I remember saying to the nurse, "How do I
hold my baby? Is it like I hold my cat?"

—Wendy

I wonder why so many of us diligently take Lamaze or birthing classes while we're pregnant, yet we do so little to learn about newborns. We follow the development of the fetus week by week and study child-birth techniques. But it is almost as if the learning process stops with the birth. As Chloe said:

I had a very successful birth and delivery. But then I didn't
know what to do with the baby. I was so scared and felt so
helpless. I cried because I didn't know how to push a stroller
up onto the curb!

Many adoption agencies do no better at preparing parents for newborn care, as Pamela found:

We had lots of great counseling, but it was largely about issues
of adoption—how to respond to whatever people say about
adoption, how to talk to your children about it. I felt very
prepared for that, but not for what to do when you finally
have your baby and have to care for her.

We often hear about the "maternal instinct," yet you may wonder where yours is. You might have thought that some innate knowledge would suddenly appear, but it doesn't. Our concept of new motherhood is sometimes bathed in romantic, unrealistic notions. We conjure up images of relaxed mothers and babies in idyllic scenes of bonding and bliss. As Erin describes, it often doesn't happen that way:

I remember when he was born and they brought him out and
put him on top of me. I'm thinking, "Okay, I feel like I'm in a

science fiction movie. In real movies, the babies are cleaned up and there's no blood anywhere, and I'm a mess, the baby's a mess. When do those maternal instincts kick in, because I'm horrified." I thought music would begin in the background and this huge glow would happen and I'd be in this fairy-tale world. When would that start?

When this innate mothering knowledge doesn't appear, many mothers become frightened. They feel incompetent in a role that they believe is their most important in life, as Patricia describes:

I was totally terrified, and I just kept thinking, "When is the mom coming home, because she's not here right now!" I was scared. I cried a lot; the baby cried a lot. Pregnancy had been so wonderful, and then I had this baby and everything was falling apart. Things had always fallen into place so nicely my whole life. I had a great husband; I had a great job. I knew how to do things. I just thought this would fall into place nicely, too. But it didn't.

Go to your birthing classes and prepare for that experience, but do take time to learn about newborns and infants. After all, you will spend just several hours in childbirth, but you will be a parent forever.

I observed when I was living in developing-world cultures that these issues are less prevalent. Typically, young girls in third-world villages grow up in a world of babies, mothers, and extended family. By the time a woman conceives, she has already become adept at caring for and handling babies. Once she has her own baby, she is often surrounded and supported by a close network of experienced mothers who help her and keep her company.

In our culture, we are more likely to grow up having very little contact with babies. We also expect to be independent, strong working women who make plans and implement them. We are accustomed to being self-sufficient. Particularly if you are a Strategic Planner or Camp Counselor mom, you are used to operating according to your own agenda. The rhythms and needs of a newborn are therefore more likely to fly in the face of how you are used to operating. This little baby requires a whole new way of looking at things. He needs a mom and dad who tune in to his subtle needs and agenda, and who will mold their lives around his. The very strengths we have developed as working women may make adjusting to motherhood harder for us initially. But let's not negate our hard-won competencies. Let's embrace a broadening of our skills, emotional depth, and ability to give.

These are tips for when you first come home:

- While you're *still in the hospital* after giving birth, don't hold back on all your questions for the maternity nurses. They are there to help you and are skilled in newborn care. Ask them, in particular, about ways to soothe a crying baby.

- When you arrive home from the hospital with your newborn and you are at a loss as to know how to soothe him, one mother recommends *calling the nurses on the maternity ward* where you had your baby. They were just with your baby and know him, and they may be a great help. There is always someone on duty, so feel free to call at two A.M.

- This is the time now to turn to your mother, mother-in-law, sisters, or close friends who have gone through this experience. In cultures throughout history, women have leaned on their *sisterhood of women* when they had their babies. This is our legacy for an important reason—we need it and value it.

- Some health plans allow for a *visiting nurse* who can come help you at critical moments.

- Call *your midwife*, if you have one, for help, support, advice.

- Schedule extra time with *your pediatrician* at the two- and four-week visits. Go through all your concerns and fears. She or he can be a great support and will check to make sure your baby is doing fine. Many pediatricians have a *daily call-in hour*. Take advantage of that as frequently as you want. Your doctor is there to help you.

- Call your organization's *Employee Assistance Program* or resource and referral program if it has one. They often provide excellent free information and counseling.

MORE USEFUL BOOKS:

- *Touchpoints,* by Dr. T. Berry Brazelton
- *Parent Effectiveness Training,* by Thomas Gordon
- *Your Self-Confident Baby: How to Encourage Your Child's Natural Abilities from the Very Start,* by Magda Gerber and Allison Johnson
- *The Scientist in the Crib: Minds, Brains, and How Children Learn,* by Alison Gopnik, Andrew Meltzoff, and Patricia Kuhl

USEFUL WEBSITES:

- www.abcparenting.com
- www.parentsplace.com

The Hardest Thing Is to Just Let Go

This is where our Earth Mothers have a natural leg up. Rather than trying to exert control over their baby's rhythms and schedule during those early weeks, they know to listen to what the baby needs—to slow down and get into his rhythms. The Earth Mother may intuitively know how to go with the flow. The rest of us need to learn how to do that. One mother talked about finally learning to *just accept* that life right now is not about getting things done. Or, as Monique began to understand, the most important thing to "get done" is to sit and hold your baby:

> *I thought that my maternity leave would be a mini-vacation. We would get to go and do great little day trips—Mommy and Tyler. What a joke. He cried all the time and needed to be held. I would just sit all day. I called my mother and told her he wouldn't let me put him down. She said, "That's nice, because at sixteen he won't want you around, so just take the time now." I just took my to-do list and threw it away and said, "Fine, this is what it's going to be." I just accepted it. Once I did, it took a huge burden of stress off.*

So many working mothers are used to trying to accomplish so much, to being competent and in control. Once we have our baby, we try to keep up a neat home, take care of our newborn, cook meals, see friends, do projects—all on our schedule. The Earth Mother's best advice is to let all of that go. *"My priorities became sleep, hold my baby, and shower. I learned to let go of things, to just let them happen."*

One mother, Leah, felt that it made all the difference in the world to remember to savor and appreciate the little things about her baby during her maternity leave. She reveled in her baby's small developmental stages:

> *I have this great memory of my husband, Adam, and me lying on the floor with our baby, Samantha. She was on her stomach, and we watched her turn her head for the first time. We were lying on either side of her, and we were just watching and watching. We were so incredibly excited. Here she was, working so hard. Adam and I, to this day, talk about how amazing it was for us.*

This early time for bonding with your baby is important. If you can allow yourself to slow down and just be with him for these early weeks and months, you will be giving him a wonderful start in life. The maternity leave is a precious oasis of time for you and your baby. The pace of daily life and work will come back quickly, so take what time you can now to "just be." Learn the subtleties of your baby's temperament and daily rhythms. He will need the experience of being with you and his father, of sinking into your body and feeling your heartbeat, of feeling protected and enveloped. If you understand that caring for and bonding with your baby are the most vital parts of your maternity leave, then all the other things will seem less stressful. One mother, Colleen, initially felt frustrated that she wasn't "getting anything done" during her maternity leave until her husband pointed out that wasn't the case:

> *I remember talking to my sister about an armoire I had bought for the baby room that I was going to paint and decorate. Every time I talked to my sister, she would say, "Aren't you done with that thing yet?" And then I would tell her I hadn't done a thing during my maternity leave, and I got very down on myself. Finally my husband, Jack, pointed*

*out that yes, I was doing so much—and stuff that was so much
more important than painting an armoire. I was caring for our
baby, I was feeding him, I was taking him for walks.* I was
with him. *That was really something. Jack was right.*

Feel free to turn off the ringer on your phone and let your
answering machine take any messages. Quiet moments when you can
nap or relax are rare; don't let well-meaning friends or work colleagues interrupt them. You are already at the beck and call of your
newborn—you don't have to be at the beck and call of your phone
as well.

Here are some tips for your maternity leave:

- If you need a goal to keep you going, make it simple: that
  you will just be with your baby every day. For busy working
  women, an accomplishment may seem important. Holding,
  bonding, and getting to know your baby are your most
  important achievements for each day.

- Dramatically lower your expectations about daily life. This is
  not a contest or a race. There is no perfect way to do things.
  Simplify your life; follow your baby's rhythms.

- Tell your friends and family to bring a cooked dinner, not a
  baby gift.

- Turn off the phone ringer when the baby naps so that you
  can nap or rest, too.

- When your partner comes home, go out for a walk with him
  and the baby, or give the baby to him and go out for a walk
  by yourself.

- Don't be ashamed or embarrassed to seek help. Friends and
  family will want to help. Remember the phrase "It takes a
  village to raise a child." Or at least remember that it takes a
  helping hand to remain sane. Lean on your support structure.

- Do some small things to pamper yourself: Let your husband
  or a friend take your baby while you soak in a long hot

bubble bath, get a manicure or a haircut, go to your favorite bookstore or CD store, have a massage, buy some makeup. But don't go clothes shopping—that will only depress you, since it will take a while to get back into your original shape.

Breast-feeding Can Be Hard

I was totally set on nursing and had a really hard time with it. I remember once we got home from the hospital, I was lying on the bed and my baby was lying beside me, and he was screaming and I was crying, and I just said, "I'm the mom. I have the milk. I'm going to win. You're hungry. You know, let's just figure this out." And the windows were all open, and I'm thinking the neighbors are saying, "What is happening? The poor baby."

—Erin

For many mothers, nursing is initially difficult and painful. We have learned of the health benefits of nursing and the ultimate wonderful bond it can provide between mother and baby. These make it particularly frustrating when the experience is not easy and smooth. Monique describes the difficulty she had:

It was incredibly painful, so I would wake up twenty minutes before a feeding in anticipation and break out in a cold sweat, thinking, "Oh God, not again." I felt horrible, because all these pictures show it to be this wonderful, loving experience, and I was thinking, "Man, we could just send him over to the enemy line. He'd be a great form of weapon."

Some mothers look ahead and feel anxious about continuing to breast-feed or pump once they go back to work. In fact, many are not sure they will be able to continue. For some mothers, that makes breast-feeding during maternity leave all the more precious. Other mothers, like Stacy, find it harder to stay committed to breast-feeding while on leave:

I stopped breast-feeding after six weeks because I was so worried about breast-feeding while working. I kept thinking, "How do I go back to work in an all-male environment and continue to breast-feed? What if I start leaking during a meeting? Where am I ever going to find a place to pump?"

So my husband, Richard, and I decided that he would give Jeffrey his first bottle at six weeks. I was at the top of the stairs so that Jeffrey couldn't smell me or hear me. I was crying because I was going to lose this experience of breast-feeding. Richard put the bottle in Jeffrey's mouth, and that was it. He just took to it right away with no problem. I thought about that a lot. That seemed to represent what my life would be as a working mother. There were going to be a lot of times when I was going to have to step back and let somebody else do something important for my baby. That was hard.

If it is important to you to continue breast-feeding, don't assume that your workplace will not accommodate it. More and more mothers are pumping at work. It is your right to do so. You can breast-feed throughout your maternity leave and then, when you return to work, follow some of the guidelines in the next chapter to continue. It may make it easier for you to return to work if you know you can still nurse your baby.

Tips for breast-feeding:

- While you are still in the hospital, ask the maternity nurses to work with you on nursing so that you clearly understand how to do it.
- Know that the difficulty and discomfort go away for most mothers. If you can get through the initial stage, you will likely enjoy nursing for many months.
- Some health plans provide a lactation consultant. If not, consider hiring one anyway.
- La Leche League International is a helpful organization that helps mothers with nursing issues. Check your phone book

for a local chapter. If not, call their national number: 1–847–519–7730. They have advisers who can work with you over the phone.

- Work out a plan for what you will do regarding pumping, especially after you return to work (see the next chapter).
- If breast-feeding just doesn't work for you, move on. Think how lucky your husband or partner will now be to get up in the middle of the night and bond with the baby while feeding!

USEFUL BOOKS:

- *The Complete Book of Breastfeeding,* by Marvin Eiger and Sally Wendkos Olds
- *Nursing Mother's Companion,* by Kathleen Huggins

USEFUL WEBSITE:

- www.breastfeeding.com
- www.lalecheleague.org

Childbirth as the Impetus for Life Changes

There are many situations where the birth of a baby changes the direction of a woman's life. One woman, Amy, had her baby, Douglas, six weeks early, while she was living with an abusive boyfriend. When she and the baby left the hospital, the doctors put her in touch with an early intervention specialist. Although Amy had felt no ambition or motivation to get out before, she now wanted to turn her life around:

> *After Douglas was born, I spent most of my time alone with him in the apartment. I was very depressed. Douglas's father wouldn't let me leave the apartment, and threatened me if I did. So I'd be stuck in the apartment sometimes for days. I spent a lot of time just holding my son and hoping things would get better. I knew that I had to make a decision; I debated whether I should leave.*

Then the early intervention specialists came to look at my son. They told me that this was not a way I had to live; this was really going to affect my child. I was less concerned for me—I thought I didn't deserve better. But when I realized that my son would be affected by all of this, I knew I had to do something. They gave me the phone number of a domestic violence shelter. That was really what I needed to hear. The more I thought about it, I realized my son needed better than this.

Soon after, when her boyfriend left for a few days, Amy escaped to a domestic violence shelter. After a few months there, she signed up for courses in occupational therapy. Amy was determined to get a college degree and get back on her feet again.

Once I had Douglas, I realized that I had to be a role model for him, and that I was not going to be a welfare mother the rest of my life. Since I wasn't going to go out and just find a husband to take care of us, I knew I needed to work. I needed to have a profession. I wanted him to see me going to college and realizing that you can do things in life. You don't have to settle for what you have.

It is now five years later, and Amy is finishing her last semester of college. She will graduate this year with a degree in occupational therapy and already has a job offer. Douglas is a wonderful, bright boy in kindergarten. Realizing the responsibility she had toward her son was the impetus for Amy to make hard changes in her life to get herself, and her child, on a positive, productive path.

Postpartum Depression

I was feeling profoundly isolated and alone when I was home with my baby. I felt like I was just filling time. I lived for the kids' naps and bedtime. People would say, "Why do you have your kids in bed by seven P.M.?" But they didn't understand; I would die if I didn't have that break. Everybody wanted something from me. There wasn't any room for me. I felt like I was dying at that point. I felt like I always needed to sleep, but then I would wake up and feel like the life was sapped out of me. I could hardly function. I remember my mother-in-law leaving work to come help get my kids dressed in the morning. I couldn't even get them dressed. I was depressed, but I didn't know it. One night I just broke down and started crying and didn't stop. Eight hours later, a girlfriend took me to the hospital and they admitted me.

—Yvette

Depressions can range from mild to severe. Up to 80 percent of all new mothers feel some sort of "baby blues," during which they cry easily and feel sad, overwhelmed, or irritable during the weeks after childbirth. Seek support from your spouse and other close family members and friends during this period. Talk freely about how you are feeling.

However, 10 to 20 percent of all new mothers experience the more severe symptoms of postpartum depression, in which the mother can feel deeply depressed and may be unable to care for her infant. If you feel that you are suffering from postpartum depression, seek help. Support groups, therapy or counseling, and even medication may be needed. Don't feel that you need to push through this experience on your own. You and your baby will be much better off if you seek outside help and support.

If you think you have postpartum depression:

- *Confide* in someone close to you: your spouse, your mother, a close friend.
- See *your doctor* as soon as you can. He or she can help you find therapy and/or support groups. Your doctor may prescribe medication.
- Many hospitals and health plans have a *hot line* for those moments when you feel that you really need help fast.
- Don't hesitate to seek *professional counseling* or call your employer's counseling service or Employee Assistance Plan.

Many insurance plans cover postpartum counseling and therapy. Remember that depression is not an uncommon reaction; don't wait to seek help.

USEFUL BOOKS:

- *This Isn't What I Expected: Overcoming Post-Partum Depression*, by Karen Kleiman and Valerie Raskin
- *Mothering the New Mother*, by Sally Plackin

USEFUL WEBSITE:

- www.depressionafterdelivery.com

Start Building Your Community of Support

I think my maternity leave would have been so much better if I had friends and support around me. I honestly do. If I'd had people next door who I could go and have a cup of coffee with and our kids could be together, it would have been so much better. I don't live in a neighborhood where there are moms home or kids around, so I had nobody; I had no neighbors. I lived far from friends. I was by myself all day.

—Carol

If you are accustomed to a busy work life, interacting with other people all day long, suddenly spending long days at home alone with a newborn can be difficult. Many working mothers, since they are away at work every day, do not have a close community of friendship and support in their neighborhood. This was the case for Gina as well:

I was so alone. I was used to going to work and seeing everyone, it just felt like I was missing out on something. I felt isolated. Somehow I just couldn't ask my family for help. I couldn't ask friends. I couldn't ask, I just couldn't ask. I don't know why. But if I ever did it again, I would ask.

If you haven't already, start building your community of friends and support. As a working woman, you may find much of your community at work. With a new baby, try looking for a community of support around your home—extended family, neighbors, other parents with babies. You'll find that as your child grows, much of your family community will begin to center around other parents with children the same age as yours. Babies and young children are a great bridge to new connections and friendships. Other new parents are also looking for support and community. It's a stage of life where many friendships form as you enter into this domain of parenting. As you go for walks with your baby or to a neighborhood playground, reach out to other parents with babies. Look at the bulletin board in your local library for local play groups or events for parents and young children.

One of the most important initial sources of support for many moms is their extended family. I know that for me, one of the best aspects of each of my three maternity leaves was that I got to spend long, relaxed time with my mother, who came to stay for a while. She was a great help with all my little worries about my newborn, and I just enjoyed having some time to hang out with her. Even with my second and third babies, when I felt more adept, it was still reassuring to have her there. Particularly during the early days, when you can feel desperate, turning to a family member is sometimes easier, as Vivien found:

> It was horrible in the beginning of my maternity leave. I was tired and in a lot of pain. I was frightened out of my skull, and my mom was just so patient. She would stay all day and help me with the twins until my husband, Donnie, came home. I couldn't have done it without her. She was the voice of reason and calm, while Donnie and I were just walking around like zombies.

Having an experienced mom at your side can help you with all the skills you have to learn. Sharon felt that having her mother by her side deepened their relationship:

> My mother stayed with us after we had our first baby. She was an incredible support, and through her I got a clearer

*understanding of what it means to be a good mother. She
raised three children and had a lot of wisdom and experience.
We became closer, and I developed a different type of respect
for her that I didn't have before I had children. I saw her in a
different light.*

Don't think there is any value in trying to tough it out all alone.
You and your baby will both benefit from support. I was shocked to
hear what Shalisha told me:

*My mother and my mother-in-law both offered to come stay
with us for a couple of weeks, and my pediatrician said, "No,
absolutely not. You need to take care of that baby by yourself,
because your mother-in-law and your mother will eventually
go home, and then what are you going to do?"*

Shalisha would have loved the support and help and compan-
ionship during such a momentous time. Afterward, she might have
felt more rested and confident about caring for the baby herself.

Start building your community of support:

- Allow—no, *encourage* your friends and family into your life.
  Seek help, friendship, and support. Try to plan visits in
  phases so as to stretch them out over time. After your
  husband stays home for a while, have your mother come,
  then your mother-in-law, then your sister, then your best
  friend.
- Find a local parent support group or mothers' group. Look
  for information at local community centers, your religious
  organization, parent resource and referral agencies, hospitals,
  or your pediatrician.
- Get outside and take a walk with your baby. Sit on a bench in
  a playground. That can be a wonderful place to meet other
  mothers.
- Join a mother/baby exercise class. It's a great way to make
  friends and get a little exercise.

- If you have already identified a child care center or family child care home for your baby, hang out there occasionally, even though your baby won't actually start for a while yet. Good programs will often welcome this if you are already registered. You may get to know other parents that way, and you can benefit from watching the provider handle and care for other babies.

- If you have hired a nanny, have her start a few weeks early.

Include Your Partner in This Journey

New parenthood is a moment of mammoth change in your individual lives and in your marriage. You and your spouse or partner may both feel disoriented. Working mothers who are home on maternity leave often feel isolated. But most mothers have a partner in this initial phase. If the father is present in your child's life, both of you can travel this path to new parenthood together.

One of the significant changes when you bring your newborn home is in your respective roles during maternity leave. While you are home with the baby, and your husband or partner continues working, you are having very different experiences of new parenthood. Even if this has been the plan, the dramatic and sudden shift in roles is difficult for many mothers:

> *We were now in such unequal positions. I felt that Ralph was so lucky. He gets to go off to work, and I have to stay home with a crying baby and just give up my life.*
>
> —Patricia

> *It was very hard. My life was disrupted. But my husband would do what he would do every day. He would wake up and go to work. My life has been changed forever. His life is the same. I felt that this was not fair. All day long, I went from the baby at the breast to changing the diapers to the baby at the breast."*
>
> —Francesca

Even though it seems as though the father's role hasn't changed at all, he is actually experiencing an enormous life shift, too.

At this juncture in your life as a couple, all the dynamics change dramatically. Some of the roles are biologically necessitated if you are pregnant with the baby, give birth, and nurse. But many roles and tasks associated with a baby are not biologically necessitated, such as baby care and the increased number of household tasks: laundry; shopping for baby supplies, equipment, clothes, and food; picking up the house; feeding and bathing the baby; going to pediatrician's appointments; and looking for child care. All these can be shared.

Mothers who adapt most easily have the tremendous benefit of support—not only from close family and friends but also from their partner. Separate the baby care from the household tasks and discuss who should do what in each. Don't just assume that you will now take on all the responsibilities. Even when you are home on maternity leave, if you are planning to go back to work, figure out right from the start how to share the many new tasks. As one mother said, "I know I gave birth to our baby, and I'm the one now at home nursing him. But that does not necessarily mean that I'm now the one to scrub the bathroom." Single moms may find this needed support in close family members or friends. For married mothers, the fathers should be engaged and involved alongside the mothers.

Some fathers retreat into work at this moment. Many fathers suddenly feel an increased drive to be the family's primary economic provider. Some fathers feel shut out of the intense mother/baby bond after birth and believe that they're irrelevant at home. Fathers may also feel overwhelmed by this newborn and confused about what to do. It can be easier to go to work, where they have a clear role. As one mother said, "I think my husband was scared. And because he was scared, he worked even more—just at the time when I was scared, too, and needed him here."

It helps if your husband or partner can also take time off initially (I discuss paternity leave in greater length in the next chapter). If your partner is home with you after the birth, you can start your new life as parents together, which may prove less daunting for you and will facilitate his bond with the baby.

Fathers also need and deserve time off to absorb the depth of this transition and all the changes that come with it. The father should also experience the exhilaration of new life—his newborn. Trying to navigate this life change while continuing an intense work schedule can lead to frustration and disappointment on his side. This initial bonding will help launch his ongoing relationship with his child. Listen to this one mother, Myrna:

> *My husband, Eugene, is so close to our daughter, Bethany. I think it has to do with the fact that he was there when Bethany was delivered and stayed home with me right after her birth. He loved Bethany so much, and they're still so connected to this day. I think it's because of those first weeks, having that initial bond.*

Both mother and father should learn about newborn care so that both can be skillful at diapering, bathing, holding, soothing, and feeding. Without realizing it, Joyce started shutting out her husband, feeling that only she could do it right:

> *I felt completely and totally responsible for this baby. Nobody else could do anything for him but me. Anything my husband tried to do wasn't the way I thought it should be done, so I just took over. I got very overwhelmed. I guess I needed to be in control. My husband would try so hard. He would bring me flowers, and he would bring dinner, and he would try to help. It didn't matter, because he couldn't do for the baby what I thought he should be able to do—what I could do.*

Those early weeks center on the nursing relationship to such a degree that the father can sometimes feel pushed aside. The mom quickly becomes competent in handling the newborn, while the father gets less practice. But even though you may think your husband isn't attaching the diaper tabs just right, or talking in a sweet and soft enough tone of voice, in actuality, he is likely to be just as competent as you are in newborn care. He probably just does it differently.

Try to remember that "different" may not be "wrong." Allow your partner to develop *his* way of caring for the baby. Your baby actually benefits from two styles of care, affection, and play. There are many skills to being a good parent; if you both combine your efforts, think how your baby will benefit. As Denise found, your husband may be even better at baby care than you are:

> *The good news is that my husband is great with the baby. In fact, he is better. He seems to just know what to do; he is so calm. I remember the first time I went out to dinner with some friends after I had our baby, and somebody said, "Aren't you going to call home and see how the baby is doing?" And I said, "My baby is not with a baby-sitter, he's with his father. When I'm home all day, my husband doesn't call to see how I'm doing with the baby. He's a parent, too." There was an implication that my husband couldn't do it as well as I did. That wasn't true at all. In fact, my husband would get so angry if anyone called what he did baby-sitting. "I'm the dad!" he'd say.*

Your Marriage May Feel Stressed When You Have Your Baby

The birth of a baby, no matter how magical, can also represent a danger point in your marriage. The monumental experience of new parenthood, like many significant life challenges, can either draw you closer together as you share the ups and downs of parenting, or drive you apart as you both become stressed and exhausted. As one mother said:

> *I remember my husband leaving in the morning for work, and the second he would go, I would start to weep. I really thought that our beautiful life and our beautiful marriage were going to be completely altered, and we'd never sleep together again.*

Your marriage may be strained because of the huge amount of time, energy, and attention devoted to your new baby; lack of sleep and anxiety about the baby; concern about family finances; or all the current restrictions on your life and role adjustments.[1] One mother describes the feelings of many new moms:

There's just no end to the work—the physical tasks of diaper changing, feeding, laundry, etc.—all the things that need to be done. That eats into your couple time. For about the first six months, I just hated my husband. There were times when I would feel so resentful and so angry. Especially during the beginning of my maternity leave, when I was home with this kid who screamed all day and my husband got to go off to work. When he'd come home and say, "How was the day?" I'd want to snap, "How do you think it was?" What was I supposed to say? I knew that it was probably postpartum hormones. I was also overwhelmed by the tremendous amount of work that there is to do, and I was doing it alone.

Divorce rates spike during the early years of child rearing. By eighteen months after the birth of a first baby, 12.5 percent of all couples are separated or divorced. By the time the first child is five years old, 20 percent of all couples are divorced.[2] But your marriage may strengthen rather than fray if you actively engage with your newborn as a team, helping and supporting each other.[3]

In many cultures, there are "rites of passage" where members become tightly bonded by going through a tough or painful experience together. Becoming parents is one such rite of passage. By approaching it together, the parents can become closer. Particularly today, when so many couples marry later and have spent many years operating independently, making a concerted effort to become a *family* can bring out a greater generosity of spirit and create a stronger marriage:

Our relationship is definitely better now that we have Nate. Not that it was bad before, but we each focused on our own thing and were a little bit selfish. I think that would cause friction and stress. When Nate was born, it was a lot more of "What is the right thing for Nate?" Both of us put our own personal life goals behind what we now wanted as a family.
                                                        —Silvia

Becoming parents and being totally devoted to our children together has been an incredible bonding experience for us.

We've learned so much about each other by watching how we parent. I think we're much more aware of the land mines that sit within each other's psyche and consciousness. I've loved to see what an incredibly devoted father my husband is.

—Leah

Some mothers, like Shoshanna, talked about how both their husband and marriage were transformed:

Baruch always wanted to have kids. He was just floating on air when our son was born. Everyone said he looked brilliant. I love to see how warm and excited he is with our baby. We were looking at our baby just a few days ago and saying, "Isn't it the most wonderful thing that we have this child together," and we just hugged each other. The two of us connected again.

Many mothers delight in discovering another aspect to their husbands' personalities. Like Helen, below, they see their husbands developing and gaining greater emotional depth:

You just see that side of your husband, your partner that you've been with for all these years, and it's just a completely new angle. Ken doesn't wear his sensitivity on his shoulder, and then you see him kind of pouring it all out, see it flowing out, when his child is born. It's wonderful.

Fathers are better able to feel this excitement if they are central to the whole process. Over the last twenty years, it has become more and more common for fathers to participate in childbirth. In fact, now it is rare for a father (if he is still involved with the mother) to choose to be absent at the birth. The experience has a profound impact on many fathers. This intense involvement should continue once you come home with the baby. In fact, it's hard to imagine why the intense involvement should suddenly stop at perhaps the most critical moment—that of initial bonding with and learning to care for your newborn. For the father's sake, the baby's, and yours, he should be there during those early weeks. Help be the matchmaker so that your husband can also develop those feelings of love and responsibility.

Tips for approaching new parenthood together:

- Allow and expect that both you and your partner will care for your newborn. The father is usually as adept in newborn care as the mother; he just does it differently. Approach this as a team, but let him do it his way. Allow him to develop *his own expertise*.

- Encourage your husband or partner to take the first few weeks off so you can approach this new experience together. Fathers are also allowed by law to take a family leave (see the next chapter).

- Allow this experience to strengthen your bond. Don't be afraid to let him know you need him, that you are unsure of what to do, that you both need a shoulder to lean on and lots of hugs.

- Make sure you and your husband or partner take some time together as a couple. You have a lot to share: your feelings, your fears, your joys. Travel this experience together.

- Sit down and discuss *all the new tasks* that come with a baby. There is often more work than new parents imagine. Be thoughtful about who should do what, so no one person feels overwhelmed. Use this period of change to be open about how you will do things as a couple.

Outside Services

My health plan provided a visiting nurse for three hours a day the first week home. She would give Tyler a bath, take his temperature, make sure I was okay. I had a bit of a safety net. I knew that even if something went wrong, a nurse was coming to me every day. My family wasn't close by, so this support was valuable.

—Monique

Some mothers feel that help at home is well worth it. These services can be short-term and can make a big difference in how calm you feel. Some company health plans pay for a visiting nurse for a week or two. One of the most valued services is that of a *doula*—an experienced woman who comes to your house to help you and your newborn. She can help take care of both you and your newborn. She can give breast-feeding advice and support. She can do grocery shopping, laundry, errands, prepare meals, and assist with your older children. To find a doula in your area, contact the Doulas of North America.

DOULAS OF NORTH AMERICA:

- 1–800–756–7331
- www.dona.org

Although additional outside services can be costly at a time when newborn costs seem never-ending, they can be used for just a few weeks to help you over the initial transition. Or you can propose to friends and family that instead of buying a gift for your baby, they can supply some other valued home services. These can include:

- Housecleaning
- Meal preparation or delivery
- Grocery shopping and errands
- Laundry
- Lactation consultant
- Help with or baby-sitting older children
- Doula

What About Work During Maternity Leave?

You may have a job that is difficult to take a break from—where people depend on you or a project has been left in the middle. You may feel some pressure to continue working from home during your maternity leave and wonder how or if you should do it.

My bias is to put work aside during maternity leave if you can—at least during your initial period at home. You have only a short period where you will be with your baby full-time. The goal of maternity leave is to get to know your newborn and to learn how to care for him. It helps to be away from the distracting pressures of work. You'll benefit from a relaxed schedule where you can tune in to his subtle cues and learn how best to soothe him, how he wants to be fed, and how to put him down to sleep. You can slow down and focus just on him. You will also need this time to physically recuperate, rest, and regain your strength. Work will always be there.

Many moms talk about the specter of work always being in the background during maternity leave. That helps some to hold on to their maternity leave as a precious oasis in time. But for others, like Stacy, the shadow of work makes them feel very sad:

> *I felt that the days were just slipping by. The sand was going through that hourglass, and I was going to have to be back to work so soon. I wanted time to just stand still. And for all the anxiety of caring for him, I didn't want to go back to work. I kept saying to myself, "I don't want to leave this, I want to be here, I want to care for this child."*

You may feel confusing emotions and desires during your maternity leave. Stacy felt desperate to be with her baby, and guilty about going back to work, but she was also excited about the job she had just started:

> *When we were driving home with the baby from the hospital, we stopped at a store to buy a portable phone I could use during maternity leave. This is a terrible thing to admit, but the first picture of me in the house is on the couch holding the baby with the phone cradled on my shoulder, talking to someone at work. I wanted to stay in the loop with things at work. My job was still so new, and I was still so energized by it.*

Although I believe that staying away from work and its issues during maternity leave gives you the needed chance to just *be* with your newborn, some mothers, like Monique, appreciate the contact with colleagues and friends at work; they enjoy staying abreast with what's going on there:

> *I felt lonely during my maternity leave because my whole social system was through work, and all of a sudden I was at home all day working nonstop with this little person. I didn't have that much outside contact. Before I left work on maternity leave, I arranged to get a laptop and an Internet connection. I was then able to follow the e-mails at work. I was able to help my replacement if she needed it. The first four weeks, I checked in maybe once a week, and then as things got a little more sane at home, I was able to stay involved. I even went in for one or two client meetings, which felt good. I was able to e-mail gossip back and forth with my colleagues, and they would call me. I was paranoid that I was going to be cut out, so it helped to stay involved a little bit.*

For many of us, work is an important part of our identity. You may get a great deal of satisfaction from it. You may like staying in close touch with your colleagues. For some of you, holding on to a bit of work may feel like a lifeline during your maternity leave. It may help you to think about something other than diapers, rashes, and sleeping schedules. Many moms talk about going through a mini–identity crisis when they suddenly no longer feel like a thinking, competent, effective human being as their brain sinks into a sleepless fog. Staying involved with some projects at work may give you a balanced perspective and a bit of sanity.

Also, practically speaking, you may need to stay a bit engaged with work to keep your job from getting out of control when you go back. People may rely on you for certain essential things, and you won't want to let them down. You will be back in that world soon enough, and you want to keep those relationships strong.

But many mothers resent the intrusion of work during their maternity leave. When they are called at home or asked to come in to the office, many moms feel that it is robbing them of precious time. Leah felt that it interfered with her ability to just relax with her baby:

> *My pregnancy with Jared fell in the middle of a project I was working on that I was unable to finish before going out on leave. I agreed to take on the work during my maternity leave, which was a big mistake. I didn't want to do it, but I felt that I had to. It totally stole the maternity leave. And I didn't get the project done, either. It was a terrible dynamic all around. Five weeks after Jared was born, I arranged for a series of baby-sitters to come three days a week; I really then gave up my maternity leave. I was terribly stressed. I was exhausted. I couldn't do good work. I always felt the presence of my supervisor. It felt like she was always hounding me. I would be working and breast-feeding at the same time, and then she would call me. I felt that there was some unconscious urge on her side to ruin my maternity leave.*

Whether or not you would enjoy doing a bit of work during maternity leave depends on whether it is your decision or if you feel pressured into it. Whether or not you will want to work during your maternity leave will also depend on if, by nature, you are a work/family Blender or Separator—many Blenders enjoy staying involved a bit with work during maternity leave, while Separators may resent the intrusion of work. I go into this in greater detail in chapter 7.

It also makes a difference if you can control how and when work happens while you are home. Even if you want to stay involved, do it on your own timetable. Your newborn will demand your presence and attention according to his own needs; you don't need another set of demanding interruptions. Turn your phone ringer on only when you are available to talk; otherwise, keep it off and turn on the answering machine. You can process the requests from work and respond when it is convenient for you. You don't want to try to sound intelligent and responsive when you are frazzled and exhausted, with a crying baby on your lap.

Prepare to have your work covered while you're gone; don't commit to do any major projects while you are on leave; and once you are well into your maternity leave, decide how involved you want to be with work while you are at home. Although it may seem to you, your colleagues, and your supervisor that you will be gone a long time, very soon you will be back at work, and you all will soon forget that you were gone at all.

Elements of a Happy and Settled Maternity Leave

After listening to story after story, some themes emerged from those mothers who seemed to have a happier and easier time with their maternity leave. The mother who seemed to do well had much of the following—some of which is under your control and some not:

- *A settled, calm baby* who can be soothed easily and eats and sleeps well. Babies have different dispositions at birth. Although you can't determine your baby's temperament, you can determine how you react to it.

- *An ability to let go* of her own agenda. She sees this initial period with her newborn as a time to bond with her baby, to learn his rhythms, and how to care for and soothe him. She realizes the importance of this early bonding time.

- *A willingness to seek help if needed.* She recognizes that she doesn't have to do it alone. She is aware of what kind of support she needs and then seeks it. She leans on a sisterhood of support if she wants or needs it.

- *An engaged, supportive partner-in-parenting.* Her partner is present and involved. He or she assumes responsibility and care for the baby as well. They feel very much a team.

- *A positive attitude* about the whole experience. She sees the challenges as opportunities to grow into a new role. She views the experience as deepening and broadening, not narrowing. She focuses not on what she has given up but on what she has gained in becoming a mother.

SIX

Returning to Work After Maternity Leave

Toward the end of my maternity leave with Farrell, as I contemplated returning to work, I dreaded not being with her every minute of the day. I felt a terrible sense of mourning in leaving her. I held on to each of my final days of maternity leave as precious ones. I didn't want to see friends. I didn't want to take phone calls. I wanted only to cocoon with Farrell. I already felt nostalgic for this special period of just the two of us together. I felt the same way at the end of my leaves with Lucas and Gracie, our other two children. It did not get easier with experience. In fact, I felt the same feelings this summer as Lucas, now nine years old, got ready to visit a friend in New Hampshire for a week. I almost couldn't bear for him to leave. I understand now that the separation at the end of my maternity leave was the first of many painful separations (for me) as our children grow.

It was a complex readjustment back to work. Despite all the sadness and guilt, I would walk into the office and feel reenergized. I knew what to do, I was decisive, I was able to make things happen quickly. I was proud of our small company and wanted it to grow and be strong. Yet I had difficulty making a rapid leap from one world to the other. A few days after I had started back to work, I was deeply engrossed in a team meeting where we were grappling with some center building delays that were costing us a great deal of money. I then raced from that meeting to one with some of our center directors to go over a preschool curriculum initiative. As I settled back in my office, I realized that I hadn't thought about Farrell for the last few hours. I thought that somehow that was wrong, and I felt a pang of grief. Thus started a painful period. When I was at work, I felt guilty about not being at home, and when I was at home, I was plagued by all the work problems and challenges I had left behind.

After I returned to work, Roger took a paternity leave for one month and followed a similar pattern. He loved the island of tranquillity of his paternity leave. He easily departed from all the worries of our company and enjoyed his precious time with Farrell. When his paternity leave came to an end, he had the job of transitioning Farrell into child care. Here he was faced with a difficult dilemma. We were putting Farrell into our child care center at our office, the very first center for Bright Horizons. Both Roger and I had interviewed every teacher candidate. We had spent many painstaking hours in the design of the center and in the development of our philosophy of care and child development. She would be right downstairs from us, and we could visit her whenever we wanted. How could we be more confident of the care Farrell would receive? Yet Roger couldn't relinquish our daughter into someone else's arms, no matter how wonderful the caregiver was.

On Farrell's scheduled first day, Roger brought her into the infant room, sat with her on his lap for about an hour, and then left with her. The second day, he sat with Farrell on his lap for two hours, and then they left. On the third day, Joan, Farrell's infant caregiver, tactfully suggested that this should be a transition time for Farrell as well as Roger; she might need to venture out of his arms. Roger let Joan take Farrell, but he stayed close by her side advising her, and then after an hour, he and Farrell departed. The infant teachers then caucused with the center director. On the fourth day, the director cheerfully suggested that Roger drop off Farrell for a little while and go get a cup of coffee. Oblivious, Roger replied that he didn't drink coffee and again settled himself down in the infant room with Farrell right there on his lap. Separating was so hard.

In this chapter, I will go over the various reactions to returning to work and help you identify what is behind them. We will look at ways for you to have more choice and control in the process. I will give you strategies for easing your child—and yourself—into child care. And I will show you mothers' practical strategies for easing back to work.

EVERY PARENT REACTS DIFFERENTLY

Parents have a broad range of responses to returning to work and leaving their children in child care. This is one area where you likely will not be able to predict how you will react. Being a Camp Counselor or a Passionate Spirit will not really determine how you will feel at the end of your maternity leave.

You May Feel Excited About Going Back to Work

Some mothers are surprised to find that they actually are happy to be back at work. Abigail had been the administrative assistant in a small office for years. It was a place where she felt respected, liked, and valued:

> *I had been so emotional about going back to work. I was really dreading it. So it was odd that now it felt good to be back at work. I love my friends at work. It was a familiar job. I could handle it.*

Many mothers, upon returning to work or to school, realize how much they enjoy their job. It's a part of their life where they grow and learn in a domain separate from parenting:

> *I was excited to go back to school. I was just so happy to be thinking and discussing again—especially after having been deprived of adult community. I loved being a student, and I loved being back in school. I was so stimulated, and I wanted to take every course, and I just loved every course I took.*
>
> —Chloe

I was very excited to go back to work. As much as I adore my daughter, I just felt I would be a better mom if I were working outside of the home. I needed to be around adults. I needed to be challenged mentally.

—Shalisha

Shalisha, a product manager, had always thrived in her work world. She transitioned back to work easily, with her daughter, Amber, right downstairs in an on-site center. She continued to nurse Amber for months; the teachers beeped her whenever her baby was hungry.

Some mothers find it satisfying to make a work plan, implement it, and see the results of what they do. It is comforting to perform a role where they can see tangible results. Amanda, a financial manager, found that her structured, results-oriented work energized her for the more fluid life at home:

I loved staying home with my baby, but I also loved going back to work—adult interaction, knowing 100 percent of what I am doing. It wasn't "Why isn't she burping? Why is she pooping this color?" At least at work, I knew why I got this bill and what I needed to do with it. I felt confident.

Rebecca, who directs community affairs at a hospital, enjoyed her sense of achievement at work:

I was excited about going back to work. To have both parts of my life is very satisfying. There was something very calming about going into an office and accomplishing things, a big change from being at home. On maternity leave, you realize that if you made the bed, it was a great accomplishment. At work, it was a very, very different pace, one that was very satisfying.

Some mothers like being back in a familiar routine. They enjoy the rhythm of their workday and appreciate the structure that work creates in their lives, like Lara, a factory worker:

*I was ready to go back to work. There's a certain amount of
organization when you have to get up and go to work during
the day. I needed that structure.*

In fact, some mothers feel very guilty that they are excited to
go back to work. They think that somehow they aren't good mothers
because they don't want to stay home full-time. The stress they feel is
not having to go back to work but believing that they should want to
stay home when they really don't. Catherine, an entrepreneur with
her own trucking company, felt wrong about wanting and needing a
break from being at home with her child:

*Oh, give me all the problems at work. I don't care. Pile
them on me. Let me think. Let me talk. And I would find
myself talking constantly—blah, blah, blah. I was with other
adults. Yes, it was a relief. I was more comfortable in this
environment, where I knew how to be successful. It was
stimulating. But I felt guilty about dreading the days at
home. Isn't this awful? I felt like a bad mother for liking
work so much.*

Or You May Feel Anguish

Some mothers grieve deeply about returning to work. They may have
chosen to work, but they still anguish about leaving their children.
There are also mothers who wish they could stay home with their
child full-time. There was so much emotion around this issue that, as
I spoke to mothers, I kept a box of tissues at hand for when we discussed leaving a child to go back to work. The mother would invariably cry, and I'd find myself crying right along with her:

*I felt that I just had to buck up. But it was so hard. I would go
into the ladies' room and just keel over in the stall and sob.
I'd be thinking, "Oh my God, how is he, what is he doing?"
I just wanted to hold him.*

—Stacy

I vividly remember that first day—that feeling of my arm having fallen off, having to leave my baby. The first day back at work, I could hardly breathe. I had barely let the world in for four months. My world had been totally her.

—Leah

Although Sondra and her husband, Cody, worked split shifts in a factory so that their baby, Bryant, could always be with a parent, it was still a wrenching transition for Sondra to return to the assembly line:

I worried if they'd be okay. I was sad. I went back to work forty-five hours a week. I was tired all the time. I was working four P.M. to one-thirty A.M., and then I would have to come home and jump in bed and get up early in the morning with Bryant when Cody went to work. It was hard, and it was so sad for me.

Alena went back to work in the audit department of a hospital, and her husband and parents-in-law took care of the baby at their store. Even so, she still remembers that first day with sorrow:

I was so upset. All I knew was that somebody was pulling my baby away from me, even though it was my husband. It was torture. It was really torture. I remember that first day leaving the house, crying and crying. I just couldn't stop. I wanted it to be me so badly. It hurt so much that I couldn't let go.

It's Okay to Grieve

During my last week of maternity leave, I kept thinking that this was the last time I would give my baby his morning bath, this was the last time I would be putting him down for his afternoon nap. The thought of leaving him was overwhelming. I think the nights were the worst—saying good night and knowing that I just had a few days of maternity leave left. The first morning I got dressed to return to work was horrible, horrible. I thought I was going to be sick. I cried as I handed him over to our nanny. As I drove to work, I felt sick the whole way.

But for all that, I never really thought that I could stay home full-time. The winter set in, and all I thought was that I could never stay home all day. I'd lose my mind. I knew I needed to go back and get my own life back. As soon as I got to work, it was great to see everybody, and it felt good to put my suit on. It felt reassuring. I loved the people. I loved the job.

—Erin

Although many mothers are emotional about returning to work, many ultimately feel good about their decision. For Erin, the mom quoted above, work was important. She didn't feel she had to choose, but rather that the work role energized her for the parenting role, and vice versa.

But even if you are sure about your choice, it may still be very hard to leave your baby. The transition from baby to work can feel traumatic, and we shouldn't try to bury our emotions. Allow yourself to grieve, but also let it force you to examine your choices, and make sure you're making the right ones for you and your baby. Don't let other people decide for you.

DON'T BE FORCED INTO A CHOICE YOU DON'T WANT

Transitioning out of the cocoon of your maternity leave back into the fast-paced work world is hard, even if you know that is the choice you ultimately want to make. If that is how you feel, allow yourself to feel these emotions, then ease back using some of the tips in this chapter.

But some mothers feel terrible beyond the moment of the transition: They believe they have lost the element of choice. They may have wanted to take a longer maternity leave but cannot and, like Stacy, feel cheated of time with their baby:

I went back to work full-time after only six weeks. My boss let me work two days of the week out of my house for a while, but I wasn't happy anywhere. I wasn't doing anything right. Nobody gave me credit for working at home, so I started working very long hours there—whenever my baby was asleep. I was trying to make up for the fact that there was a perception that I wasn't working. And so then I wasn't ever being a mother, either. I wasn't happy at work; I wasn't happy at home. It was just an awful situation. I needed more time. Yes, I just really needed more time.

Have you thought about whether you really want to:

- Have a longer maternity leave?
- Go back to work part-time, at least initially?
- Stay home full-time with your baby?

Some mothers feel good about their choice to work but want to cut their hours and feel they can't—either they need to work full-time to support their family or their employers are not open to part-time work. And some mothers don't want to work at all. They want to stay home with their baby.

You may have more options than you think. Some mothers feel pressured by demands to go back to work after just a few weeks. Don't let that happen to you. Through the Family and Medical Leave Act (FMLA), you now have the right to take twelve weeks' leave for the birth or adoption of a baby if your job and your company meet certain requirements (see chapter 5). You should never feel pressured to take a shorter maternity leave. Not only is it your right, but it is critical for you and your baby to take the amount of time that feels most comfortable for you. However, the FMLA does not require an employer to provide *paid* maternity leave, and most employers don't. Mothers may need to go back to work quickly because of financial pressures.

It's hard to live with a deep regret about how much time you take for your baby. Those early moments of bonding are vital; you don't want to short-change yourself or your newborn. The first several weeks for many babies are times when they are fussy, unable to sleep for more than a few hours at a stretch, and not yet smiling and cooing. It's gratifying to traverse the often difficult first phase and then still have time at home when your baby becomes more interactive, settled, and sunny. That is a precious moment of parenthood.

One mother, Colleen, gave birth to her baby boy prematurely. She was determined to take a longer maternity leave than was originally planned, to give her baby time to become strong and settled. She sensed resistance at work but knew she had paid her dues:

> *I had been there so long, and they know me, they know how committed I am, they can wait three more months for me. I just thought if anyone gives me the remotest hard time, if anyone looks at me funny, I am going to quit. In a way, that helped, because I always felt I had an out. I wasn't trapped.*

Colleen was right—the firm realized how valuable she was and ultimately granted her the longer leave. What a shame, however, that she didn't feel support from her employer during such a meaningful time in her life. It's during critical life moments, like the birth of a baby, when we see what a difference the workplace can make. Chavonne, a single mother with two young children, went back to work with a supportive employer after the birth of each of her children:

> *There is such flexibility at my company, where I can do what I need to do as a parent. Thank God it is such a family-friendly company. Oh, I am blessed. I am telling you, I'm really blessed. That made a huge difference coming back to work, knowing I was supported as a mother.*

Give Yourself an Out

As I mentioned in the last chapter, many couples move to larger living quarters as soon as they can before or after the birth of their baby. My advice, however, is to *stay small*. Do just the opposite of conventional wisdom. After all, we don't necessarily want to do the conventional, but what's right for us. If you can, make sure you're in a financial situation where you can have the option to take a longer leave, to go back to work part-time, or to stay home.

For most of us, rent or mortgage is our largest financial commitment. You don't know yet how much you and your spouse will want to work, or how devoted to a career you will want to be, now that you have a baby. You may have more flexibility if you are not locked in to major financial commitments so early in the formation of your family.

My heart broke as I talked to one mother who desperately wanted to stay home full-time with her babies. Right before she and her husband had their first baby, they moved out of their small apartment, bought their first home, and took on much higher monthly expenses. She feels trapped, since they need her salary to cover their increased expenses. Given their current financial obligations, she can't even cut back to part-time.

I couldn't help but think that she would have been much happier to stay in their small apartment, quit her job or go part-time, be a little poorer, and do what she wanted to do in the depth of her heart. Keep in mind the need to stay flexible when you look for your dream house.

Another mother, Patricia, lived with her husband and baby in a small place in a city and was very happy with their choice. "It was really tiny. We thought of it as a wooden tent. It was tiny and old and we loved it." Later on they began to think about moving to the suburbs and finding a larger place to live. They came close to making the move, but decided at the last minute to focus on the advantages of staying small and in the city.

It's Okay to Change Your Mind

Becoming a mother is a powerful and emotional passage. Respect your emotions and deep desires. It's okay if you change your mind and decide to take a longer maternity leave, or to ease back part-time, or to quit altogether. It's also okay if you've opted to quit work and then reconsider.

When Carol got pregnant with her first child, she and her husband decided that she would quit work and stay home with her child. She had always thought that if they could afford it, that would be the way to go. But after a few months at home, she reconsidered:

> *I remember in January, I was sitting on the couch with my baby in the Snugli, where he is constantly, since he screams nonstop if I put him down. I was watching* Regis & Kathie Lee *and I thought, you know, Kathie Lee is so lucky, she gets to have a cup of coffee without anybody on her. She has time alone. She can get dressed up. Wow, that sounds so wonderful. Then my boss called with a question from work. I know he didn't want to interrupt me at home. I was walking the baby back and forth, my boss asked me a lot of questions, and I loved it! I missed that. I could answer the questions; I felt competent.*
>
> *I got off the phone, and I realized I wanted to go back to work. That was a hard realization. I felt so guilty. But I was jealous of my friends who were working. I'd talk to them on the phone. They had a list of things to do, and they could cross things off.*
>
> *I called my boss and told him I was going back to work; then I hung up the phone and cried.*

Carol cried because she felt guilty. She thought that she should want to stay home full-time, but she didn't. It's really okay to change your mind. Carol felt better about herself when she could do a good job both at work and at home. Again, choose the path that feels best for you and your child, not the one that you think society or extended family or anyone else expects.

Francesca, too, planned to quit work and be a full-time mom. She had worked long stressful hours in a construction-management firm. She didn't feel she could continue in that job and be the kind of mom she wanted to be:

> *I can't work those thirteen-hour days, and I knew I would never be able to get ahead in the company with kids. So I quit. After the birth of my baby, I visited all my relatives, all*

*my friends. But after a while I started to get so bored. I had
to do something. I hate cleaning. In fact, I don't like any
housework whatsoever. I needed to have something else to do.
So I started my own construction-management firm in my
home. I incorporated, did all the paperwork, I got a loan.*

Francesca decided to work on *her* terms. She set the rules so
that she could live her life the way she wanted. She cut back on
expenses to accommodate her reduced income. She blended work
and family during the day. Her children stayed with her a great deal.
She was up-front with prospective employees about the way work
would function in her house. She hired only people who were
attracted to the unconventional situation. She did not want to feel
stress about having her children with her whenever she wanted.

So, you may have more control in your life than you think you
have. Here's my advice:

- *Stay small;* limit your financial obligations. At this point,
  keep as much financial flexibility as you can.
- *Listen to your heart.* Disregard what all the talk shows, aunts,
  neighbors, and friends are telling you. If you want to continue
  in your job with unchanged responsibilities and hours, do so
  confidently and with pride. If you want to cut back or quit,
  know that being a little poorer, but happier, is worth it. In
  both cases, it's not a lifelong decision but one *for this phase.*
- *Don't cut off your options.* Be responsible about how you
  negotiate any changes regarding your profession, since you
  may want to revisit these decisions later.

PATERNITY LEAVE

For many mothers, returning to work is much easier if their spouse or
partner is at home with their baby on paternity leave. It's reassuring
to have the baby with Dad, and it extends the baby's time in parental
care before entering child care. It's important for both Dad and baby
to have that bonding time. The Family and Medical Leave Act allows

for both the mother *and* father to take family leave upon the birth or adoption of a baby. Although the numbers of men taking paternity leave have traditionally been small, these numbers are growing rapidly every year.

Many dads clearly would like to take a leave but feel they might be somehow penalized at work. Many men would like to be more present at home if they felt they had the option. One mother, Abigail, went back to work after three months, and then her husband, Bill, took a one-month paternity leave. He loved this time with his baby:

Oh, they had the best time together. They were quite the duo. Bill just loved being with little Garrett every minute. Bill really organized his paternity leave so differently than I did— they were off all the time, bopping around. But that was fine; Bill did it his way. I remember rushing home from work my first day back, and no one was home. No one's home! What happened? Where are they? They were at the coffee shop having coffee. Bill had left me a note that said, "Your boys are having coffee. Back in a few minutes. Relax and enjoy!" They had a blast together during his leave.

Wouldn't it be great if every father could have this special experience? And it was wonderful that Abigail understood Bill would take a paternity leave *his* way, developing his own relationship with their baby.

Leah's husband, Adam, took a paternity leave while he was working as a junior associate in a law firm. No one there had ever taken a paternity leave before, but Adam was determined to do so. It paid off, as Leah notes:

I have great respect for him having taken a paternity leave, given the pressure of his work world and being a young associate. He loved his month with Samantha. At first he got panicked about how to care for her, but then the whole experience gave him so much confidence as a parent. He just felt so blessed to be able to do it.

How Can Dads Do It?

First of all, fathers shouldn't wait until the last minute to ask for a paternity leave. Just as with a mother, it should be discussed and planned with his supervisor and coordinated with colleagues. The birth or adoption of a baby is not a surprise, so the family leave should not be a surprise as well. If the father-to-be lets his supervisor know that in six months' time he would like to take some time off for the birth of his baby, it is harder for a supervisor to discourage it on account of "work urgencies."

As I discuss in the last chapter, a new dad should try to take some time off when the baby is first born. You will always appreciate that you and your partner were able to greet this new experience together. After the initial period home, fathers vary widely in how they organize their paternity leaves. Since they do not have the issue of nursing, dads can be more flexible in how they take their leave.[1] In *Working Fathers*, James Levine and Todd Pittinsky give many practical suggestions for organizing a paternity leave. Sometimes couples decide that it is most helpful for Dad to take his leave concurrent with Mom, especially if they have older children who need to make a major adjustment as well. In Sweden, where parental leaves are common, the father typically divides his paternity leave into two parts: a week or two off with the mother when the baby first comes home, and then the balance after she goes back to work. This gives the baby more time exclusively with her parents before child care begins.

You have some scheduling options for paternity leave:

- Both the mom and dad can take family leave at the same time so they can share the experience and support each other.
- Following the baby's birth and the initial period of settling in at home, the mother and father can each work part-time. This way, they can stretch out their family leaves over more months and share in the care of their newborn baby.

- The mother can interweave the end of her maternity leave with the beginning of the father's paternity leave so they each have some transition time between work and home.
- The mother and father can sequence family leaves, with the father taking his leave after the mother's leave.

Paternity leave is still new ground for most companies, and many fathers feel subtle or not so subtle pressures to avoid one. They will need to negotiate a leave openly and responsibly with their employer for this trend to continue to grow. Fathers should consider the following issues in deciding how to craft their leave:

- Whether the mother is recovering from a caesarian section or other health complications and may need more support at home during the early weeks.
- Family scheduling. If siblings are home on vacation or are not in child care or school, having two parents around can be very helpful during the early weeks.
- How much unpaid leave the family can afford, since most companies do not yet offer paid family leave. Remember, if you make sure to "stay small," you will have more financial flexibility.
- Being responsive to work needs. Does he have the type of job where it is easier to be gone in one block of time or to cut back to part-time for a while?

Eight years ago Rebecca's husband, Carl, took a three-month paternity leave when their son was born. Even today she feels that the experience reverberates throughout her family:

Carl really loved his paternity leave. He spent half of his time with our baby, Adam, and me when I was still on maternity leave. This was heavenly, to be all together. The other half of the time Carl spent with Adam alone, when I first went back to work. This was a helpful transition for me to know that Adam was with Carl. Carl looks back on this experience as very meaningful in strengthening the bond he has had ever since with Adam. I am thrilled that Carl is such an involved dad, which has been beneficial for the whole family.

EASING IN TO CHILD CARE

I remember dropping my baby off at the sitter's that first day. It was horrible. I was totally devastated when I had to finally give my baby over to her. The baby-sitter had him in her arms, and he was perfectly happy. I just walked outside and leaned against the wall of her house and cried and cried and cried.

—Patricia

Taking Melanie in to child care that first day was probably the hardest thing I have ever done. I have a picture of her in her car seat at home as we are getting ready to go. She looks so tiny and innocent. When I look at the picture now, I think, "You didn't even know what we were going to do with you that day, did you?" When we got to the center, I couldn't even talk. The teachers must have known what to expect; they let me take my time and were very gentle. The words just couldn't come out, and the tears were rolling down my face, and I was thinking, "What am I doing?"

—Gina

For some parents, the feeling of "giving" your baby to someone else to care for is excruciating. Even if you are confident of your child care choice, the act of handing your baby over to someone else is so difficult. You may fear that your baby will shift her primary love to the child care provider. As one mother, Janet, said, "My fears were that he would bond with the caregiver, forget who Mommy is, or become confused." I want to reassure you that this does not happen. You and your husband or partner-in-parenting will be the most important people in your baby's life. But it's also wonderful for a baby to be surrounded by caring, devoted adults who can give her the feeling that the world is a safe, loving place.

Although some moms worry that their baby and child care provider will bond too much, others are concerned that the provider may not love the baby enough. One mother, Stacy, said, "I had to believe that the person who was taking him loved him or would learn to love him. I had to believe that." It can be hard knowing that you are not the one doing all the little things for your baby, and hoping that your provider will invest as much care as you would. As Stacy puts it:

I was on my way to pick up my baby one night after work, and I was overcome with fear that he would get into a car accident with my baby-sitter. I was so sad because I wasn't the one always checking to make sure the car seat was secure. I wasn't the one buckling him in. I wasn't the one making sure I was slowing down enough. I had entrusted someone enough to do that for my child, and I had to believe she would take as much care.

One mother, Evelyn, went to extraordinary lengths to first convince herself that the child care center she chose was excellent, and then that she wasn't really giving up her baby:

Once I signed up Rachel for child care, I decided that I was going to spend a full week full-time in the center. If my baby was going to do it, then I was going to do it. I wanted to find out what the center's limitations were. I helped take care of Rachel, and I helped take care of other babies, and all the while I was scrutinizing the center.

And then next Monday morning came around, and I had to go to work. Rachel was already used to this stuff. I handed her to her teacher, Ruth. I knew what the routine was. I had watched all the separation stuff all week, and I was trying to do my part. But it came time for me to say good-bye, and I started crying. Ruth had that Kleenex box right there.

I started to go to the center every day for an hour during lunch because then I felt I hadn't "left" Rachel. Basically, Ruth was a drop-off service. I dropped off Rachel in the

*morning, then I took care of her in the middle of the day, and
then she was with Ruth for another few hours while she
napped, and then I got her again. I wasn't "giving her up."
I was simply getting a couple of breaks during the day.*

You may be reassured to know that these are common, natural feelings that most mothers have, regardless of how fabulous their child care situation is. For many of us, there is no way around the separation grief. At Bright Horizons, many center directors can bring their babies and young children right to the center where they work. They can work and be with their babies at the same time. How could it get much better? But it is still excruciating for them, as this center director recounts:

*I cried all morning long the day I went back to work with my
baby at the end of my maternity leave. My husband said,
"Why are you crying? She's going with you!" And I said, "But
she's got to sleep in someone else's crib!" I still had to hand
her over to someone else. I loved the infant teacher. I had
known her and worked with her for years. I knew she'd take
great care of my baby. But it was still painful to have to say,
"Here, take her."*

Know That It's Probably More Difficult for You Than Your Baby

I had first titled this section "Easing Your Child into Child Care," but as I talked to mothers, I realized that most of the babies were adjusting fine; it was the parents who needed help. Seeing all the emotion, I started to think that we must all be making a mistake to go back to work while our children are still babies. I wondered if maybe our society and workplaces are cruel to expect moms to come back to work after a short period home, and if families and workplaces should do whatever they can do to allow a parent to stay home with the baby that first year or two of life.

Although I do believe that parents should try to take the time they want at home, I also realize that separation can be excruciating at any age. It often gets harder, not easier, as the child grows older. The transition of a toddler or preschooler to child care if she has never had the experience of nonparental care is usually much more difficult than with a baby.

Focusing on the benefits of excellent child care is key to your sense of well-being. Remind yourself that you've done a great job selecting care. Knowing that your child can benefit developmentally from quality stable care will help you feel confident of your choice. I talked in chapter 4 about how to select child care. Now let's talk about how to ease your transition into it.

Insiders' Tips

In addition to asking the very capable mothers I interviewed for their tips and strategies, I decided to turn to my other experts—Bright Horizons' directors who have helped thousands of parents and children into child care. I asked for their best advice. Over the next few pages, you'll find their tips included with my advice on how to ease into this process. I first discuss strategies for group care such as child care centers and family child care. I then talk about easing in with nannies and relatives.

In preparing for the child care center or family child care home:

- While on maternity leave, *go visit* your center or family child care home from time to time. When relatives come to town, take them there. On a rainy day, you and your baby can hang out there for a while. Both of you will become acclimated, and the caregivers will get to know you and your baby better.
- *Take some pictures* while visiting the center or family child care home and put them on your fridge. Then you can talk with your toddler or preschooler about the place, the other children, and the nice caregivers she met.
- *Focus on the benefits* of excellent child care. As one mother said, "Okay, these are some people who can help me out.

They've handled a lot more infants than I have, and I felt like it was a real educational opportunity for both me and my baby. I would learn, too, by seeing other babies and watching the teachers."

- *Bring a small book of pictures* of the family, any pet, grandparents, her bedroom, etc., that your toddler or preschooler can keep with her things to look at whenever she wants.

- *Bring tapes* of your child's favorite music. Your child will be reassured hearing her favorite tunes.

- For a baby, *bring something to leave in the crib* with home smells and feel: a crib sheet, a blanket, one of your old T-shirts.

- For toddlers and preschoolers, *bring a special "lovey" toy*—a favorite stuffed animal or blanket that she can sleep with during naptime.

- *Take your toddler or preschooler to your workplace* so she can picture where her parents are during the day.

- *Bring the grandparents to visit* the child care center or family child care home, especially if they are skeptical of child care. They may have never seen an excellent child care environment. Introduce them to the caregivers; help them to feel welcome. They may become great supporters and come often!

- *Meet other parents* who use the program. Get to know them and their children. It's helpful to have other parents to turn to with questions. They may later become part of a support network for you.

Write a Description of Your Child for Your Caregiver

Share all relevant information about your child with your provider, whether it is a child care center, family child care home, nanny, or relative. You will be developing a close partnership with your caregiver and will want her or him to understand your child intimately. Your center may provide you with a developmental profile to fill out where you can describe your child. If it doesn't have one, write up your own that you can share with your caregiver.

DEVELOPMENTAL PROFILE:

- Your child's name and date of birth
- Spoken *language* at home; any special words used
- Other *family members* in close contact; names and ages of siblings
- Your child's typical *daily schedule*, including nap times, meals, diaper changing
- Age child reached *developmental milestones* such as sitting, crawling, pulling up, walking, talking
- Times when your baby or young child is fussy, and your methods for *soothing and comforting* her
- Your methods of *behavior management* with your toddler or preschooler
- *Sleeping habits*, routines you use for putting your child down for her nap, including a special blanket or toy; mood upon waking; length of naps
- *Eating habits*, diet, favorite foods, *allergies*. Methods of feeding (on lap, high chair, at table); ability to use spoon or fork
- *Toileting/diapering habits*, type of diapers, any problems with toileting, history of rashes
- *Health* issues, including serious illnesses or hospitalizations, special physical conditions or disabilities, regular medications
- *Social relationships*, including amount of experience with other children and adults, reaction to strangers, favorite games or activities, any fears, ability to play alone
- How would you *describe* your child? What other information is relevant?
- What are your *goals* for the experience? What would you like your child to gain?

One mother, Alissa, wrote a three-page letter to the infant teachers, letting them know all about her baby, Carsyn:

> *Writing the letter made me feel like I was doing everything I could to ensure that the teachers really knew Carsyn. I was her voice, if that makes any sense. It made me feel so secure when*

one of her teachers gave me details about putting Carsyn to
sleep that matched the way I did it at home. It let me know
that she read my letter and that it was important to her.

Alissa is the office manager (and former center director) in one
of the Bright Horizons centers and works where her baby is enrolled.
Even though she is there every day, she still felt it was important to
write down all her thoughts for the benefit of the teachers caring for
her baby.

Create a Transition Plan

Make sure you allot adequate time for the transition. Don't plan to
drop off your child Monday morning and then go right back to work
full-time. Whether you have your child in organized group care or at-
home care, plan to spend the last week of your maternity leave (or
paternity leave if the father is taking one) in transitioning parent and
child to child care.

Babies often transition fairly easily (although it may be very
difficult for you). Toddlers and preschoolers need more preparation
for the transition. During the transition time, you and your caregiver
will get to know each other and start developing a mutual sense of
trust, respect, and partnership. As much as you can, go through this
transition together with the baby's father. Both of you should get to
know the child care provider, the facility, the routines, and the other
parents. Your child will also see that both parents are engaged in her
care. Susana and her husband, Antonio, took their son, Andres, to
their family child care provider a few times before she returned
to work:

We stayed a couple of hours each time and watched how the
provider interacted with the baby who was already there. We
showed the provider how we care for Andres. We met the
parents of the other baby in their care. It was important to our
provider that we all know each other, and we got to know our
provider very well. We cared for her and respected her, and
tried to partner with her in raising our child.

THE TRANSITION WEEK FOR A CHILD CARE CENTER OR FAMILY CHILD CARE HOME:

The First Day

- *Set up an appointment* with your child's caregiver to go over the developmental profile that you have written up. If you can't meet in person, set up a time when you can talk by phone. Allow her or him to ask questions. Share any fears and anxieties you may have.
- *Keep the first day's visit relatively short,* but follow your child's lead if she wants to stay longer. Bring in the items you will need to leave there: diapers, change of clothing, blanket, favorite stuffed animal, pictures. Show your toddler or preschooler her cubby or closet and where to hang up her coat. Walk around and discover the room or rooms together.
- On that first day, *be your child's caregiver* regarding diapering, feeding, or comforting. The caregivers can watch to see how you do things.
- *Quietly stay in your child's vicinity but allow her to venture forth* into children's activities when she feels comfortable. The caregiver should gently engage her in various activities.
- When your child is comfortable and engaged, *leave the room* for fifteen to twenty minutes. Let her know you are leaving in a natural, matter-of-fact way, and tell her that you will be back. *Don't sneak out* and don't waver in your decision to leave.

Subsequent Days

- *Gradually increase the amount of time* your child is in the center or family child care home and the amount of time you are absent from her.
- Before you leave each day, *give her plenty of time* to get into the children's activities. Show her that you think they're interesting and fun and let her know that you will return.
- When you return, *quietly and warmly greet your child* and congratulate her on what a wonderful job she did. Don't overdo it; just be natural.
- Spend some of your time in the center or home when other parents are dropping off. It will be helpful to *meet and get to know other parents* and to watch their routines.

A gradual increase during the week helps you both get used to the separation. You will feel strange at first without your child, but the transition week will also give you a helpful break between your maternity leave and your start back to work. Use the blocks of time that your child is there to do something for yourself: Go have a cup of tea, meet a friend for lunch, or do some last-minute shopping before returning to work. You and your husband or partner can drop off your child at child care one day that week and then go out to lunch together.

This week is also a good time to start spending small but increasing amounts of time back at work. This week will bridge your two worlds. Reconnect with your coworkers. Sort through your mail. Sit down with your supervisor and colleagues to be brought up to speed on all that went on during your absence. Start making the mental transition to your world of work and its cast of characters, priorities, and what will await you upon your full return. This transition week helps you get ready, physically and emotionally. One mother, Monique, saw great benefits to a gradual process:

> *My child care center had a mandatory phase-in process where you slowly build up your child's time there. It was a great transition. It gave me little chunks of time at first, and that was all that I wanted. I was able to mentally gear myself up for work, go buy panty hose, catch up on my work e-mails. It was good for me. It was good for my son.*

Denise used the transition week as a way to reassure herself of the quality of care her son, Jeremy, would be receiving:

> *I stayed in the classroom with Jeremy the first day. I got to know the caregivers, and I could tell them what I knew about his preferences. The second day I went to the mall for an hour, which was the first time I'd traveled really unencumbered since I had Jeremy. I came back when they weren't expecting me so that I could see what was going on. The big concern I'd had about child care was whether he'd be held and cuddled. When I came back from the mall, his teacher was sitting in a rocking chair holding him. She wasn't feeding him, he wasn't crying, she was just holding him. I thought, "Okay, maybe this isn't going to be so bad after all." I think my vision was he'd be sitting in a corner somewhere screaming, and people would be busy with other kids and ignoring him. I felt reassured.*

Cardinal Rules for Easing in to Child Care

A few principles will set the stage for your family to have a positive child care experience. Although you should try to focus on these as you begin your child care experience, they are good habits to form and continue throughout your time in child care, and later in school.

1. Maintain a *natural, positive demeanor* about the experience. If your child senses how positive and confident you are, she is likely to feel the same. If you let her know how sad you are to leave her, then she will feel the same, only stronger.

2. *Never sneak out* without saying good-bye. Your child needs to trust you. Develop the same daily routine for saying good-bye: Tell her when you'll be back and then go. Once you say good-bye, don't waver. You can always call when you get to work to get an update on how your child is feeling.

3. View your child care provider as an *important partner* in the care of your child. Develop a sense of trust, honesty, and teamwork with her or him. Work together to make this a positive experience for your child.

EASING IN WITH A NANNY OR RELATIVE

You should use many of the same approaches and principles with a nanny or a relative. Write a developmental profile of your child, and plan for a one- or two-week transition before going back to work. It's a good idea to lend your caregiver some of your most valued parenting and child development books (for a list of recommended books, see chapter 5); she or he should be learning from the same sources that you have. You might feel less comfortable advising your relative to read child-rearing books (especially if it's your mom or dad!), although you should still have thorough conversations about child-rearing philosophies to make sure you approach the care of your child in similar ways. An experienced relative or nanny will also have much to teach and show you!

Before your nanny or relative begins, develop the Caregiver

Notebook that I described in chapter 4. This document will evolve over time as your child grows and your circumstances change. Go over the Caregiver Notebook with your caregiver and keep it in a central location. Also keep in an accessible drawer the keys to the car, if appropriate, and a wallet with library and video cards and money for expenditures.

Also put a separate *notebook for daily communication* right on the kitchen counter or in a central location. Your caregiver can write down what happened during the day and any important events, milestones, or conversations. Also write down changes in schedule or anything else the caregiver may need to remember that day.

Orientation and Training

You have gone over the Caregiver Notebook and are ready to start the orientation and training week. Have your nanny or relative shadow you for a few days to observe your methods and help you at the same time. Talk to your caregiver as you go along, explaining everything that is on your mind. Use this time to begin developing a relationship of trust and respect. Your caregiver should watch how you handle your child, how you feed her and put her down for naps. Demonstrate how you soothe your child and how you play with her. For older children, talk about how you discipline. Orient your caregiver to your house and your community.

One mother, Erin, takes a full week off to train her new au pair each year (they can work only one year due to immigration restrictions). Erin's perspective on the training week:

> *I try to take everything I do subconsciously and make it conscious and speak it out loud: "Now, here's the breakfast routine." So when the kids come downstairs and there are battles over breakfast, here's how I resolve the issues. What they can eat, what they can't eat. Where they sit, since they fight over what stools they get to sit on at the kitchen counter. I always take the au pair to the doctor's office so she has met my pediatrician and knows where to go in case something comes up. I take her around the neighborhood and introduce*

*her to all the neighbors. The neighbors now know to expect it:
"Oh, here's the next one!"*

ORIENTATION TOUR:

- Show her all around the house and how all the appliances operate
- Introduce her to the key people and places in the community:
  - Friends, neighbors, relatives
  - Doctor's and dentist's office
  - Your place of work, your husband's
  - Playgrounds, parks
  - Library, museums
  - Pharmacy, grocery store, video store
  - Nearest, or preferred, hospital

Once your caregiver is well on the way with orientation and training, start leaving for varied periods of time. It's helpful to ease your caregiver into a full-day schedule over a period of days. If you leave for short blocks of time, your caregiver can experience parts of the day with your child and may have more questions for you when you return. Toward the end of the week, you might want to come home at unexpected times so that you can see what's going on at home. As one mother, Sarah, said:

I would go out in the morning and wouldn't tell my nanny when I was coming back. Sometimes I would come back a half hour later, sometimes I'd come back two hours later. I was trying to peek in and see what they were doing. And she was always doing something fun.

And, of course, you should ultimately trust your instincts about whether this situation or person is going to work out. If you have hired a nanny, take full advantage of the "probation" period. You can often sense from subtle cues and chemistry whether you have found the right person. Listen to those instincts. I believe they play a strong role in such situations.

SPECIAL ISSUES WITH A RELATIVE

It can be wonderful for you and your child to have a family member be your child care provider. Avoid some of the pitfalls, put as much energy in the transition to this option as you would any other, and you can make it work.

• *Establish good communication:* You and your family member may be close, but this arrangement adds another dimension to your relationship. Don't assume you understand each other. Talk to your relative about your views on behavior-management techniques, approach to discipline, daily schedule, toileting. Talk about use of TV and videos, play dates, and playtime outside. Your relative may not clearly know if these are important issues for you.

• *Help your relative with suggested activities:* Your relative may not have been around young children in a long time. Help your relative with a list of suggested activities and a daily schedule that can include outside play or walks, reading, games, time with friends, and naps. Find local activities and resources for your relative: a children's story hour at the library, play groups, community children's events. Subscribe to a local parent paper if there is one available. Provide a local library card.

• *Provide needed supplies and materials:* If your relative cares for your child in her or his home, make sure all the needed supplies, materials, and toys are there. If not, provide them. Stock a supply of diapers, wipes, and baby food in your relative's home. Keep a couple of changes of clothing there. Check out children's books from the local library or bring some over from your home. Evolve the toys and games as your child grows and needs more complex activities. If you are particular about your child's diet, bring a supply of healthy snacks and foods.

Together with your relative, childproof the house and remove any hazardous materials. Provide for your relative a first aid kit and a fire extinguisher if she or he does not have one. Find a local CPR or first aid class and offer to pay for your relative to attend.

• *Show your appreciation often:* Your relative is providing a wonderful gift for your child and you. Show that you value this care deeply. If your relative will not accept payment, find other ways to show gratitude—a nice gift, a dinner out, or a weekend away. Find ways to return the favor of this child care—and do it often!

• *Use available resources:* Often local child care resource and referral agencies will have resources for relatives providing child care. They may have workshops and training for "informal" child care providers. The National Association of Child Care Resource and Referral Agencies (NACCRRA) offers useful resources, education, and training, and also has a phone line and website for questions and support.

THE NATIONAL ASSOCIATION OF CHILD CARE RESOURCE AND REFERRAL AGENCIES:

- www.naccrra.org
  202–393–5501
- The NACCRRA provides a "Relative Caregiver Agreement" and brochures such as "Working Parents Want to Know: When a Family Member Cares for Your Child" and "All in the Family: Making Child Care Provided by Relatives Work for Your Family."
- The *Daily Parent* newsletter's special fall 1997 issue is devoted to child care by relatives.

EASING BACK TO WORK

Okay, so you're ready to go back to work. You know it will be difficult to leave your baby, but you're confident that she is in good hands. Mothers have found all sorts of ways, large and small, to ease their return to work. First, understand that this is a *transition*, and transitions take time. One mother, Leah, put it well:

We always underestimate the amount of time transitions can take. I remember feeling this way after living in Spain for a

year and a half. Then I got on a plane, and six hours later
I jumped back into America. It was too quick. I think the
transition going back to the work world after having a baby is
equally startling. Anything you can do beforehand to tiptoe
back in can help, even having lunches with your colleagues,
going to the office, and then maybe having lunch downstairs,
just seeing the place again before you are actually expected to
engage.

As I mentioned earlier, try to stop into your workplace for a few short visits before the end of your maternity leave. One mother, Sarah, took her nanny and baby to the office before she returned to work. She wanted the nanny to be able to visualize Sarah's place at work and understand that environment a bit. She also wanted her colleagues to meet her baby: "I wanted people at the office to see my baby to understand what I was leaving at home." This seemed like a very good strategy to help each part of her life understand the other.

One of the hardest accommodations is from baby-and-mommy mode into your world at work. Try *easing in to it gradually.* If you can avoid it, don't go back to work on Monday morning and work a full five-day week. One mother interwove the end of her maternity leave with her husband's paternity leave. For a three-week period, they each worked part-time, sharing the care of their baby. One nice aspect was that they overlapped one day a week so they could also be together that day while caring for their baby.

If you are able to take that transition week to smooth your child's passage into child care and yours steadily into work, you can get used to the new situation gradually. If you have to start back full-time, return on a Wednesday or Thursday. You may feel disoriented and emotional the first few days back. Trying to get you and the baby ready and out the door may seem impossible, and the separation may feel excruciating. If you know that you have to work only a little bit that first week back, you can make all these efforts that feel so strange, knowing that soon it will be the weekend. It may feel that you are just "going through the motions" in a bit of a fog, but even practicing or pretending to work will help you to transition back. We can learn from our Camp Counselor moms for a successful transition back to work.

The Camp Counselor's positive, can-do attitude helps her push through the difficult emotions, and she is able to focus on the positive aspects of her situation.

Focus on the logistics the first few days—getting you and the baby ready and out the door, settling your baby into child care, figuring out how to pump at work, getting used to sitting through meetings and a work conversation, making sure you don't forget to eat lunch, learning the new evening routine. These logistics will seem overwhelming at first, but if you can make them routine, they will start to feel easier.

Give yourself a pep talk as you return to work. You may feel sleep-deprived, confused, sad, and guilty. However, your supervisor will want to see you enthusiastic and committed to the job and the organization. Remember, first and foremost, that this is a workplace. Even if you are fortunate to work in a supportive work environment, the people there need you to be a dependable, competent worker who takes work priorities seriously.

People will be watching to see if you are really committed to the job; to see if they can count on you. Despite the emotional roller coaster you may be feeling, if you want and need this job, show that you can do it, as Stacy recounted:

> *My first few days back, I had the sense that I just had to pick myself up by my boot straps. I kept saying to myself, "Just put on that positive attitude, give the positive spin." It was as if I was saying to everyone there, "I'm here. I'm going to do a good job. And you watch, I'm going to be focused. I'm not going to let you down or let you see me cry." I had to buck up and make it look good.*

This is where the support of a few other working moms can help you. They can offer a shoulder to lean on during your transition back as you deal with your jumble of feelings. You can show your supervisor and colleagues that you can jump back enthusiastically into your job and your role—and then find that friend or two with whom you can let down your hair and cry, if need be. Leah found that this support really helped her:

I would go in their offices and just lean on them. Their offices were my refuge those first days back. When you go through such an important and monumental experience, it helps to share it with people who understand.

If there is a support group of working parents in your workplace, join it. As time goes on, a support group can be a resource for parenting books, doctors, schools, lessons, and advice on parenting issues. If your workplace does not yet have a working-parent group, suggest forming one to your human resources officer. Normally, it means only arranging for a room during lunchtime, then getting the word out to others in the organization. People may create a group e-mail list to communicate time and place of meetings, helpful numbers, and so on. Amanda created a small group of working moms at work, and it turned into a play group on the weekends:

There have been times where I've had to go into one of the other moms' offices, shut the door, and cry with her, "Are we doing the right thing?" It's been a great support. We are all at different levels within the company, but it makes no difference. We are all moms.

Tips on easing back to work:

- Tell only your closest colleagues the actual date of your return. This will minimize any pressure on you to produce at a fever pitch those first few days.
- Be enthusiastic and committed when you return to your job—remember that your supervisor and colleagues expect you to come back to do your job, and do it well.
- Find a trusted friend or two whom you can lean on.
- Start back midweek; it's hard to jump back Monday morning and make it a full week. Or phase back gradually during a transition week or two.
- Take a Polaroid picture of your baby each morning. It's wonderful to have in front of you a picture of your baby as

she was this morning, not last week or last month, in the outfit you dressed her in.

- Call your child care provider as many times as you want during the day. It's great knowing the little details of your baby's first days.

- Give yourself a treat to look forward to at the end of the first week—a visit to your parents, a favorite friend.

- Join or start a support group of working parents.

- Be sensitive about those people at work—women and men—who don't have children and may want to. Not everyone will want to share your joy.

Breast-feeding and Pumping at Work

I knew I wanted to pump at work, but I didn't have an office. I borrowed a colleague's office, but it didn't have a lock. I was always nervous about someone walking in. I would take off my shirt and get underneath the desk and hide in this position with both these things pumping, thinking, "If someone ever walked in!"

Sometimes I would go down into the basement bathroom at work, where there was an outlet. I would plug in my pump and then go into a stall. This pump would make a huge amount of noise. Whenever anyone would walk into the bathroom, I would think, "Oh my God, what are they thinking? There are electrical cords coming out of this stall!" I wanted to shout out that I was just pumping.

—Paige

Okay, moms, now that I may have made you a little squeamish about pumping at work, let me tell you that I think it's a great idea. Many mothers do continue to breast-feed after going back to work. Many do this by finding child care either nearby or on-site so they can leave every few hours to nurse. If that is not an option, pump at work and store the breast milk in a refrigerator or freezer. Breast-feeding can be a wonderful continuing bond with your baby, besides being healthy for her in those early months of life.

As one mother, Rebecca, explained, if she were a stay-at-home mom, her child would have the advantage of breast-feeding: "Although I was going back to work, I was determined that my baby would continue to have this advantage of breast-feeding. Psychologically, it made the transition easier to work. I wouldn't have to give that up." You can breast-feed at home in the evenings and mornings, then pump a few times at work. By pumping throughout the day, you will be able to keep up your flow of milk. Your child care provider can feed your baby the stored milk when you are not there.

Some mothers find it too difficult to pump at work and decide to nurse just in the evenings and mornings at home. If you keep to this regular schedule, your body may adjust and continue to produce milk at those times of day. Some mothers continue nursing for months this way. For more information on breast-feeding, see the resources listed on pages 216–217 in chapter 5.

Tips for breast-feeding and pumping while working:

- Find a child care provider or center close to your place of work. Give your provider your beeper number or direct telephone number so you can be contacted when your baby needs to be fed.

- During your last weeks of maternity leave, build up an extra supply of breast milk in your freezer.

- Talk to your human resource officer about designating a "pumping room" for nursing mothers. This can be just a small, private room with a comfortable chair and an outlet for an electric pump.

- If a specified room cannot be found, work with your colleagues to find a private office that you can use two or three times a day. It doesn't take long to pump.

- Store your breast milk in a refrigerator or freezer at the office. Bring freezer packs and an insulated container for the trip home.

- Of course, there is no reason why you can't pump in your cubicle if you have one. Just pin up a blanket at the opening and put up a sign that you do not want to be disturbed. One mother put up a sign: "Pumping—not iron!"
- If there are no private spaces available, you can always pump in the bathroom with a battery-operated or manual pump.

More and more offices are getting used to the idea of nursing mothers. Just think of it as your natural right. No employer should try to discourage nursing or pumping. After all, if some workers are allowed to take a break to go outside and smoke a cigarette, you should be allowed to take a break to pump! As more mothers do it, it will seem more natural and commonplace. As one mother said, "I was very casual about it. It's my choice, it's my cubicle. Just don't come in!"

I want to finish with my own personal pumping story. In the early spring of 1996, soon after giving birth to my third child, Gracie, I received a call from the White House. President Bill Clinton was convening a CEO forum at the White House on work and family issues. Seventy-five chairmen, CEOs, or presidents of major corporations across the United States were invited to a breakfast at the White House and then a full-day forum with President Clinton, Vice President Al Gore, and several cabinet members. A few representatives—myself included—from the work and family field were also invited.

Since Bright Horizons was still a fairly small, low-profile company, we were amazed to have been invited. Of course, I felt that I should go. The invitation could not be transferred to another individual, so if I didn't attend, Bright Horizons would not be represented. But I was faced with a dilemma. Gracie was only ten weeks old. I was still nursing, and I didn't want to leave her. After much consideration, I decided to travel to Washington with Gracie and my assistant, Angela, who is also Gracie's godmother. Angela could take care of Gracie during the meetings. We went down together; I settled Gracie and Angela into the hotel around the corner from the White House; then I walked the few blocks to the White House, excited about this opportunity. Since I was nursing full-time and would be gone for several hours, I packed my breast pump in my briefcase.

As I approached the entrance to the White House, I saw several corporate executives being dropped off in their limousines. I went through White House security accompanied by the CEO of Northwest Airlines, the chairman of AT&T, and the vice chairman of Texaco. They were all men in their fifties or early sixties. As we chatted politely, I handed my briefcase to the young marine guard at security. He pulled out my breast pump, held it aloft, and asked loudly, "Ma'am, what is this apparatus?" I replied calmly that it was my lactation pump. As the men with me uncomfortably looked away, the marine guard looked perplexed. Suddenly it dawned on him what he was holding. He turned beet red and looked at it with horror, shocked that he was touching it. I just took the pump from him, reinserted it in my briefcase, and said, "That's all right. I'm sure I'm the only one here today with a breast pump in a briefcase."

Although I can assure you that it unnerved a couple of men around me, it didn't bother me at all. I spent a fascinating day at the White House, ducking out of the meeting a few times to pump (that's another story—where does one pump at the White House?), then rejoined my baby and Angela in the afternoon. I felt it was very fitting to have this experience while at a meeting on work and family issues!

SEVEN

Making Life Easier
at Work

One fall day, I left work early to take our five-year-old son, Lucas, to his kindergarten soccer practice. This day came when I was trying very hard to recruit a new member to our board of directors. Bill Donaldson, whose past experience in education, public service, and business, would be a wonderful addition to our board, and I was working hard to convince him. But Mr. Donaldson, a highly sought-after and busy man, was proving to be a tough sell. I had had several long conversations with him about the company, and he had not yet committed.

Lucas and I excitedly approached the soccer field, talked to the coach and the other kids, and he settled in for the practice. Once they were well into practice, I quickly checked my work voice mail from my cell phone to see if anything urgent was on the horizon. I had a message from Bill Donaldson's secretary that he was flying to Japan the next day and could talk to me this afternoon. I thought, "Okay, this is my chance to quickly seal the deal." I called him while watching Lucas practice.

But no, it was not a quick call. Bill had several more questions about the financial metrics of the company, about the outlook of the child care industry, about some of our key challenges. While engaged in this conversation, I continued to watch my child.

Bill and I continued talking for another ten minutes. He finally accepted the board seat. We hung up, and I went on to cheer the team and my adorable little boy with the big smile on his face. I later wondered if it was a good thing or a bad thing that I combined my business call with watching my son's soccer practice. I was so grateful to have been able to witness this small but important little moment in my son's life. I also felt thrilled to get Bill's commitment to join our board before he went off to Japan. But I wondered if it was the wrong way to go about both working and parenting. After interviewing scores of other working mothers, I concluded that it wasn't wrong—I discovered that, like many women, I am a work/family Blender.

In this chapter, I will help you determine whether you are a work/family Blender—someone who combines work and family throughout the day; or a Separator—someone who establishes clear boundaries between family and work. I'll show you that either way is fine. I'll show you how being a parent can be an asset, not a liability, at work—that good parenting skills can be relevant to skills you need in the workplace. I will describe for you how friendships and a network are invaluable for working mothers. Then I'll show you a variety of flexible work schedules to get you thinking about which option (if available) can best serve you and your family as you go through different phases of parenting. If you travel for work, read how mothers have eased these burdens, and how some mothers have transformed work-related travel into a positive experience for them and their families. And finally, I will share with you how technology increasingly helps working mothers.

ARE YOU A WORK/FAMILY BLENDER OR SEPARATOR?

Many work environments do not offer employees the option of being a Blender or Separator. You may be in a job where you have to be focused solely on work when you are there; it may not be possible to handle a home issue. However, some work environments allow employees to blend or separate according to what works best for them. If you have the option, are you naturally a Blender or a Separator? Neither one is better; it's a matter of what feels most comfortable to you.

The Blender

Work/Family Blenders feel most comfortable integrating their work and family lives. They move easily between the two worlds; in fact, for many Blenders, there are not two worlds—just one integrated life with both work and family pursuits. Blenders handle home issues while they are at work and, likewise, handle work issues while they are at home. Not all work environments allow blending, but when they do, Blenders thrive. Sarah works as an academic administrator at a university and also serves as the PTO president of her children's school:

> *I'm an enthusiastic Blender. I take school calls while at work; I e-mail PTO committee members and the principal and the superintendent all the time. And when I'm at home, I check my e-mail from work and frequently take work calls. I don't find it stressful, because I appreciate that I have the flexibility I have at work. My life works better this way.*

Francesca, mother of three young children, set up her own construction-management firm in her house after the birth of her first baby. She wanted to be able to blend her work and family and keep boundaries fluid. She has created a workplace where she and her employees are all involved with one another's personal lives:

> *My employees understand that this is also a friendship. Juan, my construction manager, is more like a friend. If any of us needs a personal favor, we just ask. Juan's mother was coming to visit, and he asked if I could pick her up at the airport because his car broke down. Of course I did. Because it is a little company, we get to know each other personally. Juan knows everything; the kids love him.*
> *One day my baby-sitter couldn't come, and I had an important meeting in a downtown office building. What was I going to do with the baby? "No problem," says Juan, "I'll stay with her downstairs while you go up for your meeting." The baby slept. When she woke up, Juan called me on my cell*

phone to come downstairs and nurse her. I excused myself,
went and nursed her, she fell back asleep, and I went to finish
my meeting.

Francesca has a separate computer in her home office just for
the children. They work on their computer while she works on hers.
She has them photocopy documents and use the paper shredder.
"They play 'working.' My son thinks this is such an important job. He
is part of what I do."

Many Passionate Spirit moms are natural Blenders. Passionate
Spirit moms don't like strict boundaries in their lives; they prefer to
keep things fluid. As women of action, Camp Counselor moms are
also often Blenders. If a home issue comes up at work, or vice versa,
they quickly deal with it without getting stressed out. But as decisive,
strong-willed women, Camp Counselors can just as easily keep the
other world outside if need be. Being a Blender or Separator is on
their terms. For Francesca, a Passionate Spirit mom, blending eases
the stress in her life:

There are many important parts of my life. Instead of devoting
myself to first one, then another, and excluding everything else
for that time, I just integrate every single aspect of my life—my
children, my husband, my work, my friends, the house—you
know, the big things we all have to do.

By running her own business, Francesca can blend to whatever
extent she wants. Many other mothers are not able to do that, and
blend more on the margins. Wendy, an operations analyst and mother
of two, frequently checks voice mail or e-mail while at home. She
finds that knowing what goes on at work when she is not there
relieves stress.

I'll check e-mail, but I won't necessarily respond unless it's
urgent. I think it's almost a self-protective thing, just to see
what's on my plate—is there anything that needs a quick
response from me so that someone else can continue with
whatever they're doing?

Wendy also frequently checks in at home while she is at work. This way she never feels out of touch with either side of her life. She determines when she will check in; she chooses the interruption on her own timetable.

Blenders need to be careful to avoid working too much under the guise of blending. For some mothers who call themselves Blenders, it is all in one direction—work frequently spills into home life. Colleen, a financial planner, arranged a three-day work schedule after the birth of her baby. But work kept creeping into her two days at home:

> *The days at home can sometimes get pretty hard if there is some piece of work that I feel I really need to do. Alexander usually takes a good two- or three-hour nap in the afternoon, but if he doesn't for some reason, I just panic because I really need that chunk of time to work.*
>
> *There are days when I get frustrated being at home and being interrupted all the time by the office. I want people at work to leave me alone. I know it's hard for them to have me at home, so I try to be flexible.*

The Blender:

- Does not set clear boundaries around work and family
- Takes some time at work to handle home issues, get personal errands done, or volunteer in schools; likewise, brings work home at night or checks voice mail and e-mail and takes calls at home
- Feels more comfortable keeping a hand in both home and work matters
- Easily moves back and forth between the two domains; feels less stress by being fluid; does not feel that one domain usurps the other
- Likes the feeling of one integrated life

The Separator

Work/family Separators, on the other hand, feel much more comfortable keeping the two worlds distinct and separate. For many Separators, their modes of operating at work and at home are different. They may be hard-charging, focused, and fast-moving at work, then consciously shift to a slower, calmer mode at home. Silvia, a real estate project manager, makes a conscious shift in attitude:

> *I am clearly a Separator. My husband and I have an understanding that we do not work at home. We keep work and family absolutely separate. As soon as I reach the door of the child care center, I stop and go "Ahhh." I relax. I say to myself that work is over: "Leave it behind. This is now time for Nate."*

Some Separators talk about losing their focus or concentration if they move back and forth. Switching from one world to the other makes them feel distracted and never really "there" in any one place. Helen, a freelance consultant in an employee-placement firm and mother of two young children, feels that moving from home to work issues and back causes her to lose momentum:

> *I'm the most focused employee when I'm in the office. If I leave the office for errands, it pulls my focus, so I don't do it. If I have to go to my car and drive up and get my hair done, and then come back, I get out of the flow. It might be only an hour, but when I'm groovin', and then I stop to do that, I lose my flow.*

Some Separators also keep the people from the two worlds separate. For them, work and home are two distinct domains with different habits, modes of operating, friends, and sometimes even values. Suzanne, a corporate manager and a devoted mother, has never brought her husband to any company functions, even holiday parties. She doesn't want him to feel like the "spouse," an adjunct to her. When she is at home, she gives her total attention to her family and never gives a thought to work:

I actually feel very liberated keeping the two worlds apart. It allows me to fully throw myself into home or work and not worry about the other side. I actually feel more whole by being "separate."

I found that many Earth Mothers are Separators. They like putting all their attention on whatever activity they are involved with—whether at home or at work—and not having part of their mind on another endeavor. Jumping back and forth between worlds is not how they operate. As one Earth Mother, Shoshanna, says, "I totally separate them. Work is work, and family is family—nothing in between. Once I leave work, that's it."

Although some Strategic Planners choose to be Separators, given their proclivity for planning and thinking ahead, many will take care of home business while at work and work business while at home. Strategic Planners, however, usually make a conscious choice—given their particular work and family situation—whether they want to separate or blend, and then they stick to it.

The Separator:

- Feels more comfortable keeping work and home worlds separate

- Often uses different modes of operating at work and at home; can be hard-charging and efficient at work, and laid-back and relaxed at home

- Is better able to concentrate if the other world is not on her mind. Feels she is able to be fully "in the moment" with no distractions

- Values the momentum of staying on one track and not being interrupted

- Sometimes develops different sets of friends—one set at work and one at home—and doesn't mix the two

USE THE SKILLS LEARNED IN PARENTING TO HELP YOU AT WORK

Because I have to have so much patience with my son, I have now developed more patience with people at work. When I get these rude truck drivers who arrive at the plant and demand their deliveries, I have more understanding for them. They've been on the road a long time; they're exhausted. Now I show more respect, and I give them clear expectations for when I can get to them. I got that all through parenting my son!

—Lara

Don't you find that, as a mother, you often bring skills you have learned as a parent into the workplace to good effect? Some managers worry that once a woman becomes a mother, she will no longer be as valuable at work, but employers and workers are finding that the opposite is often the case. Let's be confident and positive that our motherhood can bring skills and attributes to help us in our work world. You may feel stronger, more centered, and more confident. You may be better able to figure out what is important and focus on that. You might have developed skills to draw out the best in people and foster their development. Maybe now you're better able to juggle multiple demands and priorities—while keeping your cool. This all can directly transfer into better performance at work. Dionna, a factory worker, felt this was the case for her:

When I became a mother, I felt more sure of myself. I began to interact with people better. Once I delivered my daughter, this strength just came over me. Little slights or problems at work didn't bother me anymore. Somehow I knew how to separate the important from the not so important.

Certainly one of the most common things I heard from mothers is how they have become more strategic and efficient at work once they have children. The boundaries on their workday help them to focus more tightly, as Colleen, a financial planner, describes:

*I now work much harder than most people, and I tend to
make the most of the time I have. I am more efficient because
I have to be. I get done in eight hours today what I used to do
in twelve. Honestly.*

Good parenting develops your levels of patience, empathy, and
understanding. Just as you encourage the development of various
skills in your children, you may find you are better able to do the
same at work. Claire, an active volunteer in her children's schools and
community organizations, feels that she has brought tangible skills
from parenting into work:

*As a parent, you learn to help your children to do things for
themselves, to become contributing members of the family. I've
brought that approach into my volunteering work and have
become much more able to delegate and to empower other
people. Also, patience is very important in parenting, both in
day-to-day interactions and in fostering your child's long-term
development. That's a new perspective I have brought to my
work in the schools. Change takes place slowly in a school
environment; I've learned to patiently but steadily nurture
progress along.*

Many good parenting skills can help you at work:

- A better sense of what is important; an ability to prioritize
- Efficient, focused work habits
- Greater patience and understanding
- Respect for the individual skills and contributions of
  employees
- An ability to support and develop skills in subordinates and
  colleagues

CLEAR EXPECTATIONS AND TIME MANAGEMENT

You want to do a terrific job at work without sacrificing your family life, and vice versa. Having a job with clear expectations and managing your time well will help you achieve your performance goals at work in the allotted time frame. In fact, many working parents have become experts in crafting a productive day where their time is used efficiently. Strategic Planner moms naturally start out with this orientation to work. But many moms from other parenting categories also find that their parenting role has honed their time-management skills at work.

Clear Expectations

If you know what is expected of you, then you will be better able to meet those expectations. Work with your supervisor to outline performance goals and define your schedule. Otherwise your day can become unbounded and unproductive. Abigail, an administrative assistant, consistently clarifies expectations and schedule with her supervisors:

> As I have taken on more new responsibilities, I've made sure that I clearly understand what they are. In return, I am really clear about my boundaries and needs. As a result, I have the ability to speak up when something is just too much of a burden for me and my family.

Irene, a senior manager, finds that it is vital to set clear expectations for those who report to her. Her advice to people at all levels:

> It's important to draw boundaries. I don't mean to draw boundaries and say, "I'm only going to do 80 percent," but establish what you will commit to, and make it reasonable, and then organize yourself to do 100 percent of it. This is important for both women and men. Increasingly, you see fathers who want flexibility in their jobs and lives and are prepared to do that kind of juggling. Yet I think people are sometimes afraid to ask for clarity.

Effective Time Management

If you are in a work situation where you have the ability to organize your own day, take control of your schedule so that you can make it work for you. You may have felt no urgency to get your work done and leave work at a reasonable hour before having children, but now you realize, as Evelyn, a research scientist, observes below, that every minute is precious:

> In a minute you can make a phone call, do an e-mail, start a letter. Don't wait, because you don't have the extra forty-five minutes at the end of the day. I no longer say, "Well, I'm going to be here until eight anyway, so I'll go ahead and stroll over and get another cup of coffee and see who I can talk to."

Mothers find a variety of ways to manage their time during the day. Silvia, a real estate project manager, makes sure not to schedule early-morning or late-afternoon meetings. Such meetings can complicate child care drop-off and pickup:

> I don't want to put that stress on my myself. If Nate is having a bad morning, I want an extra ten minutes at the child care center with him, without feeling I have to drop him to make an early meeting. I also don't want to have to get up from a meeting at five forty-five P.M. and say I have to go pick up Nate from child care now.

THE IMPORTANCE OF FRIENDSHIP AND A NETWORK AT WORK

> There's a sisterhood at work. It's amazing. As soon as I became pregnant, people came crawling out of the woodwork— all these women I didn't know before were just so excited for me. We've definitely created a wonderful camaraderie.
>
> —Shalisha

Since work takes up such a large part of your day, it's much nicer if the environment is one that you can look forward to each day. Friendships can make a difference. Dionna is a mother who works from four P.M. to one-thirty A.M. in a paint department at a factory. Over time, the workers in her department have forged a tight-knit "family" of people who are there for one another whenever necessary. It has become a strong support in Dionna's life:

> We now eat dinner together every Friday night during our shift. We all put our names in a bag. Whatever date you get, you cook the whole dinner for all fifteen of us and bring it into the plant for that Friday night. We found that it brings about such a positive work relationship. The men are just as excited as the women. They even outcook us!

These social relationships can be a source of sustenance, information, and advice. Parents find useful information on child care, pediatricians, behavioral issues, schools, summer camps, and so much more through their networks of friends and colleagues at work. One mother, Erin, a banking executive with three children, found that the common ground of parenthood helped forge closer bonds even with her supervisor:

> I work for a woman who has a five-year-old son. When she hired me a few years ago, one of the things that she was really excited about was the ability to share strategies about mothering. When I first started working here, she was just trying to toilet-train her son. She called me into her office and asked me if I could take a minute with her. She had me on the speaker phone with her nanny, and the three of us strategized a potty-training approach.

Stewart Friedman and Jeffrey Greenhaus, social scientists at the University of Pennsylvania, have studied men's and women's work lives extensively and found that friendship networks at work are particularly useful for women: "We believe that networking for women has a greater impact on enhancing self-esteem, generating a feeling of acceptance, and creating a pool of useful information and advice. In turn, those resources help make women more emotionally available and more competent in their family roles."[1]

Some mothers feel they need to focus intensely *only* on work during work hours, so they can leave promptly afterward for their family. Some never take a moment to chat or join friends and colleagues for lunch. Although efficiency and focus matter at work, don't shortchange yourself the wonderful benefits of friendship. It doesn't have to take much time. As I discussed in chapter 6, you can create a parent support group that meets regularly during lunch. Denise, a mother of two who works in the benefits department of a government agency, started just such a group that meets monthly:

> *We started out with formal luncheon discussion topics, then booted that format and continued with a less structured one. It was great to have an instant network of other parents with whom to share ideas, problems, developmental stages, resources, and even equipment. Our agency actually wound up plugging it as a benefit and put a flyer in the new employee orientation packet. It's best to ask human resources for permission and a space to meet.*

Develop *your* sense of teamwork at work. It helps if you don't feel alone. There may be some times when you will have to shift things around to go pick up a sick child or attend to another family matter. As Joanne found, if you are on a team, you may be able to help one another out a bit:

> *There are people at work who cover for me or help balance out the projects that I can't get done if I have to leave work suddenly for a sick child. But "shield and protect" is a negative term; we have a very positive dynamic. We have a group of people here who work closely together and help each other out a lot.*

TIME-SHIFTING: MAKING THE MOST OF A FLEXIBLE WORK SCHEDULE

We discussed flexible work options in chapter 3 and how to negotiate for them. Flextime is one of the most valuable options employers can offer to working parents. The needs of children and families don't often fit neatly around a fixed nine-to-five schedule.

If you are in a work environment that allows a flexible schedule, think creatively about what would work best for both your family and your workplace. If you plan ahead, you may be able to do a better job both at work and at home. This will validate to your supervisor that flexible work options make sense. It helps if you can demonstrate, and even document, how this schedule will help improve your performance or output. Periodically review your schedule; you may find that as your work and family lives change, you will also want to alter your work schedule.

As you consider your own situation, let me share with you some approaches that other mothers have created. I think of this as "time-shifting"—shifting time from one domain (work or family) to the other in order to do a more responsible job with each.[2] One of these time-shifting approaches may work for the work/family phase you are in. Some scenarios entail sharing the responsibilities with a partner-in-parenting; other scenarios work if you are managing on your own.

Staggered Work Schedules

This is probably the most common time-shifting approach for dual working parents. Many parents stagger their daily work schedules to maximize the time their child is with a parent. For example, one mother, Gina, gets up at six A.M., snuggles with her preschooler, Melanie, who is just waking up, and then goes off to work early. Her husband, Samuel, lingers with their daughter over breakfast, has some playtime at home, and then takes her into the child care center between nine-thirty and ten A.M. Gina leaves work at three P.M., picks Melanie up right after she has finished her nap, and enjoys the rest of the afternoon with her. Samuel works until six-thirty, then they all have dinner and spend the evening together. This schedule works well for them. Melanie spends a couple of hours in preschool in the morning, has a nap, and then goes home. It allows for a shorter day in child care and for each parent to spend time with Melanie.

STAGGERED WORK SCHEDULES

	6 A.M.	7	8	9	10	11	12 P.M.	1	2	3	4	5	6	7	8	9	10
Gina																	
Samuel																	

Home   Work   Child care needed

Alena, who recently switched to a similar schedule, found that her arrangement has improved both family and work dynamics:

I now arrive at work at seven-thirty A.M. instead of nine A.M. This is my most productive time at work. I can just sit there and do six hours of work in three. Since I am there almost an hour before everybody else, there are no phones ringing or interruptions.

And now I am able to leave work at four P.M. It was so much harder when I used to leave the office later. There would be just enough time to pick up the children at the child care center, hurry them home, quickly do the bath, quickly do dinner, read a story, go to bed. It was awful. Everyone was tired and cranky. I felt I was getting upset with them, but it's not their fault. I was the one with the schedule. That was what made me change everything around.

The staggered work schedule can work particularly well where parents have nontraditional work hours. Giovanna, an inventory planner, works from seven-thirty A.M. to four P.M. Her husband, Jorge, is a chef who works late afternoons and evenings:

I just wake up, shower, and go. Jorge will wake up later with our four-year-old, Leonor. They both like to sleep in. He'll give her a bath; they'll have a leisurely breakfast and morning together. They'll play, and then Jorge will drop her off at child care between twelve and one P.M. I then pick her up at four P.M. It works so well.

Paige and Larry stagger their shifts for slightly different purposes, and they alternate their schedules throughout the week. On Monday and Wednesday, Paige works an earlier shift so she can leave work in time to run errands, make the dinner, and do any needed household work. Larry picks up their two children from child care, and they arrive home to a cooked dinner and a neat house. On Tuesday and Thursday, Larry works an earlier shift to do the household chores, and has dinner waiting when Paige arrives home with the children. They like this schedule because it allows a parent to quickly finish off household chores before the children get home. The parents can then devote their evenings to family rather than housework.

Many of these time-shifting schedules have the added advantage of giving each parent some time alone with the child during the day. Many parents also mention that in staggering their days, they are able to get some periods of quiet, productive time at work in the early morning or late afternoon/early evening, when there are fewer people around and phones are quiet.

The Afternoon/Dinner Break

Maureen, a chief financial officer of a small company and mother of a one-year-old, uses a common time-shifting technique for people in jobs with long hours. She leaves work early, around four or four-thirty P.M., to pick up her daughter, Christie, from child care after her nap.

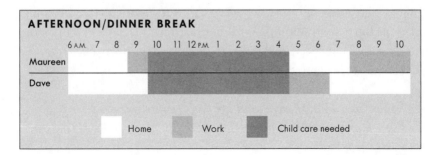

They spend the rest of the afternoon together, then have dinner with Maureen's husband, Dave. Maureen and Dave put Christie to bed at seven-thirty P.M., and then Maureen goes back to work—either at her desk at home or back to the office, two miles away. She works late and sleeps in a little later, since Dave gets up with Christie. They all eat breakfast together before Maureen heads off to work, and Dave takes Christie to child care.

> *I cherish the late afternoons with Christie and dinner all together. And then I'm working in the evening, when it's really quiet and I know Christie's asleep. I get so much work done. This schedule has actually allowed me to be much more efficient but still have a good chunk of time each day with my daughter.*

Many single mothers with demanding full-time jobs often use this strategy. By leaving work early, they can have a few hours of unrushed time with their children during the late afternoon and evening. They then finish up their last hour or so of work after their children are in bed.

Break in the Middle of the Day

Maria has two school-age children and works as an office manager for a small nonprofit agency. Her children go to a Boys & Girls Club for after-school care. Maria waits to take her lunch break at two P.M. At that time, she drives to her children's school, picks them up, and they have a snack while she has a late lunch; then she takes them to their after-school program. She likes this schedule because it gives her a chance to see her children during the middle of the day and hear about their school day while it is fresh on their minds:

> *Even though the Boys & Girls Club is fairly close to their school, and they could probably easily walk, I still like to go get them. It's a good routine. It's something nice to look forward to in the middle of the day. I just don't want to go an entire workday without seeing them.*

MIDDAY BREAK

	6 A.M.	7	8	9	10	11	12 P.M.	1	2	3	4	5	6	7	8	9	10
Maria																	

Home　　Work　　Child care needed

Overlapping Work Weeks

Myrna and her husband, Eugene, work different days of the week, overlapping on two of the days. This way, child care is necessary for only two days a week. They both work for factories that keep operations going twenty-four hours a day, seven days a week. Eugene works Friday through Monday, and Myrna works Monday through Friday. Eugene takes care of their two daughters on Tuesday, Wednesday, and Thursday while Myrna works, and Myrna takes care of the girls on Saturday and Sunday while Eugene works. The girls go to a family child care home on Monday and Friday.

OVERLAPPING WORK WEEKS

	Monday	Tuesday	Wednesday	Thursday	Friday	Saturday	Sunday
Myrna							
Eugene							

Home　　Work　　Child care needed

In another case, Justin, who works as a solo practicing attorney, takes every Friday off to be with his son, Nate, and then he works on Saturdays while his wife, Silvia, is home with Nate. Although both his parents work in demanding jobs, Nate is in child care only four days a week.

Parents may work these schedules for a period of time to economize on child care costs and to maximize the time the child is with his parents. As the child gets older and child care costs decline, the parents often move back to more similar schedules so they have more opportunities to be with each other, too.

Compressed Work Weeks

Some parents choose to work three or four ten- to twelve-hour days rather than five eight-hour days so they have a shorter, more intense work week and can spend additional days at home. Vivien, an information technology specialist, works three ten-hour days. She is away from her twin babies just three days each week yet works enough hours to qualify for health insurance and other benefits at her company. Her husband, Donnie, who works more traditional hours, drops off and picks up the children from child care when Vivien works these long days.

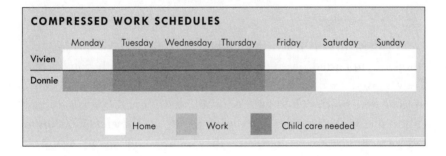

Opposite Shifts

Some couples choose to work in jobs where they can have opposite shifts—one works the day shift and the other works the evening or night shift. People who work in hospitals, factories, call centers, or other places of employment that are open twenty-four hours a day can arrange such schedules. Couples do this for a number of reasons: so that the children can always be with a parent; if quality child care is unavailable; or to economize on child care costs.

Sondra and Cody worked opposite shifts in an automotive factory the first few years after their son, Bryant, was born. Cody worked from seven A.M. to three P.M., then came home and took over from Sondra, who worked from four P.M. to one-thirty A.M. Cody spent the afternoon and evening with Bryant and put him to bed on the late side so that Bryant slept in late. Sondra came home from work at one-thirty A.M. and slept until Bryant woke up, usually around eight-thirty or nine A.M. She then spent the day with Bryant and often took naps when he napped. Sondra felt that this worked well for them the first few years: "We tried as hard as we could to stay on opposite shifts so Bryant would have one of us with him at all times. That was very important to us."

When Bryant reached preschool age, they enrolled him in a company-supported on-site child care center, and both Sondra and Cody moved to daytime shifts. Although the opposite shifts had worked well from a child care point of view, Sondra and Cody had almost no time with each other during the week. They felt good about Bryant's child care center, and they now could spend evenings together as a family.

Jeannie moved to a nighttime shift once her two children entered elementary school:

I just love being home when my kids get home from school, and I like to get them up and off to school. I like to be their bookends when they go to school. I loved that shift because I got to work when they were asleep, and then I slept while they were at school.

I am impressed by how many parents go to great lengths to arrange work schedules that allow them to be with their children. This often comes at the cost, however, of husband and wife spending time together as a couple. They can feel like "ships passing in the night." It seems to many working parents that something always has to give during those first few years: time together as a couple, unrushed time with children, unrushed time at work, or all-important sleep. This adds to the stress we feel in our daily lives. Flexible work options and a supportive employer can ease the stress but usually cannot eliminate it entirely during this phase.

Parents often choose opposite shift arrangements or overlapping work weeks only during the early years of a child's life and then move back to more traditional shifts with the child going to child care or school. No one schedule works forever. As your children grow, periodically change your work schedule to meet changing work and family needs while still maintaining or improving performance at work. You will feel better about both work and home.

TRAVEL FOR WORK

Frequent or even occasional work travel can cause stress for you and your family. You may feel guilty about being away from your children; you may be worried about things getting done in your absence. You may even wonder if people can survive without you at home. One time when I was traveling for work and Roger was at home with three-and-a-half-year-old Farrell and one-year-old Lucas, I called home around nine P.M. when I thought the children would be sound asleep. There was no answer, so I called several more times, wondering where the family could be after bedtime. On my fourth try, Farrell answered the phone in tears. I asked her where Daddy was, and she answered that he had left to go play basketball with his friends, and that she and Lucas were home alone. My heart skipped a few beats as I said, "Daddy left to go play basketball?" I told her to sit right by the phone and I would call her back. I frantically called our neighbor and friend Scott, and asked him to rush over to the house to see what was going on. I imagined all sorts of horrible things.

As it turned out, after the children fell asleep, Roger had gone to exercise in the basement. My repeated phone calls woke Farrell, and she thought that her daddy must have left, since she didn't see him right there in the kitchen or living room. She woke Lucas, and they both started to cry. Roger wandered upstairs after a nice workout to find both Farrell and Lucas sobbing; our friend Scott sitting in the kitchen with both of them on his lap; and me on the phone, frantic.

Sometimes travel for work can be hard on everyone. As an education administrator and pastor, Nichelle has to travel frequently:

Last year I was traveling over Mother's Day. The kids were not happy. We decided to celebrate Mother's Day the Wednesday after, but I couldn't even make it home by then. That really upset them. So we finally celebrated the following Saturday. I opened one of the gifts, a small picture of my two sons and my husband. My younger son said, "We got this for you, Mama, because you travel all the time, and we don't want you to forget what we look like." I just cried. I felt so bad. He said, "Mama, it's okay, we know you have to travel for work, but this way you can remember." So I took the picture and put it on my key chain, and I carry it everywhere with me.

There are ways to ease the stress of work travel. Some mothers have even found that it can actually have some positive dynamics all around, if handled right. The first and most important thing is to make sure that life at home goes on smoothly in your absence. If you are the "household manager" in charge of daily family life, write up a schedule of what needs to be done each day. Be detailed about times, locations, carpool information, what your child needs to bring, etc. Give this schedule, along with your travel itinerary, to all people who might need it—spouse or partner, child care provider, neighbors/ friends involved with carpools, play dates, etc. Include important local telephone numbers such as pediatrician, dentist, best friends. Also include your contact number and pager number, if you have one. Save all this on your computer so you can modify it for your next trip. It's helpful to have a cell phone so you can be contacted if needed. Stacy, a skilled Strategic Planner mom, is always organized regarding her frequent work travel:

I pull on every resource I can when I travel. As a single mother, I set aside my pride and ask for support. I rely on everyone and everything. I type up a schedule that says who has Jeffrey, who picks him up, and what he needs, and everybody involved gets a copy of the schedule and my travel itinerary. I send it to his teacher at school so she knows how much care, time, and patience have gone into trying to make sure that this child feels comfortable about where he's going. The teacher will play an active role. She'll say, "Oh, Jeffrey, I see on the schedule today that your nana is picking you up from school. Let's get ready for her." I call Jeffrey every night to review the next day's schedule with him.

Always arrange for a back-up person to pick up your child from school or child care in the event that your trip home is delayed. Don't just assume that your flight will arrive back on time and you'll easily be able to make it to the child care center before it closes. Make sure this back-up person is authorized to pick up your child. Many couples have a policy that one parent is always in town—they never both travel at the same time if they can prevent it.

Many mothers have a standard packing list to make frequent travel easier and quicker. Keep a toiletry kit and other travel necessities in your suitcase so you need to add just your clothes. You might even keep a couple of framed pictures of your family in your suitcase so you can set them up in your hotel room—to have a bit of home with you on your travels.

If you are confident that the kids are in good hands, you and your partner may even start to view work travel, if done in moderation, as an opportunity for the parent at home to have special time with the children. Family dynamics shift with one parent gone for a couple of days—and sometimes in ways that are nice. Roger and I have found that another side of our relationship with the children emerges when only one of us is at home. We do different things with the children. I like to have us all get in our pajamas right after dinner, then go hop in my bed, where I read books to the children. Roger likes to take the kids to the town center for an ice-cream cone after dinner, or he might organize running games out on the lawn.

If you are the household manager, maybe these trips will allow your partner to develop more skills in that arena. And if you are a "gatekeeper," think of how thrilled your partner will be to finally be able to do things *his* way. You may even learn that his way works, too, so you can be less of a gatekeeper!

In preparing to travel for work:

- Type up your child's daily schedule; include school schedule, lessons, play dates, etc., and items your child needs to bring for each event
  - List important local telephone numbers: pediatrician, dentist, key friends, teachers
  - Attach your travel itinerary with your contact number, pager number, cell phone number
  - Give schedule to spouse, child care provider, elementary school teacher, key friends
- Arrange for authorized local back-up person to pick up your child if your return is delayed
- If you can, always keep one parent in town and available for child care interruptions, etc.
- Create a standard packing list for business travel

Some mothers will leave a note or picture under their child's pillow or in the dresser drawer for a little surprise once Mom is gone. It's nice to keep a connection with your child while you're away. You can call home in the evening, or leave messages on the answering machine for your child, or send your child her own e-mail message. One mother, Barbara, a senior executive who took long business trips, would write a note for her daughter for each day she was gone, and the child would open a new letter each morning. Farrell and I have a tradition of each looking at the moon at eight P.M. and knowing the other is doing the same.

Many mothers see airplane and train travel as a rare opportunity to peacefully read a book, look through catalogs, or write letters, and they look at time in the hotel as precious alone time. Tina, an operations manager, found it pleasant to have some time with no other distractions:

I have started to change my attitude about travel for work. If you have to do it, get a good attitude. I love to go to the hotel, take a bath, and not be interrupted. I love to just have some

time to think and not have to fix meals and do this and that
and be responsible for everybody. I like to go out for dinner
with other adults and talk about adult things. Travel can
definitely be a break for me. I know the kids are fine.

Some parents will occasionally use business trips as an opportunity to do some small thing on their own. They might add a little bit of time during the trip to go visit a friend or relative. They might go shopping or get a massage—things they might not ordinarily do in their busy daily lives. They may even catch up on some sleep! Monique, a financial manager, enjoyed this time on her own:

When I travel, I bring all my workout stuff and go to the gym.
Just being in a decent hotel and relaxing and going to bed
early and getting a good night's sleep are all really nice.

There may be some trips where bringing your child or your whole family would be appropriate. If you're going to a city where you have friends or relatives, it might be a good chance for you all to get together. Some mothers go to conferences in wonderful locations where the hotel is already paid for, so they bring their family to sightsee while they are in meetings. They may add on a day or two for family vacation time. Or, where appropriate, it might be nice to bring one child with you for a special trip with Mom.

Be prepared for reentry issues when you return home from a trip. You may come home to an exhausted or harried spouse, if you have young children or a busy family schedule. Your children may be clingy after your absence. Or your spouse and children may have become nicely independent and self-sufficient, and you feel a little left out. Be sensitive to feelings on all sides, and give yourselves some time to ease back into normal daily relationships.

TECHNOLOGY CAN HELP YOU AS A WORKING PARENT

To Stay in Touch

Barbara, a public-company president with two children who are now grown, has always been a master at using technology to keep in close touch with her children. When her children were in middle school and high school and no longer had after-school care, they would each call Barbara's pager number as soon as they got home from school. They used the lighthouse code for love: 1-4-3. Her son's code was 1431, and her daughter's code was 1432. Even if Barbara was in the midst of a meeting or negotiation, she could see by the pager codes when each child arrived safely home.

Later, when cell phones became more common, Barbara bought both children a cell phone so they could call their mother or she could call them. She had a busy travel schedule, but her children always felt free to call her at different points throughout the day to check in, even when she was traveling. The children continued this habit throughout college. Barbara would frequently get quick calls from her college-age children, just to fill her in on news or to get some help with homework. Technology, in particular the cell phone, allowed Barbara to always feel in close touch with her children.

To Work More at Home

With computer, phone, fax, and e-mail, working at home has become easier for parents. Many parents work at home a day or two each week or even full-time. Some parents use the time that they save on the commute to volunteer in their child's classroom. A telecommuting day or two also can give some relief from interruptions at work, and many people, such as Susana, feel they can be more productive on those days:

I use telecommuting days to handle bigger projects that require some thinking and uninterrupted time. The other thing telecommuting gives me as a mother is silence—time when no one needs me, time when it is completely quiet and I can think. And you can stay in your pajamas if you want.

But the technology that allows you to work at home can bring disadvantages as well. As Leah points out, work can be harder to turn off:

Although working at home can be much easier on you as a mother, it can be much harder on you as a professional. Work is always there in front of you; the phone and fax don't necessarily stop when you want to stop. I find that I work at nights and on the weekends, whenever I can find a free moment.

Doing most or all your work at home requires thought, planning, and organization. There are several excellent books and websites that can serve as important resources if you want to set yourself up to work at home.

RESOURCE BOOKS FOR MOMS WORKING AT HOME:

- *The Work-at-Home Mom's Guide to Home Business*, by Cheryl Demas
- *The Work-at-Home Balancing Act*, by Sandy Anderson
- *How to Raise a Family and a Career Under One Roof*, by Lisa Roberts

USEFUL WEBSITES:

- www.wahm.com
- www.en-parent.com
- www.hbwm.com

To Help Spouses Coordinate

Many busy working parents rely on e-mail and voice mail to stay in touch with their spouse or partner during the day, particularly if they have changing schedules and frequent travel. If all the family logistics are handled through e-mail during the day, then the evening can be free of family scheduling. It's also great to use for a sweet message or "I love you" during the day. And with the advent of handheld computers and schedulers, spouses can "beam" schedule information into each other's Palm Pilot or other handheld device.

To Stay in Touch with Schools, Teachers, and Child Care

Many teachers now communicate with parents by e-mail. More and more classrooms and schools have websites where parents can get and give needed information. Registration for schools and camps is happening more frequently on-line.

One mother I talked to installed her Palm Pilot software on her home and work computers. Her nanny was able to input events for her: school assemblies and closures, scheduled pediatrician and dentist appointments, etc. She could even input play dates. The mom then downloaded this information onto her Palm Pilot in the evening.

More and more child care centers are using technology in creative ways. Some offer Internet viewing of the classrooms so parents can log on at work and watch special activities or just see their child during the day. Some centers digitally scan in children's artwork or photographs and then send these "portfolios" via the Internet to parents. The parents are able to receive this information whether they are at home, at the office, or on a business trip. These same portfolios can also be sent to grandparents or other relatives.

Some child care centers and schools take digital photographs of activities and learning throughout the day. The parents arrive at the end of the day and receive a wonderful visual collage of their child's day. One mom has her nanny occasionally e-mail her digital photos of her daughter during the workday, just for fun.

To Help Children with Their Schoolwork

If going to the town library is difficult because of your work schedule, help your children do school research on the Internet in the evening if you have a home computer. Books and resources can be ordered on-line.

Barbara, who traveled with a laptop, told me how her middle school and high school children would e-mail their research papers or compositions to her when she traveled. She would edit them and e-mail them back.

To Use as a Parenting Resource

Parents can go on-line to access parenting information, to research children's products and equipment, to investigate schools and camps, to learn about medical information, and so on. There is practically no subject that cannot be researched on the Web.

There are also many useful chat rooms on-line for parents, working mothers, divorced and widowed mothers, and more. Parents are tapping in to on-line communities for both information and support.

USEFUL WEBSITES:

- www.parentsoup.com
- www.parentsplace.com
- www.parentstages.com
- www.abcparenting.com

EIGHT

Creating a Strong Family Culture While Working

It's so rewarding to see our family as its own unique unit, growing together, laughing together, learning together—I wasn't sure we could do it with our busy work lives. Yup, it's not always a joy ride, we fight together, too. But there's a feeling that's different when we're together. There are no words to adequately describe our pride and joy. We're family— we're there for each other.

—Irene

There's one thing every working mother I know wants: a strong family life. A strong family is one with a deeply felt connection, a sense of belonging and security, and unconditional love. A sense of family is defined by these values, not by any particular configuration of individuals and roles. I saw an incredible array of family models among the mothers I interviewed—married with both spouses working full-time; part-time working mothers; part-time working fathers; single mothers; extended families with grandparents or grown siblings living together; lesbian couples; older parents with young children. A rich family life can be created in any of these or other configurations, and regardless of whether a mother works.

In this chapter, I will show you how parents have created strong family lives while working. I will go over the importance of family culture, what creates a strong one, and how work can add to it rather than take it away. I will discuss the importance of rituals and traditions in family life and how to adopt them. I will tell you how busy working parents create intimate connections with their children and partners, as well as homes that reflect this intimacy.

As working mothers, we may worry that we are sacrificing family cohesiveness because we are gone during the day. A vibrant family culture can help you to feel close even if you work long hours and time together seems rare or rushed. For many of the mothers I interviewed, their families have evolved a strong culture and identity despite the pressures of working. As I tried to understand how they forge this feeling of family, I found that many of them are doing three things: 1) They accept themselves, and their children, for who they are; they let go of trying to be perfect. They allow their personalities and interests to be part of the family, and through that, a family identity is created. 2) They share their world with their children, including their world of work. 3) They have developed their own unique set of family rituals and traditions. These are often small and simple, but they help to create a family identity and bond.[1]

I would like to share with you in this chapter many of the wonderful and interesting things I saw parents doing to create a strong family culture while working. This will be an important backdrop for the chapters that follow on daily family routines.

ACCEPT WHO YOU ARE

Don't let the guilt of being a working mother make you try to be something that you are not with your children. Take the pressure off; you don't need to be perfect. Since you are gone from your children during the day, you may feel that you need to hide your feelings and needs to devote yourself fully to them in the time you have together. But by trying to be selfless and impervious to difficult emotions, you set up a model that is impossible to live up to and not even desirable. As one mother, Dionna, says:

> *Hey, I'm a real person, and my little girl needs to know that. She needs to know that it's okay to make mistakes and that mommies make them, too. I remember growing up, my mother*

always seemed to have her ducks in a perfect row. I always
felt that I had to live up to that model and do everything
just right, and if I didn't, I was inadequate as a person.
By showing my little girl that I am a real person with my
strengths and my flaws, I feel that I am allowing her to
develop herself as a whole person, too. I don't want her to
have an unrealistic expectation of perfection.

If you liberate yourself from attempting to follow some ideal model of motherhood, you may feel more relaxed to find your own style of mothering; and your family culture becomes stronger in the process. Denise spends long days at work, and she often feels rushed to get everything else in. However, she has always been a woman who loves to laugh, and she has brought her personality and sense of fun to her family:

We always have plenty of fun moments together every day.
Especially when you work, it's easy to lose sight of the light
moments; sometimes there is not that much fun. There is not
that much time. I want my kids to grow up with the sense
that there is so much to be happy about in the little things
of everyday life. I like to joke around a lot and tease. I like
to be playful. When I lighten up, we just all have a really
good time together.

Family life flourishes with intimacy and honesty. By showing your children the breadth and depth of your emotions, you allow them to develop a broader range of emotional reactions as well. By seeing you as a real person, not just someone who cooks, drives them places, and picks up after them, your children will understand and respect that their parents are also people with needs and desires. Elizabeth, a mother with two young children, described a morning when she had to leave for work and her husband was sick in bed:

I was running out early for an important meeting, and the
kids were fighting with each other. I told them that I had to go
to work, that Daddy was not feeling well and needed to sleep,
and they just had to get along and cooperate until the nanny

*came. Daddy really needed them to be good. They listened
to me with wide eyes. Before I knew it, they became very
cooperative; they started working on a puzzle together, and
they were very sweet. I think it's important for them to see
that not everything can be provided for them, that their
parents have needs sometimes, and that they have to help
their parents, too.*

Children can enjoy learning about your life, including stories
from your own and your partner's childhood. This becomes part of
your family culture. Children will love hearing stories of the important people, events, and traditions of your past, and even some of your
childhood exploits. My husband's story of a neighborhood bully who
put a clothespin on Roger's nose and made him sit with it on for an
hour fascinates our children. They have asked him to retell it over and
over. It helps them to see that their father had childhood struggles,
too. After reading fairy tales and storybooks, our children often ask us
to tell them stories about our childhood. This is also part of their
childhood literature.

We can share not only our childhood stories but some of the
life lessons we have learned along the way. Particularly as your children grow older, they can benefit from some of your life wisdom, and
grow to know and understand you more. One single mother, Maria,
dropped out of school when she was seventeen and got pregnant.
Although she leads a happy, productive life now, she regrets many of
her early actions and often shares her life's past with her children:

*I tell them I messed up in school big-time, and there's no way
you can get it back, there's no way. So before you make an
error, double-check what you're doing, because there are some
things that you cannot fix, and you can't go back. I didn't
really know anything about life while growing up. So I make
sure that my kids know everything that they ask. I teach them
through my life.*

A rich family culture is created out of your and your partner's
interests and values. It reflects your personalities and your passions.
Not only do the parents create and affect the family culture, but so do

the growing children with their different interests and approaches to doing things. Jaclyn, a mother with a grown daughter and grand-daughter living with her, her husband, and their three small adopted children, describes her approach to family life:

Always show a lot of love toward one another, and respect one another's decisions and beliefs even if they are different from your own. I look at each individual, see what their gifts are, and try to focus toward that. I try to focus them on their gifts— the positive things they can do to help themselves, and then the family grows as well.

Your children can gain immeasurably from your interests, whether work or extracurricular. Patricia and her husband, Ralph, love to camp and hike. Ralph grew up overseas, and his mother lives in Europe. Patricia and Ralph started to share their passion for travel and camping even when their children were very young. The children now love these pursuits, which have become cherished family activities.

A lot of stuff that Ralph and I love to do, we do with the kids. These things are now favorite family interests. We just went camping for a week, and the kids loved it. We've gone to Europe many, many times with them to visit Ralph's mother. We don't stop our interests because of the kids. We've tried to include them.

Your children can benefit and grow from sharing your world. A few years back, I went to Kosovo on a program to examine the plight of young children in the aftermath of a brutal war. Although our children might have been worried about their mother going to such a troubled spot, instead they became part of the adventure. Each day I sent back a daily dispatch by e-mail. Farrell and Lucas, my two older children, were very engaged in the trip. When I returned, they initiated a campaign at our church and their schools to collect bookbags of school supplies to send to several elementary schools in Kosovo. They benefited greatly from the experience, and we loved participating in the endeavor together.

Sharing your interests, needs, and emotions with your children:

- Helps them develop empathy and respect for you—to know that you do not exist just to meet their needs
- Allows and encourages your children to develop a breadth and depth of emotional responses
- Can help you seem more real and accessible
- Can model for children constructive ways to handle anger, sadness, disappointment
- Can open new worlds to them as you share your interests and passions

SHARE YOUR WORLD OF WORK

Work takes up a big part of your life. Your family culture can include this world—the people, the personalities, the experiences. Many working parents believe that when they leave work at the end of the day, they need to leave it completely behind *for the sake of their children*. In fact, some mothers are afraid that their work will compete with their children's affections, so they talk about it as if it's something they wish they didn't have to do, although they actually may enjoy it very much. In trying to show their children that they are the most central and cherished part of their lives, they may disparage their work or never mention it.

But children can benefit from gaining a window into your work world. For many mothers, work carries many positive benefits—deriving a sense of accomplishment, earning a living, using different skills, creating friendships, relishing challenge. Children may find these aspects uplifting. They can learn about the productive world outside their home and begin shaping their views of what they want to be when they grow up. They can be proud of their parents' achieving something they have worked hard for. And it can give them a positive view of what their own future may look like. But work is not always positive. Children can also learn from stories of how you have handled conflicts and obstacles. You can model constructive ways to handle disappointment.

For better or worse, Roger and I have always shared a fair amount of our work world with our children. They have been most fascinated with our difficult or disappointing experiences at work. When we or our company have really struggled, the kids have been full of questions about how we can "fix" things, how bad was that loss and does it make us sad or mad, what do we do about that person who was really mean to us. They want to understand who could fire us and how it might happen. I believe it helps them as they think about their own struggles. The challenge is to share the ups and downs in an appropriate way, without making them anxious or worried.

Ellen Galinsky, president of the Families and Work Institute, recently wrote a book, *Ask the Children: What America's Children Really Think About Working Parents*, based on a large national survey. She found that children in general do not think their parents' jobs are a negative element in their lives. They just wish their parents could enjoy their working lives more. By leading our children to think that we don't want to go off to work, we may be telling them that we're unhappy with our life choices. It may discourage children about their own future. Galinsky goes on to state:

> *[The study's] findings make it clear that mothers and fathers are not adequately communicating how much they like their work. . . . The byproduct of such behavior is that we are not fully teaching our children about the world of work, particularly that we can care about what we do to earn a living. Our interviews with children make it clear that children think it's positive for us to care a great deal about our jobs, just as long as these feelings don't eclipse our feelings for them. . . .*
>
> *When we don't share our feelings about work constructively, we are missing a chance to help frame our children's views about their own work in the future.*[2]

Galinsky also noted that when we consciously or subconsciously relay negative feelings about work, our children worry about us. If it's appropriate, occasionally take your children with you to work. It's a great way to share that experience with your children and helps them visualize what you do with your day. Some parents invite colleagues over for dinner. Many parents participate in Take Your Child to Work day each April. One mother, Amy, found that her son loves to go with her to the college where she is completing her degree in occupational therapy: "It's important that Douglas understands what I do with my time. I talk to him about it, and he helps me study sometimes. Now he wants to be a doctor."

Your children will appreciate learning about the characters and personalities that populate your day. These people also become part of the family lore as you share ongoing sagas of their lives. As they see you interact in your work world, your children get to know you in a fuller, richer way. When your children tell you about their day, tell them about yours, too.

When you share your world of work with your children, they can:

- See the positive personal benefits you gain from working
- Begin to glimpse the world of work and start forming views of their own future
- Understand the value of hard work and effort
- Learn from stories of how you handle conflict, struggle, and disappointment
- Visualize what you do with your day
- Find out about other important people in your life

IMPORTANCE OF FAMILY RITUALS AND TRADITIONS

To this day, my husband and his family remember and talk about how Ron's dad had this daily ritual of making the kids breakfast. Even though his father had a job with long hours, and his mother stayed at home with the children, Dad would get up early and make the breakfast every day. That's the thing I have heard most about—Dad's breakfast for the kids.

—Natalie

You may feel as busy working parents that you don't have time or energy to develop family traditions. But cherished family traditions don't have to be elaborate. Like Natalie's example above, some of the most memorable family rituals are simple: This busy working father made breakfast for his children, not elaborate or time-consuming, just a breakfast. And all the grown children still remember it fondly. Perhaps even more so as a busy working parent, creating a small moment of magic that becomes a ritual can sweetly punctuate an otherwise harried day for you and your children.

Family traditions become the stuff of cherished memories, marking childhood with the sense of the special. When I was growing up, my father would make a big batch of milkshakes every Sunday night after we had our baths. We would drink the milkshakes and watch *Wonderful World of Disney*. Dad would always experiment with flavors, and every Sunday we would sing out, "Best yet, Dad. This is the best yet"—even if ingredients like raw eggs went into them. My siblings and I still lovingly remember this little tradition. Family rituals become part of your unique family culture, which helps to make a child feel part of something intimate and special.[1]

The importance of rituals and traditions in a family life:

- Helps to shape a childhood and becomes an important part of childhood memories
- Adds a bit of specialness to a daily routine; pulls us out of the ordinary
- Can connect a child to his broader family and history
- Enhances a child's and family's values and belief system

Holiday celebrations can involve cherished traditions. Pamela, an artist and choreographer, uses her passion for art and music to craft family get-togethers that are infused with beauty, color, and aesthetics. Her family loves to celebrate many holidays. They work together on centerpieces for the table and decorations for the house. As Pamela says, "For me, I love to create a whole sense of an event—a celebration—the food, the decorations. It's the aesthetics as well."

And, as Pamela indicates, it's not just the holidays that are observed in this household:

> *We have our big ritualistic breakfasts on Sunday mornings, since we often can't sit down together as a family during the week. We have long conversations during these special meals. You know, I see a lot of kids in restaurants who cannot sit and have a meal for longer than a few minutes, because that's probably how their family's lifestyle is, but we linger.*

Rituals need to be special to your family, emanating from family interests. Think about the little things you and your family do during the day, week, or year that you all seem to enjoy. Then make them rituals that you will all come to expect and savor. They can add a unique feeling to your family life.

A sampling of family rituals:

- Special Monday-morning breakfast to launch everyone into the week
- Dancing to favorite music after dinner
- After-dinner walks with the dog
- Nightly tickles on the bed after baths
- "High tea" following the school- and workday
- Lighting a fire in the fireplace after dinner
- Friday-night family video with popcorn
- Saturday-morning cuddles and books in the parents' bed
- Sabbath-eve dinners together
- Weekend pancake breakfasts
- Popovers on Sunday morning
- Saturday- or Sunday-morning walks to church or synagogue and then pastries afterward in the neighborhood bakery
- Spring planting together as a family
- End-of-school-year camping trip

- Annual visit to a cherished grandparent's gravesite and then a picnic in a beautiful spot nearby

What small events do you all enjoy that you can make into family traditions?

FINDING TIME FOR YOUR CHILDREN

Sometimes children of working parents feel they have to compete with work for our time and attention, and they need a chance to know that they matter, too. This is an area where we can learn from our Passionate Spirit moms, who seem to have a natural ability to stop and embrace the little and big experiences with her children. She is better able to put aside her to-do list and savor the little moments that all add up to important child development. Whether it is stopping to really listen to what your toddler is trying to say to you, or to sit down and listen to the piece your nine-year-old wants to play on his bugle, or to let your four-year-old explain all the details in his drawing, focus your attention on those brief moments. As one mother, Gina, said:

Just when I'm rushing into the house after work and have a million things on my mind, my daughter will say, "Mommy, will you play dolly with me?" And then I think, "Uh, playing. That means I can't get dinner made." But to her, play is for five minutes, and then she's on to something else. It's so important to stop and smell the roses, no matter what it is, whether it's looking at that bug she just found on the sidewalk or whatever.

One strategy many working mothers use (as well as any mother and father) to keep a close connection with their children is to carve out some *special one-on-one time* with each child. It can be as simple as lingering at bedtime to talk and cuddle, giving each child time to bring up whatever is on his mind.

Tina and her two children have a tradition where either child can ask for "mommy time" whenever they want it—no matter what they are doing. During mommy time, Tina takes the child on her lap in the rocking chair, and they rock and cuddle as long as the child wants. Tina's children know that mommy time is inviolable time that is just for them:

We started mommy time when they were real little and felt out of sorts and didn't know why. I would always ask, "Do you need some mommy time, some mommy love?" We would just sit and hug—always in the rocking chair. Even now if my ten-year-old daughter, Kiesha, is upset, I will ask her if she needs mommy time. She always says yes.

One educator and mother, Linda, loves the approach of "special playtime." The child always gets to choose the activity. During this time, the parent doesn't answer the phone or doorbell but pays exclusive attention to her child. The father or a friend can be with any other children, or if they're old enough, the others play independently and have their own special playtime at another point. You can give an hour each week to this special playtime, perhaps on Saturday morning, or even every other week.

Working mothers find ways to offer their children focused time even during busy days at work. Barbara has always kept a demanding work and travel schedule, but she had an iron-clad understanding with her two children that they could call her at work or on the road and she would take the time for them, either at that moment or soon after. These calls continue today:

Often it is just to touch base, just to say hello and know that I am there for them. Each child would call for different reasons, and they continued to call me throughout their teens and even now, in their twenties. Tommy just called me from work so I could help him calculate if he'll have enough money in his 401(k) plan when he's sixty-five years old!

Barbara's children are now grown, but she talks to each child every day, sometimes several times. When I asked her twenty-one-year-old daughter, Alison, about this relationship, she responded:

*I am much closer to my mom than my friends are to their
mothers, and none of their mothers works. It's ironic, isn't it?
I wonder if it's because I always had the habit of calling her
frequently whenever she traveled. I knew she was always
there for me—even if I called in the middle of the night, which
I did a few times during finals!*

Some parents create special one-on-one outings with a child
on the weekend, when they have more time. The outing can be one
that your child chooses, or you can come up with the idea. Even if it
is nothing out of the ordinary, it feels special for both of you to have
this alone time together. You can often see a different side to your
child when you have him all to yourself. One mother always brings a
camera so she can document the moment. Jane, a good friend of
mine, still talks with affection about the trip she and her father made
together when she was twelve. Her dad took each of his children on
a special trip when they reached that age.

A sampling of special one-on-one outings:

- Bike rides to the bagel store together
- Saturday-morning visit to the playground or park
- Weekend swim at the Y
- "Date" night with a movie and dinner
- Leisurely errands on Saturday afternoon with a stop for hot chocolate
- Special playtime at home with no interruptions
- Breakfast out before drop-off at child care or school
- Special pickup at school or child care for a lunch out
- Visit to the reading room at the library
- Camp out together in a nearby campground

CREATING INTIMATE SPACES AT HOME

I talked in chapter 5 about staying "small" in your choice of home. I advised this mainly so a couple just starting to have a family can have maximum financial flexibility on how much they want to work. But another reason to stay small is that young children will just stay in whatever room you are in, particularly during the first few years. During many of my interviews, the mother would describe to me how she and her spouse had set up a playroom for the children in the basement or in some other area of the house, but the children played in the kitchen anyway.

Young children love to be around other people, most particularly their parents, and they are drawn to cozy corners and nooks—intimate family spaces. Do you ever find that your family tends to congregate on a small window seat, on your bed, on a carpeted stair landing, or around a small kitchen table rather than in the dining room? None of these spaces requires money to create, just a sense of capturing these natural family gathering spots. When I was on pregnancy bed rest for four months with Gracie, our family life revolved almost entirely around our bed. Although I got tired of sleeping with a bed full of cookie crumbs and Play-Doh, we all have warm memories of that winter curled up in the bed, playing board games and reading.

There is even a growing movement within the architectural field of the "not so big house."[3] Instead of "bigger is better," many architects are designing for smaller, more natural family gathering areas: alcoves and nooks, chairs gathered around a window, a small play area in the corner of the kitchen, a window seat. One of my favorite childhood poems, "Halfway Down," by A. A. Milne, is about just such a small space—a stair. The poem begins:

> Halfway down the stairs
> Is a stair
> Where I sit.
> There isn't any
> Other stair
> Quite like it.

In quality environments designed for early childhood education, spaces are explicitly designed for small gatherings of a few children and an adult—to read books, to draw pictures, to play games. We call these "interest areas," where we might have a small table and a couple of chairs with a box of writing supplies, markers, paper. In another corner, we might have a small carpet with a couch and a bookshelf where a teacher and a couple of children can cuddle and read a book. The smallness of the space makes it feel especially inviting.

I love to visit the homes of early childhood educators who have young children. Many of these mothers have carried these concepts into their homes with great effect. One mother, Susan, stocks a small cupboard adjacent to the kitchen counter with art and writing supplies so her child can draw and color while she makes dinner. In the corner of her living room, she keeps a small quilt with cushions on the floor and a basket of books for a reading corner. In her daughter's bedroom is a basket with dress-up clothes on a small carpet for a make-believe area. In her very small apartment, Susan has created inviting spaces for her child to pursue play activities while they stay close together.

When Lucas and Farrell were two and four years old, they would occasionally have "meltdowns" when we arrived home after a day in child care. One of our wise toddler teachers, Lorraine, suggested we create a snug reading corner with cushions, security blankets, and books that we could go to right away when we got home. While still in the car on the way home, we would talk about going to "our cozy corner." Farrell and Lucas would each think about what stuffed animal or book they would take to the corner. This little ritual transformed our reentry home. The spot felt intimate, contained, and warm. Our ten or fifteen minutes there launched the initial mood of our evenings.

Considerations for your home:

- Young children like to be where parents are. Create a small play area in the corner of your kitchen and living room. As they get older, they will learn to play more independently.

- Children gravitate toward small, cozy spaces: corners, nooks, alcoves, stair landings.

- Determine the natural family gathering spots in your household. Make them more inviting by adding seating, cushions, and lighting.

- Create two small spaces for your young child: a *writing area* and a *book area*. This emphasizes the importance of reading and writing and gives your child his own space.
  - Writing area: can be a corner of your kitchen counter with a box of pencils, crayons, markers, paper, envelopes so your child can draw and write whenever he wants
  - Reading area: create an inviting book area with a basket or shelf of children's books and a comfortable cushion or chair

TELEVISION AS A PART OF YOUR FAMILY LIFE

As a working parent, your time with your children is limited; don't let TV dominate their time at home. As an occasional break, television for children can serve a useful purpose—if you closely monitor what they are viewing. Many working parents use television as a transition between child care or school and home, or let their children watch TV while they are trying to prepare dinner.

But children will ultimately do better if they learn how to have downtime on their own, or how to make this transition from child care or school to home, without the television. If your child is in a structured child care or school situation, some unstructured playtime at home, without resorting to the TV, would be much better. As you think about creating a strong family culture, think about alternative activities to watching TV.

Also the content of television shows and videos has become increasingly violent. Let's look at some media facts:[4]

- Children's television shows contain about twenty violent acts each hour.

- Even G-rated movies and videos contain too much violence: On average, there is a total of ten minutes of violent acts in each G-rated film.
- Children spend an average of three hours each day watching television shows or videos.
- Less than half the parents report watching television with their children, though it's important to filter what the child sees and then talk about it.
- More than half of all children under the age of eight have a television set in their bedroom, and 29 percent have a VCR in their bedroom.

Some young children have difficulty discerning fantasy from reality. Violence on TV leads many children to believe that the world is a mean, scary place. Watching a great deal of TV during the preschool and elementary school years influences children during a time when they are just establishing their habits for social interaction and conflict resolution. Television programs often model violent and aggressive ways to solve problems, which some children carry over into everyday life. Even if it's good guys killing bad guys, the message for children is that violence, injury, and killing are the ways to solve problems.

In my view, the most critical reason to limit television and

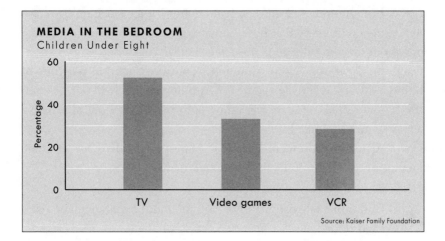

MEDIA IN THE BEDROOM
Children Under Eight

Percentage

60

40

20

0

TV   Video games   VCR

Source: Kaiser Family Foundation

videos is that they use precious time during which children could be otherwise involved in more productive activities. Childhood is the time to learn how to interact with other children, to use the imagination in creative play, to develop fine motor skills in drawing, and gross motor skills in physical play, to practice reading skills, etc. These are critically important activities that foster social, emotional, and intellectual development during the formative years.

Having said all this, many responsible parents do have good reasons to allow their children to watch *limited* TV and videos. Not all TV programs and videos are violent; there are certainly some good programs. Entertainment and relaxation are an enjoyable part of life. Also, some parents, such as Silvia, below, have found some real value in allowing their child a short video as a time to wind down, just as many parents watch a little television or read the newspaper as a way to relax:

> *Early childhood educators are so adamant about not having videos for downtime for kids. However, that is how we get through certain periods of time. If we are all a little bit stressed and we have just come home from child care, we let Nate sit and watch a Scooby-Doo tape. Time to just chill out a little bit. My husband likes to come home and put his nose in the newspaper. That is his chill time. So why can't Nate have his?*

It's the excess of viewing time, the unsupervised watching, and the violence of the programs that are the problem, not TV itself. The American Academy of Pediatrics recommends that children under the age of two not view television at all and offers the following advice to parents of preschool and school-aged children:

- Carefully select specific programs for your children to view. Plan the viewing times in advance so your children will understand how much TV they are allowed to watch.
- Watch the program with your children to filter and discuss what is going on. Teach critical viewing skills: "Do you think there is a better way for him to solve this problem than punching him?"

- Do not permit TV watching during dinner.
- Do not allow a TV set in your child's bedroom. Keep the TV in a central place where viewing can be monitored.
- Set a good example: Limit your TV watching, too.

Help your child develop some other habits to wind down after child care or school. Instead of watching a video, perhaps he can quietly color or play with his pet or stuffed animals, or even better, you can read some books together. Contrary to calming a child down, TV more often will serve to stimulate and agitate him. Over time your child can learn to see TV and videos as a special treat, not a daily habit.

USEFUL WEBSITES FOR REVIEWING MOVIES AND TELEVISION PROGRAMS:

- www.kidsnet.org
- www.parentstv.org
- www.moviemom.com
- www.screenit.com

STRONG MARRIAGES/PARTNERSHIPS ARE A FOUNDATION OF THE FAMILY CULTURE

A strong family culture can be created in any family configuration—single or married, reconstructed families with stepparents and stepsiblings, grandparents caring for children, and others. When there is a single parent, the family culture is created by the parent, children, and partners-in-parenting. With two parents at home, there is an added dimension of the parents' marriage or partnership.

If a marriage exists, the strength of this relationship is crucial. A strong, happy partnership creates a positive family climate, and that in turn will promote healthy child development. The best predictor of a child's ability to forge lasting relationships as an adult is the strength of his parents' relationship. You model, day in and day out, relationship dynamics, and your example instills in your child lasting values, roles, and habits.

But even in the best marriages and partnerships, there are disputes and problems, even crises. These can also serve an invaluable purpose, in modeling for your children constructive ways to problem-solve and settle conflicts. They can see how you handle difficult emotions and positively negotiate solutions. Let your children observe how you share responsibilities, love each other, resolve problems, plan together, express conflict, and have fun. Whether you like it or not, your partnership is a schoolhouse for your children's future relationships.

Loss of Marriage Intimacy

As I mentioned earlier, marriages are at higher risk in the early years of child rearing. Your normal way of operating in the world is thrown into disarray; there is a great deal of stress as you and your partner adjust to new roles, learn how to parent, and balance work and family pressures. Separation and divorce rates go up during these early years.

One of the biggest challenges to the marriage after the birth of a baby is loss of intimacy. You seem to have so much less time for each other, you're exhausted but still have to get up and work, and much of your emotional energy is now transferred to your child, as this mother describes:

> *We're not as intimate now because we can't be. There is another person living in the house with us now. I miss the relationship my husband and I had over those many years. It has changed. We don't have as much time alone together. To be exhausted just sitting on the couch is spending time together, but it's not spending time together like we used to.*

Or, as another mother put it aptly:

> *There has definitely been some loss of intimacy. Let's just say there is no way we will have any more children, because we are never in bed at the same time, nor are we ever awake at the same time.*

Because there seems to be just a small sliver of time between when the children are in bed and when you go to bed, it doesn't seem long enough to have meaningful discussions and relaxed time together, especially if you have work on your mind and a busy day ahead. Working couples are often on different work and sleep schedules, and overlap during only a few family moments. It sometimes feels easier to not get into any intimate discussion—and certainly easier to avoid thorny issues. As one mom says:

We just don't have time together. All our time is spent pretty much with our children or at work, so I guess communication has broken down a little bit. We tend to get impatient with each other more quickly. We have misunderstandings about little things more often. It's hard for us to just pick up and start talking at night when the kids are in bed. I mean, we do, but it's mostly about small stuff. We don't start talking about the important stuff that needs to be hashed out because we know that takes a long time. We tend to avoid those subjects.

Keeping the Flame Alive

Working parents find that they have to make more of a concerted effort to find time for themselves as a couple. Before children, those intimate times may have just happened, but now they take a special effort, especially if there are demanding work pressures. The most common strategy couples use is to set up a *regular date night* where they can simply be with each other. Some couples purchase tickets to a theater or musical series; others go out to the movies and dinner, either together or with other friends. Some just go out for a long walk together—without children. If it is a regular date night, the children will expect it as a normal part of their routine. Helen and her husband, Ken, have a Thursday date night that has become an enjoyable evening for both parents and children:

We have a dear friend, Lisa, little Brett's godmother, who comes every Thursday at six-thirty P.M. We usually don't leave

the house until seven-fifteen. We hang out, we do the baths
together. I talk with Lisa, and then we go out. When Ken and
I finally sit down together, it's so refreshing. It's quiet, it's
relaxing, and we're communicating. I now can't imagine not
having our Thursday nights.

The children love Lisa, so it's great for them, too—they
look forward to "Lisa night." I tell them right when I pick
them up from child care, "It's date night, and Lisa's coming
over!" and then they're psyched. That just sets the stage.

Helen mentions another important thing—establishing children's expectations in advance. If you set up a predictable routine, the children will expect it.

Many couples work hard at *adding a little romance* to their time together. Carrie and her husband, Andrew, often don't eat dinner until their young children are in bed. The food may be simple, but they will light some candles and turn the lights down low. Chloe and her husband, Seth, pour themselves a glass of wine, put on soft music, and light a candle after the children are in bed. The setting lends to the mood of intimacy, and they love to linger. "It creates a sleep problem, but we treasure having that time," says Chloe.

Nichelle, a busy education administrator and pastor who travels a lot for her job, has found that she and her husband, James, have reverted to their old ways of courtship:

Before we got married, my husband used to send me love
letters twice a week. So now we have e-mail, and we e-mail
each other love letters. Last week I was picking up my e-mail
while on the road, and up pops this note from James. The
heading was "Hey, girlfriend, sure do miss you." He wrote all
these sweet little things like he used to do when we were
having a long-distance relationship. He tells me that he's
learning to court me all over again.

Gina and her husband, Sam, have made a pact to remember to hug and kiss each other every morning and every night—a simple thing that they had often overlooked. Their daughter has now gotten into the pact as well, and they have regular family hugs throughout the day. Some mothers told me how they occasionally *do the unexpected*. Make an impromptu lunch date with your spouse. Leave a note in his briefcase or pocket. Leave a special voice-mail message at work.

It is often the *small gestures* that make a big difference—doing something that is loving or considerate for your partner, like bringing a cup of coffee into the bedroom in the morning, giving a backrub, getting a favorite dessert. The daily life of working parents is so full of the mundane that stopping briefly for a gesture of kindness can mark the day with a little bit of magic. As Wendy explains:

> *It's just the little things one does every day that make all the difference. That's why I married my husband, because he did all the little things—the little hugs, getting me a cup of tea, etc. It's not about bringing home that big bouquet of flowers or whatever. It's just the day-to-day of how you treat your spouse. I think that's what kind of makes up your life—it's all the little gestures.*

Stopping to *seize a special moment* in the midst of the routine can also create a halo of intimacy. Passionate Spirit moms are especially good at this. One mother told me about how she and her husband, who are apart a great deal due to work travel, suddenly left a wedding reception and took a long walk together to prolong a special conversation and feeling they were having. Or perhaps you find yourself in a wonderful conversation just as you're about to go to bed. Don't lose that special moment, even if it means less sleep for one night.

Many men, however, may understand intimacy differently than women. Understand not only what you need for intimacy but what your partner needs as well. Each of you must be sensitive to your partner's needs and desires and find ways to express that intimacy.

Mothers' tips for keeping intimacy:

- Regular date night; semiannual or annual weekend away together

- Add an element of romance: Eat a candlelight dinner after the kids are in bed, relax on the couch with wine and soft music after the children are in bed, sit outside under the stars—and bring the baby monitor
- Focus on the small gestures, acts of generosity and consideration
- Keep your sense of humor and playfulness
- Write a letter or note to express your feelings
- Allow time for an important conversation—don't cut it off even if it means schedules go awry
- Physical expression of love each day—even if it's just a sweet hug between events
- Lunch date together if you can leave work
- Go to bed at the same time and make love!

Support and Appreciate Each Other

Stewart Friedman, a researcher and author of *Work and Family: Allies or Enemies?*, finds that working husbands and wives each seek greater support—but in different areas of work and family. Women look for support from their husbands with child care and household tasks. Men look for support from their wives on personal and emotional growth.[5] I found in my interviews that wives and husbands are seeking, in particular, more acknowledgment in those areas where they have taken on additional roles that are relatively new for their gender. Mothers want to be celebrated and praised for managing to work and have a family. They want sensitivity for all they are doing at home while also trying to hold down a job. Fathers want consideration for doing so much with the kids, and for doing it willingly:

> *It's important for Peter to be acknowledged for all the dad stuff he does. I don't know if this is true of all men, but I think it probably is, and he really thrives on acknowledgment. He's the dad who goes on field trips, the dad who volunteers in the classrooms. You should see how other mothers praise him.*
>
> —Selena

I have noticed that my husband will stand up at the lecture podium at the university to publicly state, and then apologize, that he has to leave at 3:40 to get the kids. "I thought I could stay later, but my wife has a meeting, so I have to pick up the kids by 4:00." Then all his students say, "He is such a great professor. He is so committed to his kids." His assistant will tell me later that, at 3:45, then 3:55, people are telling him to hurry and wrap up or he'll be late getting the kids. If it was a woman up there, she would be all sweaty because people would feel that she is not committed enough to her work. If a woman mentions the fact that she has kids, she is going to lose the respect of the audience. But for men, it's considered great.

—Francesca

Although this seems to Francesca like a double standard, the public acknowledgment of a devoted dad reinforces her husband's growth in this new area for men. This is just as important as hoping, and expecting, that you will be acknowledged in taking on all the roles that you have. When that support does come, mothers greatly appreciate it, as expressed by Nichelle:

James promotes and encourages me like nobody I have ever known. When I received my promotion at work, I seriously considered turning it down because of my responsibilities with the children and with our church. But James said, "Nichelle, you put a lot of things on hold because of the children and church. I really think this would be a good opportunity for you and a good career move. Do you think I am not capable of taking care of the boys? Because I am. They will still have a parent here when you are out of town." I so appreciated that support.

Keep What's Important to You

To build on your partnership or marriage, support each other's interests. Take time for yourself and allow your partner the same. Working mothers often feel that since they are gone for the better part of the day, their remaining hours should be dedicated to children and family. It's ironic, but by taking some time for yourself, as Wendy found, you may feel that you have more time for your children:

> *Vigorous exercise really helps me. It takes about an hour and a half to go to the gym, work out, and then come home, but it gives me more energy. I feel like it gives me more time in my day. I also feel like I am setting a good example for my daughter.*

While you should simplify and try not to take on too much, taking some personal time may help you to reenergize, so that you can reconnect with your family in a more positive and relaxed manner. Parents feel better about their lives and their parenting if they have some time for themselves.[6] Many moms work hard to trade off with their partner so that each can pursue an individual activity. One may head off to play tennis on Saturday morning, and the other may go jogging on Sunday. Monique, like many moms, has a favorite activity that is simple and short:

> *I love to take a bubble bath at night. Even if it's just a fifteen-minute bubble bath and a facial, I feel so much more relaxed. It's a real reward after a long day at work. And it's right before bedtime, so I'm relaxed for sleep.*

Single mothers in particular suffer from lack of time for themselves, but it is equally important for them and may require more determination and planning. Stacy, a single mother with a seven-year-old son, Jeffrey, feels that she is better able to be an energetic, positive mother after she has had this time:

> *I will often get our neighborhood baby-sitter to play with Jeffrey for an hour while I go to the gym and work out. I think for Jeffrey, that one extra hour, he's going to be out playing with his friends in the neighborhood, and I'm going to be so much healthier and feel so much better if I get home at seven P.M. having made it to the gym versus getting home at six. It's*

amazing how I'll come home feeling like I have so much more energy, and I'm happier. I feel like I then have more of me to give to my son.

Dionna, a single mom, gave every free minute outside of work to her four-year-old daughter, Jamilla. Over time, she started to put on weight, and she seemed to always be exhausted. Before she had Jamilla, exercise and athletics were central to her life. She knew she had to get them back again:

I started to get depressed. I love my baby, but I was starting to get irritable, and she was starting to get on my nerves. I was always really, really tired. I had stopped exercising, feeling like I couldn't take that time for myself. I started to think that there was something really wrong with me. I went to the doctor, but all the tests came back normal. I then knew. I had to get back to my old life of working out and being in shape. So I started exercising again. I just changed my attitude—that I wasn't depriving Jamilla by not being there every second, but instead that I was giving her a better mom by allowing myself to be a healthy person again.

Since Dionna works the evening shift in a factory, she goes to the fitness center on-site at one or two A.M. after her shift is over. She works out five days a week, as she did before she had Jamilla. While Dionna works out, Jamilla is asleep at the company child care center:

I go get Jamilla after I have worked out. I am so happy to see her. I just kiss her all over her face, even though she's sound asleep. I feel more alive now and am a more enthusiastic mom.

Do you have a cherished activity? How can you start fitting it back in your life? Talk about it openly with your partner and your children and make it a routine. That way they will come to expect it and accept it as part of your and their daily lives. As your children develop their own talents and interests, you are role-modeling the same.

A sampling of mothers' cherished activities:

- Regular exercise
- Piano lessons
- Manicures or pedicures
- Playing on or coaching sports teams
- Shopping or visiting with girlfriends
- Solitary walks
- Spiritual time
- Teaching at a local community college
- Serving on community boards
- Massages
- Meditation or yoga
- Reading/book clubs

What could be yours?

Creating a healthy family culture is perhaps more natural than you might believe. It is more about letting yourself go, accepting who you are and who your partner and children are, and letting your personality, interests, humor, and even eccentricities flourish. If you think more about intimacy and connection, and less about achieving an expected ideal, your family life will evolve in its own warm, unique way. One mother, Alena, summed it up well:

I feel like it's such an accomplishment that we really kind of have it together as a family. It's not something I'm going to wave the flag at and say, "Yahoo, I've got the cleanest house and the best kids in the world," but to say that we've created a loving environment for them, that this is their home

whatever way it looks, and this is where they will be
unconditionally loved and accepted.

This discussion of family culture is an important backdrop as we explore, in the next two chapters, the prolonged times during the weekday when we see our family. The morning and evening routines may feel like the most rushed parts of our lives, but it is also the time where family culture is developed.

NINE

Making the Most of Prime Times: The Morning Routine

One morning when our baby, Gracie, was seven months old, she woke up earlier than usual. It was a beautiful morning, so I thought that this would be a wonderful opportunity to take her outside for a stroll—a chance to have some "quality time" together before work. So I bounded out of bed and into her room. I wanted to quickly nurse her, change her diaper, and get her dressed so we could take off. No sooner had I gotten her dressed than she spit up all over her clothes. I felt frustrated having to take yet more time to change her again, and I found myself getting more rushed and determined. As Gracie lay there on the changing table, she caught my eye and burst into a giant smile that seemed to take over her entire body. She wriggled and gurgled and reached up. As I bent over her, she grabbed my hair and pulled me close. As she gave me luscious wet kisses, time seemed to freeze. I just stayed bent over her as we both kissed and nuzzled and laughed. I stroked her belly and legs; we both slowed down. What started as a quick diaper change to get on to something else turned into a slow, relaxed moment where we played, kissed, smiled, and laughed—and somewhere in the process, her diapers and clothes got changed. We never ended up going on our walk, but I realized that this diaper-changing moment offered as much or more quality time than the walk.

In the early childhood field, we teach our caregivers never to underestimate the value of routine caregiving. Child care teachers learn not to rush through diapering and feeding in order to get to "the important stuff." The routine caregiving *is* important—this is our "prime time"* with children. When you feed your child, when you bathe her and clothe her, when you change her diapers, you have wonderful opportunities for loving, caring interactions. These are precious moments where you can focus all your attention on her. Routine caregiving is also an opportunity for teaching young children self-help skills, such as tying shoes or zipping a jacket.

For working parents, prime time with children during the week is in the mornings before work, school, or child care; and in the evenings at home again. These two periods that wrap around our workday often feel stressful for us as we rush to get through all the tasks in what can be a very short period of time. We usually don't think of these times as quality time to enjoy—more like something we endure, as Gina observes:

> *I get up and rush through the morning; then I come home and rush through the evening. It's the same old thing, day in and day out, one day after another. Monday, the clock starts, and it doesn't stop until Friday. The day goes into the week, which goes into the month, which goes into the year. And if you stop to think about it—oh my gosh, where have the last four years gone?*

How we spend our early mornings and evenings becomes the architecture of our family life. Can we learn to enjoy our prime times?

In chapters 9 and 10, I am going to attempt to reframe how we think about these two periods of our day. I will share with you mothers' strategies, attitudes, and tips for easing the stress during the routine. I will show you how parents develop elements of their family culture, as described in the last chapter, in these short but consequential times during the week.

---

* Jim Greenman, senior vice president of education at Bright Horizons, has developed this concept in his book, *Prime Times*.

BUILD IN MUCH MORE TIME THAN YOU THINK YOU NEED

It helps to really look at and understand how each child enters and exits the day. Each child is different; each one needs a different approach.

—Leah

Getting the whole family up and out the door in the morning can be challenging, particularly if you have very young children. Every family member has different needs, rhythms, and moods in the morning. It can often seem like you're at the center of a little tornado, with everything swirling around you. As you feel your stress level and voice rising, you sometimes wonder if there isn't a better way. You would like to have each family member launched in a happy and settled mood. Is that possible? Sure it is—maybe the morning won't be perfect, but it certainly can be a little easier.

First let's look at the rush factor: Don't just factor a few extra minutes into the time you and your husband took to get ready in the morning before having kids. Maybe add another hour. I'm serious—especially if you have young children or a baby. If you include enough extra time, the morning won't feel like a mad rush, and it can actually become a time you and your family enjoy. As your children get older and are able to get themselves ready, you may not need as much.

Some mothers get up an hour before the rest of the family. They treasure that time for themselves. They may exercise, read the newspaper, have a cup of coffee, check e-mail, take a shower, or get ready in peace. They may get the children's backpacks ready or the breakfast set out. As one mother, Helen, said, "I'm up at five A.M. As a working mom, I consider that time to myself priceless—to gather my thoughts and have my coffee before my children are jumping all around." Another mother and her husband get up early so they can have quiet morning time together before the busy day begins.

Some young children want and need to start the day slowly. It is more difficult for them to switch into high gear immediately. If you can give them a little extra time to get going, that may positively affect their morning mood. In one family, the children all climb into bed with the parents, then slowly wake up together. It's nice to start the day by catching your last few winks in bed cuddled with your warm child, reading aloud a favorite storybook, or holding her in the rocking chair for a few minutes. One mother wraps her sleepy, slow-waking little girl in a blanket and puts her on the couch in the family room. Her daughter wakes up gradually while she watches the family activity. I notice that each of my three children likes to begin the day very differently. Eleven-year-old Farrell jumps up and bustles with activity, energy, and song. Nine-year-old Lucas loves to snuggle quietly with our beagle in front of the heater in the kitchen. Four-year-old Gracie likes to stay in her pajamas as long as possible, find her magic wand with streamers, and dance about and bestow magic while she gets dressed. It's important to understand what works for each child and respect that.

If your evenings are too busy or if you aren't all on the same schedule, Denise recommends having a sit-down family breakfast instead of, or in addition to, the family dinner:

> Our mornings are leisurely. I know that I get up at five A.M. to pay for that, but that's okay because we all eat a nice breakfast together. Breakfast is our family time. We're all in much better moods in the morning than we are at dinnertime. With that routine, we start our day happy.

Dionna, who works from four P.M. to one-thirty A.M. in a factory, makes a hearty breakfast with her daughter, Jamilla, their main meal together:

> Either I'll make her pancakes with sausage, or we'll eat grits, eggs, toast. It's really our bonding time. We'll sit down at breakfast, and I ask her how was her day. I can't say "today," because it's a new day. That's our time to talk. I don't answer the telephone. I also try to tell her some things about my day.

Although many mothers feel like they never have enough time in the morning, there are some who actually feel like they have too much time because their children are such early risers. They then need to figure out what to do with that time. One mother, Amy, and her active five-year-old go to the local YMCA at six-thirty in the morning for a swim. It burns off a little energy for her son, and she gets some needed exercise before she heads off to school and he goes to child care.

Mothers' tips for getting up in the morning:

- Understand the *different rhythms and needs of your children.* If one is slow-moving in the morning, give her extra time.
- Think of the morning routine as an *important moment of parenting.* Build in some cuddle time first thing if you can. It's valuable to have some quiet time to connect before the busy day begins.
- Also *understand what you need.* If it's alone time, try getting up before the family to do whatever feels good for you: exercise, reading a book or newspaper, a leisurely shower and makeup routine, an extra cup of coffee, time alone with your partner.
- *Create a morning family ritual,* particularly if you're an early-rising household: a family breakfast, a cuddle in bed, a book, a walk with the dog.

However, many of us hate getting up early. You may need to know that the sun is up before you contemplate doing the same. For many mothers, it is also impossible to add much time in the morning. If you are on an early shift at work or if your children's school starts early, you all may have to move into high gear pretty quickly. In that case, do as much preparation the night before as you can. Using some of the tips in this chapter will help keep things rolling.

If your child stays at home with a nanny or relative, you will not have to get her up, dressed, and fed before you leave home. You can let her sleep in or stay in her pajamas if she wants to. However, you will probably want to spend time with her before you go—whether it's a snuggle in bed, a book, or breakfast together.

KEEP A SENSE OF HUMOR

Humor goes a long way in a family, or in any relationship. Little children (I guess like all of us) can sometimes wake up grumpy. Attitude and humor can help immeasurably. Many mothers talked about resisting getting drawn into the grumpy mood or the intransigence of their young children. Rather than getting angry with a young child who will just not get dressed, try redirecting her attention to something she will like to do: "It looks like you're having a hard time getting dressed right now. Why don't we go check the thermometer and see how cold it is outside. Then we'll come back and know what to wear."

You can make a game of getting ready. One dad makes a dressing game with his four-year-old. They race to see if they can get dressed before the toast pops up. One mother, Natalie, lays out the clothes on the floor as if on a person. Then she does something silly, like putting the underwear where the head should go:

> *"What's that—an undie head?" Then we talk to the clothes. We tell them to get up. "What are you doing lying on the floor? You're supposed to be on me!" We try these anti-stress measures to get the kids to get up on the right side of bed. If they get up laughing, that really helps.*

Children are naturally playful. You can keep things moving in the morning with a humorous, affectionate attitude. Attitudes are contagious. Here, our Camp Counselor moms can show us the way. They seem to have the easiest time with the morning routine. Camp Counselor moms just stay upbeat and happy, and eventually the children get caught up in the mood. They try to have fun or play a game while they are getting the kids ready.

CONSISTENCY WILL HELP THINGS MOVE ALONG

Young children thrive on routine. If you have the same one each morning, the children become accustomed to it and will move along more naturally and easily as time goes on. You can have a daily routine that goes something like this:

- Each child gets dressed (perhaps with some help if they are very young).
- They make their beds and put away their pajamas.
- They wash their hands and face.
- They have breakfast with a couple of the same choices each day.
- They put their dishes in the sink or in the dishwasher. They put away the milk and cereal boxes (with help if very young).
- They brush their teeth.
- Then, with everything done, they are free to play until it's time to leave.

Perhaps use an incentive, such as drawing with favorite markers once your child is ready, to encourage getting dressed and eating breakfast. My son, Lucas, adores playing with his LEGOs. He's an early riser, and he knows that once he is ready for school, he can play with his LEGOs until school. He is motivated to move along so that he can have some playtime.

Mothers talk about keeping things moving so a child does not get "stuck" on an activity. Since young children may struggle with transition, you can gently prepare them for the next task: "After we tie your shoes, let's go have our breakfast. Would you like cereal or toast this morning?" A daily routine makes it easier to keep forward movement. One mother, Leah, says:

I think in a series of stations in the morning, moving them from one station to the next: "Okay, now they're all dressed, we need to get them their breakfast. Okay, now we need to move them from inside to outside, to get into the car."

Young children have a budding sense of autonomy. Support that by giving them some choice in what they do and how they do it. But limit the choices to a *couple of acceptable options*. Rather than asking a question that requires a yes or no answer, ask a question that presents a limited but attractive choice. Instead of asking, "Are you ready to get dressed now?" (you know what they'll say!), ask, "Do you want to put on your own shirt this morning, or would you like me to help you?" And later you can say, "Would you like to wear the red or blue hat to school this morning?" By focusing on the choice for the next event, you can keep things moving along and give your child a role in the process.

Mothers' tips for the morning routine:

- With your child, choose and set out her clothes the night before. Then she will know what to put on in the morning.

- Also set out *your* clothes before you go to bed, which can save you some time.

- Pack the children's bags for child care at night: extra change of clothes, diapers, can of formula, etc.

- Lay out the breakfast dishes and cereal the night before. It's one less task to do in the morning.

- There's nothing wrong with dressing your young child at night in a clean shirt and underwear for the next day, especially if she dislikes dressing in the morning. Some young children just don't like to get out of their comfy, warm nightclothes. Do you blame them?

- Follow the same consistent routine each day. Your child will become used to it and expect it.

- When getting dressed is a battle: Try putting the clothes in the dryer for a few minutes. If they're toasty, they will be more inviting to put on.

- Create an incentive for getting ready: Once they are all ready, they can play their favorite game until it's time to leave.

- For older children, establish some commonly understood cutoff times: The alarm is set at six-thirty, but if she's not out of bed in fifteen minutes, she won't have time for a shower. Set cutoff times for young children as well: She should absolutely be out of bed by seven A.M., with breakfast done by seven-thirty and out the door by eight.

- Set a musical alarm for the time you need to head out the door. Kids will learn the cue, too. Also sing your own made-up songs for getting out the door: "This is the way we leave the house, leave the house . . ."

ENCOURAGE SELF-HELP AND GROWING INDEPENDENCE

One of the tasks of early childhood is gradually learning how to do things for oneself. Although you may be tempted to do everything for your child to keep things moving quickly, slow down and let her develop self-help skills. It's amazing how some young children who are obstinate about getting dressed or going to the potty suddenly become more enthusiastic if they have some control in the process. One mother, Colleen, explained:

> *Alexander is now getting to the point where he wants to put his socks on by himself, which I try to encourage. But then it takes much longer, so we have to allow extra time for that. I try very hard to be patient; it doesn't really take that much longer, and he feels so proud. He exclaims, "I did my own SOCKS!"*

Actually, I have a real thing about socks. It seems as though each of my children had such a struggle with socks when they were little. They never seemed to feel just right. Our four-year-old, Gracie, now painstakingly tries to get "the bumpy side" (otherwise known as the seam) to line up exactly with the tips of her tiny toes. It's a tricky endeavor, because you might get it just right, but it quickly slips out of place when you put on the shoe. In fact, it's a nearly impossible feat. We finally came up with the "five-minute system," in which she'll try to wear the imperfectly placed sock and shoe for five minutes, and then if she wants, we'll try it again. Once she starts prancing around, she immediately forgets about the bumpy side in her shoe.

Some children, however, are truly more sensitive to fabrics, seams, and tags than others. While it may appear that your child is making a ridiculous fuss about how her clothes feel, she might be particularly uncomfortable with a certain fabric or texture. Try to tune in to what textures bother her. She will likely grow out of it over time.

Back to self-help skills. The first thing young children usually love to do for themselves is pick out their own outfits. This morning, Gracie arrived at breakfast in tights with hearts, a jeans skirt layered under a purple ballet skirt, a plaid flannel shirt with a tank top over it, and multiple colored clips and barrettes in her hair. It is truly a great aesthetic event for her to craft her individual expression for the day. My son Lucas absolutely adored his black cowboy boots and Batman outfit with cape when he was three years old. For six months, that was what he chose to put on every day that they were available. As Amy, mother of a five-year-old, said, "Sometimes Douglas looks kind of goofy walking around with the outfits he chooses, but it's his choice. It's only clothes." Don't worry that your child will always want to dress that way. Young children are fascinated by colors and patterns and love to experiment with what seems like outlandish combinations. It's typically just a phase that will pass in elementary school.

I am admitting to my personal bias here, since I have never been too concerned if my children choose to wear unusual combinations of colors and patterns. If they are clean and dressed appropriately for the weather, I enjoy letting them make their own decisions. I understand, however, that many parents feel differently. As Dionna said:

> It's very important that my daughter go out of the house looking neat and well put together. My child is a reflection of me; she's also the representative of the family. I want her to

have a positive self-image. As she gets older, I don't want her to walk out of the house looking any kind of way.

If you want your child to look a certain way, have a limited wardrobe in which your child can mix and match tops and bottoms that all go well together. One mother, Stacy, has a system in which she and her son, Jeffrey, pick out his week's outfits together on Sunday night:

We have hanging in Jeffrey's closet this cloth cubby that I ordered from Lillian Vernon that has "Monday" through "Friday" on it, with slots. On Sunday night after dinner, we go up to his room and pick out five pairs of pants and five shirts, and he stuffs this thing. In the morning he goes right to his cubby and pulls out his clothes for the day and gets dressed. Then there's never any argument about "This shirt doesn't go with those pants."

Yet another way to help your child with independence skills is to sit down with her and decide together what the morning routine should be. She can help generate the guidelines with you. These rules can include items like: make the bed, get dressed before breakfast, put the dishes in the sink, get milk money. Write the rules on a large chart or blackboard so your children can check them off when finished. If she is not yet reading, have her draw a picture beside each rule. One mother, Gina, did that with her four-year-old daughter, Melanie, and it was a big success:

We sat down together, and Melanie dictated some of the morning guidelines, and I made up some of them, and then I typed them up. Melanie drew pictures by each one. She's been adhering to them ever since. We have morning rules and nighttime rules. One was so funny. She dictated, "Close the bedroom door when you're dancing to loud music, 'cause you keep me awake!"

Self-help tips for children:

- Allow your child to get up with her own alarm clock. This can help her feel independent.

- Create the morning schedule with your child. Put the major tasks on a blackboard or chart so she can check them off.

- Put the breakfast cereals, bowls, spoons, etc., in a low, accessible cupboard. Even a young child will enjoy being able to pour her own cereal. Put milk in a small pitcher with a lid that she can pour herself.

- Even a three-year-old can put her bowl and spoon in the dishwasher. You can adjust it later.

- Let her choose her outfit. If she does it the night before, it can save a long process. Choose your battles wisely.

Teamwork

You exist in a family unit. There is no reason why you need to do everything for everyone. Both parents can chip in. Older children can help younger children. Younger children can help out by putting their dishes in the sink or dishwasher and doing some of the dressing themselves.

You can sit down as a family and devise a morning routine that works for all of you, with each member of the family pitching in. Children as young as three or four can have some simple responsibilities and chores, such as gathering clothes for the hamper or putting away the cereal boxes. If you start early with a family ethic of everyone being responsible for a smooth family routine, then it is easier to give children increasing responsibilities as they grow older. Children should not feel that parents will do everything for them. Responsibilities can be revisited semiannually or annually as children develop greater capability to help out.

LUNCHES

A rule of thumb that many parents use is to minimize the number of tasks in the morning. Try packing the lunches at night. Cook larger portions of dinner so you can pack the extra into lunch containers for the next day. Making the lunches then becomes part of the dinner clean-up routine. Some parents have just two or three choices for lunch sandwiches that they alternate through the week. However, I did come across a few mothers who insisted on making the lunches in the morning so the sandwiches would still be fresh by noon. Selena recalled: "There were five kids in my family growing up, so my mother made the lunches the night before, and to this day I still remember how soggy they were. I make the lunches in the morning!"

Mothers' lunch tips:

- Have just two or three lunch alternatives that you alternate during the week. This cuts down on planning and decision making.
- Prepare two days of lunches at a time. Don't add the bread and condiments until that morning.
- Make extra portions of dinner at night. As you are cleaning up, put the extra servings in containers for lunch the next day.
- Buy precut fruits and vegetables to reduce preparation time.
- If your child buys lunch each day, on Sunday night, put the daily lunch money in five baggies in a jar for the week.
- While you're preparing the lunch, add a sweet little note or picture for your child to discover.

The following is a list of lunch suggestions that we give to parents at Bright Horizons. For young children, everything should be cut into small, bite-size pieces.

LUNCH IDEAS

Cold Sandwiches	Canned Fruit	Fresh Fruit	Vegetables	Miscellaneous	Hot Meals (in Thermos)	Foods to Avoid
Ham and cheese	Applesauce	Bananas	Carrots	Yogurt	Pasta dish	Sweets
Turkey	Peaches	Oranges	Cucumbers	Cottage cheese	Rice dish	Soda
Chicken	Pears	Strawberries	Celery	Hard-boiled egg	Leftovers	Nuts
Tuna fish	Pineapple	Cantaloupe	Sweet red peppers	Salad	Chicken nuggets	Salty junk food
Peanut butter and jelly	Fruit cocktail	Apples				
Egg salad		Peaches				
Hummus		Blueberries				

GETTING OUT THE DOOR

Since many young children struggle with transitions, your child may say she doesn't want to go to child care in the morning, even if she loves it. If you know that you have selected high quality care and that your child enjoys it once she is there, don't let her resistance unnerve you. Don't try to debate with her. In a firm and friendly way, just keep things moving along.

Tips for getting out the door:

- Talk about some activities she will do that day or some friends she will see. It will help your child visualize where she is going and remember why she likes being there. Make a plan for when she arrives at child care: "When we get there, do you want to finish the picture that you started yesterday?" or "I bet your friend Joshua is waiting for you. Let's go see him."

- Your child can take a favorite stuffed animal or object from home. That can provide a connection with home that will offer some security and familiarity. You can also make a plan to show it to her caregiver: "Shall we take your stuffed bear to show Rosa today? She'll love seeing how you dressed him this morning."

- Give your child an element of control when making a transition. Perhaps she can pick out a cassette to listen to in the car, or she can pick out a book or an activity to do once she is buckled in.

- Give her some important jobs that will help make her feel like an essential part of the process: "Can you turn out the kitchen lights before we go?" or "Will you open the door for me while I carry the bags out?"

THE COMMUTE

Commuting to child care or school has become a fixture in the daily life of a working parent. Rather than thinking of it as an annoyance, look at it as an opportunity for special time with your child. As Helen discovered, quality time becomes whatever time you can really focus on your child:

> *It's a twenty-five-minute commute to child care each way; that's an extra fifty minutes that I get with the kids. They're in their seats, there's no television, we are focused, and we can really communicate and play and talk and sing. This time is priceless.*

Commuting tips:

- Use this time to go over *the day's plan*. Prepare your child for any changes in your normal routine: "Do you remember that your aunt Jean is picking you up today instead of Mommy?" Also explain what you will be doing that day. It will help her visualize you while you are not there.
- Review *the drop-off routine* so she will know what to do when you arrive at child care. Make it a consistent daily routine. If you have a baby, review the drop-off routine for your benefit. Plan how to transition, then stick to the plan.
- Develop your *favorite commuting rituals* or games. Riding in a car is a good opportunity to develop your child's observational skills: identifying all the yellow houses, looking at road construction, counting trucks.

- Sing songs together or listen to *favorite cassettes* of music or stories. Make up rhymes and silly jokes.

- Take out a *child's book-on-tape* from the library. She can listen to the tape while following along in the book. It's a wonderful prereading activity.

- Riding in a car can be a wonderful *time to talk*. A child can sometimes bring up fears or difficult issues more easily when you are not face-to-face yet she has your full attention. Some of my best conversations with my children take place spontaneously in the car.

- Many car seats come with *attachable trays*. Your child can use one for activities: coloring, car board games, sticker books. Baby seats often come with attachable toys.

- *Take turns* making the commute with your spouse or partner. It is helpful for each of you to have this time with your child, to get to know the child care situation, and to give each other a break.

- *To snack or not to snack:* Parents have different feelings about this. Children love to eat in the car, and it can make the ride easier, but you may not want her snacking between meals. If you do allow eating in the car, make sure the snacks are healthy: cut-up fruit, toast, dry cereal (Cheerios is a favorite), milk or a juice bottle with a lid. A bottle can soothe your baby during the ride.

SEPARATION: AT CHILD CARE OR AT HOME

Whether you are dropping off your child at a family child care home or a child care center, or leaving her with a nanny or relative, the two most important watchwords for the daily separation are: *positive attitude* and *consistency*. Many young children struggle with being left with a caregiver and separating from their parents. Your child may cling to you, cry, and beg you to stay. It can be heartrending to leave while your child is crying, arms stretched out to you. Understand that this separation anxiety, as long as it is not extreme, is actually a healthy aspect of child development. Understanding that she is separate from you is an important step for your baby's or young child's development. You will want your child to develop a healthy and secure attachment to you. You will also want her to develop a healthy bond with your caregiver. One experienced educator, Linda, has this to say about the separation tears:

> *I don't think it is necessarily a bad thing that a child cries when his parent is leaving. The child is sad to be away from this person he loves dearly. Tears do not mean that the departure is going poorly. Rather, the caregiver can talk to the child along the lines of "I can tell you miss your daddy very, very much. He is going to work now, but he will be back later. It is okay that you feel sad. You are welcome to cry in my arms until you are ready to go play." A child whose feelings are acknowledged will then be able to change gears and engage with the caregiver or other children.*

Young children do not yet have a good sense of time. It may take a while for your child to understand that a routine departure will be followed by a routine return. You also may be very sad to leave; let's acknowledge that this is hard. Your tears are okay, too—although it is best if you hold back those tears until after you have left.

Have a Positive Attitude

Your attitude during the separation will be important. If you have researched and selected your child care option well—whether it is a center, family child care, a nanny, or a relative—then you will be confident of the care and should express this during separation. If you show that you are happy to arrive at child care or to see the nanny, and enthusiastic about what the day will bring, that attitude will likely be contagious, and your child will ultimately follow your lead.

Maintain Consistency

Young children respond well to consistent daily routines. If you follow the same steps each day, she will know what comes next. It may help if you can stay with your child until she becomes engaged in an activity before you leave. That will also send the message that you value what she does while you are gone.

Your separation routine for your *baby*—at child care or at home—can go like this:

- Don't rush the separation. Your baby will pick up on your stress and may become agitated, too.
- It's nice for you to do the first diaper change of the day. Your baby starts out clean and dry, and you can have a moment of sweet interaction with her.
- At child care, sit with your baby for a while so she can take in the activities and people in the room. If your baby is crawling, she may want to venture out of your arms to explore.
- Talk with your caregiver and describe your baby's night and morning. Discuss any changes in today's schedule.
- If there is a daily notebook, write any needed information for the day.
- When your baby seems comfortable, let your caregiver take her. It's nice for her to be in a devoted caregiver's arms when you leave.
- Kiss and hug your baby good-bye and then go. Don't waver; that only becomes confusing to your baby.
- If your baby is crying when you leave, or even if she is not, feel free to call your caregiver when you arrive at work to see how she is doing.

Your separation routine for your *toddler or preschooler*—at child care or at home—can go like this:

- At child care: Greet the caregiver and other children as you enter the room. If your child has brought something from home to show her caregiver, she can share it now. With in-home care: Together with your child, cheerfully greet and engage your caregiver in an activity with you and your child—perhaps finishing breakfast or drawing a picture.

- At child care, first spend time helping your child into an activity before engaging in extensive conversation with the caregiver. Children love to interact with their environment, so involving her in a play activity will help her transition more easily.

- Let your caregiver know how your child is doing that morning and if there is any change in her schedule.

- Write in the communication notebook any important information for the caregiver: what time you will return, any medication to be given, child's mood this morning.

- Once your child is settled and happy, move to your good-bye ritual (see below).

- Be friendly and firm, hug, say good-bye, and leave. Don't waver at this point. Once at work, always feel free to call the caregiver to find out how your child did after you left.

Create a Partnership with Your Child Care Provider

Talk to your caregiver each morning. She or he will want to know how your child's night went, what her mood is, if there are any new issues. Go over any change in your return schedule. Your provider will become a close partner with you and your spouse in the daily care and education of your child. Invest in this relationship; it is one of the most important ones in your family life. Listen to this caregiver, Beth:

> *I think building fifteen to twenty minutes into the morning routine can make all the difference. It slows the pace and allows everyone to ease into the routine of the morning, rather than the dreaded "drop and run" that we see quite often.*
>   *The added advantage of this time is that it facilitates real, personal relationships among parents and caregivers. They can get to know each other and form a bond that is deeper and more meaningful, and this can only translate to*

the child as a relationship of caring and trust. I often wish that parents would realize how the gift of respect and affection for caregivers colors the rest of their child's experience. Quality child care is all about relationships—and relationships deserve time to develop.

Build a Community of Families

As a new mother, you may be feeling very alone. Reach out; there are other parents who probably feel the same way. As your child develops friends, get together occasionally on the weekends with their families. I often found myself lingering at the child care center during drop-off or pickup and chatting with other parents. We would trade strategies on sleep issues, toilet training, and simply life as working parents. For many parents, child care has become their new neighborhood. Find opportunities to get involved. Serve on a parent committee. Help organize get-togethers.

Create a Departure Ritual

Never sneak out without saying good-bye. That will undermine your child's trust in you, and she will fearfully watch to see if you are leaving. Develop a departure ritual that you try to follow each day, whether it's at child care or at home. Soon this ritual will become familiar and she will be comfortable with it. Let your child know when you or your partner will be returning in a way she will understand: "Daddy will pick you up right after your nap" or "I'll be back after snack time in the afternoon." Don't belabor your exit. Be happy and confident that your child will be happy, too, say good-bye, and leave. Don't keep coming back into the room if your child is crying. That becomes confusing to her, and she will think that if she cries, you will stay. This is where your attitude and actions will make a difference. If you are anxious and sad about leaving, then your child will be, too.

Possible departure rituals:

- Sit down and read one book with your child, then hug and leave.

- Draw a picture with your child, seal it with kisses, and let her keep it while you leave.

- Let your child hold a picture of the family or something of yours as you leave. That may feel like a secure connection to you.

- Sit with your child while she engages in an activity (art project, block area, puzzles, computer game, etc.) with a friend. When she is fully engaged and settled, give her a hug and kiss and leave.

- Have the caregiver bring your child to the window or door to wave good-bye while you leave.

One center director, Jennifer, describes how the children in her preschool classroom developed their own unique departure technique:

The children in our center have the ritual of "pushing" their parents out the door. I love that it gives the children the chance to make the decision that they are ready for Mom or Dad to go. Please envision a three-year-old pushing on Dad's behind, and Dad overemphasizing the push and pretending to zoom forward from his child's strength. Daily, children are laughing at their parents being silly as they leave, and parents of course love leaving their child laughing and in total control!

If your child is struggling with separating, and has a sibling at the same child care location, perhaps have her visit her sibling after you leave. Just knowing family is right there can help. Let your caregiver help with the separation: Signal when you are ready to leave, and she can hold and comfort your child if she is crying. Also, caregivers are ready to strategize about the departure routine so that you become a team in this process.

YOUR TRANSITION TO WORK

After I've dropped off the kids, I'm then back in the car. I make this mental shift. Okay, the kids are in their respective

*places; they're safe and sound. I now take off my mom hat.
I'm now starting to get my brain squared away to what I need
to do when I get to work.*

—Patricia

It's nice to have a mental break between children and work; consciously make that shift. Some mothers like taking a short walk or ride from child care to work. They, like Anna, find it relaxing to be by themselves for a few minutes:

*I love seeing my kids off at the bus stop. I'll then start walking
to work, and as the bus goes by, I see their little faces in the
window, and we wave, and that's precious. And then I keep
walking. It's a mile to work. That's my favorite time. It's
peaceful, and my thoughts can sort out before I get to work.
It's relaxing. It's meditative.*

Allow yourself to relax. You can then turn your attention to your work plan for the day. Paige drops off her two girls at child care, then takes a commuter train to her job as a graphic designer. She loves this time between family and work: "It's like my twenty-five minutes of peace. I get my coffee and doughnut and newspaper. I sit there and relax. I wouldn't trade it for anything."

Some couples commute to work together after child care drop-off, which provides a special moment for the two of them. If you are on a fixed work schedule and have to arrive by a certain time, factor in extra preparation and drop-off time so that you can get through the occasional child tears or tantrum and not be totally stressed out about arriving late. If you have control over your schedule, avoid scheduling early-morning meetings at work. That will relieve pressure on you.

Now let's switch, in the next chapter, to the other important prime time in your work week: the evening routine.

TEN

Making the Most of Prime Times: The Evening Routine

Our evenings? It's get home and put my roller skates on.
—Alena

Evening is a stressful time for me. I leave work at five-forty-five, and I race into the child care center to arrive right before the six P.M. closing time. Then there's talking to the teachers and prying little Jeremy out of the center. Then, with our forty-minute commute, it's already quarter to seven by the time we get home. Everyone is tired, grumpy, and hungry. My husband doesn't come home until right before the kids are in bed. I always feel like it's hurry, hurry, hurry. I want to get them fed, give them a bath, and get them in bed at a reasonable hour.
—Denise

Do you think of your evenings as a series of tasks that must get completed and checked off as quickly and efficiently as possible—dinner, clean-up, bath, stories, bedtime? Do you feel like you're racing the clock all evening to make sure things are getting done on time? Are you yearning for the moment when the kids get in bed so you can collapse? Perhaps this is a part of our day where we can benefit from the attitudes of our Earth Mothers and Passionate Spirits. Let's learn from them how they relax, enjoy this time, and capture the moment as a family. The evening, like the morning, is an important time for family—a prime time of parenting. How you define it will go a long way toward defining your family.

The goal of this chapter is to help us think differently about our evenings. I will try to show you how some parents create their evenings as a time of intimate regathering after the family has all been out in the world for the day—the parents at work, the children at child care or school. I will share with you mothers' tips for easing the stress and enjoying this time more. But before we get to specifics, here are some guiding principles for this important time:

Remember that routine caregiving is the main stuff of parenting

Try to think of your evening routine not as just a series of tasks to be completed but as precious moments of parenting. Rather than rushing through the bath so that you can sit down and read books, think of the bath as quality time with your child, too. The tasks probably won't take much longer, but your attitude can make a difference in how you enjoy this time. Says Leah:

We really linger over the bath. The whole family ends up in the bathroom. My husband and I chat and play with the kids, and they just love it. I suppose that's a funny way to have family time, but we always seem to do it.

Allow yourself to capture those important moments

Although you need to keep things moving so the children get in bed in time for a good night's sleep, be willing to stop occasionally and capture a moment if it is particularly special. Remember that this period is your main time for family during the week. One mother, Brenda, recounts:

Sometimes I will linger at bedtime because my ten-year-old daughter will use that time with me alone to ask questions about "Am I developing breasts yet? What's going to happen?" or "I really don't like boys, but . . ." Those times are very, very special. Then the clock doesn't matter.

Our four-year-old, Gracie, is a whimsical little girl who has fantastic flights of imagination. She will often come up with "the wonderfulest new dance" to show me, or a new piece of mischief that her imaginary friend Emily just enacted that she has to tell me about in great detail just when the phone rings, I'm trying to get dinner on the table, and our puppy is barking at the back door to go out. I'm rushing to get things done, but she needs me for a few moments, and I have to remember that for both of us, it's important to stop and listen to her (maybe just let the puppy out first!).

Cut down on some tasks, or include your children in them

You may try to tackle an unbelievable number of tasks in the evening. It is exhausting and stressful trying to be Supermom. But you're a mother; you're not Supermom. Let's let go of trying to get everything done. If need be, let your household standards slip a little; avoid picking up the Martha Stewart magazine in the checkout line; and just don't invite anyone over who needs to see an impeccable house. As Silvia says:

> We became pretty relaxed about household tasks once we had Nate. If things are a little messy, I don't worry about it. I'm not going to try to be the perfect mom with the perfect house. I go down that route every once in a while and get really psyched and try to iron everything. Then I get myself back in check: "Hello, girl—let it go!" If Nate wants to play a seventh game of Candyland tonight, we might just do the dishes tomorrow night.

But of course, there are household chores that do have to get done (see chapter 11). Doing chores together can be an important part of family life. You shouldn't feel that you need to do everything for your children, get them to bed, and then start on all the household clean-up. Children can participate in household chores from a young age. They may not be a great help at first, but you'll get them into the habit. Your toddler might love to go with you to the Laundromat and help throw all the clothes in the washing machine, then put in the quarters. Your preschooler will most likely enjoy being your kitchen helper and set the table for dinner. Particularly after dinner, everyone can pitch in to clear and wipe the table and sweep the floor. This way, children feel that they are a useful part of the family.

Young children thrive on routine

If you organize your evenings in a consistent way each night (but allow yourself to make exceptions for special moments), children will feel comfortable knowing what comes next. It can also make your evenings easier. If your child knows that after his bath, it's into bed, he will begin to move from one thing to the next without resistance (or at least with less resistance). Even babies adjust comfortably to predictability. My husband, Roger, came up with something our kids call "the system": After dinner, the children know they have to brush their teeth, go to the bathroom, get into their pajamas, and be ready for story time. Children naturally like to test limits, but they feel relief if the limits are clear, as Theresa found:

> Erica knows that she gets to pick out two books, gets her water, and then into bed. I read her two books, and then she goes to sleep. I don't keep rubbing her back for hours or keep getting her drinks of water. I think that is just setting her up for more stalling. I definitely have set routines for her, because I think they really help.

"One Glass of Water" is a wonderful children's song by Si Kahn that reminds us what can easily happen:

> Just one drop of water
> Just a small glass of water
> Just a tall glass of water
> Then I'll go to sleep
> Just a pitcher of water
> Just a barrel of water
> Then I'll go to sleep!

Team up with your partner

With two adults in the household, the evenings can go more smoothly if both participate. Particularly if you have a baby or toddler, one of you can hold and feed the baby while the other one makes the dinner or runs the bath. Or if you're a single mother, an older child can perhaps help out. I heard a great variety of ways that couples pitch in during the evening. Melinda does all the drop-offs and pick-ups of her two-year-old, Brian, while her partner, Diane, goes home and starts dinner. Since Diane doesn't have Brian with her on the way home from work, she can stop at the grocery store, if needed. Another mother, Amanda, cooks dinner while her husband, Joe, cleans up; he reads to their daughter and puts her to bed while Amanda packs lunches and gets organized for the next day.

If both parents participate, it not only makes life easier, your children also benefit from two styles of care and affection. Children often look to parents for different things, and, as Joanne found, each parent will often bring a different focus during the evening:

> *If I do the books and bedtime, I'll read one or two stories and I'm out of there. My husband, Tom, will spend a lot more time reading with the kids than I will. They get a lot out of that time. From a fairness standpoint, I think it's good that we trade off, but from a quality standpoint, it's even better because he gives them something very different than I do.*

WHAT ATMOSPHERE DO YOU WANT IN THE EVENING?

We can't and don't want to do everything in that short time. In my interviews with mothers, I asked them to paint a picture of their evenings. I would leave the conversation with a real sense of the atmosphere of their household. I was struck by how differently families live their evenings. What kind of tone is most important to you as a family? When your children are grown up, how would you like them to remember these evenings? The atmosphere will cultivate in them certain values and your family culture. Since your time together in the evening is short, think about the one value that you would like to establish. Here is what some families focus on:

- Morgan: *a laid-back, calm, unstructured evening.* Her days as a heavily scheduled, hard-driving attorney, and her daughter's days in a structured full-day preschool program, led her to want a very relaxed evening where she and her daughter cuddle, build block castles, and just hang out together.

- Sarah: *learning and family togetherness.* Sarah and her husband, John, each go off with one of their boys after dinner. They work together on homework, then do number and learning games. They finish the evening with a family board game.

- Alice: *security, serenity, and routine.* Alice and her son's life together is sometimes challenging. He has severe health issues, their extended family is frequently in crisis, and she struggles as a single mom. She likes to create an evening atmosphere of serenity for her son and herself. They love to bake together and enjoy how those smells fill the apartment. Every night Alice carefully goes over the next day's plan for Jimmy so he will have the security of knowing what to expect.

- Erin: *fun, active, controlled chaos.* Erin and her husband, Brian, are fun-loving, humorous, active people with a zest for life. They thrive on boisterous activity, and their evenings are full of active games and loads of laughter.

- Patricia: *a leisurely family dinner* with an emphasis on good, well-prepared food. Patricia's husband, Ralph, loves to cook, and they both value a delicious, healthy dinner with their three children. Dinner and conversation dominate the evening.

As I present practical tips and strategies to help you live your evenings, think about how you want to develop your family traditions. Think about what rituals (however simple) would feel special for you, and what tone you want to set in your home. Now let's get to the practical stuff—starting with departing from work.

LEAVING WORK AT THE END OF THE DAY

That little walk from work to child care is kind of like my detox from work, because once I hit the door at child care, work goes out the door. It's a nice little walk to have. Just the fresh air is good.

—Joanne

A good transition is just as necessary for you as it is for your child. Just as you want to be focused at work on doing your job well, you will want to do the same for your children when you see them. A meaningful shift from work to kids and home will help, particularly since the operating modes are often so different. At work you may work fast and efficiently, focusing on results. At home you will want to gear down to a more "pokey" kid mode, in which you can allow yourself to stop and smell the roses. One mother, Helen, found that if she changed her clothes before leaving work, she could more readily make the mental shift from work to play. "I always make a quick pit stop in the bathroom to change into jeans. Then I'm ready for anything!" It's also a good idea to change clothes, since when you see your children, you'll want to hug and hold them without worrying about Play-Doh, paint, sticky fingers, or drool.

Mothers' tips for shifting from work to home:

- Before you leave work, make a list of tasks you'll focus on at work the next day. That way you can put work out of your mind for the night.
- If it's practical, change into casual home clothes before you leave work. That can help you make the mental shift into home mode; also, it's hard to change when you first get home.
- As you travel from work to child care or home, consciously wind down and put work behind you. Start to think about your family and how you will spend your evening.

- Take a cup of herbal tea with you for the commute home. That can also serve to help you wind down.

CHILD CARE PICKUP

I would get to the center just before six P.M., and my kids would just melt down. They couldn't help it; they had been there so long. Then it's another twenty minutes to extricate the kids and try to control them, and all the while the clock is ticking and we're paying late fees.

—Brenda

Your children may save up all their emotions and pent-up fatigue from the day and then volubly unload them on you. They feel most natural, secure, and unconditionally loved with you. They know that with you, they can "let it all out." And don't let their end-of-day meltdown lead you to think they had a miserable day. They can have an absolutely enchanting day and still "break down" when they see you.

In fact, your child's reaction when you arrive can be pretty unpredictable. Your child may want to jump into your arms, receive loads of hugs and kisses, and have your undivided attention. Or your child may stay engrossed in his activity and ignore you. Respect that, and move gently into his universe of attention. Your child might throw a tantrum and become very obstinate when he sees you, which may mean that he's just blowing off steam at the end of a busy day. Or it may mean "Why did you pull me away from the middle of this activity that is so important to me? Why do I have to drop everything to keep to your schedule?" He could also be testing to see if you or his caregiver will set some needed limits for him. If you stay loving and firm, he will soon learn that this behavior doesn't get him anywhere.

Many of the same guidelines used for drop-off should also be used for pickup at the end of the day. Validate your child's experience by letting him show you what he did that day. Your child will be proud to show you his artwork or a project he has been working on. Show interest in his experience; it will then seem more important to him.

Don't pull him out in the middle of an activity. Let him finish what he is doing. That also shows respect for his endeavors.

My four-year-old, Gracie, and I have a policy that when I arrive in her preschool classroom at the end of the day, I will sit with her while she completes whatever activity she is involved with. She then shows me what she did that day, we talk to her teacher, and we leave. She should be able to finish what she's doing, but she shouldn't add "just one more" activity. This way, we respect each other's needs.

At the end of the day, always touch base with the caregiver to find out about your child's day. Once you've made the decision to leave, *you also* should avoid having "just one more" conversation. If you don't want your child to keep doing one more thing, then you shouldn't, either.

Leah talked about giving her children "jobs" as a way to motivate them to leave. It gives them some control and responsibility in the process:

> *I would say, "Guys, I need your help. Would you go get your lunch boxes?" That physically moves them from their activity, and they race to get their lunch boxes. "Guys, I need you to go open the door for me," so they run.*
>
> *If I can set their sights on a physical milestone, they will run through that playground without stopping and playing on the equipment. "Could you go out, sweetie, get to the gate first, and open it? I have all this stuff to get through." So Samantha runs out there, and she opens the gate, and then my two-year-old, Jared, just wants to be there, too.*

Tips for child care pickup (child care center or family child care home):

- As you arrive at child care, put work behind you and be present for your child.
- Warmly and calmly greet your child. Sit down with him while he finishes what he is working on. Let him show you what he did that day. Respect and validate his experience.

- Touch base with your child's caregiver. Find out about your child's day, his interests, his issues or concerns.

- Also touch base with other parents. It's wonderful for you and your child to develop a sense of community and friendship at child care.

- Help your child make the mental transition by talking about what you will do when you get home. Talk about a favorite home activity that he can look forward to—reading books, getting out his favorite toys or art projects, playing with pets, etc.

- Develop a consistent departure routine. Say good-bye to the children and caregivers. Be friendly but firm about leaving.

- Give your child some control and responsibility in the departure process. Let him gather up his artwork and lunch box, have him open the door or find the car. It can always help to make a game out of leaving.

THE COMMUTE HOME

The commute home can be a time when you purposely move out of your rushing mode and allow yourself and your child to slow down a little. Especially if you're a Camp Counselor mom and are used to vigorously and enthusiastically following your own agenda, you may want to consciously move into your child's universe rather than plunging him into yours. If your child has been in a fairly structured schedule during the day, it will be nice to have a more relaxed approach to your departure and return home, as Monique found:

> Our toddler, Tyler, needs a bit of a transition. Because we have about a block-and-a-half walk from child care to home, sometimes he'll poke. Yesterday, for example, he just sat down on a stoop, and I sat down right next to him while he was eating his box of raisins, and then we sang "Itsy-Bitsy Spider" for five minutes until he was ready to get up again. I try not to rush that time.

The trip home is a nice time to hear about your child's day. If you have talked to your caregiver before leaving child care, you will have an idea about what your child did that day and whether he had any special interests or concerns. Use that knowledge to prompt the conversation: "Ani told me you made an amazing block castle! Tell me about that." I always asked Farrell's teacher what she did during the day at preschool so I could ask her questions about specifics. If I didn't know and just asked her what she did that day, she would often reply, "Oh, nothing. I just wandered around."

Tell your child a little bit about your day, too, in a way that is interesting and easy to understand. That way you are both sharing. He will learn that you are your own person, with different activities and tasks that you do during the day. This creates a little window into the outside world that will grow over time.

It's during the ride home, when your child's day is fresh in his mind, that you may hear both his excitement about his activities and friends or any concerns. However, some children may want quiet time to listen to a favorite music or story tape and just wind down. It's helpful to talk through what you will do when you get home. That way your child can visualize the next step.

On the commute home:

- Don't rush the trip. After a structured day, let your child slow down a little.

- A healthy snack for the trip home helps if he's hungry and gives you some extra time for dinner preparation.

- Have some favorite music or story tapes for the ride home. Don't be surprised if you are asked to play the same tape over and over again. Young children love repetition, and it's actually an excellent way to learn words and tunes.

- Talk about what you will do when you get home so your child can visualize the next step.

ARRIVAL HOME

I remember walking in the door at six P.M. when the kids were home with our nanny, Michael. Josh was an infant who loved nursing and had a harder time with a bottle. So he was starving by six, and Aaron, our three-year-old, was extremely needy by then. I hadn't even taken my coat off, and the two little ones were screaming and crying and holding on to me. I just sat right down on the floor in the hallway in my winter coat, with my briefcase still over my arm. I pulled up my shirt, started nursing Josh, and put Aaron on my other knee and hugged him. We just sat until everyone calmed down. Michael looked on helplessly: "Is there anything I can do to help?"

—Sarah

Children may have been happy at home or in child care and school, but you are the mom. They want your full, undivided attention when you are back together. What *they need* can seem to fly in the face of what *you need* to do. You may feel the pressure to get the dinner going, get the car unloaded, get changed. Particularly if you are a Strategic Planner, you may have been thinking of your big to-do list all the way home, and you feel pressure to get going.

Well, give all that up for a few moments. As one little girl kept saying to her mother, "I want your full face, Mommy." She didn't want to be talking while her mother was looking over the mail or peering in the refrigerator to decide on dinner. One mother, Tina, had this to say:

I had my plan to come home and cook dinner between this time and this time, then read stories, take baths, yada yada, and then one day both my kids were crying, and I was standing there at the stove, saying, "I can't do this. I just can't do it." So I turned the stove off, picked them both up, and went and sat in the rocking chair and put up my legs and just sat there for a few minutes and rocked them. And it got calm.

I'm trying to make them fit into my routine. This isn't the

*routine that works for them. They needed about five minutes
of me sitting there. I was coming out of the traffic, all uptight,
and saying, "Okay, let's get everything out of the car, empty
the bottles, get everything ready for the next day." I wasn't
taking time to spend with them. That's all they needed—five
minutes of me, and then they were jumping off to go play.*

If your children have been home with a nanny or relative, first
stop to reconnect with them before engaging with the caregiver.
Remember that they yearn for your presence and are excited to see
you. If you explain this, your caregiver will know to give you all some
time to reconnect. Erin describes her typical arrival home after work:

*It's wild once I open that door at home. They all rush to me.
The kids see who I hug first, because they say that whomever I
hug first I must love the most, so I'm trying to hug them all at
once. There are some nights when I don't talk to the nanny for
fifteen to twenty minutes because I get caught up doing
something with them. Then I usually try to change, and they'll
all come up with me. I'll change, and then we'll snuggle and
play on the bed for a while. Once we physically reconnect,
they feel better.*

After you've had plenty of hugs and kisses, and looked at and
admired whatever they want to show you, you will then need time to
talk to your nanny. One mother, Sarah, finds that this end-of-day
communication is essential to both her and her nanny, Michael:

*Michael will always hang around and recount the day to
me. I will want to know if it was a good day, if there was
any conflict that may have arisen, any new exploits, any
adventures, anything that we can talk about at dinner, any
conversations he may have had with one of the children's
teachers or instructors. I just want to know it all.*

Create Your "Settle-In" Ritual

Once you are home and the nanny has left—or once you have arrived home from child care—just sit and cuddle with your children for a while. Settle in and read a book or talk with them about the evening. Get their favorite stuffed animals and security blankets to snuggle. Do something to set the mood: Put on quiet music, light a fire in the fireplace, turn down the lights. The settle-in activity can become an important ritual that everyone looks forward to and expects. Helen found a great settle-in activity for her children:

We pull into the driveway, and the minute we walk in the door, off come the clothes. We are on our way up the steps and into the tub. They lounge in the warm water, and everyone calms down and is happy. Then, after the bath, it's into jammies. They're feeling very cozy and relaxed. It makes the evenings more homey.

If your children are home with a caregiver, she or he can start the settling-in before you get home, so they are not all wound up when you walk through the door. As one mother, Elizabeth, described:

Everybody's usually pretty calm and cheerful when I get home. Our nanny is kind of in the background. She would start a wind-down at the end of the day, and be reading to them or just playing some little, quiet game. That's one of the greatest things—that she gets everybody very mellow.

Possible settle-in rituals:

- Sit in the rocking chair and snuggle
- Hold and play with pets
- Go to a "cozy corner" with cushions and read a book or two
- Collapse on the bed with the kids for a snuggle

- Give the kids a bath before dinner
- Light a fire in the fireplace
- Get everyone in pajamas for the evening—even you
- Put on soft lights and quiet music

Have a Healthy Snack

Children sometimes feel hungry and depleted at the end of the day. Feeding them a healthy snack gives them some nourishment and allows you time to prepare a meal. Chloe always puts out cut-up vegetables—carrots or celery sticks—on the kitchen counter when everyone gets home, and the children are allowed to take what they want. Alissa, a single mother who lives with her parents, comes home with her children, and her father serves little plates with cut-up fruits and vegetables—their "happy hour," as they call it.

Patricia and her husband, Ralph, have three children, two of whom are in elementary school. Because of Ralph's work schedule, they don't eat dinner until about eight P.M. Patricia and her children have a daily ritual of what they call "high tea." In the late afternoon, after work and school, they get out china teacups, put milk in a pitcher, and have milk, toast, and fruit:

It gets dark early here. It's cold, and there's nothing the kids like better than to go home and have "tea." Before they have to do anything—all their tasks, their homework, the piano practicing and everything—we try to relax a little bit. We might read something or talk about what happened during their day. We kind of ease in to the evening.

Other tips for arriving home:

- Put the lights and heat on timers so they are on when you arrive home. It's nicer than arriving to a cold, dark house—especially if you live in the North.
- Have siblings do separate activities at first. That gives them time to wind down without the never-ending challenge of

sharing and cooperating with a brother or sister. Later they can find each other to play.

DINNER

The kids know that dinner's ready when the doorbell rings for Chinese takeout.

—Evelyn

I guess if I have a regret, it is that we don't sit down and eat together as a family. I look back, and I think that a lot of the openness my parents and my brother and I have with one another is because of that time and that communication. It worries me that we don't have that kind of family dinner. I hope I don't live to really regret it in terms of a communication breakdown later.

—Helen

So many parents feel guilty because they don't have the idealized sit-down family dinner. But if you finish work at five-thirty, six, or later, rush to child care to pick up your children, then commute home, you never have enough time to cook a real meal and then sit down and eat it. Even if your children are home with a caregiver, you may arrive home too late or too tired to think of cooking a meal. So it just does not happen. Yet we often hear social commentators talk about the loss of the family dinner and what that means for families.

In most societies around the world, coming together around meals is central to tradition. From the most simple to the most sophisticated, cultures have created ritual and significance around meals. Even when I worked in a destitute Cambodian refugee camp, when I stopped to visit a family in their hut, it was important to sit and share a meal with them, however simple.

The ritual of food preparation, the symbols of nourishment and sustaining life, and the joining together over a meal are pivotal to every society. Many parents believe this intuitively, and although their families may not have a prepared sit-down dinner each night, they might aim for a family dinner a couple of times each week. Through the use of a Crockpot, or preparing the dinner on the weekend, or a variety of other techniques outlined later in this chapter, the family dines together once or twice weekly. Many families shift the ritual meal to the weekend. They prepare a traditional Shabbat dinner for Friday night, or they have a traditional Sunday midday meal after church, or a pancake breakfast on Saturday or Sunday morning. It is the ritual that is important to the family, whether it is the Sunday meal, the holiday meal, or the Wednesday-night meal.

One couple, Giovanna and her husband, Jorge, have quite unusual family dinner practices that work well for them. Jorge is a chef and has a true passion for gourmet cooking—both on and off the job. He works afternoons and evenings in a restaurant in the middle of a city. On Friday and Saturday evenings, Giovanna and their four-year-old daughter, Leonor, wait up until Jorge finishes working. They often go to a large bookstore near his restaurant and read books until closing at ten-thirty P.M. They then pick up Jorge at the restaurant and go home, where he cooks a wonderful meal that they eat around midnight. They go to bed very late and sleep late in the morning. On Saturday they love to go to the farmers' market, where they can look over and choose fresh produce. Jorge doesn't work on Sundays, so they try out new and unusual restaurants together. Leonor is being brought up in a culture of interesting cuisine, and it is not unusual for her family to spend a couple of hours at a restaurant on Sundays. I am sure Leonor will always remember her unique family dinner traditions.

So let's figure out this whole family dinner thing and try to eliminate the guilt. I'm going to first share some strategies that parents use to make dinners happen in a way that is positive for parents and children. This can be nightly or once or twice a week. Then I will give you an alternative to the family dinner.

Guidelines for Dinners

Family dinners should be age-appropriate

If you have very young children—babies and toddlers—it is unrealistic to imagine a sit-down dinner with everyone seated at the table for the duration of the meal. Little children have short attention spans, fidget if they sit in one place for long, and are picky eaters. Dinners for young children can be simple and healthy. They should eat and then be allowed to leave the table. As they get older, you can build in greater expectations that include sitting at the table with the whole family and conversing.

Let your children participate in dinner preparation

Children love to participate in the real work of families. Your children will be underfoot while you make the dinner anyway, so why not engage them in the process? Let them "help" you. It can be a shared activity, and they can also gradually learn real skills. Children can be your "finders" of all the things you look for in the refrigerator and the cupboards. They will learn about foods and condiments this way. They can sit at the counter and grate cheese, measure and count ingredients, stir things, put caps back on, put things away, wipe the counters, set the timer for cooking, set the table. This time can be fun and educational as they develop counting and measuring skills and fine motor skills (stirring, grating, chopping). Amy and her five-year-old son, Douglas, cook dinner together every night:

Douglas helps me pick out whatever we need for dinner. We use that time to discuss the food groups and nutrition. He likes to read the labels and figure things out. He will say that we have the starch, the meat and the protein, but we need a vegetable. He'll get a stool and get the stuff out of the cabinets for me. He'll put the timer on if we're cooking pasta. We open up the oven to see if something's browned enough. We're a real team. He loves it. He has to read the recipes to me, because I'm not a very good cook!

Not only can your child participate, but so can your spouse or partner! Many mothers share dinner preparation with their partners. Paige and her husband, Larry, split the week: Paige makes dinner Monday and Wednesday; he makes dinner Tuesday and Thursday; on Friday they go out to a neighborhood restaurant. Nichelle and her husband, James, make the dinner together, and their boys do the cleanup. Susana's husband, Antonio, cooks the dinner each night ("The best part of my day," she says), and she does the cleanup.

Dinner preparation tips:

- Post a weekly or biweekly menu on the refrigerator that you regularly follow (or, as my mother did, a monthly menu). That will simplify both shopping and preparation.

- Buy in bulk so you shop only every other week and do a quick fill-in when needed.

- Look for labor- and time-saving purchases: precooked chicken and other meats, precut vegetables, frozen casseroles, prepackaged rice or noodle or meat dinners, prewashed salad, bottled pasta sauces, healthy frozen entrées.

- Cook enough for two meals, then have leftovers the next night.

- Prepare some dishes for the week over the weekend: pasta sauces, casseroles, meats, soups. Freeze in small containers to defrost one meal at a time.

- Have the occasional "breakfast for dinner"—pancakes or waffles with fruit; omelets with vegetables; cereal. It's simple and healthy, and kids think it's fun to have breakfast at night.

- Prepare a Crockpot dinner at night and plug it in the next morning. Arrive home to a cooked meal (Crockpots really do still exist!).

With a little effort, you can make a dinner seem special

One friend of mine who is a professor and a single mother of two teenage children has a wonderful dinner ritual. She arrives home at six P.M. after an intense day and often has no idea what she's going to make for dinner. Even if it is warmed-up leftovers, she quickly creates a wonderful atmosphere: She puts a tablecloth, cloth napkins, and candles on the table, then picks out a special ceramic bowl or serving platter. She puts on soft jazz and turns down the lights. Suddenly she has transformed their simple dinner into a special family moment. They hold hands, and she sings the grace. It's a tranquil moment in the midst of a busy family life—and it entails minimal preparation. In fact, healthy frozen entrées and prepared foods are available at most supermarkets. You can pick up a prepared meal, take it out of the cartons, and serve it nicely, and you will still gain the positive effects of a family dinner.

Part of the beauty of a family dinner is the feeling of ritual and intimacy. You may be surprised at how the atmosphere changes when you exert a few small efforts to make it beautiful. Our son, Lucas, always makes sure the candles are lit and the whole family is seated before we say grace and eat. Gracie has added her own ritual of holding hands after grace and following a pattern of squeezes. These are now little rituals. Music will affect the mood. Perhaps you can put out a special centerpiece that your child has created. Small efforts that do not require much time or expense can contribute to an atmosphere of enchantment.

Have an occasional night out

Many families go out to a neighborhood restaurant once in a while. They usually choose a simple and inexpensive place where children are welcome. They get to know the staff. One mother has a tradition, every Wednesday evening, of taking her children out for dinner, then going to the library afterward. An occasional dinner out will feel special, even if it's inexpensive. It's a good opportunity to practice table manners, is a nice break from cooking and cleaning, and presents no distractions such as TV and telephone.

Dinner tips:

- Create a special atmosphere for even a simple dinner: Use a tablecloth, pretty napkins, soft music, nicely set table, child-created centerpiece, or special serving dish.
- Over dinner, have each person recount to the family something of their day. This creates a feeling of intimacy as each one shares a bit of the outside world. Allow everyone to talk, even the smallest.

- Ask each child what was the best and worst part of his day. That may elicit some surprises and honest discussion.

- Turn off the ringer on your telephone and put on the answering machine. Only telemarketers call during dinner, anyway.

- Change the dinner venue occasionally to make things special: in the backyard, in a park at a picnic table, or on a spread blanket in warm weather; a "romantic" dinner in the dining room with candles and mood music; a "cozy" dinner at the breakfast table or kitchen counter.

- If one parent works late, wait and have dessert with him or her.

- Everyone can participate in the cleanup. Wait and have dessert once everything is cleaned.

- As you are cleaning up, pack the next day's lunches using the leftovers.

TRY THESE COOKBOOKS FOR QUICK MEALS:

- *Mom's Updated Recipe Box, 250 Family Favorites Made Quick and Healthy*, by Donna L. Weihoten, R.D.
- *Once-A-Month Cooking*, by Mimi Wilson and Mary Beth Lagerborg
- *Discover Dinnertime*, by Susan Dosier and Julia Dowling Rutland
- *Lickety-Split Meals*, by Zonya Foco, R.D.

THE ALTERNATIVE TO FAMILY DINNER

Now let's look at an entirely different approach. For many families, a family dinner is just not possible—due to work or school schedules, age of children, and preferences. If that's the case, don't worry about it. Let me give you an alternative. First let's think about why the "experts" think the traditional family dinner is so important: It is a time for the whole family to come together as a unit, when everyone can settle down in one place and focus on one another. It is a daily ritual that each member can come to depend on. There is often the sense of the special. I soon came to discover that working parents are creating their own alternatives that embody many of the same values but work within the structure of their family life. Here are some:

- A later-evening gathering for herbal tea, hot chocolate, or milk and cookies, during which the family sits and talks together in the living room
- A family walk around the neighborhood before bedtime
- A gathering together of the whole family for reading and talking
- Once everyone is home, family dessert with a nicely set table and conversation
- Sitting on the porch swing at night before bed with everyone in their pajamas
- An interactive board game or charades
- Evening prayers and blessings
- Bringing a cup of tea downstairs to Grandma and visiting before bedtime

In many of these families, these are ritualized nightly events. I found it uplifting and reassuring that so many families have found a personal way to come together when sitting down at six P.M. for a fully prepared meal wasn't going to work for them. There is certainly no reason to feel guilty. Think about what nightly ritual would work for your family—your alternative to the family dinner.

AFTER-DINNER ROUTINE

For most families with young children, the after-dinner routine includes bath and bedtime stories. Now, I have to confess that I'm not as focused on baths as many parents. A regular nightly bath is fine if you all enjoy it or if your children get dirty every day. But you shouldn't feel obligated to bathe them each night. Kids don't *always* get that dirty, and it's probably better for their skin not to soap them up each night. If it happens to be a struggle for your children, let it go until they need it. If your children love it, then do it. It could be a soothing and calming routine for them.

The Importance of Reading

As busy as today's working parents are, many place emphasis on reading with their children. The percentage of working parents has increased dramatically over the last twenty years, but parents are reading to their children even more today. In fact, a recent study showed that in 1996, 59 percent of three- to five-year-olds had a story read to them at least three times a week, compared to 40 percent in 1991. That seems to be one daily ritual that parents are determined to maintain day after day. One mother, Lara, has completed only her high school education. Once she had her son, Tyrol, she focused on reading and education for both of them:

> *Without knowledge, you're in the dark. The foundation for knowledge is reading. I remember hearing somewhere, "Anything you want to know is at the library. Anything you want to do is at the library." That really stuck with me. So we do the library at least once a week. In order for Tyrol to get in the habit of reading, I have to get in the habit of reading. So I go to the library for myself, too. I like to read to Tyrol. It's our time.*

Reading is critical for a variety of reasons: Reading to young children is directly correlated with later academic success in school. It has a direct impact on a child's vocabulary, thinking processes, and eventual reading capability. If there is one thing you can do that will have an impact on your child's learning and school success, it is reading often and regularly. Your child will probably become fascinated with reading if he sees that you are, too.

Reading to your child is also a time to be physically close. You can hold your child on your lap while you share a book. Children can engage in the story with you, and you can discuss the emotions and events. They can try to predict what will happen. One mother, Shoshanna, describes her husband's reading routine:

> *Baruch loves to read stories to the kids. He gets so involved, and they do, too. He'll read a section that is really funny and jump up and act it out. Then the kids are laughing, and they do the same. Or he'll play a game of making up a different ending to a story that they know well. They will try to catch him in the act and correct him by recounting the real ending.*

One-on-One Time

For many parents, the after-dinner time is a special opportunity for alone time with a child. Francesca's husband, Carlos, keeps a special journal with their four-year-old son, Raoul. Raoul tells his dad about his day, and they draw pictures of it together, with Raoul dictating the text. Says Francesca, "My son is the quiet one the whole day, but at night, he has the biggest story."

Sarah and her husband, John, go off with one son each after dinner for some individual time:

> *We divide up after dinner. Aaron usually has a half hour of homework plus trombone and then twenty minutes of reading. Josh doesn't have any real homework, but we'll sit with him and work on his numbers and letters. We each like to have alone time with a child after our busy days.*

BEDTIME

Bedtime is a wonderful opportunity to connect with your child. Many mothers recounted lovely bedtime routines that include talking with each child as they tuck them in bed. Even if the children share the same room, you can tuck in each child individually and spend time talking or snuggling. Pamela observes:

> *Bedtime takes a long time. That's when things will come out, since I'm not there after school. So that's good, but I have to*

wait for it, and that takes a long time, too. My daughter's just not going to say, when I lean over to hug her good night, "Mom, I was kind of upset about . . ." I have to lie there for a while—and sometimes I fall asleep!

One friend, Paul, brings his guitar into his daughters' bedrooms at night, and they sing folk songs together. My husband, Roger, has a tradition of telling bedtime stories. He has a few characters—BoBo the Beaver, Scaredy-cat Wolf, and Owl—that he has developed over time, and he creates all sorts of adventures for them. Our children get involved by specifying the type of story. They sometimes get fairly demanding about its design: "Dad, can you make it scary, but not too scary? Can there be a hero who also does some funny things? And end the story tonight; don't keep us hanging until tomorrow."

For school-aged children, this is often a time for conversation. With an open-ended question like "What's on your mind tonight, honey?" you may open up issues about friends, growing up, development, fears, philosophical musings, or school. Your child feels safe and loved with you right there. Some parents rub or massage their child's back while they talk. For some children, it's easier to talk if they aren't looking directly at you.

Bedtime is also a good time to review what is happening the next day. Knowing what to expect gives young children a sense of security. As Alice says:

Because of our busy, somewhat stressful lifestyle, Jimmy's anxieties tend to catch up to him at night. It helps for him to know exactly what the plan is for the next day. I sit on his bed and go over the whole plan. I go over the after-school schedule, who will be caring for him, what we are doing for dinner, etc. I let him know where I will be. Knowing makes him feel more secure.

Bedtime tips:

- Create a predictable bedtime routine for your child so he will know what to expect—two or three books, a drink of water, and lights out.

- Sometimes young children will say they're hungry when they go to bed. I don't recommend feeding them at this point. It is often a way to delay bedtime and sets up bad habits. They will soon learn to eat enough at dinner so they won't be hungry later.

- View the bedtime as a moment to connect individually with your children. They will often open up about concerns and fears.

- Review the next day's plan. That can give a sense of security. Let your child know if there is a change in the normal routine.

AFTER KIDS ARE IN BED

Parents do a variety of things after the kids are in bed. Some parents just crash after a busy day. Some hit the housework and do laundry and cleanup. Others prepare for the next day. Some get on their computers and finish up office work. I was impressed by the extent of parents' commitment to their families while also balancing their work demands. But as I discussed in chapter 8, time with a spouse or partner can get neglected. Often one spouse goes to bed early while the other stays up later, working or watching TV. They live on separate schedules.

The couples who are able to maintain a focus on their relationship seem to follow a few guidelines. Sometimes they set a deadline for finishing up office or housework. One couple sets nine-thirty P.M. as a time to stop working and spend time together, even if it's just reading or watching TV. Some couples team up to do the laundry or cleanup so it is finished more quickly and they can spend time together. Others have a tradition of sitting down with a cup of tea or glass of wine or beer to catch up and talk. If they don't carve out that time, it will not happen.

And going to bed at the same time can make a big difference. Having that personal and physical connection at the end of the day is important for any relationship. I worry about the number of couples who seem to live on very different schedules, with no time for intimacy. And by all means, make love! Even falling asleep holding the person you love can make the next day feel brighter.

A WORD ABOUT WEEKENDS

At first I thought that families' weekends were too individual to draw many conclusions. Every story is a little bit different, reflecting the ages of the children, the families' interests, where they live, and so on. Families do a wide variety of things during the weekend: relaxation, household chores and errands, family outings, time with extended family and friends, and attending religious services.

However, even though weekends are unique to each family, many embrace a few common values and goals. I have highlighted some of the common elements that you can use to spark your thinking about your own weekends.

Friday-Night Reunion

Many families have a Friday-night tradition that becomes an intimate family reunion after a busy work and school week. It is a way that you can relax, wind down, and reconnect as a family.

> *On Fridays, we'll stop at the video store on the way home and rent movies. My two children and I like to snuggle up in my bed and watch movies. It's our snuggle time. Sometimes we'll all end up sleeping together in my bed.*
>
> —Chavonne

> *On Friday nights, we always go for a family swim at the Y. We all get in the pool, so there's some nice physical time together as well. After swimming, the kids shower and get in their pajamas at the Y. They are all cozy and comfy when they get home, and we just curl up and watch a video. That's the beginning of our weekend.*
>
> —Natalie

Friday night is our "game night." Jimmy and I will pick whatever game we want: Monopoly, a card game, whatever. We'll make popcorn and play our game; it's always our time after a busy week. We'll order something fun to eat that we don't have to cook—subs or pizza.

—Alice

Family Breakfasts

Many working parents cook a big family breakfast on the weekend, sit together as a family, and have a leisurely prepared meal.

Every Sunday, and sometimes Saturday, I make a big breakfast for the family. That is just something that we have always done. In fact, this comes from my husband's family. They always did that growing up. It's nice, because we don't often have a leisurely dinner together during the week.

—Sondra

Make Errands and Household Chores Fun

For many working parents, the housework and errands have to get done on the weekends. Instead of treating it as an onerous chore to rush through as quickly as possible, some parents organize house-cleaning as a lively, fun family activity, with everyone pitching in (wishful thinking? many claim it works!). They sometimes choose something fun to look forward to after the household chores—a trip to the park or some other favorite spot.

On Saturday mornings, the whole family pitches in to clean the house. Even the little ones have their jobs: dusting and putting away toys. We try to sing, talk, make it fun. We're done by eleven A.M. and ready to go outside.

—Jaclyn

Even running errands can become a family outing if you engage your children in the process—letting them help you find things in a store, learning about products and prices and how things work.

You can stop for a bagel along the way, or finish up at the playground. Be spontaneous about things you see as you go along—stop to watch workers at a construction site, to look at the fire engines as you walk past the firehouse, to listen to street performers.

> *Our kids love to run errands with my husband. He always takes them along when he goes to the hardware store or Home Depot. They all have a blast. They always stop to do special things. Believe it or not, it's something they all love doing—errands with Dad!*
>
> —Claire

> *My son, Douglas, and I will go to the supermarket together, and I make it a learning experience. We try to decide which product is cheaper. He knows about unit prices; he tries to figure out how much money each thing costs, and which one has a better nutritional value. It takes about two hours, but it's fun. We take our time and don't rush.*
>
> —Amy

Unstructured Playtime

During the week, many children are in structured child care or school settings. Therefore, many parents like to let their children have some relaxed time at home over the weekend. Children can benefit from playing on their own, using their imaginations to devise a make-believe game, creating their own rules and guidelines together with a sibling or friend. In fact, unstructured playtime can enhance your children's development as they learn to cooperate, share, negotiate, and, most important, develop their imaginations.

> *On Saturday mornings, the girls just chill out and play. They don't have to get dressed. They just hang out in their pajamas and enjoy each other. That's my day to constantly say to myself, "You don't need to hurry them. It's not a school day. Leave them alone. Let them enjoy their free time." I feel like I'm always rushing them during the week.*
>
> —Alena

The kids spend most of their weekend in their underwear, running around outside in our backyard. They run in and out of the house. I'll read and garden, and my husband does his projects. We spread out. It's relaxation. It's decompression time, and the kids just play.

—Evelyn

ELEVEN

Ah, Yes, Those Household Chores

It's depressing to come home from work and child care at six-thirty and the house is still the disaster that we left it in the morning. I'm so tired, but after the kids are in bed, I have to start in on the housework. There are no little elves around the house who are going to do it, are there?

—Joyce

One of the greatest sources of stress for working mothers is housework. It is so hard to come home at night, exhausted from a day's work, and feed the children, bathe them, and put them to bed—and then tackle mountains of laundry, a sticky kitchen floor that needs to be mopped, late notices for your electric and heat bills, and the sudden realization that you are out of diapers for the next day.

The Strategic Planner moms were brimming over with ideas about how to be more efficient and effective with chores. I've listed their advice below. But these tips and strategies are not meant for just the moms. All members of the family should pitch in. In this chapter, I describe the typical split in roles in two-adult households. I share strategies for how couples effectively share the housework, and how children, depending on age and ability, can also participate.

TIPS, STRATEGIES, AND SHORTCUTS THAT WORK

Use the tips below to prompt your thinking about how to make chores in your household easier and simpler.

Family Organization and Planning

- Put a large central calendar in the kitchen where all family events and work travel are noted.

- Next to the calendar, hang a bulletin board where you can post school news, birthday invitations, library notices, dry-cleaning slips, and shopping lists.

- Keep a file box in a handy spot in your kitchen. Set up files for items like lessons, school information, summer camp information, clubs, ideas for family activities, bills to be paid. Or use a big binder with pockets and dividers with tabs.

- During the late spring or summer, call the school superintendent's office for the following year's school calendar. Put vacations, school closures, parent/teacher conference days, and other important dates in your calendar.

- Research and plan vacations on-line. Airplane and train tickets and vacation packages can also be purchased on-line.

- Save time and buy tickets for entertainment, movies, plays, and sports events on-line.

Streamline Dinner Plans

- Create a weekly or biweekly menu that you consistently follow. You can change the menu every month, or whenever you're ready. Post it on the refrigerator.

- Write the name of the cookbook and page number by the menu items. Stock up on any missing ingredients when you shop each week.

- Introduce your children to one-dish dinners: pasta dishes, casseroles, salads, soups, pot pies, stews.

- Eat out or get takeout once a week.

- Frozen entrées and side dishes are a lot tastier and healthier than they used to be. Discover what a time saver they can be.

Grocery Shopping Made Easier

- Write up a list of your food and supplies staples. Organize by aisle in your supermarket. Make several copies, and you can just check off what you need each week. Shopping is quick since it's organized by aisle.

- Give yourself extra time at the supermarket when your children are with you. Include them in the tasks. They can find things for you, check for lowest prices and good nutritional value, and taste free food on offer. Make it a fun, participative event, but give yourself time.

- Buy in bulk. Look for sales of nonperishable items, and buy several weeks' worth.

- Buy groceries on-line, to be delivered right to your home— unless all those on-line grocery companies have gone out of business by now.

Clothing and Gift Shopping

- Shop on-line for clothes and gifts. Add your favorite websites to your web "Favorites" list.

- Set up computer reminders of key birthdays and anniversaries.

- Shop by catalog. Put your name on the mailing list of your favorite catalogs to receive notice of their sales. Stick your catalogs in your backpack or briefcase and do your browsing while waiting for a meeting or on the airplane for a business trip.

- Keep a holiday gift list from year to year; it helps speed up the process by reminding you what you did last year.
- Have a couple of favorite stores in which you concentrate your shopping.
- Buy a supply of children's birthday presents and keep them in a closet so you don't have to make a special shopping trip each time your child is invited to a party.
- Buy a year's supply of birthday cards for family and friends.

Simplify Clothes Management

- Take a seasonal clothes-shopping trip with your school-aged children. Make it a special one-on-one outing with each child. Go out to lunch together.
- Keep bins or large bags, labeled by age, in the basement or attic to facilitate hand-me-downs. Also have bins for summer and winter clothes.
- Buy children's clothes from secondhand stores; children outgrow clothes so quickly.
- Emphasize unisex clothes—like jeans, sweats, and polo shirts—and wrinkle-free fabrics.
- Buy lots of identical socks for your children so if one sock is lost, you can still use others. But buy a different brand or color for each child so they don't get mixed up.
- Hang a low bar in the children's closet so small children can hang up their own clothes.
- If children are too young to fold, they can roll up their clothes and put them in drawers.
- Never buy "dry-clean-only" clothes for children.

Laundry Tips

- Keep a hamper with three bins by the washing machine: whites, darks, colors. Everyone can sort and put his or her own laundry in bins.
- Fold the laundry as soon as it comes out of the dryer—it cuts down on ironing.
- Or don't buy clothes that need ironing.
- Children can fold and put away their own clothes.
- Children can pull sheets off their beds each week and put them in the washing machine.
- Buy lots of socks and underwear. That way you can stretch out laundry cycles.
- Your local Laundromat probably has a service to pick up, wash, fold, and deliver clothes for a modest fee.

Mail-Sorting Tip

- Sort the mail daily. Have baskets beside you: one each for bills, catalogs, and personal correspondence. Junk mail goes right in the recycling or trash.

Keeping the House Picked Up

- Have receptacles around the house: shoe basket, hat basket, book basket, and so on.
- Never go upstairs or downstairs empty-handed. Place things next to the stairs for the next trip up.
- Establish a family principle that whoever uses it puts it away; whoever makes the mess cleans it up.

Bill Paying Made Simple

- Arrange for direct deposit of your paychecks.
- Set up direct deduction from your checking account of regular household expenses, such as phone, heat, electricity, insurance. You will still get the itemization and be able to review it, but direct deduction prevents late payments and fees and saves time.
- Set up on-line bill paying (Quicken or other) to save time and mailing hassles. Use automatic payment of bills that stay the same each month: rent or mortgage, lessons, memberships.
- Use only one credit card. You'll save time and money spent on fees.
- Carry your bills in an envelope in your backpack or briefcase. If you have to wait for an appointment or are on a flight, you can use the time to pay bills.
- Set aside the fifteenth and thirtieth of each month to pay bills, or write the check as soon as the bill arrives and place it in a sorter by date. Mail when due.

OUTSOURCING SOME HOME SERVICES

Many working parents at a variety of income levels hire outside help for some household functions. My mother, who was a homemaker with five children, did everything herself around the home. One of her wisest pieces of advice when Roger and I had our first child was to get some help if we could afford it. If we could offload even a little bit of the housework, we could give that time to our family; be a little poorer but saner. Maybe go camping or visit friends or relatives on vacations instead of a more expensive vacation trip. Use the money saved to outsource some services.

The most common chores to outsource are housecleaning and cooking, but practically any domestic task, from gift shopping to transporting children, can be contracted out. Decide what tasks you would like to outsource, calculate your budget, then look in the Yellow Pages or a local parent newspaper or magazine.

Services that some families outsource:

- Food shopping
- Meal preparation
- Housecleaning
- Laundry
- Errands
- Window washing
- Lawn maintenance
- Child transportation
- Pet care
- Birthday-party planning
- Clothes shopping
- Academic help or tutoring
- Vacation planning
- Gift shopping and wrapping
- Waiting for repairmen
- Garbage and trash removal
- Dry cleaning pickup
- Dog walking

HOUSEHOLD CHORES ARE EVERYONE'S RESPONSIBILITY

That's right. They are not just yours. Every family member beyond the early childhood years can participate. All members can have specific responsibilities and chores.

Be Conscious About Roles at Home

While fathers participate in household chores and caregiving more today than ever, mothers often wonder why they still carry the heavier burden at home. Often, although not always, mothers do more tasks around the house. Also, mothers and fathers typically do different kinds of chores, as Denise found:

> Both my husband and I do the household chores, but I recently realized something important. I do the things that the clock is ticking on. They have to be done at a certain time, and you can't let them slide. Like there's no decision about whether you feed the kids today or tomorrow. But he can pay the bills today or tomorrow. My husband has the responsibility to dust and vacuum the house, but he may not do it for weeks on end. But I can't decide to put off cooking dinner and cleaning up the dishes and sweeping the mess on the floor.

Also, as I discussed in chapter 2, the mother is in many cases the household manager, regardless of the hours she spends at her job. At work, she thinks ahead to what errands need to be done on the way home and what after-school activities her child needs to go to. She maps out dinner preparation and evening plans. This kind of mom is always psychologically on call, as Carol points out:

> House and family are always on my mind—whether I'm at work, at home, or at the dentist. I'm thinking of everything and planning everything. I do resent it sometimes. I remember saying to my husband one night, "I don't know any more about managing a house than you do. Why do I have to think of everything?"

Don't Think Dads Can't Do It!

Mothers take on the household-manager role through cultural expectation, out of guilt because they are not home with the children, or because they like the control. Some rationalize this division of roles by saying their partner is not capable of doing such tasks. Even if their partners are extremely capable professionals and managers at work, somehow they think they are not able to do it at home. One mother whose husband is a highly skilled attorney said this:

> *I plan and decide things, and he participates. It's not so much due to gender but our individual natures. He's very organized, and he's able to do that at work, but I think it's not his nature at home.*

Another woman's husband is a financial analyst in a fast-paced job where he handles multiple accounts at once. However, she believes he loses those skills at home:

> *He's one of these guys whose brain is not equipped to think about all this. He's very smart, but he can only focus on one thing at one time, so I purposely try not to overload his brain with things. He simply cannot multitask. It's just impossible for him to do it. So there are times when I wish he would not be sitting there reading, but I have to bite my tongue.*

Another husband is a manager at a consulting company in charge of planning and managing complex consulting projects. His wife thinks that he, too, is unable to bring these skills home:

> *I don't mind being the planner in terms of our daily life. You know, it takes a lot of thought, and he's not good at that. He forgets things. I don't mind having it all under my control, because I couldn't let it go and trust him, so it's just as well.*

With all this incompetence, it is amazing that men have managed to succeed at all! Of course, someone needs to be the household manager. And there is nothing wrong with you playing that role. But don't do it because you think your partner is incapable. He may manage the household differently from the way you do it, but he very likely has the skills to manage the job. And don't forget: Your way isn't the only way.

Both of you should be aware of what the "household manager"

role entails, then make a decision about who should fill it. As in all managerial roles, the household-manager role carries some power, authority, and control, but it also carries extra responsibilities. In work settings, managers are trained to understand that empowering, valuing, listening, and appreciating are effective management skills. These have the same value at home. Very likely your partner does not appreciate having a to-do list handed to him with the expectation that it will be done your way and on your timetable.

Who should be the household manager?

- Designate one parent to fill the role with the clear understanding of what it entails.
- Or you can split household management responsibilities, with each parent being responsible for a separate domain (daily family schedule, vacation planning, social life, household repair and maintenance, nanny or baby-sitter management, finances, etc.).
- Or trade off this role depending on changing phases in the family and work life.

Whoever is the household manager should be sensitive to management style. Involve the other parent in decision making and time frames.

DOES PART-TIME AT WORK MEAN FULL-TIME AT HOME?

One question that many working mothers grapple with is whether having greater responsibility for care of the children also means primary responsibility for household chores. Some couples decide they don't want their children in full-time child care; they would like their children to spend at least part of their week at home with a parent. One parent, usually the mother, may cut back to part-time work so she can spend time with the children. What inevitably happens is that most of the household chores end up on her shoulders. Many mothers resent that. Mothers talked to me about their decision to take a step back in their careers so they could spend more time with the children. They did not take a step back in their careers to do the laundry and clean the bathrooms. As Leah said:

> This whole part-time-motherhood thing is hard. You end up doing everything full-time. Because you're the part-time person, you have to deal with all these home chores—because you supposedly have the time. Of course, the time you have at home is with your kids, so you don't have the time to do anything.

As I said previously, parents should not expect a nanny or a relative at home caring for your children to take on all the housecleaning. You have hired this person to take care of your children; you have not hired a cleaning lady. You want her to focus on your kids. Logically, that should also be the case for the mother who stays home just a day or two during the week to be with the children. She is not home with free time on her hands; she is home to care for her children. There are some things that she can do fairly easily, like throw in a load of laundry or get dinner started. She and the children can pick up the house together and fold the laundry and put it away. But the expectation should not be that all the household chores are now hers. Child-caring tasks should be separated from housecleaning and maintenance, and then spouses can sit down and decide who should be responsible for what.

Deciding and Acknowledging Responsibilities

Warren Farrell, an author on men's issues, believes the discussion of the "second shift" of work at home is often made without factoring in many of the extra contributions men make for the family. If the father has primary breadwinning responsibility and works longer hours to carry it out, Farrell says, this should be acknowledged and included in a discussion of responsibilities. He also believes that many of the father's household chores are never counted, such as shoveling snow, assembling and installing appliances, carpentry, remodeling, or planning for college education.[1] Let's try to avoid a war on the home front with a constant tit-for-tat approach. Instead, let's respect the various contributions made by both partners and create a situation where neither one has an undue burden.

Some of the moms I interviewed have figured out with their partners a fair and balanced system for getting the housework done. These are their guidelines:

1. Sit down together and list all the household tasks that need to get done (see pages 396–398).

2. Prioritize the list. You may find that you've included things that aren't really that important to either of you—for example, some parents don't really care if the beds get made every day. Eliminate these tasks.

3. Group the tasks into daily, weekly, biweekly, monthly, and seasonal. Discuss the time frames. Maybe tasks you put in the weekly category can get done every other week—for example, the weekly grocery shopping can be done every two weeks if you buy in bulk. You may both decide that dusting every two weeks is sufficient.

4. In each category, each of you should first choose the things you enjoy doing. As for the things neither of you likes doing, divide them up, eliminate them, or outsource them.

5. Relax and don't keep the tally too closely. Help each other out. Periodically revisit to see if the system is working.

It may help to relax standards a bit now that you have children. You may prefer to focus your limited time at home on family rather than on your former standards of neatness around the house. As Myrna said:

I have become more laid-back about the apartment now that we have children. Right now I have two laundry baskets in the living room, and there's a comforter in the hallway that is on its way to the Laundromat. And I don't stress out about it. The kitchen has to be clean, and the bathroom has to be clean. We're relaxed about the rest.

If you start by deciding who enjoys doing what, you may be surprised by the outcome. Listen to the breakdown in tasks with a few different couples:

> *Laundry is something that doesn't stress me out. I like it, fine, I'll do it. It's all mine. My husband really likes food shopping, and it would always frustrate him that I don't use coupons more. So great, that's his job. For some reason, making our kids' lunches gives him great pleasure. It's his way of feeling that his children are well cared for at child care. So lunches are his thing. The things neither one of us likes doing, we just split down the middle.*

> *I put the dishes in, and he takes them out. I put the laundry in, and he folds. He finds it relaxing, I don't. So he folds. We just started doing things we like; then we formalized it.*

> *My husband cleans the house, vacuums, cleans the bathrooms. I do the cooking and laundry and dishes.*

> *My husband is interested in design and colors. He does all the clothes shopping, even for me. He works downtown, where all the retail stores are, and I work where there are absolutely no stores. So he also buys the birthday presents and holiday presents. I pay the bills and take the kids to their doctors' appointments.*

INCLUDE YOUR CHILDREN IN HOUSEWORK

Children benefit from actively participating in the work of the home. Chores teach a sense of responsibility and industriousness and help children learn to be self-reliant. Children also learn best from example. If they see both father and mother participating fully in the care of the children and the upkeep of the house, they will learn to do the same. You and your partner will be teaching them that these are important values for both genders, not just women. You will be giving them skills that will help them as adults when they are on their own or in their own domestic relationships.

Many children are already learning to clean up after themselves at child care; this sense of responsibility can continue at home. In well-functioning child care centers or family child care homes, caregivers teach children to work together to clean up after an activity. They clear their lunches; they wipe up spills. How many times has your preschooler burst into singing the cleanup song at home? Here are some guidelines for engaging your children in the work of the home:

Start young

You can start your children as early as three or four by having them do simple chores such as putting their toys and clothes away. Establish early on that children clean up after themselves. Chores can be expanded for them as they grow and develop greater capabilities. Four- and five-year-old children can make their bed, put away clothes and toys, help set the table, put their dishes in the dishwasher or the sink. By eight or nine, they can help after dinner by clearing the table, putting away food, loading the dishwasher, wiping the table, and sweeping the floor. They can feed and walk the dog. By ten, they can start doing some of their own laundry and make their own lunches.

When children do chores, they also learn basic skills. For young children, setting the table is a counting exercise. Sorting laundry helps them learn colors. Caring for a pet teaches nurturance and responsibility. When finished, they have a sense of accomplishment.

Do it together

I discussed in chapters 9 and 10 that routine caregiving (diapering, feeding, bathing, dressing children) should not be viewed as unpleasant or unimportant tasks to get through as quickly as possible; they are a central part of the caregiving relationship. Household chores, likewise, don't have to be viewed negatively. Maintaining a household is part of the effective functioning of every family. We can look on chores as part of creating a healthy family life. If every member participates—in both the planning and the doing—they can become an enjoyable shared activity, as Amy found:

We take about an hour on Saturday morning, doing household chores like dusting, polishing, vacuuming, washing the floors, washing the tub, the toilet. We do it together. My five-year-old, Douglas, scrubs the tub. He does the vacuuming by himself. We're a team. We're talking throughout all of it.

As always, children will work better if they participate in the decision making. You can all work together on Saturday or Sunday mornings as a family. Small children can dust and put things away. School-aged children can vacuum, sweep, mop, change sheets.

Make it fun

Make it a game, put on fun music, go on a fun family outing after you are all done. Make it more of an event, not something unpleasant to get through.

Guidelines for deciding family responsibilities:

- Assume and expect that *all family members will actively participate* in household chores—children, mother, father, any other individuals living with you.

- *Have a family meeting* where the issues are discussed—or a parents' meeting, if the children are too young. Encourage participation about what chores should be done, who should do them, and how they should be done. The process will not be as successful if Mom decides everything and then tells everyone what to do.

- *Decide on standards.* Is it important for you to have a very neat and clean house? Or are you content to let standards slip?

- *Value what each member contributes.* Show appreciation. Don't keep a constant tally.

- *Occasionally do for your partner* what he or she is typically expected to do. It will be greatly appreciated and sets a spirit of generosity. He can sew her ripped hem; she can change the flat tire on his car.

- *Make household chores a family event.* You can all work together on Saturday or Sunday morning with lively music, rotating responsibilities, and then top it off with something fun—a walk to the bakery, a family outing to the park.

The following is a list of typical household chores and tasks. Don't let the length of the list overwhelm you; it includes many things that you probably don't do or want to do. There may be items that you would like to add. Just use it as a way to prompt your thinking on what needs to be done in your household. You and your partner can make your own list and then sit down and decide who or how each task will be done.

HOUSEHOLD TASKS AND RESPONSIBILITIES[2]

Daily
Child Care/Education
Prepare bottles and formula
Feed children
Dress small children
Make lunches
Drive children to child care or school
Drive children to after-school activities
Arrange play dates, carpools
Keep track of daily discipline, playtime, cuddling, reading books
Homework help
Oversee children's chores
Bathe children
Put children to bed
Read school information and notes

Family Life
Maintain daily family schedule and who needs to be where when

Household
Make beds, tidy rooms
Empty dishwasher
Sort mail
Plan and prepare dinner
Set table

Clean up dinner dishes, pots, and pans
Wipe down table and counters
Sweep floors
Take out garbage and recyclables
Pick up clutter
Feed pets
Walk dog
Change kitty litter

Weekly
Child Care/Education
Arrange children's activities
Wash hair
Clip nails

Family Life
Schedule weekend activities
Plan social life
Rent and return videos

Household
Do laundry
Iron clothes
Change sheets
Shop for groceries
Wash floors
Clean bathrooms

Empty wastebaskets
Vacuum, dust, polish
Fill gas tanks in cars
Water plants
Clean out pet cages
Mow lawn
Maintain garden
Go to dump
Put trash, garbage, recyclables out for collection
Drop off clothes at dry cleaner

Monthly
Household
Wash car
Pay bills, balance checkbook
Manage family budget
Clean kitchen appliances

Seasonal
Child Care/Education
Attend parent/teacher conferences
Coach children's teams
Buy clothes and shoes
Sort clothing by size and season

Family Life
Plan holiday celebrations

Household
Clean out closets and cupboards
Organize garage
Wash windows
Replace batteries in smoke detectors
Perform routine car servicing and oil changes
Turn mattresses

Regular Ongoing
Child Care/Education
Teach children skills: reading, letters, tying shoes, riding bike, etc.
Volunteer in school, extracurricular activities
Make and keep dentists' appointments

Fill out school forms, pay fees
Get haircuts
Take care of first aid, sick-child care, doctors' appointments
Drive children to birthday parties, buy presents
Attend school and sports functions
Buy school supplies
Mend clothes, remove stains
Select and enroll children in extracurricular activities, lessons, etc.
Communicate with teachers and coaches
Send letters and packages to children at summer camp
Purchase or borrow books, toys, equipment
Determine what activities are appropriate:
    Determine TV, computer, phone usage
    Decide appropriate games and videos
    Monitor friends; determine degree of independence

Family Life
Set family goals and priorities
Plan vacations
Schedule social life and entertainment
Remember birthdays, anniversaries
Keep in touch with extended family, friends

Household
Buy bulk food and supplies
Wash pets, take to vet
Weed yard and garden, fertilize, prune
Submit medical insurance forms
Deposit checks, withdraw cash

Yearly

Child Care/Education

Make and attend annual pediatrician
appointment

Plan birthday parties

Investigate summer camps, sign up

Family Life

Do holiday gift buying

Maintain memberships

Household

Get registration, inspection of cars

Pay income taxes

Make insurance payments

Plant garden

Shampoo carpets, wax floors

Defrost and clean refrigerator

Clean heat and AC filters

Arrange yearly maintenance on boilers

Pump septic tank

Arrange for chimney sweep

Clean out gutters

Occasional/As Needed

Child Care/Education

Deal with first aid, medical and dental
emergencies

Research and select child care/schools

Household

Fix car

Schedule and wait for servicemen

Make appliance, computer, furniture,
home purchases

Purchase car

Do home maintenance and repair

Pick up prescriptions

Organize household improvements and
remodeling

Paint house

Shovel snow

Assemble furniture, toys, appliances

Hook up appliances, computers

Do carpentry

Kill insects, rodents

TWELVE

The Pressure of the Early Years

*All of this working-mother stuff is just so hard. You know,
there are times when I have wanted to pack my bags and
leave—just hop in my car and drive away. Those times aren't
as often as they may have been in the first years. But I would
say it's that little thread. You're on the edge, and you're just
holding it all together—hoping the little thread won't snap.*

> —Gina

*I think that this whole thing is hard—really, really hard. They
do not teach you this at school—how you balance your life and
make everything work. And the balance changes all the time.
Sometimes your job changes, sometimes things with your
husband change, and the kids change all the time. Life can
feel crazy. I'm doing the best I can, and I haven't done it all
perfectly. I know I've made mistakes. It's really, really hard.*

> —Selena

I think Gina and Selena have summed up well what so many of us
feel as working mothers. Just when you think you have gotten
everything together, something changes and your routine and life are
thrown into disarray.

In this chapter, I will talk about the way some mothers manage
these early years—the focus of this book—and show you how they put
these years in perspective. I will share with you some of their tools,

such as family meetings and goal setting, that help them navigate ongoing family growth and changes. I will focus on a few specific sources of stress in the initial years of a working parent's life. I will talk about the arrival of the second child: Although usually planned for and celebrated, it is often at this point in a working mother's life when she feels the greatest stress. I will also talk about what to do when young children get sick and parents need to work, and how to manage this pressure point. I am not covering all sources of stress and pressure in a mother's life. Other areas of great challenge—divorce, loss of job, illness, death or disability of a family member, etc.—are beyond the scope of this book. If you are facing these challenges, I encourage you to seek specialized support in these areas.

THE FIRST YEARS ARE EXHAUSTING, BUT IT DOES GET EASIER

For many working mothers, the first years seem overwhelming. As a new working mom, you are suddenly plunged into uncharted and sometimes frightening territory as you try to figure it all out. The physical exhaustion of the first years takes its toll. Babies and young children have nearly constant needs and demands. You no longer can count on a full night's sleep, and the continual sleep deprivation can erode your strength and optimism. You may be creating a family at the same time you are trying to get established in a job or profession. It's tough to meet this intense pressure both at home and at work.

Although the goal of this book is to provide you with a variety of strategies to ease your daily life in the early years, the fact remains, as Selena says above, juggling work and family is really, really hard. Although there are difficulties at every stage of family life—sometimes enormous—many parents find the initial massive adjustment to parenthood and all the exhaustion, sleep deprivation, and complete dependence of young children to be one of the hardest times—until, of course, the adolescent and teenage years. Add the pressure and demands of working, and this phase can be overwhelming.

Fortunately, it is also fairly short-lived. By the time your youngest child is three, things begin to ease up at home. By then, your youngest child will be able to verbalize and may be able to explain to you what is bothering her rather than just throwing a tantrum to demonstrate. She will now begin to play somewhat independently without constantly demanding your help and attention. She will be out of diapers, or soon ready to be. She probably sleeps through most nights: a huge relief. I don't want to underemphasize the effect of loss of sleep—of dragging yourself through a workday after being up most of the night with a baby or toddler. For me, at least, sleep deprivation puts a gray cast over how I see everything in my life.

If you have more than one child, by the time your youngest is three, the older child has become much more self-sufficient and can actually be a help with the younger one from time to time. Remember that during these early years, you are forging your life as a family. Although the early years are exhausting to live through, many parents look back at them with nostalgia. You are so central to your child's life—you are her world. Although it seems cliché, it is true that these years pass too quickly, and your children become so independent so soon.

SIMPLIFYING YOUR LIFE

Many working parents find that a good strategy during these initial years is to narrow in on work, family, and just one or two other priorities in your life. I know for Roger and me, when we consciously simplified our lives during the early child-raising years, we found that we eliminated all sorts of things that didn't really interest us, anyway. We really "cocooned" when Farrell and Lucas were little. We were just starting to emerge and spread our wings a little when we had Gracie, five years after having our last child. Whoops, back into the cocoon we went! Having a baby again made us realize how much easier life could be if we didn't try to branch out too much.

The intensity of these early years can smooth your evolution into parenthood. It helps you figure out what kind of parents you want to be. Trying to work while having babies and little children forces you to prioritize. You can't do it all, so you figure out what is most important and focus on that. You may realize that what you value most is the company and support of extended family. Getting outside and being active may be where you and your family feel best, or your religious or spiritual community might be where you want to spend your family time. You start creating your family culture in these early years. Family life begins to take on more of a rhythm once you have established your rituals and traditions.

This initial phase of trying to figure out a work routine while parenting is also hard, but as I have discussed throughout, your routine as a working mother becomes easier as you create strategies and habits that help you through the day. Both parenting and working can be full-time occupations, so combining the two has to become a learned habit. Before I had children, I felt tremendous pressure to jump up and get to work early in the morning. I would look at friends of mine who had babies, and I could not imagine how they could manage to get out of the house with a baby and focus on work at a reasonable hour. Somehow, though, we figured it out, and now it is just a routine. As our working-mother strategies become habits for us, life becomes easier.

FLEXIBILITY IN HOME LIFE

Although I frequently mention the advantages of routines, now I'm going to tell you not to get too attached to them. One strategy that many mothers swear by as they manage the pressure points of working family life is to remain flexible. Children and families change constantly, as do jobs and work schedules, and child-care solutions. A well-thought-out routine can help your life as a working mother, but be ready to ditch it and create another one when you need to. As Chloe says:

> There are five growing individuals in our household, and things change all the time. One of our "secrets of success" is that we keep on changing our routine. It requires a constant flexibility.

Roger and I often come up with a strategy that suits our family and work needs; then in six months, we have to throw it out as our children's schedules or our work demands change. I think of it as driving on the highway: We are generally (or hopefully) going in one direction, but we have to constantly make little adjustments in steering and speed.

This is where your family culture will help you along. As you make your adjustments, your family priorities will be your signposts along the way—they will help you maintain direction.

Liberate yourself from feeling that you have to get it perfectly right. You can never predict your children's needs exactly, just as you cannot predict yours or your partner's. Tune in to your family's changing dynamics and then be flexible. As Natalie says:

> *I'm constantly struggling with "Am I balancing it right?" I don't think we've got it exactly right, but we've got it mostly right. The basic infrastructure is there. There may be daily things that happen that I don't feel good about, but I think overall, the choices that we have made have worked.*

You'll see that children's developmental stages make for a very different family life from stage to stage. As we talked about earlier, the baby and toddler years are a time when you pull in, simplify, and prioritize, learning how to be a parent while working.

The elementary school years can be a time of slowly opening back up to the world. In this period, your children form values and learn about the world. You can help them discover it by embarking on small and large adventures together. Although you are still the primary influence in your children's lives, they are growing in independence. Each stage requires flexibility to adjust to its challenges and beauty.

SOME NAVIGATIONAL TOOLS: FAMILY MEETINGS AND GOAL SETTING

How do you address the challenges of each new phase? How do you figure out your routines? Here our Strategic Planner moms have strong advice. They are used to being thoughtful about each phase in family life. They think it through, decide what they want, and craft a new direction. Maybe we can learn from their example. Many of them talked about the value of family meetings as a way to work through challenges and find solutions together.

As your children get older, try creating this tradition of family meetings. Especially since you are at work during the day—when frequent issues come up and decisions are made—it can help you all to know there is a set and regular time when you can sit down, air family issues, and make decisions.

Some families have weekly meetings to go over upcoming plans, to talk about Mom's or Dad's travel schedule and who will be taking care of the kids. You can use this time to make sure your children understand what's coming. In a family meeting, each member can bring up issues of concern. Meetings can start when children are four or five; many parents, such as Selena, appreciate learning how to discuss things as a group:

> *We have a family meeting every Sunday night. I travel almost every week, so it's a good opportunity to get everyone prepared for what's ahead.*
>
> *One of the things we have real battles about is who gets to talk. So we use a Beanie Baby during the family meeting. The person who is holding the Beanie Baby is the person who gets to talk, and when it's time for the next family member to speak, that person will pass it. It's a good way to teach children how to be good listeners.*

If a weekly meeting seems too much for you, maybe do it occasionally when big things come up. Some families use their meetings to discuss how the family functions. Maria, a single mother of two school-aged children, started monthly family meetings when her children were young and her daughter was being harassed by a neighborhood bully. She found that the meetings were a good way to draw out her children on important issues:

> *I was still on welfare and would baby-sit at night to make some extra money. This neighbor girl would come over to take care of my kids for a few hours, but she was really mean to*

*my daughter. I sat my daughter down and started to talk to
her about how we should handle this situation, and then my
son started joining in. He was a little thing, but he'd chime in.
Then we just started making monthly meetings. Sometimes we
have emergency meetings when big things happen. Anyone
can bring a topic to the table.*

Try having weekly, monthly, or occasional meetings when
issues arise.

Setting Goals for the Family

As children grow and life gets increasingly complicated, some parents
try to sit down and set family goals. Our Strategic Planner moms lead
the way on this one, too. They may periodically review how successful their work and family balance is. They think about overarching
goals in their work life, in their home life, and maybe for each of their
children. One mother, Leah, makes this an annual tradition with her
husband, Adam:

*We have a ritual each New Year's Eve of having a very frank,
thoughtful, meaningful discussion about the year gone by and
the year to come. We write out our resolutions for the year in
a book that I keep. We bring out this book each year.*

Some moms take planning even further. One mother and her
spouse developed a "vision statement" of how they wanted their family to develop. It included values, ways of relating to one another in
the family, skills development, and family priorities.

Another mom, Wendy, and her husband, Walter, took a life-
planning course based on Stephen Covey's *Seven Habits of Highly
Effective People.* They defined their various roles—in Wendy's case,
mom, business professional, wife, daughter—and focused on their
goals within each role:

*The process helped us to think about what kind of people we
want to be and what kind of kids we want to raise. What are*

the values that we think are important? I look at the goals
every couple of weeks or so. At the beginning of the year, we
go over them. What have we done? Did this work?

You may never get to that level of planning—and you may not even want to. But you might find it helps to think through some general goals as you traverse your busy, ever-changing work and family lives.

Some parents include their children in the goal-setting process. At the beginning of the school year, children can think about what they would like to accomplish, what skills to learn, what new goals to set, what friends to make. Then the parents set goals on what they would like to help each child focus on that year.

The goal-setting process:

- Find a natural time each year to sit back and reflect on the past year and what you want for the year ahead—can be New Year's or the beginning of the school year.
- The goals can include categories such as personal improvement, work goals, skills acquisition, friendships, family activities, or conflict resolution.
- Together you can create goals as a family and as individuals. Children enjoy participating in this process. You and your partner can continue in greater depth later.
- Write out the goals and post them or keep them somewhere special so that you can review them from time to time.

In my conversations with working mothers who have young children, I heard about two subjects in particular that seemed to be particularly difficult during the early years—the arrival of the second child, and what to do when children get sick and parents need to work. For many moms, the arrival of their second child is no less life-changing—and pressure-filled—than the arrival of the first.

THE ARRIVAL OF YOUR SECOND CHILD—WHILE WORKING

The arrival of a child is such a celebrated, precious, and often long-awaited event. But as wonderful as it is, we can't ignore the fact that it can also bring stress and exhaustion. For a working mother, the arrival of the second child can be the moment when she feels like that fragile little thread holding her life together is ready to snap. Suddenly it seems so easy to have just one child. You can't imagine how you are going to manage with two, especially getting up and off to work. If your first child is a toddler or preschooler, she also still depends on you for most of her needs. As Leah said:

> *As I sat in the hospital after I had our second child, I knew it was going to get crazier and more chaotic at home. I remember distinctly the pleasure of being in the hospital with him, knowing that when I went home, it was going to be wild. I felt no urgency to get home.*

You may deeply desire this second baby but still feel sad for your first child. When you're a working mother, time devoted to your children can seem so limited—and now you have to share it with two. As Leah continued, "Here we had only Samantha, she used to be our only child. She had both of us doting on her. She's not going to now, the poor thing."

Prepare the Older Sibling *Before* the Baby Arrives

As you think ahead to the arrival of your baby, and all the changes in your work and family routine, help prepare the older sibling for this change. She is used to a particular morning and evening schedule. A toddler or preschooler cannot imagine what it means to add a baby to this routine. As Sarah said, "Aaron thought he was the center of the universe, and it was a rude awakening."

Roger and I worked hard to prepare Farrell when I was pregnant with Lucas. However, we made one big mistake. We explained that she would stay with our friends Chip and Ingrid when I went to the hospital to have Lucas. Farrell was two and a half years old at the time and loved Chip and Ingrid like family. We showed her where she would sleep at their house. We packed up her clothes. We showed her where I would stay in the hospital. We neglected to tell her, however, that we would both return after just two days. She suddenly started waking up at night and getting clingy. Whenever I left her to go to work, she wailed so forlornly—as if I were leaving her forever. It took a couple of weeks before she blurted out that she didn't want to lose us and live with Chip and Ingrid forever. Don't assume that your young child understands what may seem obvious to you.

There are wonderful books (mentioned on page 409) for young children about the arrival of a new baby brother or sister. If you are so inclined, find out the gender of the baby and go ahead and name him or her. It will start seeming more real if you can all talk about baby Jennifer. Your child can stroke your belly and feel her kick. She can talk and sing to her. Our son Lucas was four years old when I was pregnant with Gracie. Every night before he went to bed, he would put his head on my belly and sing to her the song "You Are My Sunshine." Both Lucas and Gracie claim that they remember his doing that.

Many mothers advise that if the older sibling has been in a crib, it is a good idea to move her into a bed long before the baby is due. You don't want her to feel that she is losing her cherished crib to the baby. If she moves into a big bed several months before, and you take all her things out of the crib and move it to a different place, she will have forgotten that it was hers by the time the baby is born.

Despite all your best efforts, don't be surprised if your child regresses a bit before or soon after the birth of the baby. That is common. Unless it is extreme, you shouldn't worry. Your child may suddenly start waking in the night, wetting her bed, using baby talk, behaving in a clingy or anxious way. Some children start asking for the bottle even if they have long moved on, or they may need to go back into diapers for a while if they start having numerous accidents. It may seem that you are now going to have two extremely needy babies to get ready in the morning.

This is a moment when your child care provider can be a stable, calming influence. Talk to your caregiver about your child's issues or fears around the new baby; together you can come up with strategies. Particularly if you are distracted by pregnancy complications or adoption proceedings, health issues, or fatigue, your caregiver can step up during this period. If your child regresses, don't shame her or be shocked. She needs reassurance at this stage. The regression is typically short-lived. Once the baby is born and life settles down again, the older sibling will usually move out of this phase within a few months.

When I was pregnant with Gracie and confined to bed rest for four months, Lucas's preschool teacher, Zoe, was a bedrock of support for him—and for me. Lucas became focused on drawing and "writing" during this period. As he drew picture after picture of his changing family, Zoe was able to get him to talk about what was on his mind through his pictures. Since I was unable to visit the classroom, Zoe regularly called me during nap time to fill me in on Lucas's experience there and all his growing interests, skills, and friendships.

CHILDREN'S BOOKS ON A NEW BABY IN THE FAMILY:

- *I Love You the Purplest*, by Barbara Joosse
- *Julius, Baby of the World*, by Keven Henkes
- *Welcoming Babies*, by Margy Burns Knight
- *A Baby Sister for Frances*, by Lillian Hoban
- *The Berenstain Bears and Baby Makes Five*, by Stan Berenstain and Jan Berenstain

---

The Second Baby Will Not Be Like the First

Each baby has her own disposition. Just as you may have been surprised with your first baby, be prepared to be surprised by your reaction to the second. Even if you have two calm babies, they may have different sleeping and nursing schedules. I remember feeling so successful when our first baby, Farrell, started sleeping through the night at three weeks. I thought that this whole sleep business was so overblown; you just needed to know how to do it right. Then our second child, Lucas, nursed every two hours around the clock for the first nine months and didn't sleep solidly through the night for over two years. My first few months back at work were just a hazy fog of sleeplessness. Or, like Susana, you may have had a calm first baby and a colicky second baby:

> *Cristina was not at all like Andres. She did not sleep. She wanted to eat constantly, when we used to have to wake Andres to eat. Two weeks into it, I was a complete wreck. She was so tough, my mom said she could take care of Andres, but Cristina was a one-woman show.*

This kind of situation may complicate matters for a working parent. You may have found a child care situation that has worked beautifully for your first child. But you might not be able to continue with the same child care center or family child care home due to the disposition of your second child, if your second child is more prone to illness, or has difficulty with noise and commotion. Or your nanny or relative may not be able to handle both children, especially if one is very challenging. Since it's much simpler for you to have both children in the same place, you may have to find a new solution.

It is hard to plan ahead, since you will not discover your baby's disposition until she is born. Also, a colicky newborn may settle into a calm older infant. If you suspect that you will not be able to include your second child in your existing child care, start researching an alternate during your maternity leave (see chapter 4). Many moms will research another child care solution but not make a switch until they have given their existing provider a good try. Some parents can turn to a family member for help. If Grandma or Grandpa can take care of your new baby a little bit, you may be able to ease her in slowly to full-time child care when she is more settled and easier to handle.

Once the Baby Is Home, the Older Sibling's Reaction May Be Very Strong

> *"I never really wanted a brother! I wanted a fish!"*

So said Jeremy, Denise's first child, when his baby brother was born. As fine a job as you have done in preparing your child for the baby's arrival, you may still see a strong negative reaction once you are home with the newborn. Your child's world has been turned upside down. Young children see the world as revolving around them; it's hard to understand all the attention now going to this baby. To add to the challenge, many parents have their second child when their first is just a couple of years old. Your firstborn may be entering toddlerhood, where, even if you didn't have a newborn, she has learned to say no, to be stubborn and negative, or to have difficulty controlling her now strong emotions. Toddlers' emotions are far ahead of their verbal abilities. She may not be able to express what she is feeling and may frequently dissolve into frustrated tears, as Helen found:

> *The first day in the hospital, Molly, my two-year-old, came to visit with my parents, and it was awful. She wouldn't look at the baby, she wouldn't look at me, she wouldn't touch him. I remember the evening when we came home with Brett, we were just starting to have dinner, and I had Brett in my arms. I was putting him into the bassinet, and Molly fell at my feet in tears, wailing, "My mommy, my mommy," as if she had lost me forever.*

I remember very clearly trying to get ready for work on the frequent mornings when Roger was traveling for work. Lucas was a baby, and Farrell was a toddler. I found that I could take a quick shower if I put Lucas in his baby seat right by the shower and kept the curtain open a bit so he could see me. I could prevent his crying if I talked and sang to him nonstop. But then Farrell, who was feeling very needy after the arrival of her little brother, would stand there wanting me to get out. At times, all three of us would end up drenched, and at least two would end up crying.

This is a stage where the father or other partner-in-parenting can play a vital role. He can take the baby while you play with your older child, read her books, do projects. Or he can take the older child off on some adventures while you focus on the newborn. I remember Dr. Berry Brazelton telling me that the newborn will make sure all her needs are met. You don't need to worry about that. But the older child is more aware. Focus on her at this moment.

At home, engage your older child with the baby a little bit. Let her hold and rock the baby. Let her hold the bottle. She will then feel part of the process, not excluded from it. Of course, follow her lead. If she has no interest in getting involved, don't force it. Let her come to it at her own pace. If she wants, give her important "jobs." She can be the one to get the diaper, the wipes, the spit-up cloth. She can choose the baby's outfits. Some mothers give the older child a "newborn" doll. She can take care of her baby while you take care of yours. Parallel play is something that delights young children.

One thing Farrell and Lucas used to love to do was sit on either side of me in bed while I held baby Gracie. Gracie would coo and gurgle and look around at Farrell and Lucas as I "translated" her coos: "Oh, Farrell and Lucas, I'm so glad you came to see me this morning. I missed you all last night. You wouldn't believe how I kept Mom up all night. I really kept her pacing the floor!" They would then get into the game and also start translating her sounds.

Talk through what you are doing with the baby and why. That will help your child to understand the needs of a baby. "There she is, waking up, and I can tell by her cry that she is so hungry. And right while we were sitting down to read a book! Isn't that always the timing? Let's go get her up together and bring her in here. Maybe I can nurse her while we continue reading. Will you save our place in the book?"

Many working mothers keep the older child's routine the same after the arrival of their second. Even when you are home on maternity leave, you may want to keep your older child in child care, at least part-time. Helen advises maintaining that regular routine:

> It's enough of a dramatic change for your first child that you don't need to start pulling her out of school and away from her friends and changing her day-to-day. It's important to keep that continuity for the first.

Her familiar routine at child care may feel very comforting to her when her life at home is changing so much. Child care is *her* world, one that she knows how to navigate. She has her friends and her activities that give her a break from the baby and allow her to ease more slowly into the new home situation. If she is in child care a little during the week, that also gives you a much appreciated break during which you can focus just on your newborn.

WHEN YOUR CHILD IS SICK AND YOU NEED TO WORK

My four-year-old, Timmy, has had a cold for a week. When he woke up yesterday, his eye was crusted. So I wiped it away and checked his eye. It looked pretty good. "Okay, now do I go to work, where I have three really important meetings today, or do I call in sick and stay home with him?" I decided to drop him off at child care. At eleven, they called to tell me that Timmy was sick. Well, that was not a surprise! When I went to pick him up, I couldn't believe that I had gone to work. He looked miserable. I should never have taken him to child care. I should have called the doctor first thing. All those "shoulds." This is when I feel so guilty. Guilty if I take him to child care, but also guilty if I miss these meetings where people are depending on me.

—Cynthia

Sound familiar? A child's illness can create a small crisis in the life of working parents. By its very nature, illness is unpredictable in duration or severity. Your supervisor or coworkers may not be supportive if you suddenly have to leave work for a sick child or don't show up in the morning. It can also be a point of contention with child care providers. A desperate parent who feels she has to go to work may give her child Benadryl or Tylenol to mask symptoms before taking her to child care. By the time the medicine wears off and the symptoms reappear, the parent has long since gone on to work. This is doubly stressful for the child care providers, as they worry about contagion and about the welfare of your sick child. You feel trapped between the demands of work, the rules of child care, and the needs of your child. It is one of the greatest sources of stress and guilt for a working parent.

To compound the problem, young children get sick a lot. In fact, a rule of thumb used in child care is that *you can expect a child to be sick twenty days during the first year in a group situation*—whether that is a play group, family child care, a child care center, or elementary school. Not all twenty days will fall on workdays, but you can count on a large percentage of them doing so if you work full-time. If you have a nanny or a relative taking care of your child, you will need to plan on that person getting sick, too, and have a backup for your child's care.

A well-prepared back-up plan for child care interruptions can reduce your stress significantly. A child's illness can disrupt your work, but if you have supportive employers, you or your partner can try to take the time and stay home. It can be reassuring for both the parent and child. To curl up with your child on her bed and read books and color when she is feeling feverish and needy can be a wonderful moment for the two of you.

Don't just assume that you will be the one to stay home with a sick child. Talk in advance with your partner about how you can share this responsibility, then make your plan. Some parents allocate between themselves five or ten personal or vacation days each year for sick children or child care interruptions. Some parents will split the day, with one staying home in the morning and the other staying home in the afternoon—if the employer allows this option.

Some parents can work from home for a day or two while their child is in bed. They stay connected to work by phone, e-mail, and fax. If they have the flexibility, a parent may stay home with the child during the day and then go to work in the evening when the other parent can stay with the child.

Establish back-up support before you need it. Perhaps you have a relative, friend, or neighbor who can care for your child if you cannot. Advertise in local newspapers or put up notices for back-up care. You may have success finding a local person who does not work and would like to perform this occasional care. Get to know this person before you need her or him. Parents have often developed this relationship into a regular baby-sitter.

Check and see if there is a "mildly ill center" in your community where you can bring your child if her illness is not too severe.

Often these centers are connected to hospitals and draw on the nursing staff. Many cities even have specialized organizations you can call for care in your home if your child is sick or your nanny or family child care provider is suddenly no longer available. Look in the Yellow Pages under child care, or in a local parent newspaper, or call the local child care resource and referral agency. However, make sure you check references before you have to use them. Ask how they will make your child comfortable in this situation.

More and more employers are creating back-up centers that families can use when their nanny is sick, quits, or is on vacation or when school is closed. Register in advance for these services to make sure you have submitted the proper health forms and paperwork. Most agencies and back-up care centers want to see that your child is adequately immunized.

But in all cases, *be prepared.* It will be less of a crisis if you can put a plan into action in these sudden needs for extra help.

Ways to handle sick child care (or interruptions in your normal child care or school settings):

- Decide in advance how you and your partner will share this responsibility
- Allocate a week of sick, personal, or vacation days each year for sick child care
- Split the day with your spouse or partner
- Go into work in the evening when your spouse or other source of support can care for your child
- Telecommute
- Line up someone locally who can care for your child on short notice
- Find an area "mildly ill center"; register in advance of any need
- Find a local service provider that specializes in sick-child care or emergency back-up care, or see if your employer offers such a service; register in advance.

THIRTEEN

Ongoing Involvement in Child Care and Elementary School

Be respectful and loving toward the people who care for your children. You need them, and you love them. I would do anything for my children's caregivers. They are very, very special people and very important to us.

—Francesca

Working parents treasure excellent child care providers when they find them. They embrace the central role the provider plays in their children's and family's lives. In this chapter, I will talk about the gifts to working parents that a caregiver can offer—most important, another devoted adult in your child's life and a source of parenting and child development expertise. I will share advice for building a strong relationship with your provider and getting involved with your child care center or family child care home on an ongoing basis. I will suggest ways to build and maintain a strong relationship with your nanny. And finally, I will discuss ways to get involved, as a working parent, with your child's elementary school.

ANOTHER DEVOTED PARTNER-IN-PARENTING

My family child care provider taught me so much about being a mother. We are now best friends. I remember her saying to me, "You'll always be your child's mom, and I will just help you to be the best mom you can be." I care for her deeply and am so appreciative of all she has done for us. We were partners together in raising my child.

—Stacy

Many mothers express this notion of partnership. Your child is capable of loving several adults—as parents are capable of loving several children—and this relationship does not take away from the attachment your child has for you. In fact, it can augment your relationship and help your family function well. Susana enrolled her baby, Andres, in a family child care home run by a mother and grandmother. Susana and her husband had recently moved to a new city and had no network of family and friends:

They were truly like family to us, as we were to them. I loved the fact that Andres loved them and was so happy to see them every day. It felt very reassuring. In fact, the relationship we had with these women is one of our happiest memories of Andres's infancy.

Lara, a factory worker, is a single mother. Her four-year-old son, Tyrol, has been enrolled in the factory's child care center since infancy. Over the years, both Lara and Tyrol have forged close bonds with the caregivers:

When Tyrol was in the toddler room, the teachers did a project where they had each family put together a Family Book for their child. In addition to family, I also brought in pictures of the teachers in his classroom to include. I felt like they were also our extended family.

EXPERTISE IN PARENTING AND CHILD DEVELOPMENT

Many families today live far from extended family and cannot turn to them for daily behavior issues. Many adults arrive at parenting with very little prior experience of babies and young children. As Helen mentions, a close relationship with your child care provider can offer you parenting support:

> *I have a great bond with my daughter's teachers in the center. I'm a new mom. It's all a new thing for me here, taking care of a baby. The teachers have been around babies and children for so long, so they are helpful and informative. I've learned invaluable parenting techniques from them.*

This support can cover a broad range of topics, from bathing and diapering to potty training and sleep issues. Child care providers—from nannies to child care teachers—can also explain how babies and young children develop and help parents understand cognitive, emotional, and physical development.

When my son, Lucas, was three, his talented preschool teacher Zoe explained to me how relevant his scribbles were as he intently covered page after page. She had him dictate the story that he was "writing," and Zoe wrote the words right next to his scribbles. She then showed me over time how Lucas's scribbles took on greater shape until they separated into little forms that looked like letters. He had understood that letters look like separate scribbles and that letters put together made words. Lucas then began to "write" stories in which he sounded out and wrote the first letter of a word and then scribbled out its remaining shapes. Zoe faithfully wrote down Lucas's dictation of his more developed story, and they "published" it in a bound book with his illustrations. How proud Lucas was; he wanted us to read the book to him over and over. Zoe gave me a window of understanding into his development.

You can turn to your child care provider for advice on the everyday care and health of your baby and child. It can feel reassuring to know that you have an experienced caregiver whom you can turn to for the big and little questions. As a new parent, Myrna at times felt lost in the terrain of caring for a baby and all the little things that need attention:

Mrs. Johnson, my family child care provider, was the best. She was so kind and so gentle with me. She would never say, "This is what you need to do." Instead, she would say, "Well, you know sometimes babies get these little bumps on the back of their legs and bottom, and that A&D ointment is really good for that." She wouldn't say, "You dummy, your baby has diaper rash!" She was just right there for me.

Many parents learn behavior-management techniques from child care providers. Parents watch experienced caregivers using many effective approaches with the children. Alena found that these techniques helped her at home:

We're trying to instill in our children a sense of responsibility at home. Much of what I do here, I learned at child care. I find myself saying, "Use your words" when the children start grabbing things from each other. They're used to hearing that at child care, and then they start talking about what they want instead of grabbing. They are used to cleaning up after themselves at child care. I don't think it would have clicked with me that my daughter should be able to take her plate and put it in the sink or the dishwasher, or that she could put her coat away and put her boots on the mat. She learns about responsibility at child care, and now I've learned that we can bring this notion home, too.

YOUR INVOLVEMENT COUNTS: CHILD CARE CENTERS AND FAMILY CHILD CARE HOMES

Get involved with your child's experience at child care—you will be sending him the message that what he is doing during the day is important and interesting. This will help set the stage for later involvement in your children's schools. In fact, a role that we believe we serve at Bright Horizons is to help train new parents to be lifelong advocates for their child's education. We try to engage them early and help them see that they play a role in the center and in their child's experience there.

Get to Know the Director

Take the time to get to know the director who runs the center. Being on a friendly basis might make it easier to address concerns you may have down the road. Don't be afraid to speak with the director about your concerns. Give the people who work with your child the opportunity to make corrections and changes.

—JoAnne, center director

The director is the key to a smoothly running child care center. A good one will want to get to know you and understand what is important to you. Many centers have a parent committee that meets regularly with the director. This is an opportunity for the director to learn if the program is meeting parents' needs. You can express any interest in adding additional programs to the center—such as a dance or gymnastics class, a music class, or a swim program in the summer. You can work together to devise varied summer activities and field trips.

Feel free to make observations about the center to the director, to notice when things are added or the space or program has been improved—or needs to be improved. You may have a skill or talent that the center can use. One father who is a dentist offered to come to the center regularly to provide dental care for children right on the premises. Parents may know of local resources that the center could use—from local repairmen to artists who could plan enrichment programs for the children.

Develop a Strong Relationship with Your Child's Caregiver

As I discuss frequently, you should develop a positive relationship with the teacher or family child care provider who cares for your child each day. Caregivers understand that working parents may not be able to make lengthy visits to the center or family child care home. But if you communicate well at the beginning and end of the day, you and your caregiver will establish a strong rapport.

Communicate to caregivers that you value these conversations. Otherwise, the caregivers may feel it is not their place or right to offer unsolicited information. Caregivers may sense that you are rushed, and they will not insist that you take the time. Linda, an insightful educator, advises the following:

> *Caregivers are often intimidated by highly competent and educated parents, and if parents can set the caregivers at ease, and let them know they value them and respect their thinking, I think they are more likely to forge a very positive ongoing relationship. We all know how busy working parents are and how much they juggle. I don't think anyone expects a huge time commitment from parents, but it's helpful when they use the time well to converse about their child.*

Parents often ask what they can do for the caregivers who are so devoted to their children. Like people everywhere, what caregivers appreciate is recognition of their good work—a thank-you, a card, or a small gift—especially when they have gone the extra mile for your child. Of course, care providers do these special things as part of their job, but they are still nice to acknowledge. One caregiver, Christine, advised:

> *Thank a caregiver for the extra care rendered during an episode of sickness or family crisis. Write notes of thanks and appreciation; these will be saved and valued long after a family has left. They serve as reminders to caregivers of parent appreciation when "the going gets tough."*

Caregivers also want parents to respect the rules and guidelines of the family child care home or center. It shows respect for both the caregiver and the children. If your child care setting has a no-shoe policy, then please, for goodness sake, take off your shoes before entering—for even a moment. And don't just hand your child across the threshold to avoid having to untie and tie your shoes.

Caregivers often issue food and snack guidelines that limit the amount of sugar for the children—even during birthday celebrations. It may be hard to settle children down for a nap after a parent has delivered a rich, sugary chocolate cake on a birthday.

Read and promptly respond to the frequent written communication from child care centers. Caregivers work hard on classroom curricula, plans for field trips, and new projects. They feel validated when parents read these notices and answer enthusiastically.

If you have a concern about a caregiver or a classroom, bring it directly to the caregiver or the director, rather than to the other parents. That way, the center faculty feel supported rather than undermined.

Get Involved in the Child Care Setting— Even Just a Little

Since the center was right here on-site, I could often zip over for fifteen or twenty minutes between meetings. I have to say, the teachers loved it. So I might go over and read a story and have three kids on my lap, and I loved that. All the kids knew all the parents by name, and they would call, "Alena, can you come over here and do this?" or "Can I show you a picture?" or whatever. I was and am very much involved.

—Alena

Alena was lucky to have a child care center at the hospital where she worked. She also had control over her schedule and was frequently out of her office at meetings. She could easily squeeze in a short visit during the day. Not many working parents have this flexibility or the availability of an on-site center. But parents can occasionally use their lunch break to spend time with their child at the family child care home or center.

It is easiest to drop in if you have an infant. Infants are not on any set schedule, and almost any time is good to come in for a cuddle. Most younger babies will not have much trouble separating when you leave. It is perhaps hardest to drop in on toddlers, the age when a child has the greatest difficulty separating. It may be too traumatic to undergo more than one separation during the day. In child care centers, most preschool classrooms welcome parent visits. Talk to the caregivers first about their preferences; they may not mind impromptu drop-ins. In fact, parents can be a willing extra set of hands. Other caregivers prefer that you let them know in case they have special projects or programming going on. One educator, Kathy, gives this practical advice about dropping in on your child care setting:

> Be nonassuming when you arrive. Come and just sit down
> with a child and read a book. Listen to children, for they want
> to be heard. Bring a towel or quilt and sit with children
> outside. Include yourself in their activities rather than
> expecting them to be an audience for your activities.

For a family child care home, first explore with the provider her views about drop-ins. Many parents would never imagine that they would come by and visit their child during the day. But most family child care providers would welcome your participation in the group. If the provider is doing a special project with the older children, she may appreciate your help with the younger ones, or your company at any point during the day.

Many parents love to bring the grandparents by for a visit. Grandparents may have no idea what goes on in a group-care setting. I have heard many stories of disapproving grandparents who were delighted to see the richness, learning, and sense of community in a good child care situation. Many grandparents will start spending time at their grandchild's center or family child care home, sometimes just to sit and rock the babies.

If you are in a work situation where you cannot spend much time in your child care setting, you may be able to come in occasionally to do a project with the children—cooking, art, sharing a cultural celebration from home. Don't think this happens only in a center; it can happen just as easily in a family child care home. Show the children a hobby or just come in and read a book. Reading is the simplest and probably most effective activity all around. You will also want to make the effort when your child is in elementary school, so it helps to get used to those routines now. Gretchen, a child care provider and parent, offers this insight:

> *Ultimately, I think that parent participation, like so many other aspects of our work, depends on the parent and the child. There is no universal recipe for perfect parent participation. I think it is important for us as providers to remember that what works for one family may not work for all families.*

If you are not able to spend any time at child care, you can be involved by reading the caregiver's notes and journals of your child's day, listening to what your child has to say about his day, taking interest in the projects he brings home, and treasuring his artwork. You can invite his friends over for play dates and get to know other families that way. One mother recounts:

> *I am rarely able to visit my child at child care. However, I am involved through him. He shows me interesting things at the end of the day. Since I have squirreled away every single daily report and piece of work that my child has done, I feel quite close to his experience.*

Engage when you can in the center classroom or family child care home:

- Spend a little time at drop-off and pickup. Talk to the children, parents, and caregivers. Just sit and observe.
- If close by, have lunch with your child from time to time.
- Go on field trips when you can.

- Invite the preschoolers on a field trip to your place of work, if appropriate.
- Visit to read a book or do a project.
- Invite the grandparents to visit the center or family child care home.

Understand the Program and Curriculum

Your child will develop and learn a tremendous amount these first years of life. A good child care program offers a curriculum that fosters cognitive, social, emotional, and physical development. The more you can learn about the curriculum and how it works, the better able you will be to understand your child's development.

If you haven't reviewed your center's curriculum, ask to see its statement of educational philosophy, or ask the family child care provider to discuss her educational approach. If the center has a written curriculum or program goals, read through and ask any questions you might have. Many centers have documents or workshops explaining how specific children's activities foster learning and development. For example, two children using a "choice board" to decide on an activity are actually learning relationships between symbols and objects. They are observing the flow of sequence of events. And they are learning cooperation and negotiation, as they see that another child may have preferences that are different from their own. They are learning to make independent choices.

If a center offers a curriculum evening for parents during the year, try to attend. If you can't, ask for the written materials and follow up with a phone call for discussion. Many caregivers will post a weekly curriculum that shows the planned activities, the skills addressed, and the process they will follow. Read all of this. You will be amazed.

When you drop off your child and pick him up, wander about the center classroom and look at the learning centers. In the morning, look at the activities set out to engage the children. In the evening, check out the completed projects, artwork, and works in progress. Ask caregivers what went on during an activity. If your child is in a family child care home, ask about the activities during their day as well.

A family child care home usually won't have a formalized curriculum, but a good one will provide just as much learning and development. Talk to the provider about the activities she has going on during the week. Ask her about your child's evolving interests and skills.

Bring your child's artwork, projects, and "writing" home. Ask him to tell you about it. Take it seriously. It is a concrete manifestation of his developing skills. Display the artwork. Frame it. Show him how important and wonderful it is.

As our public schools increasingly focus on children arriving at kindergarten "ready to learn," with preacademic skills in place, you will want to find out how your child care provider accomplishes this with your child. In particular, providers should focus on language, social, and self-help skills to get the children ready for elementary school. Expect that this learning is taking place and try to understand how it happens.

Understand the curriculum your caregiver provides:

- Read the center's statement of educational philosophy and any available curriculum materials.

- In a family child care home, talk to the provider about her educational philosophy.

- Look at how the rooms are set up and at the activities going on. Ask questions about what is happening.

- In a child care center, look at the posted curriculum plans and anything else that is posted. Go to any parent curriculum nights or workshops. If you cannot attend, ask for the materials.

- Read the caregiver's notes and journals on your child. Write back any observations you may have.

- Bring home your child's artwork, projects, and writing activities. Ask him to tell you about them. Appreciate the work and display it. Even your baby's finger painting is a masterpiece!

Start Your Journey as Your Child's Advocate in Education

High quality child care is designed to focus on each child's individual development. There is no one right pace at which to proceed. Good caregivers nurture each child's abilities. One child may be particularly adept at small motor skills: drawing, writing, cutting, carefully fitting objects together. Another child may have great social and emotional skills of empathy, understanding, cooperating, and negotiating. Every child has strengths that should be embraced.

You and your caregivers can work together to understand your child's pace and style of development. Strategize together on growth in certain areas. Your involvement in your child's development during these early years is a first step along the entire path of your child's educational journey. You will discover, as your child enters elementary school, that part of your role as a parent is to be your child's advocate through the educational system. Begin now by understanding your child's early development.

NANNIES

If you have a nanny, this person will likely become one of the most important people in your child's life and in yours. But how do you define that relationship? The nanny is obviously your employee. But isn't the nanny often like a family member? Perhaps like a friend or adviser? Sometimes like another big child to take care of? What I include in this section is mothers' advice on several key areas of ongoing nanny management. For further information on nannies, consult the books listed in chapter 4.

Treat Your Nanny Professionally

One of the biggest complaints among nannies is that often they are not treated and respected as professionals. Your nanny should have a job description and a set of written terms and conditions of the job (outlined in chapter 4). As the job progresses, if any major element changes, such as hours or duties, the two of you should sit down and discuss it. You can both decide if it is fair and realistic, and whether the salary should be adjusted accordingly.

You and your nanny will want to set aside times at regular intervals to sit down and thoroughly discuss your children's development and how the job is going. Plan these meetings for calm moments without your children present. Ask the nanny how she or he feels about the job and whether anything should be adjusted. Likewise, share your views. Since children change and develop so rapidly, these regular sit-downs will be a good opportunity to discuss how routines should change at home to reflect your children's increased abilities and changing interests. Discuss your children's evolving capabilities with household chores, practice on musical instruments, homework time, and the like.

Just as you would with any employee, you will want feedback on the nanny's performance from those who are familiar with her or him. Talk to other mothers in play groups that the nanny goes to or talk to the teachers at the preschool or elementary school your child attends. Let your nanny know that you will be doing this so it will not seem that you are secretly investigating.

Some mothers create supportive employment benefits for their nanny. Elizabeth does everything she can to create a generous work environment for her nanny, Roberta:

> *When Roberta had her baby, I gave her three months'*
> *maternity leave. I have tried to create a professional position*
> *with the same benefits we have at the office in terms of paid*
> *vacation time and paid holidays off. I think that is very*
> *important.*

Elizabeth treats Roberta with respect: "If I really disagree with something Roberta does, I'll speak to her about it privately so that she knows I think of her as a professional. I don't criticize her actions in front of the children."

Finally, as in any employment situation, you should provide an annual review of performance and a salary adjustment (a raise!). If you have clearly laid out the parameters of the job at the outset of employment, you can review your nanny's performance against these expectations.

Treat Your Nanny Well—REALLY Well!

If you have a great nanny, treat her or him like gold. Be generous, be kind, go the extra mile. Mothers told me all sorts of horror stories of nannies who didn't work out and the havoc that created in their lives. The cost to your life in nanny turmoil—worry about your children, money spent, and time lost at work—can be tremendous. You soon realize that a great nanny is a precious gift in your life.

Some parents offer financial interests to stay on for a specified period of time. Other parents spontaneously give a bonus for a job particularly well done. Mothers figure out what can make a real difference for a nanny, and then they try to provide that. Irene found when her youngest child went off to preschool that she didn't need her cherished nanny, Margarita, full-time anymore. At the same time, Margarita had become interested in completing her college degree. Irene couldn't bear the thought of losing her completely, so she figured out a generous solution to keep her on:

We decided to send Margarita to school and are supporting her financially to get her degree. In return, we get excellent part-time child care, great loyalty, and someone who is like part of the family.

Don't feel that you have to offer such a large financial incentive to keep your nanny happy with you. Erin figured out that her au pair wanted friends and relatives to be able to come and visit. She enthusiastically supported that desire:

There are times when I've had a whole crowd staying here with the au pair—two visiting friends, some with brothers and boyfriends. We love to open our house, and our au pair really appreciates that. Friends sometimes tell us that we are operating a "bed and breakfast"!

Selena believes it is the little gestures of kindness that can make a big difference:

> I have been very lucky that I've been able to keep my nannies a long time. I don't pay more than other moms do, but I treat my nannies really well. I'm clear about how important they are to me, and I let them know that. I not only give them lots of acknowledgment, but when I travel, which is a lot, I bring them little things. Once in a while I give them a gift certificate or take them out to dinner. I'm still very close to the three nannies I have had over the years. One woman moved back to Sicily. We went and visited. We will go back again when her daughter is married. They become important people to me, and I become important to them.

Make the Job Conditions Attractive

Try to make the daily life of the job manageable and attractive. Sarah realized that the job of caring for her two active little boys would sometimes be exhausting for her nanny, Michael. She enrolled her older child in an after-school program at their elementary school two afternoons a week. She did it in part to give her son a socializing experience in a good program. But she also did it to give Michael some "mental health time"—a short break from a demanding job.

One of the biggest challenges of the job is the isolation. Perhaps help your nanny join a neighborhood play group with other nannies and/or parents and babies. Check to see if there is a local baby music or gymnastics or swim class where your nanny can get out of the house and be with other people. Town libraries often have a story hour for young children. Think about the things you would do to get out of the house and meet other people. Help your nanny to find them.

Erin made a point of introducing her au pair, Hanna, to the neighborhood moms and nannies, and she facilitates and encourages their friendships:

> Hanna has become friendly with the moms whose kids are in the preschool program. She goes walking with some of the

*neighborhood moms in the morning. She has become
incredibly involved with the community. She arranges all the
play dates with other moms.*

*She and the other moms are able to lean on each other.
One day Hanna was really sick and couldn't take care of the
kids. She arranged for all three kids to go to different homes,
and everybody stepped up. In fact, Hanna has done more of
that relationship building than I have.*

ENGAGING IN YOUR CHILD'S ELEMENTARY SCHOOL

Soon your children will be out of child care and into elementary
school. I remember feeling a sense of shock when our first child, Farrell, left child care and entered public school kindergarten. I was so
used to being intimately involved in her daily experience. I had a
close relationship with her caregivers, and I felt comfortable going in
and out of her child care center whenever I wanted. When she entered
public school, I no longer had this freedom. However, I quickly
learned that elementary schools welcome and depend on active parent participation: I just had to learn a new system. How do you
become actively involved in elementary school if you work full-time?
How do you become an advocate for your child's education?

Working parents have come up with creative solutions to get
involved in their child's elementary school experience. The first step
is to get the annual school schedule early. There is usually a lot on
that schedule that you will need to get into your calendar. One
mother, Barbara, calls the school superintendent every spring to get
the following year's schedule. Don't wait until the fall, when it is dis-
tributed. If you can put all the vacations, school closures, parent/
teacher conferences, and early-release days in your calendar far in
advance, you will have a greater chance of planning effective backup
and participating in important events. Often schools will plan a curriculum night early in the school year. Make sure that makes it into
your calendar as well.

One mother, Erin, stops into the school every year, the day
before it starts:

I always know the teachers will be in the school that day, so I'll pop in and say hello. It's hard for me to think of Bobby getting on the bus and going to see someone I don't know. The teachers usually are very friendly, even if they don't have a lot of time. It's a nice way to make an initial contact.

The spring before our oldest child, Farrell, started elementary school, I made an appointment to observe in a kindergarten classroom, then met with the school principal. He explained the structure of the curriculum, gave me tons of material to read, and asked about my child. That one conversation launched a wonderful relationship that developed over the years our children have been in elementary school.

Once the school year starts, ask your child's teacher for any other known dates of the semester: school assemblies, plays, field trips, etc. Many parents use the school drop-off as a time to check in with the teacher. You can walk your child to his classroom and have a quick conversation. Although it may be unusual for parents to come in at drop-off, there is no reason why you cannot do that. Most elementary school teachers love to have parents volunteer in the classroom. Although that may be difficult for working parents, some workplaces have a time-off policy for volunteering in schools or attending field trips. If you can't do it during the day, there are many ways you can volunteer outside work hours, as Erin found:

I sign up for anything that doesn't involve me being there during the day, so I'll do the night or weekend events or phone work. I think it's important for the kids to see that I'm involved.

I'm helping to plan a school event this Friday night, and we sent out a last-minute reminder. It was a big flyer, and at the bottom, it said if you have any questions to call one of these two moms, and one of them was me. Bobby came home and said, "Mom, I'm reading this thing and I see your name, and I'm thinking that's my mom! You're on this piece of paper that everyone is getting!" It was such a little thing, but he was so proud. As they get older, I want them to know that it's important to be involved.

Join the PTA, the school advisory council, or the after-school-program board. These groups usually meet outside work hours. Tina, a single mother of two children, describes her involvement:

I became part of the principal's advisory group. I just bring my kids with me. I don't ask, I just bring them for the evening meetings. They sit out in the lobby and do their homework while we meet with the principal.

Tina finds other ways to contribute with the limited time she has. She has brought the notion of job sharing to school volunteer positions. She signed up with one friend to be a co-classroom parent and with another to be a soccer coach for her child's team. That way, if one of them can't make it due to a work commitment, there is back-up. This year she and three other women are sharing the position of Girl Scout troop leader for a large troop.

Some parents invite their child's teacher to a special event or home for dinner. A group of parents in our elementary school put together a principal's fund and did fund-raising for school projects and purchases.

You can take your available time, however limited, and craft a way to get involved. Good schools want and appreciate parent involvement. Know that whatever you do, no matter how small, will make a difference for your child.

Ways to engage in your child's elementary school:

- Get the school calendar before the academic year starts. Mark all vacations, school closures, early-release days, and parent/teacher conferences on your calendar.
- Meet your child's teacher before school starts.
- Make an appointment with the school principal.
- Once the school year starts, ask the principal or teacher for the dates of school assemblies, plays, field trips, etc.
- Ask your child's teacher for as much advance notice as possible on classroom events, so that you can plan your work calendar around them.

- Drop your child off in his classroom—if only occasionally. Chat with the teacher.

- Volunteer in the classroom if you can take time off from work.

- Or volunteer to do work outside of school hours: evening or weekend events, phone calling.

- Join the PTA and school committees.

- Job-share school volunteer positions: classroom parent, coach, even PTA president.

- Create your own project reflecting your interests or skills.

- Invite your child's teacher to an event or home for dinner.

Become an Advocate for Your Child's Education

Many public school systems are large and not designed to focus on an individual child's needs and circumstances. This also applies to many private, parochial, and charter schools. Much of a school curriculum is designed to educate the "mean"—the average child. If your child differs significantly from the mean, the teaching may not work for him. Teachers follow their own style, which may work well for some children and not for others. You will play an important role throughout your child's education as his advocate in learning and education.

As your child progresses in school, you will discover your child's particular learning style, what works and what doesn't. Some children need a great deal of structure in a classroom, while others wither under too much. Some children thrive in a challenging, fast-paced environment, and others do better in a quieter, nurturing environment. Stay close to your child's situation; don't expect the school to figure it out for you.

Since you are a working mother and may not be able to spend time in the school while it's in session, you will need to be more proactive about getting to know the teachers and the school environment. Many working mothers have figured out ways to advocate what works best for their child. One set of parents always sets up an early-morning meeting with their child's teacher soon after school begins.

Another parent writes a long letter in the fall, describing her child's learning style and his challenges.

Some parents actively investigate the teachers in the grade ahead and write the principal a letter each spring describing what kind of classroom would work best for their child. Even if you cannot request a specific teacher (this is usually the case), principals and teachers really do want to find the right match and appreciate information that helps them make appropriate assignments.

If your child is struggling in the classroom, set up an appointment with the teacher or guidance counselor. If your child has a special circumstance in his life that affects his school experience, communicate that to the teacher and strategize together. One mother, Stacy, went through a difficult divorce the spring before her child went to a new elementary school. She was worried about how that would affect Jeffrey's school experience:

I met with the teacher and principal right away and told them about the divorce. They were fabulous. The teacher said to me, "We're going to focus on the things Jeffrey will need to make this adjustment. He's great academically, so let's focus on getting him comfortable socially in a new school." I'm so glad I talked to them about it, because they've been great.

The parent/teacher conference is an opportunity to sit down with the teacher, discuss your child's progress, plan any new directions. Though these conferences often take place during the workday, many work environments now allow employees time off to attend them. If not, teachers may help working parents by scheduling a conference early in the morning or during a lunch break. One mother always scheduled with the teacher considerably in advance, before the notices went out, to ensure that she found a time that would work for her. One set of parents always tries to schedule the last conference at the end of the day. That way they have more time with the teacher to discuss their child.

One mother, Tina, felt there were some subtle racial issues going on at the elementary school that were affecting her children and others. Through contacts at work, she found a diversity consultant to come into the school and do some sensitivity training with the teachers. The principal was very receptive. Another mother, Jane, brought in an expert on bullying to address the classrooms and a parent group when the school experienced some problems on the playground.

Nichelle felt that her elementary school was labeling her child a "behavior problem" unfairly. She felt there was a bias against her child, whom she had adopted from a difficult foster situation. She also felt her son's teacher was biased against her, since she was a working mother. Nichelle, an educator herself, began to communicate more actively with the teacher and started dropping off her son so she could touch base with the teacher each day. Once she started showing up in the classroom and actively communicating with the teacher, she felt that the teacher's attitude toward her child changed:

> *I knew that the only way my child was going to be successful at school was for me to be visible. I needed to show that I was right on top of the situation and that I cared.*

Public-school systems have programs to evaluate children for any special needs. A team of specialists then addresses a child's special needs by devising an education plan. You may need to really advocate for these services; a school can be slow to respond to your child's circumstance. Once your child starts receiving services, remain actively engaged in the program. For a working parent, it may be hard to be present in the school frequently, but you can more than compensate by phone or through e-mail.

Be an advocate for your child:

- Make an appointment with the teacher early in the year. Discuss your child's learning style and interests. Keep in touch throughout the year.

- Write a letter to the principal in the spring describing your child's learning style, academic interests, and what kind of classroom atmosphere would work best.

- Communicate early on about any circumstances in your child's life that could affect his classroom experience, such as

a death in the family, a divorce, a recent move, a change in
job, a health issue, etc.

- Schedule your child's parent/teacher conference early.
  Arrange for a slot when you can have adequate time to
  discuss your child and his progress.

- Address any problems you see at the school: bullying, racial
  issues, hazing, or other.

- If your child has special needs, be actively engaged with the
  school around his plan and services.

Relationship Between Working and Stay-at-Home Mothers

During the years when your children were enrolled in child care, most
or all of the other parents also worked. Some mothers find it a shock
to go from that community of mothers working outside the home to
an elementary school community, where many mothers are at home
during the day. Elizabeth feels complicated emotions of both envy
and pride:

> *I feel like I am a little luckier than the stay-at-home moms
> because I have this great identity and job that are very
> important to me. But in other ways, I feel like I have to prove
> myself as a good mother. I always feel envious of them
> because they are staying at home. I don't think anyone can
> honestly not be ambivalent.*

Don't assume that mothers at home are any different from you
in their major concerns about their children and the school, or that
they'll necessarily be more involved because they don't go off to work
each day. As one mom, Brenda, puts it: "You tend to have a group of
committed people, whether they're working or not; they'll give what
time they can." School and teacher issues, playground issues, social
and development issues with children are usually the same for all parents. If you are blessed to live in a community with many stay-at-
home mothers who are active volunteers in your child's school, thank
your lucky stars! Many communities aren't so lucky. Appreciate them

and thank them for all that they do for your school and community life.

And for many mothers, caring for children full-time is a phase of life, not a way of life. After all, most mothers work at some point. They may be planning to go back into the paid workforce at some later point, or they may have recently left it. Patricia puts it well:

> *Among the stay-at-home moms I know, there is probably some envy in both directions. There's a certain amount of "Gosh, it must be great to go to an office and work." Just as much as there is "Oh, it must be great to stay at home with your kids." But I don't think that we're all that different. Life is full of phases. Who knows what we each will be doing in five years.*

FOURTEEN

Building Communities of Support

When Roger and I lived in Khartoum, Sudan, during the mid-eighties doing emergency relief work, we soon grew accustomed to always putting out extra food and plates when we sat down to dinner. Invariably, Sudanese or foreign friends, neighbors, and colleagues would arrive at our house in the late afternoons and often stay for hours. No one had telephones, and many did not have cars. People walked where they had to go. It was understood and expected that late afternoons were a time for visiting and sharing—for community. In the western province where we worked and lived, movement of Sudanese villagers between huts and family compounds was fluid and easy. During the drought and famine, many people shared food, seed, and supplies and took care of the disabled and sick. It was shameful to hoard resources. Within a village community at its best, there was a strong sense of mutual responsibility. People took care of one another.

In 1999, when I visited Kosovo in the aftermath of the war, I fully expected to see massive problems with orphans, but there were few. A child who lost his parents was absorbed and sheltered by his strong extended family system—the family community. More than half the homes in the region I visited were destroyed in the war. Surprisingly few families moved into shelters set up by the international relief community; most moved in with relatives and neighbors. They worked together to rebuild their homes. This strong community of support sheltered and buffered the children and helped families recover and rebuild. Maybe because of the hardships these cultures have endured, they have learned to lean on one another—or perhaps they have just learned the value of community through both the good times and bad.

Much of this book is about building more support in our lives. As working mothers, we don't have to do it all alone. Although much of American culture has been constructed around a notion of rugged individualism and independence, many of the mothers I interviewed thrive on exactly the opposite. They take no pride in trying to go it alone. They see how communities make parenting easier and family life richer. Surrounded by caring adults, children can grow up feeling love and attention all around them.

In this final chapter, I will talk about the many places mothers have found community. Each of the three pillars can be a source: You may find it at your workplace, around your child care setting, or among the partners-in-parenting in your life. You may also find it in your neighborhood, at your church, temple, or mosque. Your extended family may offer you the most important friendship and support.

You may want to be enveloped in a large community, or you may want a small one that you can lean on from time to time. I will offer you some examples to help inspire you to the place you might find yours. Although surrounded by people, many working mothers feel lonely. If you are feeling overwhelmed by work and young children, you may not have the time to seek out others. If your job has required you to move, you may be starting afresh in a new place. Being at work all day may keep you away from your neighborhood and school communities. But listen to these working mothers. The paths they have found may illuminate some direction for you.

FAMILIES DO THRIVE IN A COMMUNITY OF SUPPORT

Claire, a mother of three and an active volunteer in her children's schools, sums up well how community has helped her family:

*There are many adults in my children's lives who offer them
something unique and special. My children are very close to
my parents and their aunts and uncles. From them they get a
wonderful sense of unconditional love—they can do no wrong.*

*We also have three or four families in the neighborhood
whom we are close to—like family. When our kids are not with
us, they are watched closely by my best friends. The kids can't
get away with any mischief, and I think it gives them such a
sense of security and safety. They also see other role models
who have been important for them.*

*We have an older friend, Ruth, who has always been a
big part of our lives. Ruth was over last week, and my son
told her all about these little naughty things he did. He really
trusts her. I think that all these relationships give my children
a sense that the world's a good place.*

Other close, trusted adults can help open the world to your
children in ways that augment what you offer. They may expose your
children to different skills, interests, and pastimes. We have a neighbor, Barry, a former physics professor, who has become a mentor and
friend to our son, Lucas. Lucas has a passion for science, and Barry
plans afternoon or evening science sessions with him from time to
time. My daughter, Gracie, spends a great deal of time with her godmother, Angela, her two grown children and four grandchildren, and
her large extended family in the community. Since most of our
extended family lives far away, Angela has given Gracie the security
and love of a large family of four generations nearby.

Not only can children benefit from the example of other close
adults, but you as parents can, too. You can learn from watching other
models of parenting, from watching how other children are developing. Parents can help one another during difficult times and share in
the fun moments. Knowing that there are people who know you and
care about you can give you a sense of belonging.

For some working mothers, their community comes from just a
few people—their mother or sister or a best friend who lives nearby—
their closest partners-in-parenting. One single mother, Estelle, has
three children. When she had each one of her children, her support

structure was small but strong. She gave birth to her first when she was in graduate school. In the graduate-student housing where she lived, Estelle found strong support from a few other mothers. They took care of one another's children and shared many afternoons and evenings together. Seven years later she gave birth to her second child while living and working as a teacher in New York City. Her mother and sister lived there and provided a constant presence in her and her children's lives. Nine years later, their church notified them that a young girl in the community needed adoption. Estelle and her older children decided together to adopt this child. Estelle and her sixteen-year-old son attended parenting and adoption classes together. Together with her family, Estelle is raising this little girl. A community of support does not have to be large to be effective.

> A community can be small or large and still give you important support.

Although some mothers feel more comfortable in an intimate community, other mothers thrive on large, overlapping networks, and they tend to build community wherever they go. One mother, Chloe, has done just that:

> *We have some close friendships from our children's preschool that we have maintained over the years. We also have current and former neighbors with whom we're friends. Now we are developing good friendships with some of the parents of our kids' elementary school friends. We have very active grandparents. We have good friends from our temple. We have many friends from work. We have good friends from all parts of our life.*

It Can Be Difficult to Build Community

Especially if you are working full-time while parenting, how can you find the time to meet people and develop friendships that lead to mutual support? Some people have family or friends who naturally fulfill this role, but what if you do not?

Roger and I moved to a new community just months after we had our first baby, Farrell. We knew no one in this new town and were under a lot of work stress. We were fearful that Bright Horizons would collapse, and at the same time we were trying to figure out how to be good parents. It was hard to come home in the evenings with all our worries and have no one to turn to. When I went to the hospital to give birth to our second child, Lucas, we had to take Farrell to close friends who lived thirty minutes away. There was no one in our community who knew us well enough to take her for a few days.

What a difference it made to have a community of support by the time Gracie, our third child, was born five years later. By then, we had made a close group of friends through Farrell's elementary school. By chance (or persuasion), two sets of our closest friends from years before moved into our neighborhood. Farrell and Lucas enthusiastically went to Mary and Scott's house while I was in the hospital with Gracie; it was a fun adventure for them. Soon after Gracie's birth, my sister, Lisa, and her family moved around the corner. Barely a day goes by when we don't see or talk with each other, and my children are able to grow up with their cousins. Important life moments are made to be shared; our lives felt immeasurably richer and happier in the fertile ground of community.

But it is particularly difficult for working mothers to nurture these communities when they are both absorbed and exhausted by work and young children. Adah, a mother of two, travels a great deal selling education services to corporations. When she and her family moved to a new city, she wanted a network of friends but found she had little time to develop one:

> *It's tough, because I'm in this intense period of both working hard and having two little children. It's hard to find time for trivial relationships. But how do you know if the relationships can develop beyond the trivial? You suddenly are prioritizing everything from your friendships to your phone calls. For example, I'm thinking of calling a girlfriend of mine whom I haven't talked to in so long. But I know that will be a forty-five-minute conversation, and I don't have that time. So maybe I'll send her an e-mail just to keep the contact. Or I'll call and leave a long message on her answering machine at a time when I know no one is home.*

Some working mothers, like Wendy, have many acquaintances but not enough time to become truly close friends:

I don't feel alone, but I don't feel like I have that close connection with one or two really close girlfriends, like when I was younger. I had a minor car accident recently, and there wasn't one person I could call, other than my parents. That's when I realized I was missing something.

Many Single Moms Are Showing Us the Way

Many of the single mothers I interviewed have built strong communities around themselves and their families. Once they were on their own, many determined to create a network with other parents, friends, and extended family. One single mother, Stacy, feels that she actually has more support now than when she was married:

I have way more girlfriends now than when I was married, way more. I now rely on everybody and everything—my ex-husband, my mother, neighbors, friends. I now have a great support system.

Dalila, a nursing assistant in a hospital and the mother of three-year-old Elijah, turns to his father's large family as well as her own for support. She moved into a small apartment near an aunt, a cousin, and a close girlfriend who is also a single mother. They are with each other almost every day.

Once Yvette separated from her husband and was on her own with two little boys, she became proactive:

It's probably the first time in my life that I've had a sense of community. I purposely went out to create it. I no longer feel alone; I have a lot of people in my life. My mother, my boyfriend, another single mom who lives right downstairs from me—in fact, this whole apartment complex is a great community. During the summer, everyone will sit outside in the evening. When I come home from work, I'll just pull up a chair and sit and talk for a half hour before I go in to start dinner. There are about ten little kids between the ages of four and seven who play together all the time. My boyfriend calls them the Rugrats. Because of this community, I won't move.

Although many of these mothers got motivated to develop a network after becoming single, we can all benefit from a community, whether we're single, married, have a large or small family, work full-time or not at all.

HOW TO FIND AND CREATE COMMUNITY

Communities are formed in many different ways—from play groups, around preschools and elementary schools, through hobbies or sports, clubs, old friendships, extended families, neighborhoods. Even if you feel lonely now as the busy working mother of a young baby, you may start building a community as your child grows. One of the wonderful things about children is that they attract other children—and community follows. As one mother, Pamela, said:

When I first had children, I felt that I didn't really have a lot of women friends. Babies require so much time and focus, and then working on top of that made it seem impossible. There was just no time. Then you start developing friendships with the parents of your children's friends. You naturally spend time together. You start picking and choosing the ones you relate to. I made many new friends that way.

> Finding friends: Notice where you feel a natural connection or spark.

I was at a barbecue recently and listened to two women animatedly talking to each other. They explained to me that they had become good friends as they both waited for their four-year-old daughters in a Saturday gymnastics class. They spent that hour together every week, and out of that grew a lasting friendship.

Abigail felt that once she had her son, she started spending more leisurely time outside in the neighborhood, which she had not done before. She felt more receptive, and her son actually became a vehicle for meeting other people at her stage of life:

> Children can be a bridge to friendships.

I now have two close friendships in the neighborhood that I've made over the past two years. I didn't have any before that, and it really bothered me. My child has opened some doors to other parents who are in the same boat.

Mothers' tips for creating communities of friends:

- Be proactive; remember that other working moms want and need a community, too.
- Reciprocate favors: Cook a dinner, take care of another's child.
- Stay open to new friendships—you never know when or where they will spring up.
- Invite small groups over to your house for a potluck meal. It's not much work, and people appreciate the hospitality. Then they will want to reciprocate.
- Find common areas of interest—children are the natural one.

Selena offers this advice:

Whenever I enter a new situation, I have an explicit strategy of creating a community of other women who will help out in a pinch in different ways. I've just been very, very focused on always identifying the other working moms—if it's in gymnastics or any other after-school activity—so that we can cooperate. It's not hard to figure out who the other working moms are. There's a certain look, you know, a slightly harried look.

Whenever I initiate it, the other mom is always very

receptive to the idea of helping each other out. Reaching out like this is one of the ways of creating a community. Most working mothers have the same issues and are generally willing—no, thrilled—to support other working moms.

> Don't be afraid to initiate— other moms will appreciate it.

Where have mothers found communities? I'll take you through some of the most common sources below. Use these stories to think about where you might be able to create your own.

The Extended Family as Support

Before we had children, my husband and I decided to move away from our hometown. We felt our families overwhelmed us; there were too many demands on us. It was really nice at first. But then I had my baby, Andres, in our new city. I felt alone. I didn't have my support network. They were now far away.

> Value and cherish your family. You need them now.

I started to think about what I needed for my life—and for our child's life. My family came for all the big things—the birth, his baptism, his first birthday. But all the little stuff together, we couldn't do. I started to really want and need my family around.

Now we are so happy to have moved back to our hometown. Both sets of grandparents are so involved and are a part of our children's lives. I value their support so much.

—Susana

Some families invite grandparents to live with them once they have children. Ingrid and her husband, Chip, built a small wing on their house for Ingrid's parents. They all feel that it has enriched their lives. Either Ingrid's mother or father is home in the afternoon when the children come home from school, and the entire family eats dinner together most evenings.

Lara, a single mom, often has to work mandatory weekend overtime at the factory where she is employed. Her mother and aunt care for her four-year-old son, Tyrol:

> *When we leave the child care center on Friday evenings, we go straight to my mother and aunt's place and stay the night there. I get up and go to work early on Saturday, and Tyrol sleeps in. Sometimes when I come home, they're getting him out of the tub or he's just playing. He's happy and feels at home.*

This kind of support makes all the difference to working mothers. Amanda works as a financial manager and frequently has urgent last-minute work to do at the office. Both her mother-in-law and sister-in-law can quickly step in to pick up her daughter, Julie, from child care. They love doing it, and it gives Amanda peace of mind: "I don't think I would be as sane as I am if it weren't for my in-laws. I'll come home all frazzled, and everyone will be settled happily at home."

Some family members help out in nontraditional ways. Chavonne's father was her labor coach when she delivered her first child. Gina's dad finds any way he can to spend time at their house and with his beloved grandchild, Melanie:

> *My dad cleans our house, does our laundry—every single week! He often picks up Melanie from preschool. He is absolutely smitten with her, and she loves him, too. So it's nice for both of them. And of course it's great for me.*

These relationships are beneficial for both children and parents. Silvia describes her family dynamics this way: "The relationship between my husband, Justin, and my mother is wonderful, wonderful. I always tell people if Justin and I ever got divorced, my family would give me up and go with Justin! They just love him."

Jaclyn and her husband, Clement, adopted three abandoned babies from a homeless shelter over the course of four years. They were able to care for them using a network of extended family support:

Clement was home on disability, so he was able to take care of the house and do all the cooking. My whole family helped out with the babies. Our grown daughter, Desiree, was living with us, and she helped out. Clement's mom came over every day to care for the babies. My sisters and my brother, they all helped out. These little babies had a whole family caring for them.

The Community Around Child Care

Your child care setting may be the first group you are intimately involved with as a family. It's a good time to reach out to others. As new parents, this may all seem so foreign to you. Chances are that other parents feel the same way; they want and need friendship and support, too. Many family child care homes and child care centers become communities of friendship for families. In fact, one wise center director, Wilma, expressed what many feel—that a child care setting can be a primary source of support:

> Child care—a community waiting to happen.

People move around so much, they don't have extended family around. When the mom and dad work more than eight hours a day, five days a week, they don't know their neighbors, either. The center can provide that neighborhood. We have potluck dinners and have created an environment where parents can hang out and talk when they pick up their children from school. It's important for us to do that for families.

Outside Farrell and Lucas's child care center was a little picnic table where, on nice evenings, families would linger and talk while the children played. We would often go to a little coffee shop at the corner for dinner. The owner loved that her place was the community hangout, and she would have plates of cookies waiting for us. She opened up a room in the back where we could eat and the kids could play together.

Paige, a graphics artist with two young children, built extra time into her commuting schedule to hang out in the child care center both in the morning and at pickup in the evening:

We're all here in the same place, and I think it's important to get to know other families in the center. I feel like they're my "neighbors," even though they're coming in from different places. Our kids spend all day together. They know each other like siblings.

Paige, her husband, Larry, and their children often socialize with other families during the weekend. Paige recently took care of two children of a friend she made in the center when her friend delivered her third child.

> Look for ways to help each other out. People will do the same for you.

Wendy believes that getting to know other mothers through the center not only facilitated friendships for her son but helped her through watching their parenting techniques: "I feel that I learn a lot by just seeing how other families operate, by seeing other kids develop, too. How do my kids fit in? What are things that I could try?"

Friendships are also created through nannies. One mother, Selena, found support by sharing a nanny with another family:

To me, that's another way of creating a kind of community, because there is now another family who is part of your life. It was also nice when we just had one child. Our daughter had a much better time when she had another little girl her age to play with during the day. The little girl is her "best friend" in life. They've been friends since they were three months old.

> Communities can come from all sorts of places.

Sarah had a nanny, Stella, whom she and her husband adored. When Sarah and her family moved to a larger house with a few rooms on the top floor that they didn't need, they invited Stella and her husband, Michael, to move in:

Not only did Stella and Michael move in with us but also two of their friends and their dog. We loved having them live with us. It was great for our son, Aaron, to have all these loving adults around. In fact, when Stella eventually went on to school, Michael then became our nanny. Our son knew and loved Michael and was even in their wedding. And as Stella said, "Michael can change both diapers and the oil."

The Elementary School Community

For some families, elementary school may be the first time their children are with other groups of children. In fact, kindergarten becomes an important time for both children and parents to form new friendships. Our

> The kindergarten year: Reach out; others will too.

children's public school actively fosters involvement by hosting a parent coffee on the first day of kindergarten. Two of the mothers I met on that very first day became close friends. Over the years, we have created a close group of women friends. We take care of one another's children, we vacation together, and we accompany one another through the small and big events in life.

Sarah and her husband, John, strategized to create their main community around their children's elementary school:

We really want to get to know the families of the children our kids play with. That's extremely important to us, because these children are going to be important parts of their lives, and they're going to be with them through twelfth grade. They are spending more and more time at their houses, so I'd like to know these people.

That investment has paid off for Sarah, as she now knows many mothers who all call on one another to help out with school pickups or in a pinch.

Pamela felt that she finally was able to create a strong community once her children started elementary school. As a choreogra-

> Find ways to reciprocate favors.

pher for school theatrical performances, she often has to work late afternoons and evenings through different periods of the school year. Moms in the school community have willingly taken her children when needed:

> *I actually get more support from nonworking mothers than I do from working mothers. Like me, the working mothers in the community are not the ones you see very often. Moms in my kids' classrooms have all helped out. Last year, when I had problems with my child care, the other moms would take the kids after school. They've always done things like that. Then, between performances and during the summer, I try to pay back by taking their children as much as possible.*

This community doesn't just happen. Parents have to reach out to create these relationships. Elizabeth realized when her children started elementary school that she didn't really know any of the other parents.

Be proactive.

Be proactive.

Be proactive.

She formed a lunch group of moms who get together regularly. She organizes the lunches downtown near her office, and people enjoy traveling into town for this get-together.

Communities Around Places of Worship

Many mothers value this community because they are with people of like values and beliefs. Others value it due to the sense of tight community. As Natalie says:

> *A lot of people with children go to our church, so it's nice for both the kids and parents. I joined the religious education committee; it's a good way to connect with other parents.*

Volunteer for committees or projects—a chance to get to know others better.

Olive credits her temple with providing her and her family's most important community of friends:

This group of friends is still my closest; they have been for over twenty years. When each of my parents passed away, I didn't have to worry about a thing. I knew they would talk to each other and they would get whatever we needed. We sat Shiva for seven days, and they brought all the food, they organized all the dishes. They took care of everything.

> Take care of each other—especially in times of need.

When my children were very young, we started a Jewish co-op preschool in our temple with four of these couples. It became extended family. We talked very consciously with our children—"If you ever need anything and your parents are not available, or you need somebody else to confide in, these are people you can turn to." The kids were all like cousins.

When my daughter got married, all my women friends from our temple worked together on the wedding canopy for two months. We created a beautiful appliqué and calligraphy canopy for her.

Neighborhood Communities

Although we hear so much about the breakdown in neighborhood communities, many mothers still have wonderful support in their neighborhoods. One mother, Isabelle, now looks to families there as her main social and support group:

I don't know how it happened, but we have this tradition in the summer called "stoop night." Every Thursday night we'll all have a beer on our stoop, and the kids play tag in the neighborhood. Our

> Organize a block party; invite people over to your home.

neighbors just wander by. They all know that if it's Thursday, everyone will be congregating. We'll get pizza or order Chinese food, and we'll all just sit out on the stoop and eat.

Shalisha talks about her neighborhood as a *Leave It to Beaver* type of setting:

We live on a great dead-end street, and the kids are always outside playing. We know everyone on our street. It's an incredible neighborhood. You can walk into town, you can walk to the train. The older kids watch out for the younger kids. The women on the street formed a neighborhood book club, and we get together once a month.

Spend time outside, and be friendly.

You don't have to live in a quiet suburb to have this atmosphere. Patricia and her family live in an urban environment, and they also feel that closeness:

We live in an urban working-class neighborhood, and we know everyone up and down our street. There are a lot of older people who love our kids, and there are also kids from our neighborhood who are friends and go to the same school. It is a community.

A Community at Work

At other points throughout the book, I talk about the value of community at work. Tina realized its incredible power when she was pregnant with her first child and had to spend her last trimester on bed rest:

I quickly used up all my available sick and vacation time, but there were people at work who donated their vacation time to me to help pay for my leave. I had really gotten to know everyone in our building, and they just gave me their vacation days. It was a great community.

Alice's work community helps her frequently. Her son Jimmy, who was born with hemophilia, is often unable to attend school. Alice works as an infant teacher in a child care center, and she feels very comfortable bringing the ten-year-old to the center with her:

Jimmy loves coming here. He loves all the other teachers. The children even know him, especially the older ones. Whenever the children see me, they say, "Where's Jimmy? Where's Jimmy?" If I were in a different work situation that wasn't so supportive, I don't know what I would do. Everyone is so good to Jimmy here. They really love him.

Networks of Old Friends

Sometimes a mother's closest network doesn't live or work nearby; it may be comprised of friends from previous phases of life. Myrna values her close girlfriends who have stuck with one another over the years:

> Don't let go of those old friends.

Most every day we talk on the phone. One of my girlfriends just had a baby. I was there at the hospital with her as her labor coach. A couple of days later, she had to check back in to the hospital. I kept her baby for almost two days.

Irene has a close group of college friends who have vacationed together annually for twenty years. Now spouses and children have all become close, like "an extended family," in Irene's words. Shoshanna and her husband, Baruch, moved here from Israel several years ago and have forged close friendships with a group of couples:

Here in the States, it seems that friends can take the place of family. One of the couples we're close to invited us over this Saturday, and I said, "Who's going to be there?" and she said, "The family." And yes, it is our family here—this group of three or four couples.

One of my friends, Sally, has a "Full Moon Group," a group of close women friends who have gotten together during every full moon for nearly fifteen years to share all of life's ups and downs. Another mother, Erin, still counts her college friends as her closest some twenty years later: "They are lifetime friends, and they are becoming more important as time goes on."

Communities Around Hobbies, Sports, Interests

Communities can also form around your interests. Wendy has a group of friends who get together regularly to work on family photo albums and family history. Paige was a committed athlete and participated in a wide variety of sports before she had children. Now she plays on a women's softball team that she's been on for eighteen years:

> *I can't imagine not playing with this diverse group of hilarious, somewhat talented softball players. Over the years, there have been weddings, births, deaths, divorces, and "coming out" events. And while our team is sponsored by a bar, with free beer, we rarely go there after games. Postgame activities consist of sitting in the parking lot, watching another game, and chatting about our lives.*

> Do what you love, then look for the connection.

My husband, Roger, formed a band with some close friends in college over twenty years ago. They have played gigs and occasionally recorded CDs over the years. Twelve years ago, another friend, Mark, joined. This group and all the wives have close friendships that go back years. We have helped one another through pregnancies, adoptions, moves, and various life issues. We have a common bond around music and frequently go to hear music together—including the band wives trailing the band to hear the music and dance together. This group has become a ballast in all of our lives.

Communities come in all shapes and sizes. I hope some of these stories will spark a thought about where you can create a community in your life. It's hard to parent without social support, even with a committed partner-in-parenting. But what you may need or want will be unique to you. It may be one best friend that you can talk to in the evenings, or your mother who is available when you need her. Or maybe you thrive with lots of people cascading into your life, all of you participating and sharing. Having close connections with others can give your life greater meaning and enrich your child's growing-up years. As Selena stated earlier, "Most working mothers are willing—no, thrilled—to support other working moms." Let's look out for one another and build a sisterhood of support wherever we can in our lives.

Notes

Chapter 2: A Partner-in-Parenting

1. James T. Bond, Ellen Galinsky, and Jennifer E. Swanberg, *1997 National Study of the Changing Workforce* (New York: Families and Work Institute, 1998), 72–73.
2. The 2000 Radcliffe Public Policy Center survey found that 70 percent of the men surveyed wanted to spend more time with their families and would be willing to give up pay to achieve that. *Life's Work: Generational Attitudes Toward Work and Life Integration*, conducted by the Radcliffe Public Policy Center with Harris Interactive, Inc. (Boston, MA: 2000). Also several studies reported in James A. Levine and Todd L. Pittinsky, *Working Fathers* (New York: Harcourt Brace and Company, 1997):
   - In 1993, a national study conducted by the University of Illinois found that the large majority of men now "seek their primary emotional, personal, and spiritual gratification from the family."
   - A 1996 consumer survey center poll found that 84 percent of men stated that "success" in life means being a good father.
   - A 1991 Gallup poll reported that 59 percent of men "derive a greater sense of satisfaction from caring for their family than from a job well done at work."
3. Elizabeth H. Pleck and Joseph H. Pleck, "Fatherhood Ideals in the United States: Historical Dimensions," Michael Lamb, ed., *The Role of the Father in Child Development* (New York: John Wiley & Sons, Inc., 1997), 33–48.
4. Ibid.; Kyle D. Pruett, M.D., *Fatherneed: Why Father Care Is as Essential as Mother Care for Your Child* (New York: Free Press, 2000); Ross D. Parke, *Fatherhood* (Cambridge, MA: Harvard University Press, 1996).
5. *The Role of the Father in Child Development*, chapter 6: "The Development of Father-Infant Relationships," 120.

Chapter 3: A Supportive Employer

1. For a fuller discussion of family-friendly companies, refer to the following:
   - Stewart D. Friedman and Jeffrey H. Greenhaus, *Work and Family: Allies or Enemies?* (New York: Oxford University Press, 2000).
   - Ellen Galinsky and Arlene Michaelson, *Reframing the Business Case for Work-Life Initiatives* (New York: Families and Work Institute, 1998).
   - James T. Bond, Ellen Galinsky, and Jennifer E. Swanberg, *1997*

National Study of the Changing Workforce (New York: Families and Work Institute, 1998).

- Rhona Rapoport and Lotte Bailyn, *Relinking Life and Work: Toward a Better Future,* a report to the Ford Foundation, November 1996.
- Ellen Galinsky and James T. Bond, *The 1998 Business Work-Life Study: A Sourcebook* (New York: Families and Work Institute, 1998).
- Rima Shore, *Ahead of the Curve* (New York: Families and Work Institute, 1998).
- *Working Mother Magazine,* October 2001. Special issue: "100 Best Companies for Working Mothers."
- Articles by Robert Levering, The Great Place to Work Institute, 286 Divisadero Street, San Francisco, CA, 94117, 415–503–1234.

2. *1997 National Study of the Changing Workforce;* chapter 6: "Workplace Characteristics," 97–110. *Reframing the Business Case for Work-Life Initiatives,* 11–18; *The 1998 Business Work-Life Study: A Sourcebook,* 58–64; Linda Duxbury, Ph.D., and Christopher Higgins, Ph.D., *Supportive Managers: What Are They? Why Do They Matter?* Richard Ivey School of Business, University of Western Ontario. Article published by the Minnesota Center for Corporate Responsibility.

3. *Two Careers, One Marriage: Making It Work in the Workplace* (New York: Catalyst, 1998), 30.

4. For a fuller discussion of negotiating flexible work options, see Pat Katepoo, *Flex Success: A Proposal Blueprint and Planning Guide for Getting a Family-Friendly Work Schedule* (Kaneohe, HI: Work Options, Inc.); www.workoptions.com; and *Flex Jobs: The Smart Mom's Guide to Finding and Creating a Great Flexible Job,* by Nancy Collamer, www.jobs andmoms.com.

5. *1997 National Study of the Changing Workforce,* 95.

6. Stewart D. Friedman, Perry Christensen, and Jessica DeGroot, "Work and Life: The End of the Zero-Sum Game," *Harvard Business Review,* November–December 1998, 119–29.

7. *Reframing the Business Case for Work-Life Initiatives,* citing the U.S. Bureau of Labor Statistics (1997), 1.

8. *Work and Family: Allies or Enemies?,* 9.

9. Current population reports, *Fertility of American Women: June 1998* (Washington, D.C.: U.S. Census Bureau), 8.

10. Ibid., 9.

11. *Work and Family: Allies or Enemies?,* 9.

12. Ibid.

13. *Two Careers, One Marriage: Making It Work in the Workplace,* 43–45; *Reframing the Business Case for Work-Life Initiatives,* 9–14; "Work and Life: The End of the Zero-Sum Game," 119–129.

14. *Reframing the Business Case for Work-Life Initiatives*, 4–14; *Flex Success: A Proposal Blueprint and Planning Guide for Getting a Family-Friendly Work Schedule*; JPMorgan Chase internal study on workplace practices, conducted 1998–2001.

15. Peter M. Senge, *The Fifth Discipline: The Art and Practice of the Learning Organization* (New York: Doubleday, 1990), 310–12.

16. *Life's Work: Generational Attitudes Toward Work and Life Integration*, conducted by the Radcliffe Public Policy Center with Harris Interactive, Inc. (Boston, MA: 2000).

17. *PricewaterhouseCoopers International Student Survey*, www.pwcglobal. com, May 1999.

18. To name a few studies that look at men's attitudes toward work and family:
    - *Life's Work: Generational Attitudes Toward Work and Life Integration.*
    - *Two Careers, One Marriage: Making It Work in the Workplace.*
    - Louis Harris and Associates, Inc., *Women: The New Providers*, Whirlpool Foundation Study Part One (New York: Families and Work Institute, 1995).
    - *Work and Family: Allies or Enemies?*

19. For information on the economic performance of companies with supportive workplace policies, refer to the Great Place to Work Institute, 286 Divisadero Street, San Francisco, CA, 94117, 415–503–1234; or the Families and Work Institute, 330 Seventh Avenue, New York, NY, 10001, 212–465–2044.

20. *Work and Family: Allies or Enemies?*; Allison Sidle Fuligni, Ellen Galinsky, and Michelle Poris, *The Impact of Parental Employment on Children* (New York: Families and Work Institute, 1995), 29.

21. *The Fifth Discipline: The Art and Practice of the Learning Organization*, 307.

22. There are many studies that look at the impact of workplace practices on children. To cite a few:
    - *The Impact of Parental Employment on Children.*
    - *Work and Family: Allies or Enemies?*
    - Federal Interagency Forum on Child and Family Statistics, *America's Children: Key National Indicators of Well-Being 2000* (Washington, D.C.: U.S. Government Printing Office, 2000).
    - Rosalind C. Barnett and Caryl Rivers, *She Works/He Works* (Cambridge, MA: Harvard University Press, 1996), 98.
    - Adele Gottfried and Allen Gottfried, *Maternal Employment and Children's Development* (New York: Plenum Press, 1988).
    - Suzanne W. Helburn, ed., *Cost, Quality, and Child Outcomes in Child Care Centers* (Denver: Department of Economics, Center for Research

in Economic and Social Policy, University of Colorado at Denver, 1995).

- Ross D. Parke, *Fatherhood* (Cambridge, MA: Harvard University Press, 1996).

23. Allison Sidle Fuligni, Ellen Galinsky, and Michelle Poris, *The Impact of Parental Employment on Children* (New York: Families and Work Institute, 1995), 27–33.

Chapter 4: Excellent Child Care

1. Jack P. Shonkoff and Deborah A. Phillips, eds., *From Neurons to Neighborhoods: The Science of Early Childhood Development* (Washington, D.C.: Committee on Integrating the Science of Early Childhood Development, Board on Children, Youth, and Families, National Research Council and Institute of Medicine, National Academy Press, 2000), 383–415; discussions with Dr. Susan Hockfield, professor of neurobiology at Yale University; Rima Shore, *Rethinking the Brain: New Insights into Early Development* (New York: Families and Work Institute, 1997), 1–69; *The Science of Early Childhood Development*, Zero to Three Bulletin, April/May 2001, Vol. 21, No. 5; Pam Schiller, *Brain Development Research: Support and Challenges*, Child Care Information Exchange, September 1997.
2. Suzanne W. Helburn, ed., *Cost, Quality, and Child Outcomes in Child Care Centers* (Denver: Department of Economics, Center for Research in Economic and Social Policy, University of Colorado at Denver, 1995), 308.
3. Ellen Galinsky, Carollee Howes, Susan Kontos, and Marybeth Shinn, *The Study of Children in Family Child Care and Relative Care* (New York: Families and Work Institute, 1994), 81.
4. Ibid., 45–47; Susan Kontos, *Family Day Care: Out of the Shadows and into the Limelight* (Washington, D.C.: Research Monograph of the National Association for the Education of Young Children, Vol. 5, 1992), 68–69; Allison Sidle Fuligni, Ellen Galinsky, and Michelle Poris, *The Impact of Parental Employment on Children* (New York: Families and Work Institute, 1995), 21.

Chapter 5: Living Your Pregnancy and Maternity Leave

1. Ross D. Parke, *Fatherhood* (Cambridge, MA: Harvard University Press, 1996), 40.
2. Ibid., 39.
3. Ibid., 41; Michael E. Lamb, ed., *The Role of the Father in Child Development* (New York: John Wiley & Sons, Inc., 1997), chapter 6, 104–120.

Chapter 6: Returning to Work After Maternity Leave

1. As discussed in James A. Levine and Todd L. Pittinsky, *Working Fathers: New Strategies for Balancing Work and Family* (New York: Harcourt Brace and Company, 1997), chapter 5, 127–59.

Chapter 7: Making Life Easier at Work

1. Stewart D. Friedman and Jeffrey H. Greenhaus, *Work and Family: Allies or Enemies?* (New York: Oxford University Press, 2000), 63.
2. Stephan Rechtschaffen, *Time Shifting: Creating More Time for Your Life* (New York: Doubleday, 1996). Dr. Rechtschaffen uses the notion of time-shifting a bit differently in his beautiful book. Here it refers to the distinct rhythms embodied in different situations.

Chapter 8: Creating a Strong Family Culture While Working

1. Thomas Moore also talks about the importance and beauty of family rituals, traditions, and culture in his book *Soul Mates: Honoring the Mysteries of Love and Relationship* (New York: HarperCollins, 1994).
2. Ellen Galinsky, *Ask the Children: What America's Children Really Think About Working Parents* (New York: William Morrow and Company, Inc., 1999), 234–39.
3. Sarah Susanka, *The Not So Big House* (Newtown, CT: Taunton Press, 1998).
4. *Kids & Media @ the New Millennium: A Comprehensive National Analysis of Children's Media Use*, Henry J. Kaiser Family Foundation, November 1999; Policy Statement of the American Academy of Pediatrics, *Children, Adolescents, and Television (RE0043)*, Vol. 107, No. 2, February 2001, 423–26; Policy Statement of the American Academy of Pediatrics, *Media Education (RE9911)*, Vol. 104, No. 2, August 1999, 341–43; Jane M. Healy, Ph.D., "Understanding TV's Effects on the Developing Brain," *American Academy of Pediatrics News*, May 1998; "AAP Discourages Television for Very Young Children," press release from the American Academy of Pediatrics, August 1999; Fumie Yokota, M.S., and Kimberly M. Thompson, Sc.D., "Violence in G-Rated Films," *Journal of the American Medical Association*, May 24–31, 2000, Vol. 283, No. 20.
5. Stewart D. Friedman and Jeffrey H. Greenhaus, *Work and Family: Allies or Enemies?* (New York: Oxford University Press, 2000), 87.
6. Ibid., 80.

Chapter 11: Ah, Yes, Those Household Chores

1. Warren Farrell, *Women Can't Hear What Men Don't Say* (New York: Jeremy P. Tarcher/Putnam, 1999), 85–122.

2. Marjorie Hansen Shaevitz, *The Superwoman Syndrome* (New York: Warner Books, 1984), 286–302; *Women Can't Hear What Men Don't Say*; and interviews with mothers.

Index

About the Author

LINDA MASON is chairman and cofounder of Bright Horizons Family Solutions, an international provider of workplace child care and early education, named by *Fortune* magazine as one of the "100 Best Companies to Work For in America." For her work with young children and working parents, she was selected by *Working Mother* magazine as one of the "25 Most Influential Working Mothers in America." Prior to Bright Horizons, she ran refugee relief programs in Africa and Southeast Asia for victims of war and famine. She lives in the Boston area with her husband and three children.

Please join our community of working mothers on-line at: www.bright horizons.com/workingmothers